7-97

The Wilderness Campaign

The Wilderness

Military Campaigns of the Civil War

Campaign

Edited by Gary W. Gallagher

The University of North Carolina Press   Chapel Hill & London

© 1997

The University of North Carolina Press

All rights reserved

Manufactured in the United States of America

The paper in this book meets the guidelines for

permanence and durability of the Committee on

Production Guidelines for Book Longevity of the

Council on Library Resources.

Library of Congress Cataloging-in-Publication Data

The Wilderness campaign / edited by Gary W. Gallagher.

p.   cm. — (Military campaigns of the Civil War)

Includes bibliographical references and index.

ISBN 0-8078-2334-1 (cloth : alk. paper)

1. Wilderness, Battle of the, Va., 1864.   I. Gallagher,

Gary W.   II. Series.

E476.52.W55   1997

973.7'36—dc20   96-35006

CIP

01 00 99 98 97   5 4 3 2 1

For

Jack Kyle Cooper

and George W. Woodard,

from whose love of history

and generosity

I have benefited greatly

Contents

Introduction

The battle of the Wilderness inaugurated an epic confrontation between Ulysses S. Grant and Robert E. Lee that would continue unabated until the Army of Northern Virginia surrendered eleven months later at Appomattox Court House. On May 5–6, 1864, the preeminent commanders of the Civil War first tested each other in the dismal clutches of a vast scrub forest spreading south from the Rapidan and Rappahannock rivers. Horrific fighting over the two days produced more than 30,000 casualties and afforded ample evidence that each of the generals faced an opponent unlike any in his prior experience. Lee learned that this Union general, in contrast to so many of his predecessors, would not withdraw after a major bloodletting; Grant discovered that the Army of Northern Virginia and its leader could absorb massive punishment, respond with telling counterstrokes, and retain the ability to maneuver effectively as the Army of the Potomac shifted southward. Although neither Grant nor Lee ever conceded the other's full stature as a military leader, both knew by the time their armies marched toward Spotsylvania Court House on May 7 that the war in Virginia had taken a striking turn away from old patterns.

They knew as well that the fighting in the Wilderness drew the attention of untold thousands who devoured newspaper reports for signs of which commander had gained the upper hand. Although many modern scholars argue that events in the Western Theater wielded greater influence on the progress of the war, there can be no doubt that in the spring of 1864 most Americans, whether in the North or South, focused their attention on Virginia. Northerners looked to Grant, who had been given the sainted Washington's rank of lieutenant general, to solve the puzzle of how to beat Lee and his redoubtable army. As Grant's chief of staff John A. Rawlins put it, the "Congress must have created and the President must have bestowed the rank of lieutenant general upon Grant the better to clothe him with power for a trial of prowess and leadership with Lee." Lee had understood for some time that the Confederate people placed their greatest hopes for independence in him and his soldiers. In the wake of Gettysburg, he had written to Jefferson Davis about "the unreasonable expectations of the public" concerning the Army of Northern Virginia. A woman in Louisiana revealed those expectations in mid-May 1864 when she reacted to unconfirmed reports about the battle of the Wilderness: "A great battle is rumored in Virginia, Grant's first fight in his 'On to Richmond,'" she wrote in her diary. "He is opposed by the Invincible Lee, and so we are satisfied we won the victory."[1]

The maelstrom in the Wilderness yielded no clear-cut winner. Neither side was driven from the field, and a majority of the soldiers in both armies probably believed they had bested their opponents. Typical was Walter H. Taylor, who observed from Confederate headquarters that "in the Wilderness we enjoyed several victories over vastly superior numbers." Behind the lines, civilians trying to make sense of what had transpired generally remained upbeat. The day after the battle, Secretary of the Navy Gideon Welles described "fragmentary intelligence . . . of a conflict of the two great armies. The President came into my room about 1 P.M., and told me he had slept none last night." Two days later Welles still had no definite news but had concluded that "there can be no doubt, the Rebels have fallen back, and our forces have advanced." A woman in New York recorded essentially the same conclusions on May 8: "News has arrived from the Army of the Potomac, and it looks as though we should be victorious. . . . Grant is driving Lee back from the Rapidan, which he has successfully crossed." Watching events from Silver Spring, Maryland, Elizabeth Blair Lee noted on May 10 that Grant conceded his failure in the Wilderness "to achieve much he intended doing." Still, he had gained an edge on "the enemy—who are . . . forced to retreat & are whipped." From the other side of the Potomac River, the rebel war clerk J. B. Jones wrote on May 8 that "Grant remained where he had been driven, in the 'Wilderness,' behind his breastworks, completely checked in his 'On to Richmond.'" Jones added that Grant "may be badly hurt, and perhaps his men object to being led to the slaughter again."[2]

Grant's memoirs conveyed his attitude about the Wilderness in typically laconic fashion. "More desperate fighting has not been witnessed on this continent than that of the 5th and 6th of May," he affirmed. "Our victory consisted in having successfully crossed a formidable stream, almost in the face of an enemy, and in getting the army together as a unit. . . . As we stood at the close, the two armies were relatively in about the same condition to meet each other as when the river divided them. But the fact of having safely crossed was a victory." For his part, Lee expressed little admiration for his new adversary's first battle in the Eastern Theater. Grant had experienced the phenomenon—unprecedented among Lee's earlier opponents—of having both his flanks turned on May 6, a fact that left Lee with a sense of unfulfilled opportunity. If his subordinates (especially Richard S. Ewell) had not failed him in the Wilderness, remarked the former Confederate chief in 1868, the Army of Northern Virginia "would have crushed the enemy." Lee also spoke somewhat dismissively about "Grant's gradual whirl and change of base from Fredericksburg to Port Royal, thence to York River and thence to James River, as a thing which, though foreseen, it was impossible to prevent."[3]

Few people in May 1864 dwelled on the Wilderness as a distinct event because so many other battles followed in rapid succession. It remains most often treated as one part of a much larger whole—the opening act in the sprawling drama of the Overland campaign. The tactical story of the Wilderness has been told often, most effectively by Gordon C. Rhea in his recent *The Battle of the Wilderness, May 5-6, 1864*.[4] Yet it is instructive to examine the engagement within the framework of Union and Confederate expectations in the spring 1864, to explore trials of high command in armies that underwent dramatic reshaping between March and June 1864, and to sift through conflicting evidence to reconstruct and reinterpret some of the most gripping incidents of the two days. As a group, the essays in this volume address various elements of the Wilderness campaign, combining broad and specific approaches to expand understanding of one of the war's major military confrontations.

Brooks D. Simpson leads off with a discussion of what northerners expected from Grant and the Army of the Potomac and how they reacted to the carnage of early May. Weary of Lee's ability to thrash the republic's largest army and to escape crippling defeat when seemingly vulnerable (as after Antietam and Gettysburg), the northern public saw in Grant a new champion who could meet the wily rebel on even terms. They hungered not only for success in Virginia, but also for a climactic Napoleonic victory that would sweep away two years of frustration and open the way to Richmond and reunion. When Grant could not supply that type of triumph in the Wilderness or at Spotsylvania the following week, newspapers failed to convey the full story of what had happened in the bitter woods of the Rapidan and Rappahannock valleys. Secretary of War Edwin M. Stanton's role in that failure, together with Abraham Lincoln's realization that the unvarnished truth about the fighting of the first two weeks in May might damage northern morale, are two of the many threads Simpson weaves into his essay.

Expectations within the Army of Northern Virginia also were high in the spring of 1864. The second essay counters the common notion that southern white morale sagged irretrievably following defeats at Gettysburg, Vicksburg, and Chattanooga in the summer and fall of 1863. Confederate successes at Olustee, Mansfield, Plymouth, and elsewhere loomed much larger at the time than they do now, lifting spirits across the South during the late winter and spring of 1864. Despite severe shortages of food and matériel, Lee's soldiers retained a solid faith in his leadership and hoped that a major victory in the upcoming campaign would depress northern morale and assure Confederate independence before the end of 1864. Sometimes upset with civilians who seemed unwilling to sacrifice as much as they, Lee's soldiers typically exhibited determination to see the war through to a successful conclusion even if it meant temporary compromises regarding states' rights and cherished personal freedoms.

John Hennessy sketches an Army of the Potomac beset with more doubts than its Confederate opponent but cautiously optimistic that Grant might hold the key to victory. The soldiers passed a winter of 1863–64 markedly different from the troubled one that had followed the battle of Fredericksburg in December 1862. They lauded George G. Meade's decision not to launch an offensive against Lee's strong positions at Mine Run in late fall 1863, accepted with minimal grumbling the consolidation of the army into three large corps (a process that involved significant shuffling of senior commanders), and benefited from excellent army administrative work that kept supplies flowing smoothly to the camps. The men also sensed stronger support from the home front, witnessed less political bickering between their generals and Republican politicians in Washington, and turned in increasing numbers to religion. With two of three infantry corps and the Cavalry Corps under problematical or untested commanders, however, it remained to be seen whether the army's ranking officers would supply leadership worthy of their men's steadfast service on the march and in combat.

The winter and spring of 1864 brought new faces to top positions in the Army of the Potomac's mounted arm. Philip H. Sheridan, who had forged a successful record as an infantry division commander in the Western Theater, replaced Alfred Pleasonton in charge of the Cavalry Corps, and James Harrison Wilson took over one of the three divisions in the corps. Although considerable renown lay ahead for both men, Gordon C. Rhea demonstrates that they failed badly in their assigned roles at the Wilderness. Sheridan smugly believed he knew best about how to use cavalry and ended up wasting a good part of the corps during early May. Wilson groped toward trouble on May 5, neglected to look after the most elementary functions of cavalry, and found himself dangerously separated from the bulk of the army on May 6. Together Sheridan and Wilson committed enough errors to compromise the entire Union effort. Rhea suggests that anyone seeking to understand what went wrong for the Federals in the Wilderness must accord the cavalry considerable attention.

R. E. Lee believed that two of his corps commanders also performed less than adequately in the Wilderness. He thought Richard S. Ewell lacked decisiveness, especially in fumbling an opportunity to strike Grant's right flank on May 6, and held A. P. Hill responsible for the disintegration of two Third Corps divisions on the morning of May 6. Peter S. Carmichael challenges a number of influential historians in defending Ewell and Hill, both of whom, he argues, suffered the lingering effects of unfair criticisms of their actions at Gettysburg as well as invidious comparisons with Stonewall Jackson. Carmichael questions the value of Henry Heth's and John B. Gordon's memoirs, which have been cited repeatedly to criticize Ewell and Hill at the Wilderness. More important, he argues that Lee placed Ewell and Hill in untenable positions by failing to concentrate his army before the battle and by issuing vague orders once the armies were engaged.

The collapse of A. P. Hill's line in the early morning hours of May 6 set up an encounter between R. E. Lee and the Texas Brigade that quickly took on the aura of legend. Robert K. Krick draws on a wealth of wartime and postwar testimony to construct the most detailed account to date of this famous scene in Catherine Tapp's overgrown field along the Orange Plank Road. He shows that Lee trailed behind the Texans rather than leading them (artists have preferred to portray Lee in front of the troops, dramatically riding toward the enemy) and breaks down the episode into four phases that, once understood, explain how eyewitness accounts seemingly at odds with one another actually refer to different stages of the action. Beyond the sheer drama of the moment, Lee's encounter with his Texans illustrates graphically the bond between him and his men that produced such stunning accomplishments on so many fields. The scene also indicates that Lee thought it necessary to take a more personal hand in directing the army. Perhaps he doubted Hill's capacity to handle his men in a crisis (Lee moved to safety soon after James Longstreet arrived). Or he may have seen the crisis as so profound as to warrant his presence as a symbol for the men. Whatever the reason, the Lee-to-the-Rear episode marked the beginning of a new pattern of behavior for Lee on the battlefield.

Although Lewis A. Grant's Vermont Brigade of the Union Fifth Corps participated in no scene as gripping as that in the Widow Tapp's field, it fought with distinction on both May 5 and 6. No unit better exemplified the determination with which the Army of the Potomac entered the campaign, yet, as Carol Reardon's essay explains, the brigade's contribution went relatively unnoticed within the army and among Vermonters back home. Grant's soldiers suffered 10 percent of the army's casualties in the Wilderness but saw their accomplishments and sacrifice obscured by a chorus of praise for Winfield Scott Hancock's Second Corps. The Vermont legislature voted a resolution of thanks for George J. Stannard's 2nd Vermont Brigade for its brief but eye-catching role in helping turn back Pickett's Charge at Gettysburg. A similar resolution for Grant's 1st Vermont Brigade was tabled. Reardon's essay reconstructs the superior performance of Grant's men, analyzes the response to that performance within the army and behind the lines, and reminds modern readers that a unit's postwar reputation may not reflect accurately its wartime service.

Lewis Grant's Vermonters felt the impact of James Longstreet's flank attack against the Federal left on May 6. Robert E. L. Krick's essay probes the origins, execution, and results of Longstreet's assault, concluding that few attacks during the war better demonstrated the power of a small flanking column (two Confederate brigades did most of the work) to spread chaos through a much larger defending force. Inevitably compared to Stonewall Jackson's famous attack against Joseph Hooker's right flank at Chancellorsville on May 2, 1863, Longstreet's maneuver involved far fewer men but yielded comparable results. Like Jackson, Longstreet was shot down by his own men while attempting to maintain the momentum of his success. Confederates at the time and many later writers speculated that Longstreet's wounding denied Lee an opportunity to drive the Army of the Potomac against the Rapidan River. Krick concludes otherwise, stressing several factors that would have militated against such a decisive result.

As with earlier volumes in the Military Campaigns of the Civil War series, these eight essays revise or enhance existing work and highlight some of the ways in which the military and nonmilitary spheres of the war intersected. Collectively, they draw on research in manuscripts, obscure printed materials, and more prominent published works and suggest that in terms of sources and approaches Civil War military history offers a spacious field in which to consider the past.

The contributors to this volume made editorial tasks easy. Peter Carmichael, John Hennessy, Robert E. L. Krick, Bob Krick, Carol Reardon, Gordon Rhea, and Brooks Simpson submitted manuscripts that required minimal revision, suggested illustrations, prepared mock-ups for the maps that accompany their essays, and otherwise behaved in an exemplary fashion. Individuals who helped each of them are thanked at the end of individual essays. George Skoch, who has become the Jedediah Hotchkiss for this series, did his usual excellent job with the final maps. As with other volumes in the series, the Research and Graduate Studies Office of the College of the Liberal Arts at Penn State provided support for maps and illustrations. I thank one and all for their help and encouragement.

NOTES

1. Herman Hattaway and Archer Jones, *How the North Won: A Military History of the Civil War* (Urbana: University of Illinois Press, 1983), 517 (quoting Rawlins); R. E. Lee to Jefferson Davis, July 31, 1863, in R. E. Lee, *The Wartime Papers of R. E. Lee*, ed. Clifford Dowdey and Louis H. Manarin (Boston: Little, Brown, 1961), 565; Kate Stone, *Brockenburn: The Journal of Kate Stone, 1861–1868*, ed. John Q. Anderson (Baton Rouge: Louisiana State University Press, 1955), 284.

2. Walter H. Taylor to Bettie Saunders, May 15, 1864, in Walter H. Taylor, *Lee's Adjutant: The Wartime Letters of Colonel Walter Herron Taylor, 1862–1865*, ed. R. Lockwood Tower (Columbia: University of South Carolina Press, 1995), 160; Maria Lydig Daly, *Diary of a Union Lady, 1861–1865*, ed. Harold Earl Hammond (New York: Funk & Wagnalls, 1962), 295; Elizabeth Blair Lee to Samuel Phillips Lee, May 10, 1864, in Elizabeth Blair Lee, *The Civil War Letters of Elizabeth Blair Lee*, ed. Virginia Jean Laas (Urbana: University of Illinois Press, 1991), 379; Gideon Welles, *The Diary of Gideon Welles*, ed. Howard K. Beale, 3 vols. (New York: Norton, 1960), 3:25–26; J. B. Jones, *A Rebel War Clerk's Diary at the Confederate States Capital*, 2 vols. (1866; reprint, Alexandria, Va.: Time-Life, 1982), 2:202.

3. Ulysses S. Grant, *Personal Memoirs of U. S. Grant*, ed. E. B. Long (1885; reprint of 2 vols. in 1, Norwalk, Conn.: Easton Press, 1989), 408; William Preston Johnston, "Memoranda of Conversations with General R. E. Lee," ed. Gary W. Gallagher, in *Lee the Soldier*, ed. Gary W. Gallagher (Lincoln: University of Nebraska Press, 1996), 29 (the conversation took place on May 7, 1868).

4. Rhea's book appeared in 1994 (Baton Rouge: Louisiana State University Press).

The Wilderness Campaign

BROOKS D. SIMPSON

Great Expectations

ULYSSES S. GRANT, THE NORTHERN PRESS, AND

THE OPENING OF THE WILDERNESS CAMPAIGN

Ulysses S. Grant and William T. Sherman met in early 1863 to discuss how to capture Vicksburg, Mississippi. Unhappy with the Army of the Tennessee's position on the west bank of the Mississippi River, Sherman urged his superior to retrace his steps northward to Memphis, Tennessee, establish a base of supplies, and then approach Vicksburg from the north. It was not bad advice. Grant later admitted that it was what the experts on strategy would have recommended. But he rejected the suggestion. It would look too much like a defeat, he explained; at least that was how the press would interpret it. Better, he concluded, to work something out from where they were.[1]

This story, which ended with the surrender of Vicksburg on July 4, 1863, is noteworthy because as Grant pondered his next step, he took into account how the public and the press would interpret his actions. What a general might deem necessary to improve the chances for a successful attack could be characterized by the citizenry as an admission of defeat. In a conflict where so much rested on mobilizing and retaining public support, such perceptions were crucial. Abraham Lincoln seized on public perceptions of Antietam as a great victory to make known his plans to issue the Emancipation Proclamation; later, much to Grant's chagrin, the president cast the battle of Stones River as a Union triumph because it raised people's spirits in the aftermath of a series of military setbacks.

Never was the link between what was happening on the battlefield and what the public believed was happening so critical as in the spring of 1864. Lincoln was up for reelection. Although some Republicans were not pleased with the prospect of another four years in the White House for Honest Abe, the incumbent had done much to secure his renomination. The major threat to his reelection came from members of the Democratic party who would highlight any battlefield reverses as a sign that the administration could not achieve victory. How the public perceived the course of military operations and the prospects for success would determine the outcome at the polls in November. It was in these circumstances that Grant accepted overall command of the Union armies.

Although Grant knew what was at stake as he traveled to Washington in March 1864 to accept his commission as lieutenant general, he was not yet entirely aware of what was expected of him. Indeed, not until he arrived at the nation's capital did he begin to comprehend the task before him. Sherman had warned of a city filled with devious politicians awaiting their chance to snare the unwary; Grant himself harbored some distaste for partisan politics even as he was aware of their importance. Once at the capital, he discovered both why he wanted to get away as soon as possible and why it was important that he abandon his initial preference to conduct operations from the West. People were still discussing the Joint Committee on the Conduct of the War's investigation of charges that George G. Meade, the commander of the Army of the Potomac, had wanted to retreat from Gettysburg, only to be prevented from doing so by the course of events and the acts of several subordinates. At Willard's Hotel and a White House reception, Grant learned that everyone wanted something from him. If he dreaded such meddlesome activity, he soon realized that he must endure it or someone else would be subjected to it, and the result might be fatal to his plans. As he later explained, "When I got to Washington and saw the situation it was plain that here was the point for the commanding general to be."[2]

Robert E. Lee's presence in Virginia was another reason why Grant would have to establish his headquarters in the Eastern Theater. Simply put, Lee had become the foremost symbol of Confederate success in northern eyes. His Army of Northern Virginia had foiled the efforts of a series of Union generals to defeat it and take the Confederate capital of Richmond. By 1863 Lincoln had singled out the defeat of Lee's army as the most important objective of Union military operations in the East. The reason was not difficult to understand. Time and again Lee had upstaged Union successes in the West, primarily because so many Americans looked to the East as the theater of decision. The major northern newspapers, especially the influential New York dailies, provided exten-

Lt. Gen. Ulysses S. Grant.
A photograph taken in the field shortly after the battle of the Wilderness.
National Archives

sive coverage of operations there. The drama of a theater containing national capitals barely a hundred miles apart proved quite compelling to a public reared on the notion that to seize the enemy's capital was virtually to win the war—although the American military experience provided sufficient examples to disprove this notion.

It did not matter that Grant and other generals had succeeded in regaining control of the Mississippi River valley and had made significant inroads into the Confederate heartland over the past two years while the contending forces in northern Virginia found themselves merely several dozen miles southwest of where they had been in 1861. As Lincoln had remarked in August 1862 in the aftermath of the Seven Days, "It seems unreasonable that a series of successes, extending through half-a-year, and clearing more than a hundred thousand square miles of country, should help us so little, while a single half-defeat should hurt us so much."[3] Yet it did. If Lincoln was to win reelection, something had to be done about Robert E. Lee, and Ulysses S. Grant was Lincoln's choice to do it.

Many studies of the military campaigns of 1864 focus on the confrontation between Grant and Lee between the Rapidan and Richmond and assess the results according to rather traditional standards of victory and defeat, despite claims that Grant brought to the American military tradition new ways of waging war. One gains a far better appreciation of what happened in the spring of 1864 if one sets that campaign in the context of Grant's overall strategy both in Virginia and against the Confederacy. What did Grant hope to achieve? How did he seek to defeat Lee? How did the campaign in Virginia contribute to his grand strategy? And how did the northern public perceive his progress? What did it expect? For how northern voters assessed the success or failure of Grant's plan would go far to determine their choice for president in 1864. Did they understand how Grant made war, or were they wedded to more traditional measures of victory and defeat? One of the best ways to answer these questions is by examining newspaper coverage leading up to the crossing of the Rapidan and during the first two weeks of battle. One need not make the common mistake of confusing press coverage with public opinion; it is enough to recognize that daily newspapers and weekly publications provided a large portion of the northern public with a primary source of information and interpretation about military events. Both the Lincoln administration and Grant realized the important role that the press played in shaping public opinion, even if they did not always welcome it. That role would be highlighted during an election year.[4]

A comparison of what Grant expected to accomplish against Lee with what the northern public anticipated reveals crucial differences between how each viewed making war. Grant subordinated the clash of battle to the larger objectives of his campaign, but northern civilians remained wedded to the notion of the climactic confrontation. Seeking early and decisive victory, northerners were ill prepared for what unfolded in the spring of 1864. Initial declarations of victory offered by newspaper correspondents, editorial page analysts, and the War Department deepened the public's eventual disillusionment. The war Grant and Lee fought in the spring of 1864 was unlike anything Americans had ever seen. Newspapers insisted on rendering the struggle in terms far more suitable to their images of Napoleonic warfare capped by Austerlitz and Waterloo, with Grant and Lee engaged in a clash of titans. Northerners were bound to be disappointed. As a result both Grant's reputation and Lincoln's chances for reelection suffered.

On his first trip east Grant spent two nights in Washington, journeyed down to visit the Army of the Potomac, and then stopped in Washington once more before heading west on March 11. He made several critical decisions during this period. Impressed by the force of political pressures on Union generals, he discarded any notion of establishing his headquarters in the West. Instead he would take the field with the Army of the Potomac to shield it from further disruption. Sherman would take his place in the West, with James B. McPherson assuming command of Grant's old Army of the Tennessee. At the same time Grant decided to retain George G. Meade as commander of the Army of the Potomac, rather than naming as his replacement William F. Smith, whose actions as chief engineer during the Chattanooga campaign had so impressed him. Eventually Grant assigned Smith to command a corps in the Army of the James.[5]

In deciding to come east, Grant acted against personal preference. The previous August he had welcomed news that he would not have to travel east to assume control of the Army of the Potomac: "Here I know the officers and men and what each Gen. is capable of as a commander. There I would have all to learn." His arrival in Virginia coincided with the publication of George B. McClellan's report of his military campaigns, the reaction to which among several officers of the Army of the Potomac suggested that for some people, at least, Little Mac always would be their general. It would take some time for Grant to get used to his new surroundings and to overcome the doubts of others—doubts sometimes succinctly expressed in the comment that Grant had yet to meet Bobby Lee.[6]

Grant also began to devise a plan of campaign. It proved to be a variation of a proposal he had forwarded to Washington the previous January at the request of then general-in-chief Henry W. Halleck. In the West he wanted Sherman to bear down on Atlanta and the Army of Tennessee, commanded by Joseph E. Johnston. Grant hoped that before long a second Union force would be able to launch a strike into the Confederate interior after taking Mobile via an amphibious landing, using soldiers currently detained on an expedition into Louisiana. This plan only slightly modified his January proposal. More radical was how he adjusted his original musings about operations in the East. In January he had advised Halleck to launch an invasion of North Carolina designed to force Lee to abandon his position in Virginia in order to check the threat to his source of supply. Halleck had rejected the plan, in part because he did not think sufficient manpower was available. He also had told Grant that Lee might counter by invading the North, and he doubted that an Army of the Potomac reduced in size to raise the North Carolina force could stop such an offensive. Like Lincoln, Halleck deemed Lee's army the primary objective of operations in the East—overlooking that Grant's proposal contained within it a way to dislodge Lee from Virginia and force him to come to battle. "But little progress can be made here till that army is broken or beaten," Halleck concluded. Whether Lincoln actually learned of the proposal is unclear; however, Halleck's reasoning reflected the president's own perspective on how to approach the problem of Lee and Virginia.[7]

Rather than simply give in to Halleck, Grant refashioned his plans for Virginia. Abandoning the North Carolina proposal, he transferred its objectives to an army to be mobilized at Norfolk with orders to sail up the James River and threaten Richmond and its connections to points south. That such an operation might bring to mind George McClellan's 1862 campaign bothered him not at all, although he knew that Halleck and probably Lincoln were sensitive on that point. Besides, it would be only one of four strike forces. A second column, stationed in West Virginia, would advance into southwest Virginia, destroying railroads and saltworks before heading toward the rail junction of Lynchburg. A third command would sweep south through the Shenandoah Valley, denying it to the Confederates as both a source of food and an avenue of invasion while forcing them to defend it. Finally, the Army of the Potomac would seek to engage Lee's Army of Northern Virginia.[8]

What Grant sought to do was relatively simple. By simultaneously striking at several of Lee's lines of supply, he hoped to force Lee to hit back at one of the columns or to retreat toward Richmond, whereupon the Army of the Potomac would pursue in the hopes of catching the Confederates in the open and on the move. The principle was the same as he had proposed in January; he had simply adjusted the means of menacing Lee's rear in order to placate the administration. At the same time, he hoped to make certain that Lee could not replicate the Confederate initiative of September 1863 by shifting forces westward to gain local superiority against Sherman's command. If all went well, Lee would have his hands full in Virginia. How the campaign would unfold depended in large part on how Lee responded to the Union advances.[9]

Grant planned to open the campaign by accompanying Meade and the Army of the Potomac. He found his options limited in choosing commanders in Virginia. Lincoln had placed Franz Sigel in charge of the Department of West Virginia in February; Benjamin F. Butler directed army operations along the James River. To remove either man would cost Lincoln political support. Although Grant resigned himself to Sigel, he came away from his first encounter with Butler impressed with the general's intelligence—perhaps in part because Butler revealed a plan that resembled Grant's own. Grant sent both generals a series of rather detailed dispatches in April outlining their roles in the forthcoming campaign. In assigning Smith to Butler, he intended to provide the Massachusetts Democrat with a skilled subordinate.[10]

Grant's instructions to Meade were straightforward: "Lee's army will be your objective point. Wherever Lee goes, there you will go also." The second sentence reflected Grant's belief that Lee would have to choose either to stand and fight along the Rapidan or to march south to counter Butler's thrust at Richmond. As it turned out, the movements of the Army of the Potomac determined where Lee would go. Although Grant had not yet decided in early April whether to move against Lee's left or right, he observed that a march by the right flank might result in a juncture with Butler, and he made plans to establish supply depots along the way. In the end the logistical advantages offered by a move against Lee's right proved decisive in the choice of that route.[11]

Grant did not expect a short spring campaign. Believing that the Confederate armies would put up a fierce resistance because they were aware of the stakes, he told Frank Blair to anticipate a "long hard desperate fight." He also considered the possibility that the campaign might result in a siege of Richmond and Petersburg. Preparing for such an eventuality, he instructed Halleck to put together a pontoon train and sent staff officer Cyrus B. Comstock to Washington to discuss the need for a siege train. He also informed Butler that the two armies would probably unite outside the Confederate capital. He intended "that with the forces here I shall aim to fight Lee between here and Richmond if he will stand. Should however Lee fall back into Richmond I will follow up and make a junction with your Army on the James River."[12]

There was little in Grant's plan to suggest that prior to the commencement of operations in 1864 he embraced a war of attrition against Lee's army. He thought it possible but not probable that Lee might suffer a decisive defeat in the field. The different offensive thrusts were designed to force Lee to choose between counterattacking, defending Richmond, or abandoning Virginia altogether. There was very little to suggest that Grant sought battle in the style of Joseph Hooker at Chancellorsville, although, like Hooker, he appreciated the value of threatening the Confederate rear. In any case, by keeping Lee off balance he would deprive the Confederate commander of the ability to turn the tide of affairs in an effort to counter Union successes elsewhere. Grant did not insist that victory come in Virginia. He did insist that wherever it came, it would be in time to keep Lincoln in office for another term and thus ensure that the war would be fought to a successful conclusion.

Newspapers praised Grant's rise to overall command as a sign that at last the Union was on the way to victory. "With Lieutenant General Grant at the head of military affairs, our people have renewed hopes for the spring campaign," correspondent Noah Brooks told readers of the Sacramento *Daily Union*. The *New York Herald*, still cherishing hopes of a Grant presidential candidacy, agreed. The new lieutenant general "inspires the public confidence to a reasonable anticipation of quick work and great results." Many northerners joined the *New York Times* in awaiting the conflicts of the spring: "In all probability they will be the decisive battles of the struggle." Several editorials praised the idea that Union military operations finally would be coordinated under one commander. Still, it was the confrontation with Lee that most papers welcomed. To those who pointed out that Grant had never faced Robert E. Lee, the *Times* replied, "That is true enough. But do these people ever think that, if it be true that Grant has never fought Lee, it is equally true that Lee has never met Grant?"[13]

In light of this concern, and reflecting the interest in military operations in Virginia, most previews of the coming campaign concentrated on the fate of Lee's army. All but the Democrats agreed that it was doomed. Where these armchair prognosticators disagreed was over how soon northern victory would come. "It would not at all surprise us, if the next Fourth of July should see the war transferred from Virginia to a narrower field far South, and Gen. Grant pressing the defeated enemy in his last strongholds," speculated one *Times* editorial. Not everyone embraced this vision of a short and decisive campaign. Some newspapers recalled how painful that delusion had been. "Let us, as sensible men, remember how uncertain the event of every battle is, and not take leave of our common sense by declaring that we must and shall win," urged *Harper's Weekly*. The notion of immediate and decisive victory was a delusive one: "Three years of fierce civil war, as they have made us sadder, should certainly make us wiser men." To expect Grant to achieve so much so soon was counterproductive, noted *Harper's Weekly*, and would end in replacing unreasonable hopes with unwarranted criticism.

"Let him not be impeded nor embarrassed in his work either by speeches or articles, advice or criticism, until we shall have given him a fair trial," offered the *New York Tribune*. "If he proves a do-nothing, a hang-back, a mistake, let us in due time get rid of him; but first let him have a fair chance to prove he is the man for his work. Let him not be condemned for one miscarriage, if there shall be one, but generously trusted and sustained until he shall have decisively shown that he can or cannot put down the Rebellion." Elsewhere, however, the *Tribune* showed signs that it, too, anticipated something grand. Reporter Charles A. Page proclaimed, "This campaign into which the Army of the Potomac is just now to be launched probably holds the pivotal battle that shall be an era for all time"—it would be, suggested Page, an American Waterloo or Marathon. In the actual event, it was more like a marathon than a Waterloo.[14]

The *New York Herald* raised the stakes of the entire campaign by claiming that anything less than a decisive victory would be a disastrous defeat. "If, with General Grant at the head and the struggle as it now is, we cannot put the rebellion down in the coming summer, we can never put it down," it proclaimed on March 18, adding the next day, "for if we do not end it now we never can." It left no doubt of what was at issue: "We are on the verge of a decisive campaign—a campaign which will bring the rebellion to an end or cover with disgrace and confusion the government and the loyal States." Out west the *Chicago Times* also spoke of one last battle on which everything depended.[15]

Three years of war apparently had taught the northern public little about the patterns of war. The quest for decisive battle had proven a fool's errand, especially in Virginia, where the contending forces were encamped about fifty miles southwest of their positions in 1861. The Union's most impressive triumphs to date had come in the West, especially at Vicksburg, where some 30,000 Confederates had surrendered the previous July 4. In light of all that had happened, it seemed unreasonable for anyone to harbor notions of an American Waterloo bringing the war to a close. Yet this was exactly the vision that several newspapers embraced. Discerning readers might have recalled that such hopes also had appeared in print the previous three springs.[16]

A closer examination of the sources for such comments suggests that politics helped to shape perceptions prior to the campaign. Republican papers such as the *New York Times*, the *New York Tribune*, and the *Chicago Tribune* were willing to accept the idea of a prolonged campaign in part to guard against the consequences of anything less than early and decisive success, although each at times gave in to the notion of a swift triumph. The *Times*'s Henry Raymond was a staunch supporter of the president's bid for a second term; Horace Greeley of the *New York Tribune* and his equally mercurial Chicago cousin, Joseph Medill, pondered the possibility of a candidate more acceptable to the radical wing of the party, but their loyalty to the party was unquestioned. In contrast, newspapers that espoused Democratic or conservative positions proved much more impatient for victory, albeit for different reasons. James Gordon Bennett's *Herald* saw a quick victory as essential to the success of his scheme to make Grant president. In contrast, by promoting an "all or nothing" theme, Democratic papers hoped that early battlefield setbacks would lead to disenchantment with Lincoln and the Republicans.[17]

Partisanship was also evident in discussions about whether Lincoln and his subordinates were interfering with Grant's plans for the spring offensive. People who claimed that Lincoln had tied McClellan's hands now feared that Grant would suffer the same fate. "Will General Grant be hampered and harpied by politicians, as General McClellan was, or will he be permitted to do what he thinks ought to be done?" asked the *Herald*. It deplored possible interference with Grant by Lincoln: "His political fortunes, not less than the great cause of the country, are in the hands of General Grant, and the failure of the General will be the overthrow of the President." An editorial headline expressed its point succinctly: "The Certainty of our Success if Grant is Left Alone."[18]

Supporters of the administration dismissed such charges, as did the *Times*. Lincoln himself implicitly alluded to them in a last letter to Grant on the eve of the opening of the campaign. "The particulars of your plan I neither know, nor seek to know," the president remarked, adding, "I wish not to obtrude any constraints or restraints upon you. . . . If there is anything wanting which is in my power to give, do not fail to let me know it." Fully aware that Lincoln and his advisers had indeed restricted his freedom of action in several areas, Grant also understood the political import should such disagreements with the administration become public. With that in mind, his response, if not exactly accurate, nevertheless would quell such rumors. Claiming that the administration had never obstructed "my vigerously prossecuting what appeared to me my duty," Grant added that he had been "astonished at the readiness with which everythin[g] asked for has been yielded without even an explaination being asked. Should my success be less than I desire, and expect, the least I can say is, the fault is not with you."[19]

Grant was fully aware of what the northern public believed was at stake. "I know the greatest anxiety is now felt in the North for the success of this move, and that the anxiety will increase when it is once known that the Army is in motion," he wrote his wife as he made final preparations. Meade reported that Grant was "very much annoyed" with press commentary about the coming campaign. A newspaperman, eager for a scoop, asked Grant how long it would take him to get to Richmond. "I will agree to be there in four days," Grant dryly replied, "that is, if General Lee becomes a party to the agreement; but if he objects, the trip will undoubtedly be prolonged."[20] There was more to this comment than a simple joke at a reporter's expense. Grant realized that the conduct of campaigns was shaped by decisions made by leaders on both sides. Much would depend on how Lee responded to Grant's opening moves. Perhaps he would rush to defend Richmond; perhaps he would confront Grant in battle. Whatever Lee decided to do, Grant stood ready to respond and was determined to seize and retain the initiative.

On May 4 the Army of the Potomac commenced the spring campaign. By nightfall the Second and Fifth Corps were south of the Rapidan and Rappahannock; the Sixth Corps remained astride the Rapidan at Germanna Ford; Ambrose E. Burnside's Ninth Corps, under orders to protect Grant's lengthy supply train, remained north of the river. "Forty Eight hours now will demonstrate whether the enemy intends giving battle this side of Richmond," Grant telegraphed Halleck.[21]

In less than twenty-four hours Grant learned that Robert E. Lee did indeed intend to give battle. On the morning of May 5 lead elements of Richard S. Ewell's Second Corps engaged Gouverneur K. Warren's Fifth Corps along the Orange Turnpike west of Wilderness Tavern. Grant directed Meade to pitch into the advancing Confederates. By midday the battle was well under way. For the rest of that day and all of the next the two armies traded blows, each coming close to achieving a decisive advantage, but neither securing it.

Many who watched Grant during his initial clash with Lee remarked on his cool composure. They noted that he whiled away the hours whit-

Grant composing a message indicating his army had crossed the Rapidan River, May 4, 1864 (sketch by Alfred R. Waud).
Library of Congress

tling and puffing a cigar. Reporter Charles A. Page painted just such an image for his readers: "Gen. Grant is smoking a wooden pipe, his face as peaceful as a summer evening, his general demeanor indescribably imperturbable." In fact, however, Grant was a bit anxious about the Army of the Potomac. Although he had grown somewhat familiar with the army and spoke of it in positive terms, there remained the true test of battle. "I was new to the army, did not have it in hand and did not know what I could do with the generals or the men," he later explained. The fact that Grant first appeared in the Wilderness with sword, sash, and gloves—not exactly his usual field uniform—suggested the degree to which he was still uncomfortable with the army, as if he had to dress to impress. The whittling and smoking, far from displaying calmness, were signs that he was struggling to soothe his nerves. That in slicing away at pieces of wood he cut up his gloves and that in puffing away he went through twenty cigars in one day far more accurately suggests his state of mind than did descriptions of an almost stoic commander. Only once did he reveal something of what was going on inside. When a Confederate assault on the Union right on the eve-

Grant whittling on the afternoon of the first day's fighting in the Wilderness (sketch by Charles W. Reed).
Library of Congress

ning of May 6 scored initial success, a staff officer excitedly exclaimed that Lee was about to sever the army's line of communications. Grant stood up, removed his cigar, and snapped, "Oh, I am heartily tired of hearing about what Lee is going to do. Some of you always seem to think he is suddenly going to turn a double somersault, and land in our rear and on both of our flanks at the same time. Go back to your command, and try to think what we are going to do ourselves, instead of what Lee is going to do."[22]

Grant already had done some thinking about what he was going to do. He did not expect to fight the decisive battle of the campaign in the Wilderness and rested satisfied that his command had crossed the river and repelled Lee's assaults. His efforts to launch an offensive of his own on May 6 had failed to crush Lee's right; the nature of the terrain and the fortified defenses thrown up by the Confederates deterred him from trying again. Better, he decided, to move once more by Lee's right, to force the Confederates out of the trenches that blocked a Union advance on Richmond. The terrain around Spotsylvania Court House was far more open and offered a better chance to damage the enemy. Such were Grant's thoughts on learning that his early morning attack on May 6 had failed to roll up the Confederate right. On the morning of May 7 he issued directives in preparation for a night march.[23]

In short, Grant had achieved what he wanted to achieve, although he had failed to gain any additional advantage. Standing by itself, the battle of the Wilderness was neither victory nor defeat. Viewed in the larger context of Grant's plan of operations, it was merely the first of what he envisioned as a series of clashes with Lee's army. Comparisons to Hooker's experience the previous year at Chancellorsville missed the point entirely. Hooker had sought to crush Lee in one dramatic blow, whereas Grant accepted the fact that Civil War armies, especially veteran forces, possessed too much strength to be destroyed in a single battle.[24]

None of what happened in the Wilderness would be known in the North for several days. In fact, few people understood much about Grant's campaign plans. The general-in-chief had kept them confidential, leading to great speculation in the press. The people "will wait with intense solicitude, and yet with strongest expectations," the *New York Times* told its readers. "They look for great things, and with reason." The Washington *National Republican* predicted, "Every hour may now bring us news of a battle, but we are inclined to the belief that it will be a foot race for Richmond. The Rebel Capital will undoubtedly be flanked and invested, should Lee's army occupy its defenses, and the country may reasonably hope that this time Richmond will fall." Noting such expectations, the editorial page of the *Tribune* cautioned against excessive zeal about Grant's prospects: "Vex him with no impatient criticism, no angry reproach, if at one point or another there is failure or delay, but while we profoundly feel that under his guidance the war approaches a tremendous crisis, let us await the development and result of the *general* plan which he seeks to put in execution."[25]

Among those anxiously awaiting word from the front was Abraham

Lincoln. At times he resorted to humor to alleviate stress. In responding to a congressman's inquiry, he remarked, "Well, I can't tell much about it. You see, Grant has gone to the Wilderness, crawled in, drawn up the ladder, and pulled in the hole after him, and I guess we'll have to wait till he comes out before we know just what he's up to." At other times, however, he paced the halls of his living quarters, "his hands behind him, great black rings under his eyes, his head bent forward upon his breast," as the artist Frank Carpenter recalled. At the War Department, Ethan Allen Hitchcock looked up to see Secretary of War Edwin M. Stanton's fingers tremble as he reached for a piece of paper.[26]

May 5 passed without word of any action. So did the day of May 6. Lincoln sat in the telegraph office at the War Department, "sickening with anxiety," according to one observer. It proved to be a sleepless night for the president. But in the early evening hours word reached the War Department that a correspondent for the New York Tribune wished to contact Assistant Secretary of War Charles A. Dana, who had once worked for the paper. Stanton demanded to know what was going on with Grant. When the reporter, nineteen-year-old Henry Wing, insisted that he first be allowed to send his story to New York, the secretary threatened him with arrest. After Lincoln intervened, Wing promised to share his information, but only after he wired the Tribune. The president assented, and Wing boarded a special train to Washington. Arriving at the capital in the early hours of May 7, he found himself rushed to the White House, where he told Lincoln and several cabinet members what he knew—which was not much, as he had left at the close of the first day of battle. Wing did have a special message for the president from Grant himself: "He told me to tell you, Mr. President, that there would be no turning back." It was just what Lincoln wanted to hear. In his joy he actually kissed Wing. But there was precious little else to celebrate. As Secretary of the Navy Gideon Welles noted, Wing's account was "not full and conclusive."[27]

The anxiety was understandable. Just more than a year earlier another general of great promise had led the Army of the Potomac across the Rapidan and Rappahannock. For days neither Lincoln nor anyone else knew of the progress of Joseph Hooker's grand offensive. "Great uneasiness and uncertainty prevail in regard to army movements," Welles had observed in his diary. "I think the War Department is really poorly advised of operations." Encountering Lincoln at Stanton's office, the navy secretary noted that the president "had a feverish anxiety to get the fact; was constantly up and down, for nothing reliable came from the front." For days Lincoln worried: "His fears," Welles noted, "are the result of absence of facts, rather than from any information received." In the end, news of defeat had proven quite painful to the president. "The press had wrought the public mind to high expectation by predicting certain success, which all wished to believe," the cabinet minister jotted in his diary. To endure the same sort of anticipation a year later was truly trying.[28]

In fact, Grant had kept his superiors informed of the course of events. Shortly before noon on May 6 he telegraphed Halleck that while no decisive result had been obtained, "all things are progressing favorably."[29] But it took time for his dispatches to make their way northward and be deciphered. Grant differed little from his predecessors when it came to sharing news. By now the image of a president pacing as he awaited word from the front was a familiar one, as were the all-night vigils at the War Department's telegraph office.

Perhaps a little irritated by the silence from Grant's headquarters, Lincoln and Stanton decided to send Assistant Secretary of War Dana to field headquarters with instructions to keep the administration apprised of events. Arriving at Grant's camp on the morning of May 7, Dana commenced sending dispatches to his superiors, but the messages did not reach Washington immediately. "Our whole thought has been hanging over the military movements of Our Armies & Fleet—in a breathless suspense—with scare rumors enough to make one take a long breath," remarked Elizabeth Blair Lee of the famed Blair clan. Noting that no dispatches had arrived at the War Department, she added that Stanton was dismayed: Grant must be "busy—too much so to think of such people's curiosity or solicitude." Lincoln was still in the dark as to the course of events when he responded to a call to speak at a concert given by the Marine Band that evening. "In lieu of a speech," he remarked, "I propose that we give three cheers for Major General Grant and all the armies under his command"—thus, if the transcript recorded him accurately, forgetting Grant's new rank.[30]

The *New York Tribune* fired the first shot in that city's press wars on May 7, largely on the basis of Wing's dispatch. Although the struggle on May 5 had been inconclusive, the *Tribune* assured readers that "there ought to be no doubt that there has been a grand victory. . . . That the whole nation is in suspense with breathless expectation we well know, but we recognize it to be their duty, as it is ours, to wait without murmurs till the truth can be told with no chance of periling the success we long for." Competing papers preferred to wait and see. The editorial page of the *New York Times* admonished readers who expected too much too soon: "While we abate no part of our condemnation against those who eagerly anticipate defeat, let us not forget, if we would be wise, that there is error and danger in the opposite extreme, which blazons forth victory in advance of its achievement, and opens the way for disappointment and chagrin by prefiguring impossible exploits and supernatural successes." The *Herald* observed that while many people were anxious for immediate results, "The more thoughtful, however, came to the conclusion that a single encounter would not determine the contest, and a series of battles may have to be fought before there can be any decisive result." That attitude stood in stark contrast to reports elsewhere in the same edition that "whether the enemy has been driven into his intrenched winter camp, or down the roads to Richmond, we have yet to learn."[31]

There were good reasons for the delay in transmitting news. Confederate cavalry was doing what it could to block communications between Grant's army and Washington. Reporters had to follow Wing's example of personally carrying dispatches to the capital if they hoped to transmit news to their editors. The *New York Herald*'s Sylvanus Cadwallader and J. C. Fitzpatrick and the *Philadelphia Inquirer*'s Edward Crapsey found themselves detained by Confederates for several days.[32]

Scraps of information arrived in Washington on May 8. Welles put much stock in learning that Rufus Ingalls, the Army of the Potomac's quartermaster, had requisitioned more supplies. Newspapers knew no more than did Lincoln. Wing's dispatch proved to be the first extended description of the opening of the campaign. Other papers reprinted his column, overlooking the fact that it failed to offer anything about events after May 5. The *National Republican* teased readers with brief and sketchy assertions of victory: "Gen. Grant is master of the field. Lee is in full retreat. Gen. Grant is in hot pursuit." It declared that "the result of the fighting on Thursday and Friday is all that the most sanguine friends of the Government can desire."[33]

In New York that Sunday, May 8, the war dominated discussion. Ministers delivered sermons on war-related topics. In the afternoon crowds gathered outside newspaper offices in anticipation of bulletins from the front. There was precious little to learn, although an impression prevailed that Grant had triumphed—doubtless reinforced by what appeared in the Washington papers. Republicans cheered what they heard; some Democrats, aware of the impact of Union military success on the presidential contest, sulked. In Printing House Square one brash Copperhead denounced the government. "The discussion of the war and the late news from Virginia occupied the attention of groups of men in the hotels, eating-houses, saloons, cars and stages," observed the *Tribune*. "Large numbers of individuals were seen seated on the steps of stores and dwellings, each one with a newspaper in his hand, eagerly reading the news. . . . The glad tidings afforded great gratification to our citizens, but there was an absence of that boastfulness which has too frequently mingled with our jubilant manifestations, on the receipt of good news from the War." New Yorker George Templeton Strong, just back from a trip to Washington on behalf of the United States Sanitary Commission, reacted with ambivalence: "It is long since our national prospects looked so bright. But we may be fearfully 'disillusionated' tomorrow morning, and find that an assault on Richmond has been repulsed and that Grant and Meade are falling back on Washington or 'changing their base' to Fredericksburg and Aquia Creek."[34]

Some time during May 8 Stanton received sufficient information from the front to justify a claim of victory. Learning the news, Attorney General Edward Bates remarked that the war secretary "believes that we have gained a great victory: probably the turning point of the war." Aware of the importance of public reaction to news of events on the battlefield, Stanton determined that he would issue dispatches to inform newspapers of Union military progress. He chose to do so by keeping Gen. John A. Dix, in command at New York City, updated and by instructing Dix to share the contents of his dispatches with the local papers. This guise proved rather transparent, as Stanton also distributed copies of the dispatches to the Associated Press. His first missive judged Grant to have achieved "material success" on the battlefield. He also explained the purpose of his effort at news management: "It is designed to give accurate official statements of what is known to the Department in this great crisis, and to withhold nothing from the public."[35]

On May 9 the first concrete information about the campaign appeared in the morning newspapers. "GLORIOUS NEWS/DEFEAT AND RETREAT OF LEE'S ARMY," cheered the *Times*, forgetting its own advice about restraint. So did the crosstown *Tribune*: "Gen. Grant Driving Lee Back/REBEL DASH FOILED AT LAST" screamed one headline, while elsewhere readers learned "LEE DRIVEN AT ALL POINTS." The editorial pages now confidently asserted that "the movements and the battles of last week are an assurance of final success." Not everyone accepted the analysis. Reading the papers, George Templeton Strong noted that while Lee seemed to be retreating, the battle otherwise appeared to be "a severe and close affair . . . a drawn battle."[36]

Lincoln was ecstatic. He released a public statement asking Americans to pray, noting that the outcome of operations "claim[s] our especial gratitude to God." That evening he responded to a crowd that had gathered outside the White House to celebrate the victory. "Our commanders are following up their victories resolutely and successfully," he noted. "I think, without knowing the particulars of the plans of Gen. Grant, that what has been accomplished is of more importance than at first appears." The general "has not been jostled in his purposes; . . . he has made all his points, and to-day he is on his line as he purposed before he moved his armies." Pleased at what had happened, the president reminded his listeners that "there is a great deal still to be done" and urged them to emulate Grant by maintaining "the same tranquil mood that is characteristic of that brave and loyal man." Privately he spoke with even more confidence. "How near we have been to this thing before and failed," he told his personal secretary. "I believe if any other general had been at the head of that army it would have now been on this side of the Rapidan. It is the dogged pertinacity of Grant that wins." In various forms Lincoln's statement made its way into the newspapers. Stanton passed the news to Dix: "The belief here is that Lieut.-Gen. Grant is achieving a complete victory." "All our conclusions are one way," Welles reported, "and there can be no doubt the Rebels have fallen back and our forces have advanced."[37]

Grant's reaction was much more restrained. He had notified Halleck on May 7 of the events of the previous two days. Estimating his own losses at about 12,000 ("of whom an unusually larger proportion are but slightly wounded"), he speculated that Lee must have suffered at least as severely. "At present we can claim no victory over the enemy, neither have they gained a single advantage," he concluded. Omitted was the fact that he already had directed Meade to prepare for an advance that night. Informing Halleck of his movement the next day, Grant added, "My efforts will be to form a junction with Genl Butler as early as possible and be prepared to beat any enemy interposing. . . . My exact route to the James River I have not yet definately marked out." By now he was willing to claim that the results obtained at the Wilderness were "decidedly in our favor," although a combination of Lee's fortified position and the need to guard his supply trains "rendered it impossible to inflict the heavy blow on Lees army I had hoped."[38]

In light of what had happened the last three times Union armies had attempted to cross the Rapidan-Rappahannock line, however, the public response to Grant's advance was understandable. After Fredericksburg, Chancellorsville, and Mine Run, the Army of the Potomac had returned to its previous location. To learn that Grant was intent on continuing to move south came as a welcome change. It logically (if incorrectly) followed

Union soldiers cheer Grant as the army moves south,
May 7, 1864 (sketch by Edwin Forbes).
Library of Congress

that if Grant was advancing, Lee must be retreating. Traditional ways of assessing victory and defeat remained intact; different was the fact that for the first time a Union army had crossed the Rapidan and Rappahannock rivers without quickly retreating northward.

The news continued bright on May 10. "VICTORY!/'ON TO RICHMOND.'/Lee's Defeat and Retreat Fully Confirmed," announced the *Times.* "VICTORY!/Splendid Success of General Grant," echoed the *Herald.* Greeley's *Tribune* proved even more dramatic: "THE GREAT BATTLES/Victory for the Union/NIGHT FALLS ON A DOUBTFUL FIELD/ BUT THE REBELS FLY BY NIGHT/NO ENEMY TO BE SEEN ON SATURDAY/Lee Found to be in Hasty Retreat/OUR FORCES AT ONCE IN PURSUIT." Along with the *Herald* it reported that Winfield Scott Hancock's Second Corps was in possession of Spotsylvania Court House— a serious error—and that the end was in sight. As the *Tribune*'s editorial page proclaimed, "There is no longer any doubt. Gen. Grant has won a great victory. . . . The military power of the Rebellion has received a fatal blow." All signs pointed to more good news in the near future: "Grant is pressing on with relentless vigor and determination, with the full assurance that Lee is in his power, and that delay is the most he dare hope. . . . While, therefore, we believe it possible that another tremendous struggle is yet to be fought, we believe there is no longer room for doubt of ultimate, complete, and early triumph. The days of the Rebellion are surely numbered." [39]

The *Herald* for May 10 sounded the same themes. In common with other papers, its columns carried Lincoln's proclamation and Stanton's statement that Grant was "achieving a complete victory." Inside, the editorial page announced, "The army of General Lee, baffled and beaten at every point, is in full retreat towards Richmond, pursued by the unconquerable old Army of the Potomac." Readers learned that Lee, "leaving his dead and wounded in our hands," was withdrawing southward. The paper expressed some concern that the Confederates would destroy bridges as they made their way to North Carolina. "But the combinations of General Grant have been arranged to meet all contingencies, and from the developements already made, we may reasonably anticipate not only that Richmond will very soon be ours, but that hardly a remnant of Lee's defeated, exhausted and demoralized legions, as an organized body, will be left to tell the story." [40]

The news brought smiles to many northerners. "Everybody was in capital humor yesterday," the *Herald* observed. "The bright sunshine and the brighter news from the seat of war were reflected upon every face. Bulletin after bulletin and extra after extra were eagerly read, and as every bit of news made the fact of Grant's great victory clearer there were frequent cheers and more frequent congratulations. . . . The serious and anxious reticence of Friday and Saturday, and the comparative doubtfulness of Sunday, gave place to the assurance of success and the confidence of still greater victories." No wonder that the weekly journal *Leslie's Illustrated* declared, "The War in Virginia—The Prospect a Short and Decisive Campaign." So far as anyone knew, "the fatal hour to the rebellion is near at hand." [41]

Back in Virginia, Grant contemplated his next move. By May 10 he knew that Lee was willing to come back for more: "Enemy hold our front in very strong force and evince strong determination to interpose between us and Richmond to the last." Anticipating a prolonged struggle, Grant informed Halleck that "I shall take no backward steps but may be compelled to send back to Bell[e] Plain for further supplies. . . . We can maintain ourselves at least and in the end beat Lee's army I believe." That evening he nearly tasted victory when Emory Upton's column broke through the Confederate center, but lack of support forced the attackers to retire. [42]

As Grant moved, northerners waited for more news, primed to believe that the end of the war might be near. "A craving, uneasy feeling pervaded the community through the day," Welles scribbled in his diary on May 11. "No intelligence from any quarter received, yet a conviction pervades everywhere that much is being done." The *Journal of Commerce*, a Democratic New York daily, complained that "we have been deluged with worthless—worse than worthless, false dispatches giving false accounts, and the people have been elevated and depressed by turns." Most clearly depressed, others might have added, were the *Journal*'s readers, who knew that good news from the front was bad news for the Democrats. The *New York Tribune* advised readers to remain calm. "The only thing against which it can be necessary to suggest a caution is popular impatience. Success has come very suddenly. If the next is slower, we can afford to wait." [43]

News of the May 10 assault renewed anticipations that the moment of decision was at hand. On May 12 the *Times* announced, "Another Defeat of the Rebels/The Rebel Right Crushed." The neighboring *Tribune* agreed: "The Army of the Potomac has fought another great battle, and again is victorious." It judged Grant "the matchless soldier." Columnists looked to the Napoleonic era for parallels. "If Waterloo was a battle of giants, as Wellington said, what is this?" asked the *Tribune*. "If General Lee has not suffered a Waterloo defeat in his first encounter with General Grant," enthused the *Herald*, "his retreat looks to us very much like that of Napoleon from Leipsic, developing the same desperate resistance from point to point, but with the fortunes of the struggle as overwhelmingly against him." It seemed that Grant was indeed the general of the age. If, as the *Tribune* claimed, Grant had assured Lincoln that "I will do my utmost to fulfill public expectations," it seemed that he was doing just that. [44]

More optimism was evident in press accounts appearing on May 13. Part of the new wave of enthusiasm was due to Grant. Congressman Elihu B. Washburne, long Grant's spokesman and promoter, had accompanied his general through the first week of the campaign. As he made preparations to depart on May 11, he asked Grant if he could carry a message to Washington—preferably one that would offer some encouragement. Grant pondered the wisdom of the suggestion. "We are certainly making fair progress, and all the fighting has been in our favor," he finally replied, "but the campaign promises to be a long one, and I am particularly anxious not to say anything just now that might hold out false hopes to the people." He then drafted two dispatches, one to Halleck, the other to Stanton. "We have now entered the sixth day of very hard fighting," he told Stanton. "The result to this time is much in our favor. . . . I propose to fight it out on this line if it takes all summer." The missive to Halleck contained nearly the same declaration, but it also urged Halleck to hurry forward reinforcements. "I am satisfied the enemy are very shaky and are only kept up to the mark by the greatest exertion on the part of their officers, and by keeping them entrenched in every position they take." It looked as if the climactic struggle might well take place at Spotsylvania. Grant observed that there was no evidence that Lee was sending men south to defend Richmond from Butler.[45]

Grant miscalculated if he thought his messages would spark no false hopes. Stanton forwarded Grant's dispatch to him to the newspapers, which seized on the declaration about fighting it out all summer as evidence that the campaign was going about as well as could be expected. The *New York Herald* claimed that Grant was six miles beyond Spotsylvania Court House. An editorial in the *New York Tribune* declared, "We have abundant reason to believe that it will not 'take all summer.'" The *Tribune* believed "the catastrophe is certainly near" for the Confederacy: "We have reason to believe that a very few days now will settle the fate of the rebellion. It is staggering to its fall from the crippling blows of Grant, and cannot survive the summer." It seemed clear that the Army of Northern Virginia was on its last legs. Moreover, as the *Times* reminded everyone, "when Lee's army is destroyed, let it be remembered, the rebellion is virtually over."[46]

It was understandable that public anticipation rose in response to these heightened expectations. From Chicago, Medill's *Tribune* noted, "Our very hearts seem to pause in their beating as we listen, breathless, for the most meagre news of the conflict." Washingtonians were absorbed by the struggle. Brooks observed that "nothing else appears to be thought of but what is going forward on the debated territory between the James River and the branches of the Mattapony, where thousands of brave men are rushing to victory and immortality each hour." The waiting created incredible pressure. "The city is pervaded with a feeling which can scarcely be called excitement, it is too intense—it is an absorbing eagerness which is more fervent than excited." People grabbed extra editions as they appeared and interrogated anyone who had returned from the front. "Every loyal heart is full of joy at the glorious tidings which continue to come up from the front," Brooks added, "and citizens everywhere are congratulating each other upon the near prospect of an end of this wasteful and wicked war. The 'coming man' appears to have come at last, and Grant is the hero of the war." Lost in such discussions was Brooks's admonition that "the war cannot end this summer even if we are victorious now, but a successful issue will give us the prestige of ultimate and sure triumph." Ever sensitive to the political implications of events, Welles observed that Copperheads did not share in the celebration: "It is painful to witness the factious and traitorous spirit, but it plainly shows itself."[47]

Meanwhile Grant planned yet another blow against Lee. Encouraged by the success of Upton's assault, he ordered Hancock's Second Corps to try to pierce the enemy center. In the early hours of May 12 the battle opened. Union forces achieved major initial success, capturing nearly a Confederate division and many cannon. As the day dragged on, however, Lee plugged the hole in his position, and both sides waged a most sanguinary battle at what became known as the Bloody Angle. Once more Grant gained something, but not as much as he might have.

Newspaper reports overlooked the final result in their rush to describe the opening attack. Stories of Hancock's assault created the most excitement since the beginning of the campaign. "VICTORY!/A Decisive Battle/LEE'S ARMY ROUTED," read the headlines of a late edition of the *New York Times* on May 13. More celebration followed the next morning. "THE GREAT CONTEST/GLORIOUS SUCCESSES/Lee Terribly Beaten on Thursday/HE RETREATS DURING THE NIGHT/Grant Pursues on Friday Morning," announced the *New York Tribune*. There were rumors that Lee himself was wounded in battle and had been taken to Richmond—as if to confirm that Grant had indeed overcome the Confederate chieftain. While the *Tribune* published denials that Lee had surrendered, it added, "THE END DRAWS NEAR." *Leslie's Illustrated*, under the headline "The Clouds Lifting—The Day Breaking," predicted that Grant's operations "must speedily put an end to the rebellion" and offered its readers a large image of Grant, hand thrust in his coat in the Napoleonic fashion, consulting with Meade. It was all over for Lee: "Let it suffice that his shattered army is between two fires; that his communications and scanty supplies are cut off on every side; that while Richmond must speedily fall unless he flies to the rescue, inevitable capture or starvation awaits him in seeking a refuge within that city's defenses. Flying westward, from sheer exhaustion and destitution, his disheartened and despairing army will soon be dissolved, and in pausing to fight again he covets immediate destruction."

As a *New York Tribune* editorial observed, "The Rebel Army of Virginia has been thoroughly vanquished. Probably more of those who composed it one week ago are now wounded or prisoners than remain to be rallied again under the flag of Secession. We will not anticipate: but we believe Lee's Army as an effective force has practically ceased to exist." The

"*The Clouds Lifting—The Day Breaking.*" *Grant and Meade on the cover of* Frank Leslie's Illustrated Newspaper, *May 28, 1864.*

Times concluded that Lee's army "is being defeated, demolished, crushed and annihilated." It was "the greatest victory of the war."[48]

Even Grant held high hopes for the ultimate outcome of the battle in the aftermath of the May 12 assault. "The enemy are obstinate and seem to have found the last ditch," he told Halleck. To Julia he wrote, "I am very well and full of hope. I see from the newspapers the country is also hopeful," which was an understatement. He thought that Lee was "simply covering a retreat which must necessarily have been slow with such roads and so dark a night as they had last night." It was time to press forward to see what was going on. Dana jumped the gun, however, reporting to Stanton that Lee had withdrawn. Indeed Lee had, insofar as the Confederates had abandoned the salient; but they had merely withdrawn to a new line of fortifications erected over the previous twenty-four hours. That news was slow in coming to Grant and was even slower in being transmitted to Washington by Dana. Stanton released the former dispatch to the papers, fueling optimism that the end was near. "The Virginia campaign approaches a glorious culmination," the *Herald* proclaimed. Lee's army was shattered: "Broken down, half famished and demoralized, where can it be rallied to accept another battle this side of Richmond? . . . We anticipate that this retreat of Lee will become a rout, and have no doubt that a general stampede has already commenced at Richmond. . . . We hope to print the announcement—Richmond is Ours!—in a very few days after [this] date."[49]

Premature reporting produced a second and even more serious piece of false information. On May 14 Dana told Stanton that an advance of the Fifth and Sixth Corps might force Lee to withdraw in the direction of Lynchburg. Lincoln shared the news with his secretaries, and Stanton included it in a dispatch to midwestern governors on May 15. Only later did everyone learn that heavy rains had forced Grant to call off the advance.[50]

Rain halted effective offensive operations between May 13 and May 17. "The army is in best of spirits and feel greatest confidence in ultimate success," Grant informed Halleck. "You can assure the President and Secretary of War that the elements alone have suspended hostilities and that it is no manner due to weakness or exhaustion on our part." Nevertheless, administration officials continued to worry about Grant's progress. "A painful suspense in military operations," Welles noted. "It is a necessary suspense, but the intense anxiety is oppressive, and almost unfits the mind for mental activity." Like others, the navy secretary believed that these battles would prove decisive.[51]

That anticipation proved premature. As Grant waited for clear skies, he reconsidered the details of his pledge to "fight it out on this line." Circumstances elsewhere compelled him to ponder alternatives. News that Sigel had suffered a defeat at New Market on May 15 meant that the Confederates in the Shenandoah Valley could now reinforce Lee. Dispatches announcing Butler's failure to sever Richmond's rail links with the rest of the South indicated that Lee would be under no pressure to protect his rear.[52] Had Grant merely desired to continue trading lives with Lee in an endless war of attrition, remaining at Spotsylvania would have suited him just fine. Instead he decided to choose the alternative he always had left open: joining forces with Butler outside Richmond to commence operations against the city's links to the remainder of the Confederacy. Perhaps he could entice Lee to leave his entrenchments and attack; perhaps he could catch his opponent off balance. Whatever might ensue, it was clear that the climax of the campaign would not come at Spotsylvania.

The lull in operations also forced newspaper correspondents to reassess their analysis of the progress of Grant's campaign. Despite a week of almost continuous fighting, capped by the massive assault of May 12, Lee, contrary to initial reports, remained ready to continue the struggle. Sigel's defeat and Butler's failure to take or to isolate Richmond meant that the Confederacy was not on the verge of collapse. "Sorry to say that the feeling downtown today is despondent and bad," Strong observed in New York. "There is no news to justify it, but people have taken up with an exaggerated view of Grant's hard-won success in opening the campaign, and now, finding that the 'backbone of the Rebellion' is not 'broken at last' into a handful of incoherent vertebrae, and that Lee still shows fight, 'on the Po' or elsewhere, they are disappointed, disgusted, and ready to believe any rumor of disaster that the wicked ingenuity of speculators can devise and inculcate." Although the *Herald* dismissed the news from New Market as "a mere feather in the scale," it did give pause to one used to news of victory.[53] Yet it took some time for the newspapers to formulate a new understanding of what was going on. Readers still awaited news that Grant had achieved a decisive victory.

The War Department did what it could to keep everyone informed. Stanton's dispatches to Dix appeared in all the papers. "They have been quite free from exaggeration, swagger or prophesy," observed the *Times*. Indeed, it looked as if the War Department had made amends for its misleading dispatches during the Chancellorsville campaign. One reason the *Chicago Tribune* had not joined in the enthusiasm evidenced by the three major New York papers was Joseph Medill's suspicion about the credibility of those missives. "We must not celebrate a victory yet," the *Tribune* remarked in the aftermath of the Wilderness, "but we may rejoice in the present promise." To modern eyes its measured commentary during the first week of the campaign seems a far more accurate portrayal of what was happening. Perhaps some of this was due to its ability to sift through early reports without the pressures of competition to get the story out first. Nevertheless, by continually reminding readers of past incidents, it cultivated skepticism. But by May 14 even the *Tribune* had succumbed to the lure of imminent triumph: "As the case looks now the end seems about to be reached." The paper now believed that "our national Waterloo is being fought." One reason was that it had learned to trust Stanton's messages. That trust did not prove entirely warranted, as the secretary's incorporation of Dana's erroneous assessments in his press releases revealed.[54]

It was thus with some surprise that in the early morning hours of May 18 the editorial offices of several New York papers received a proclamation from the president calling for a draft of 400,000 men and setting aside May 26 as "a day of fasting, humiliation and prayer." The reasons given for such an extraordinary action shocked readers: Grant's campaign was "virtually closed"; Union arms had suffered a series of serious setbacks; it was yet again time to rally and regroup. The *Times* and the *Tribune* held back. The *Herald* set the document into type but hesitated to distribute its press run because editors reasoned the proclamation did not quite sound like Lincoln. Only the two leading Democratic dailies, the *World* and the *Journal of Commerce*, published the document. That proved to be a mistake. The proclamation was a forgery, the handiwork of Joseph Howard, a reporter whose earlier credits included crafting a story that Lincoln entered Washington in 1861 wearing a Scotch cap and military cloak. Howard had hoped to make a profit through manipulating various financial markets in the wake of their response to the news.[55]

Within hours everyone knew that the proclamation was spurious. The *Herald* quickly printed a new edition. The Democratic journals were not so fortunate. Lincoln directed Dix to arrest the owners and editors of the *World* and the *Journal of Commerce*, deeming their actions traitorous, and to shut down the papers. This proved to be a mistake because the papers in question did not perpetrate the fraud—although their critical stance toward the Lincoln administration perhaps rendered the editors too eager to print a document that seemingly confirmed their best hopes.[56]

Part of the reason Lincoln and Stanton were furious was that the president had indeed prepared a document calling for a draft of 300,000 men. Moreover, in the aftermath of New Market and the lull between Grant and Lee, the administration was concerned that newspaper readers might entertain growing doubts about the progress of Union arms. The quickness and energy with which Lincoln countered the fraudulent proclamation revealed how sensitive he was about public perceptions of events on the battlefield. Coming as it did after a relative lull in the fighting, the proclamation played on anxieties about Grant's campaign. The early hopes of overwhelming victory were now starting to fade, and it was evident there was to be much more fighting. Revelations of the proclamation's true source did not totally erase its impact: "The knowledge that it is a forgery has not quieted the public mind," Welles observed.[57]

One reason many northerners began to feel a bit queasy about the progress of Grant's campaign was their growing awareness that the quest for another Waterloo had proven a forlorn one. "After having cheered ourselves hoarse over the success and prospects of successes by Grant and the Army of the Potomac," Brooks wrote on May 24, "we find ourselves pausing to take breath and discovering that our successes are more prospective than immediate, at least so far as the campaign in Virginia is concerned." Second thoughts and doubts now entered more minds. "News from Virginia very good but not entitled to the least credit," Strong observed on the day after the publication of the bogus proclamation. Republican papers began to place their own spin on what had happened, and they found the answer not in military failure but in unreasonable expectations. "Grant's successful advance threw the public into its usual fever," the *Times* recalled, "and they looked for nothing less than his unbroken progress and immediate entry into Richmond."

That newspaper reports, including those in the *Times*, were the primary source of such news escaped mention. It was perhaps no surprise, therefore, that when subsequent reports modified and at times repudiated initial accounts, morale among Republicans and a good many Democrats declined. "Each of these fits of exaltation is followed by great despondency, a general disposition to abuse the Government, to doubt the General-in-Chief, and, of course, also by an upward tendency in prices," the *Times* noted. "It is hard to say . . . how much blood this Moloch of public opinion would require to satisfy it that our armies are doing nobly," the *Herald* complained. It blamed Confederate agents and Copperheads for the misshaping of public opinion, claiming that they had been circulating "an idea abroad that the silence of the war bulletins is ominous for our cause, and that we must have suffered a reverse if we cannot announce a battle and a victory every day."[58]

As for what the press was saying about his progress, Grant, who earlier in his career had been acutely aware of such coverage, claimed that he no longer consulted the papers—although his letter to his wife indicated that he was well aware of their contents. If so, it may have been in part because George G. Meade often read them. "The papers are giving Grant all the credit of what they call successes," Meade growled on June 1. "I hope they will remember this if anything goes wrong." Within a week Meade and Burnside were busy expelling reporters from the army.[59]

One person who realized that northerners had expected too much too fast was Abraham Lincoln. In a conversation with newspaper reporters in June, he remarked, "I wish when you write and speak to the people you would do all you can to correct the impression that the war in Virginia will end right off victoriously. To me the most trying thing in all of this war is that the people are too sanguine; they expect too much at once. I declare to you, sir, that we are today further ahead than I thought one year and a half ago we should be, and yet there are plenty of people who believe that the war is about to be substantially closed." Such hopes were doomed to disappointment. As they fell, so did Lincoln's popularity.[60]

Yet Lincoln had to accept some blame for the result. So did Stanton and many northern newspapers. The sober warnings against expecting too much too soon faded quickly during the opening weeks of Grant's campaign. Many northerners continued to measure success and failure in traditional terms, unaware of the ways the contest between Grant and Lee challenged these notions. Grant had not sought a Waterloo in the Wilderness. From the beginning he considered it quite possible that his forces would link up with Butler's army near Richmond. Nor had he sought a struggle of grinding attrition. Had this been what he desired, he would have held fast to his declaration to fight it out at Spotsylvania. Only once, for a few hours on the morning of May 13, did he entertain notions that Lee's army might have given way.[61]

There in fact had been candor in battlefield reports—most notably about casualty rates. There was no effort to hide the extent of the losses from the public, although both the newspapers and the Union high command overestimated Lee's casualties. Indeed, it seemed as if many northerners steeled themselves for such sad news, believing that at least progress was being made. Only when Grant subsequently commenced siege operations against Lee did critics, noting that two years earlier McClellan had begun a siege of Richmond without nearly as much preliminary bloodshed, begin to make the label of butcher stick to Grant.[62]

Regardless of its battlefield accomplishments, Grant's campaign probably was doomed to fail in the eyes of the northern public because the

Union commander could not reshape expectations about the conduct of military operations. Pinning Lee's army might reduce (although it did not entirely eliminate) the Confederate commander's capacity for creating mischief, but that did not satisfy a public conditioned to assess military events from a traditional Napoleonic perspective. Russell F. Weigley once suggested that it was a sign of Grant's military genius that he could make a victory, a draw, or even a defeat serve his larger purposes. Unfortunately Grant was unable to convey that understanding to others. The degree to which traditional ways of recognizing victory and defeat persisted became evident several months later when the North celebrated Sherman's capture of Atlanta, a victory that resembled nothing so much as a successful version of McClellan's Peninsula campaign of 1862. Even Little Mac recognized the resemblance. "Your campaign will go down to history as one of the memorable ones of the world," McClellan wrote Sherman, "& will be even more highly appreciated in the future as it is in the present." That such a triumph did far more in the public's mind to assure Lincoln's reelection over McClellan than did Grant's campaign against Lee simply enriched the irony.[63]

NOTES

1. Ulysses S. Grant, *Personal Memoirs of U. S. Grant*, 2 vols. (New York: Charles L. Webster, 1886), 1:443; John Russell Young, *Around the World with General Grant*, 2 vols. (New York: American News, 1879), 2:615–17. Exactly when this conversation took place is unclear; the version of the story told to Young suggests that it was April, while the *Memoirs* place it somewhat earlier.

2. Grant, *Memoirs*, 2:116.

3. Abraham Lincoln to Agénor-Etienne de Gasparin, August 4, 1862, in Abraham Lincoln, *The Collected Works of Abraham Lincoln*, ed. Roy P. Basler, 9 vols. (New Brunswick, N.J.: Rutgers University Press, 1953–55), 5:355–56.

4. See Herman Hattaway and Archer Jones, *How the North Won: A Military History of the Civil War* (Urbana: University of Illinois Press, 1983), chaps. 16 and 17, for an extended discussion of the clash of public expectations with military realities in the 1864 campaign. This essay examines the northern press with its primary (but not exclusive) focus on the three major New York newspapers: the *Times*, the *Tribune*, and the *Herald*. They were selected in part because each offered extended coverage of the Virginia campaign and played a major role in influencing northern opinion, both directly through its readers and indirectly as other newspapers picked up its reports. The three papers also present a spectrum of political opinion across Republican ranks, although the *Herald* sometimes flirted with the Democrats.

5. Grant, *Memoirs*, 2:116.

6. Grant to Charles A. Dana, August 5, 1863, and Grant to Elihu B. Washburne, August 30, 1863, in Ulysses S. Grant, *The Papers of Ulysses S. Grant*, ed. John Y. Simon and others, 20 vols. to date (Carbondale: Southern Illinois University Press, 1967–), 9:146, 217. On reactions within the Army of the Potomac to McClellan's report, see Charles S. Wainwright, *A Diary of Battle: The Personal Journals of Colonel Charles S. Wainwright, 1861-1865*, ed. Allan Nevins (New York: Harcourt, Brace & World, 1962), 330–32 (March 13, 1864), and Henry Livermore Abbott, *Fallen Leaves: The Civil War Letters of Major Henry Livermore Abbott*, ed. Robert Garth Scott (Kent, Ohio: Kent State University Press, 1991), 239.

7. Grant to Henry W. Halleck, January 15, 19, 1864, and Halleck to Grant, February 17, 1864, in Grant, *Papers*, 10:14–17, 39–40, 110–12. The merits of Grant's proposal have been a subject of controversy. See T. Harry Williams, *Lincoln and His Generals* (New York: Knopf, 1952), 295–97; Hattaway and Jones, *How the North Won*, 511–15; Brooks D. Simpson, *Let Us Have Peace: Ulysses S. Grant and the Politics of War and Reconstruction, 1861-1868* (Chapel Hill: University of North Carolina Press, 1991), 54–56; and David Herbert Donald, *Lincoln* (New York: Simon and Schuster, 1995), 498–99.

8. See Grant to Edward O. C. Ord, March 29, 1864; Grant to Franz Sigel, March 29, 1864; Grant to Benjamin F. Butler, April 2, 1864; Grant to William T. Sherman, April 4, 1864; Grant to George G. Meade, April 9, 1864; Grant to Franz Sigel, April 12, 15, 1864, all in Grant, *Papers*, 10:233–34, 236–37, 245–47, 251–53, 273–75, 282, 286–87. The basic outlines of this plan were drawn up in March 1864.

9. On the possibility of the transfer of Confederate forces, see Grant to William T. Sherman, April 19, 1864, in ibid., 10:331–32.

10. Cyrus B. Comstock Diary, April 1, 1864, Cyrus B. Comstock Papers, Library of Congress, Washington, D.C. (repository hereafter cited as LC).

11. Grant to George G. Meade, April 9, 1864, in Grant, *Papers*, 10:273–75.

12. Elizabeth Blair Lee, *Wartime Washington: The Civil War Letters of Elizabeth Blair Lee*, ed. Virginia Jean Haas (Urbana: University of Illinois Press, 1991), 358, 391; Comstock Diary, April 19, 1864; Grant to Benjamin F. Butler, April 19, 1864, in Grant, *Papers*, 10:327–28.

13. Noah Brooks, *Mr. Lincoln's Washington: Selections from the Writings of Noah Brooks, Civil War Correspondent*, ed. P. J. Staudenraus (South Brunswick, N.J.: Yoseloff, 1967), 311; *New York Herald*, March 18, 1864; *New York Times*, April 21, May 6, 1864.

14. *New York Times*, April 9, 1864; *Harper's Weekly*, April 23, 1864; *New York Tribune*, March 5, May 6, 1864.

15. *New York Herald*, March 18, 1864; *Chicago Tribune*, May 12, 1864 (quoting the *Chicago Times*).

16. In "'We Live Under a Government of Men and Morning Newspapers': Image, Expectation, and the Peninsula Campaign of 1862" (*Virginia Magazine of History and Biography* 103 [January 1995]: 5–28), Eric T. Dean Jr. argues that unrealistic expectations contributed to the perception that George B. McClellan's campaign to take Richmond ended in spectacular failure. One might note that McClellan's panicky dispatches also may have created that impression, to say nothing of the results on the battlefield. In any case, this essay takes issue with

Dean's contention that "it was not until expectations were lowered that generals such as Grant and Sherman could take the field in extended campaigns to grind the Confederacy down" (28). There is ample evidence that different newspapers expressed high expectations prior to the 1864 campaign; moreover, press coverage of the first two weeks of Grant's offensive suggests that old habits proved hard to break.

17. On Bennett, see James L. Crouthamel, *Bennett's New York Herald and the Rise of the Popular Press* (Syracuse, N.Y.: Syracuse University Press, 1989).

18. *New York Herald*, March 10, 30, April 1, 1864.

19. *New York Times*, April 22, 1864; Abraham Lincoln to Grant, April 30, 1864, and Grant to Lincoln, May 1, 1864, in Grant, *Papers*, 10:380.

20. Grant to Julia Dent Grant, May 2, 1864, in Grant, *Papers*, 10:394; George G. Meade to Margaret Meade, April 4, 1864, in George Gordon Meade Jr., *The Life and Letters of George Gordon Meade*, 2 vols. (New York: Scribner's, 1913), 2:187; Horace Porter, *Campaigning with Grant* (New York: Century, 1897), 43–44.

21. Grant to Henry W. Halleck, May 4, 1864, in Grant, *Papers*, 10:397.

22. *New York Tribune*, May 9, 1864 (see also *New York Herald*, May 11, 1864); Hattaway and Jones, *How the North Won*, 527; Porter, *Campaigning with Grant*, 41–42, 64–65, 69–70.

23. Porter, *Campaigning with Grant*, 65–66. Edward Steere surely errs in claiming that Grant sought "a battle of annihilation" against Lee in the Wilderness (Steere, *The Wilderness Campaign* [Harrisburg, Pa.: Stackpole, 1960], 18).

24. See Shelby Foote, *The Civil War: A Narrative*, 3 vols. (New York: Random House, 1958–74), 3:187–88, for an example of the attempt to draw a parallel between Chancellorsville and the Wilderness.

25. *New York Times*, May 6, 1864; Washington *National Republican* quoted in the *New York Tribune*, May 6, 1864; *New York Tribune*, May 6, 1864.

26. Porter, *Campaigning with Grant*, 98; Frank B. Carpenter, *Six Months at the White House with Lincoln* (1866; reprint, Watkins Glen, N.Y.: Century House, 1961), 19; Benjamin P. Thomas and Harold M. Hyman, *Stanton: Lincoln's Secretary of War* (New York: Knopf, 1962), 300.

27. George Templeton Strong, *Diary of the Civil War, 1860–1865*, ed. Allan Nevins (New York: Macmillan, 1962), 442 (May 6, 1864); Gideon Welles, *The Diary of Gideon Welles*, ed. Howard K. Beale, 3 vols. (New York: Norton, 1960), 2:25 (May 7, 1864); Thomas and Hyman, *Stanton*, 300.

28. Welles, *Diary*, 1:290–92, 294 (May 2, 4, 5, 7, 1863).

29. Grant to Henry W. Halleck, May 6, 1864, in Grant, *Papers*, 10:400–401.

30. Lee, *Wartime Washington*, 377–78; Lincoln, *Collected Works*, 7:332.

31. *New York Tribune*, May 7, 1864; *New York Times*, May 8, 1864; *New York Herald*, May 8, 1864.

32. Sylvanus Cadwallader, *Three Years with Grant as Recalled by War Correspondent Sylvanus Cadwallader*, ed. Benjamin P. Thomas (New York: Knopf, 1955), 184–95.

33. Welles, *Diary*, 2:25–26 (May 9, 1864); *New York Times*, May 8, 1864; Washington *National Republican*, May 8, 1864 (reprinted in the *New York Tribune*, May 9, 1864).

34. *New York Tribune*, May 9, 1864; Strong, *Diary*, 437 (May 8, 1864). The *Tribune* reprinted the May 8 declarations of the *National Republican*.

35. Edward Bates, *The Diary of Edward Bates, 1859-1866*, ed. Howard K. Beale (Washington: GPO [for the American Historical Association], 1930), 364 (May 8, 1864); Thomas and Hyman, *Stanton*, 301; *New York Tribune*, May 9, 1864.

36. *New York Tribune*, May 9, 1864; Strong, *Diary*, 442-43 (May 9, 1864).

37. John Hay, *Lincoln and the Civil War in the Diaries and Letters of John Hay*, ed. Tyler Dennett (New York: Dodd, Mead, 1939), 180 (May 9, 1864); Lincoln, *Collected Works*, 7:333-34; *New York Times*, May 10, 1864; Welles, *Diary*, 2:26 (May 9, 1864).

38. Grant to Henry W. Halleck, May 7, 8, 1864, in Grant, *Papers*, 10:405-6, 410-11.

39. *New York Times*, May 10, 1864; *New York Herald*, May 10, 1864; *New York Tribune*, May 10, 1864.

40. *New York Herald*, May 10, 1864.

41. Ibid.; *Frank Leslie's Illustrated Newspaper*, May 14, 1864.

42. Grant to Henry W. Halleck, May 10, 1864, in Grant, *Papers*, 10:418-19.

43. Welles, *Diary*, 2:28 (May 11, 1864); New York *Journal of Commerce*, May 11, 1864 (quoted in Washington *National Intelligencer*, May 13, 1864); *New York Tribune*, May 11, 1864.

44. *New York Times*, May 12, 1864; *New York Tribune*, May 11, 12, 1864; *New York Herald*, May 12, 1864.

45. Grant to Edwin M. Stanton, May 11, 1864, and Grant to Henry W. Halleck, May 11, 1864, in Grant, *Papers*, 10:422-23.

46. *New York Herald*, May 13, 1864; *New York Tribune*, May 13, 1864; *New York Times*, May 13, 1864.

47. *Chicago Tribune*, May 13, 1864; Brooks, *Mr. Lincoln's Washington*, 318; Welles, *Diary*, 2:30 (May 13, 1864).

48. *New York Times*, May 13, 14, 15, 1864; *Frank Leslie's Illustrated Newspaper*, May 28, 1864; *New York Tribune*, May 14, 1864. But note George Templeton Strong's comment: "All this may be true. God grant it is! But we are so schooled in adversity that we presume all good news apocryphal" (Strong, *Diary*, 445 [May 13, 1864]).

49. Grant to Henry W. Halleck, May 12, 1864; Grant to Julia Dent Grant, May 13, 1864; Grant to George G. Meade, May 13, 1864, all in Grant, *Papers*, 10:428, 444, 441; Charles A. Dana to Edwin M. Stanton, May 13, 1864 (two telegrams), in U.S. War Department, *The War of the Rebellion: A Compilation of the Official Records of the Union and Confederate Armies*, 127 vols., index, and atlas (Washington, D.C.: GPO, 1880-1901), ser. 1, 36(1):69 (hereafter cited as *OR*); *New York Herald*, May 14, 1864.

50. Charles A. Dana to Edwin M. Stanton, May 14, 1864, *OR* 36(1):69-70; Edwin M. Stanton to Governor John Brough et al., May 15, 1864, *OR*, 4:382-83; *New York Times*, May 14, 1864; Hay, *Lincoln and the Civil War*, 181 (May 14, 1864); Grant to Henry W. Halleck, May 14, 1864, in Grant, *Papers*, 10:445.

51. Grant to Henry W. Halleck, May 16, 1864, in Grant, *Papers*, 10:452; Welles, *Diary*, 2:33 (May 17, 1864).

52. Porter, *Campaigning with Grant*, 124; Grant, *Memoirs*, 2:238.

53. Strong, *Diary*, 447 (May 17, 1864); *New York Herald*, May 19, 1864.

54. *New York Times*, May 12, 1864; *Chicago Tribune*, May 10, 11, 14, 17, 18, 1864.

55. Lincoln, *Collected Works*, 7:348–49; Carl Sandburg, *Abraham Lincoln: The War Years*, 4 vols. (New York: Harcourt, Brace & World, 1939), 3:53–54.

56. Lincoln, *Collected Works*, 7:347–48.

57. Ibid., 344, contains the draft proclamation. For criticism of Lincoln's action, see James G. Randall and Richard N. Current, *Lincoln the President: Last Full Measure* (New York: Dodd, Mead, 1955), 150–52, and Welles, *Diary*, 2:35 (May 19, 1864).

58. Strong, *Diary*, 448 (May 19, 1864); *New York Times*, June 22, 1864; *New York Herald*, May 23, 1864.

59. Lee, *Wartime Washington*, 397; George G. Meade to Margaret Meade, June 1, 1864, in Meade, *Life and Letters*, 2:200.

60. Brooks, *Mr. Lincoln's Washington*, 342–43.

61. Allan Nevins severely criticizes Stanton's dispatches in *The War for the Union: The Organized War to Victory, 1864–1865* (New York: Scribner's, 1971), 34–35.

62. Hattaway and Jones, *How the North Won*, 570.

63. Russell F. Weigley, *The American Way of War: A History of United States Military Strategy and Policy* (New York: Macmillan, 1973), 139; George B. McClellan to William T. Sherman, September 26, 1864, William T. Sherman Papers, LC.

GARY W. GALLAGHER

Our Hearts Are Full of Hope

THE ARMY OF NORTHERN VIRGINIA IN

THE SPRING OF 1864

strong sense of optimism pervaded the Army of Northern Virginia as its officers and men approached the spring campaign of 1864. Although they had endured a winter marked by sometimes severe shortages of food and matériél, their letters and diaries give evidence of unshakable trust in R. E. Lee, assurance that Ulysses S. Grant would achieve no more success than had his many predecessors, and hope that a decisive triumph on the battlefield might undercut northern civilian morale and bring Confederate independence within a year. Testimony from this period also illuminates attitudes within the army toward civilian leaders, concern that commitment to the cause on the home front was wavering, and a widespread sense that God would order things for the best if white southerners held fast to their struggle for nationhood. Many of the soldiers employed language that suggests allegiance to the Confederate nation—rather than to their states or localities—motivated them to remain at their posts. Three years of bloody war had not eroded to a significant degree the army's morale; indeed, in many respects the Army of Northern Virginia in 1864 matched in confidence, if not in numbers, the force that had marched into Pennsylvania the preceding June.

Some attention to overall Confederate morale in the winter and spring of 1864 will help set the stage for a closer look at Lee's army. Bell I. Wiley suggested in *The Road to Appomattox* that defeats at Gettysburg, Vicksburg, and Chattanooga precipitated a plunge in morale from which the Confederacy did not recover until mid-1864. Those military setbacks, together with suspension of the writ of habeas corpus in February 1864 and a new conscription bill that set age limits at seventeen and fifty, sapped the will of southern whites. According to Wiley, only Confederate success in defending Richmond and Atlanta through May and into June, along with "evidences of increasing peace sentiment in the North and prospects of good crops in the Confederacy, lifted the Southern spirit from the deep despondency that had enthralled it since Gettysburg and Vicksburg." More recent work also suggests poor Confederate morale in early 1864. For example, the authors of *Why the South Lost the Civil War* note that a number of historians point to a "loss of the will to fight" that plagued the Confederacy after July 1863.[1]

Writing much closer to the events, Edward A. Pollard sketched a very different temper across the Confederacy in his *Southern History of the War*. The defeats of 1863 receded during early 1864 as news of one victory after another heartened Confederates. Often slighted in modern accounts, these successes loomed larger at the time. Brig. Gen. Joseph Finegan turned back a small northern army at Olustee, Florida, on February 20, and troopers under Nathan Bedford Forrest triumphed over Federals at Okolona, Mississippi, on February 22 and captured (and then largely slaughtered) a mixed garrison of black soldiers and white unionists at Fort Pillow, Tennessee, on April 12. In the East, Judson Kilpatrick's cavalry raid against Richmond in early March achieved nothing militarily but raised Confederate hackles when papers carried by Federal Col. Ulric Dahlgren purportedly outlined plans to assassinate Jefferson Davis. West of the Mississippi River, Nathaniel P. Banks's campaign along Louisiana's Red River ended in ignominious retreat after battles at Mansfield and Pleasant Hill on April 8–9, while on the North Carolina coast Confederates commanded by Robert F. Hoke captured Plymouth. "The spirit of the Southern Confederacy was scarcely ever more buoyant than in the month of May, 1864," concluded Pollard. "The confidence of its people in the ultimate accomplishment of their independence was so firm and universal, that any other conclusion was but seldom referred to in general conversation . . . and in Richmond and elsewhere the hope was freely indulged that the campaign of 1864 was to be the decisive of the war, and to crown the efforts of the South with peace and independence."[2]

Morale probably fell somewhere between the extremes presented by Wiley and Pollard. A chaplain who traveled through the Lower South in December 1863 and January 1864 railed against "the stay-at-homes" who cared about nothing but profit and property: "Money and their negroes appeared to be their gods, and for these they were not only willing to sacrifice their own children, who were now fighting the battles of their

The engagement at Fort Pillow, April 12, 1864. Confederates applauded Nathan Bedford Forrest's capture of Fort Pillow as one of several victories in the winter and spring of 1864; northern opinion labeled the slaughter of Federal troops an atrocity.
Frank Leslie's Illustrated Newspaper, *May 7, 1864*

country, but even the country itself." Traversing much of the same area a bit later on a medical inspection tour, Confederate physician William Alexander formed far more positive impressions. "Our Va. people are as determined as ever, & hopeful even to buoyancy," he wrote in mid-April. "This is also the case, with few exceptions, of the other states."[3]

In every corner of the Confederacy, citizens debated the merits of legislation designed to shrink the supply of paper money, tighten conscription, and limit antiwar activities. In Georgia, Governor Joseph E. Brown and Vice-President-in-exile Alexander H. Stephens loudly disapproved of the central government's actions, winning support from disgruntled individuals who believed, as one man put it, that a "bloody war among the Southern people" might ensue if some of the acts were not repealed. North Carolinians unhappy with the war clustered around William Woods Holden and others who opposed Jefferson Davis's administration and advocated peace negotiations. A majority of Confederates almost certainly agreed with Robert Garlick Hill Kean of the War Bureau, who labeled Brown, Stephens, and "their set . . . the most pestilent demagogues in the land, more injurious than the North Carolina buffaloes because more able and influential." In South Carolina a young woman spoke a common sentiment in her journal entry for March 16: "All the talk is about the unfortunate currency, and thousands and one taxes, tho few, very few complain."[4]

Newspapers generally conceded problems of morale, urged citizens to sacrifice, and maintained a hopeful stance concerning eventual Confederate victory. In January the proadministration Richmond *Dispatch* applauded the example of the men under arms, the nation's women, and most farmers and country people (the last two groups, "with a few shameful exceptions, [were] hopeful and resolute") but excoriated "the denizens of the towns, the money makers—the men who fear that further resistance may be the means of cutting off all their profits." The Charleston *Daily Courier* similarly observed that "avarice should be accounted an eternal disgrace, cowardice an unpardonable sin." Both papers called for harmony among all Confederates, and the *Dispatch* attributed "a certain degree of despondency" among the people to faithless politicians and newspaper jeremiads. The Richmond *Enquirer* alluded to hunger in the armies and joined the other papers in calling for sacrifice on the home front: "Give the army subsistence, and the army will give the people peace; withhold subsistence now, and the war is prolonged, its miseries increased, and final ruin may be the consequences. . . . The people must sacrifice their comforts, and, if necessary, endure hardships and want in order that the army may perform the duty of defending the country."[5]

Editors used volatile images of enslaved white southerners to paint a stark portrait of the consequences of defeat. The *Dispatch* spoke of Federal plans "to rob us of all we have on earth, and reduce our whole population to the condition of beggars and slaves." The question no longer was whether African slavery would survive but "whether you and your children shall be slaves," whether Confederates should become "hewers of wood and drawers of water for their Yankee masters." In an editorial calling for determined resistance no matter how long the war lasted, the Charleston *Daily Courier* cataloged Federal atrocities: "They have . . . driven helpless families out of their homes and burned their habitations, murdered their husbands in the presence of their wives, put to death gray headed men and nurslings, done violence to female virtue, destroyed farming utensils, and, in a word, committed every possible deed of baseness, cowardice and cruelty." Confronted with such an enemy, asked the *Daily Courier*, "Who would not rather die than consent to live again under the shadow of their hateful flag?"[6] The string of victories from February through April, together with encouraging reports from Confederate armies and news of increasing gold prices in the North, prompted many editors to forecast victory during 1864. The Atlanta *Southern Confederacy* thought it plausible that "the present year will close the contest. . . . The crisis of the North is near at hand. In another half year, if the South meet no further reverse, the quotations for gold will have increased at a fearful rate, and financial perplexities and distresses will accomplish what our bayonets have left unfinished." The Montgomery *Advertiser* noted in late March that the "general symptoms of the Confederacy are good. Our veteran soldiers have re-enlisted for the War, and are in better discipline and spirits than at any time before. . . . The courage and confidence of the people at home keeps pace, in the main, with that of the army, and they look forward hopefully to a bright and glorious future." The Richmond *Enquirer* pointed out that "repeated calls and drafts indicate greater difficulty on the part of the enemy in procuring men than any encountered by the Confederate authorities," and predicted that a new round of southern victories would kill the North's "War spirit, and fully and completely develop the prospect of an early peace." In Charleston the *Daily Courier* averred that never had "the spirit of soldiers and people been more in keeping with the character of the occasion than at the present time." There was no need for despondency, the *Daily Courier*'s editor subsequently predicted, if all Confederates did their duty: "Dark clouds will shortly break and roll away and under the bright shining of the sun we will march on to glorious triumph."[7]

As they read their newspapers and followed the progress of their armies during the spring of 1864, most Confederate civilians likely indulged a cautious optimism. Many looked to God. Prayer had helped to deliver the spring's victories, remarked a woman in Georgia: "What gratitude should fill our hearts as Christians for all these evidences of divine mercy!" "I have never despaired of the final issue, but I have never before felt the dawn of hope so near," she wrote. "I trust it is not a presumptuous delusion!" In Tennessee, Belle Edmondson gave thanks in her diary for Fort Pillow and Mansfield: "Oh! how thankful we are for the bright days which are dawning." From Warrenton, Virginia, which often lay behind Union lines, Susan Emeline Jeffords Caldwell assured her husband in

Richmond that rumors of wavering spirit among the town's women were false. "We are all loyal—," she stated. "We must exist and are dependent on the wretches for many things but . . . keep *true* to the South amid all our sore trials."[8] Judith W. McGuire, a refugee in Richmond, struck a common chord in combining trepidation about the future with a belief that with God's assistance the Confederacy would win. On April 25 she reported the "country in great excitement" over Hoke's capturing Plymouth. Along with the victories in Florida, Louisiana, and elsewhere, this indicated that the "God of battles is helping us, or how could we thus succeed?" McGuire knew a large Union army under Grant soon would threaten Richmond, but "with the help of God, we hope to drive them back again. . . . I don't think that any one doubts our ability to do it; but the awful loss of life necessary upon the fight is what we dread."[9]

Ulysses S. Grant's transfer from the Western to the Eastern Theater convinced most Confederates that Virginia would witness the decisive fighting in 1864. "Grant is now the presiding genius," the Georgia *Messenger & Journal* observed somewhat sarcastically on March 30, "and at the council of war which he recently attended in Washington, it was arranged that the capture of Richmond should be the primary object of the Spring campaign." This paper betrayed no doubt about the outcome of such an effort because in Lee's army "the spirit of both officers and men points but to one result—success." The Atlanta *Southern Confederacy* agreed that southern forces were "ready at all points, and especially at Richmond" to block the efforts orchestrated by "good Ulysses." In Charleston the *Daily Courier* printed a piece from the *New York Herald* naming Virginia as the primary Union target: "We dare say that General Grant has discovered that Richmond is the head of the rebellion," stated the *Herald*, "and that *a telling blow upon the head is the readiest way to finish it.*" Residents of Richmond learned from the *Dispatch* that Lee's veterans were eager for the Army of the Potomac to make its final effort. Denying Grant's greatness as a general, the *Dispatch* insisted that his past "performances bear no comparison whatever to those of Gen. Lee."[10]

Comments from outside Virginia echoed those of these editors. A Virginian whose regiment had been posted to Florida reported all his comrades anxious to return to the Old Dominion, "to which point the vast armies of the enemy seem to [be] concentrating for a final death grapple." H. W. Barrow of the 21st North Carolina wrote from Kinston that he thought "the Yankees are going to try to capture Richmond again as Grant has been successful out west and thinks he can manage Genl. Lee and his army." Believing the summer's campaign would end the war, this man predicted that Grant would "find some difference between Genl Lee and old Pemberton."[11]

Lee's soldiers also saw their role in the upcoming campaigns as crucial, and their morale in April fully justified the trust of their fellow Confederates. A lieutenant in the 51st Georgia put it succinctly less than two weeks before the Federals crossed the Rapidan River: "My opinion is that before another month rolls off a great battle will be fought in this part of Virginia and I am confident of success." Many of his comrades thought a victory would win Confederate independence—though he believed the "war would terminate by some means other than fighting." Brig. Gen. Stephen Dodson Ramseur, whose four North Carolina regiments had figured prominently in the army's operations during 1863, summed up the prevailing attitude in a pair of letters to his wife Ellen. "We are getting ready for an arduous summer Campaign," he wrote in late April. "Our hearts are full of hope. . . . Oh! I do pray that we may be established as an independent people, a people known and recognized as God's Peculiar People!" A week later he assured Ellen that every man focused on the coming campaign, that the army was in splendid condition, and that "All things look bright and cheerful."[12]

This is not to say that the Army of Northern Virginia experienced no problems in the winter and spring of 1864. Shortages of food, concern about the plight of loved ones at home, and general war weariness troubled many soldiers. Ramseur himself had confided to his brother-in-law in January that rations of ⅛ to ¼ pound of meat and 1⅛ pounds of flour per day had dampened spirits considerably. "The army must be fed," he insisted, "even if people at home must go without it." A member of the Stonewall Brigade complained in mid-January that the men drew at most only ¼ pound of meat a day and sometimes went without it altogether. The government's inability to provide adequate rations and its decision to stop allowing conscripted men to hire substitutes (which he interpreted as a desperate measure to bring men into the ranks) convinced this soldier that "the Confederacy is about to play out." Should the meat ration remain inadequate, he prophesied darkly, "I dont think that the men will bare with that way of doing much longer."[13]

R. E. Lee's letters from this period leave no doubt that he considered inadequate food and fodder the major danger facing the army. "We are now issuing to the troops a fourth of a pound of salt meat & have only three days' supply at that rate," he told Jefferson Davis early in the new year. "I can learn of no supply of meat on the road to the army, & fear I shall be unable to retain it in the field." As late as April 12 the commanding general confessed to Davis "anxiety on the subject of provisions . . . so great that I cannot refrain from expressing it to Your Excellency. I cannot see how we can operate with our present supplies." In the absence of improvement, Lee could not rule out a retreat into North Carolina.[14]

As during the late summer and fall of 1862 and the summer after Gettysburg, desertions also plagued the army—though numbers never reached a critical level. Lee speculated to the secretary of war in mid-February that "the discipline of the army is suffering from our present scarcity of supplies." Thomas J. Goree of James Longstreet's staff deplored the fact that many members of the famed Texas Brigade, while detached from the army for service in Tennessee, had "got it into their head to go across the Mississippi" to seek duty closer to home. "Shame upon the men who have gone to Texas for easy service, and have deserted their brave comrades here," scolded Goree from East Tennessee. He hoped all would be returned to the brigade to face justice. A member of the 41st Virginia of William Mahone's brigade mentioned in mid-January "numerous cases of disertion in some of the Brigades on the Rapid Ann," and Lt. Burwell Thomas Cotton of the 34th North Carolina commented on April 30 that "soldiers keep deserting. Some tried to leave our Regt. last night but they were caught before they went far. Shot two in our Brigade a few days ago." Many North Carolinians faced especially hard choices because their state nourished a strong peace movement led by W. W. Holden. Most Tarheels remained steadfast, however, as Jeb Stuart reminded his wife in early February. "North Carolina has done *nobly in this army*," affirmed the cavalry chief. "Never allow her troops to be abused in your presence."[15]

Letters and diaries frequently expressed compassion for the deserters as well as a belief that their crime merited harsh punishment. Typical was LeRoy S. Edwards of the 12th Virginia, who called the death penalty for two deserters in the 16th Virginia a "*terrible* penalty that the law attaches to a *terrible* crime." A noncommissioned officer in the 44th North Carolina reported the executions of a man from his regiment and another from the 11th North Carolina: "They was shot for desertion[.] Running away from the army is not fine work." "We are soldiers," he added, "and we have to stay as long as there is any 'war.'" An Alabamian wrote movingly of the execution of two men from the 9th Alabama, terming it "dreadful to bring out a man in good health and in a moment plung his soul into ever lasting perdition." Yet the pair "well knew the fate of deserters," he added, "but they heeded not."[16]

Determination to see the war through to a successful conclusion animated the vast majority of Lee's soldiers. Thousands reenlisted for the duration of the conflict before the Confederate Congress mandated continued service with the Conscription Act of February 17, 1864. A soldier in the 22nd Georgia described his comrades as in high spirits, "and to prove it our Regiment have all re-enlisted for the war." They expected a hard fight during the spring and summer but had "no notion of ever being subjugated, and we will fight as long as we have any territory to fight on." Another Georgian admitted "getting very tyred of this war" but declared himself "willing to stay here for three more years and live off of bread and water before I will submit to an abolition dynasty." A Mississippian responded negatively to his wife's plea that he seek a place in one of their state's local units. "I would like to be near home where I could see you and the children occasionally," he stated, "but after serving in the Confederate army Honorably for Three years I can't Riconcile it to my Pride of Honor to go Into the Malitia. . . . I am not by any means willing to yield to the federal government." A lieutenant in the 5th Virginia proudly announced to his parents that the regiment had reenlisted for the war, adding that the "troops were never in better sperits—the people to are being inspired by the same feelings and are in excellent sperits now."[17]

The example of men willing to commit themselves to a prolonged struggle did inspire civilians, as evidenced by testimony from witnesses such as Kate Cumming and Emma Holmes. "I have received a letter from an officer who is in Longstreet's corps," commented Cumming, a volunteer nurse in Mobile, Alabama. "The whole of that corps has re-enlisted for the war, no matter how long it may last. Our whole army has done the same." South Carolinian Holmes expressed delight that "the whole army is animated with the brightest & most determined spirit and almost everywhere the soldiers are re-enlisting unanimously, by companies, regiments or brigades for *the war*, (& one body added) even if it lasts 40 years." The Richmond *Enquirer* suggested in late January that the "prompt and patriotic action of the army in re-enlisting for the war . . . [helped infuse] new life and spirit into the people."[18]

Many soldiers suspected their homefolk and some political leaders lacked the army's optimism and devotion to the cause. For Georgians and North Carolinians the actions and statements of Joseph E. Brown, Alexander H. Stephens, and W. W. Holden often proved an embarrassment. A captain in the 45th Georgia read extracts in the Richmond newspapers of Brown's message pronouncing the currency and military bills unconstitutional. "I am sorry the Gov. gets at loggerheads with the administration," he remarked, "because I think now is the time . . . for perfect harmony to exist throughout the Confederacy; all dissensions or quarrels in our midst but serve to encourage the energies of the enemy." Rumors that Holden would seek to replace Zebulon B. Vance in the North Carolina governorship prompted one officer to fume, "Surely, Surely, North Carolina is not so low, so disloyal, as to bow to Holden as Gov- If so—then Good bye to the old State."[19]

Holden's crusade for a negotiated peace spread enough disaffection among North Carolinians that Vance visited Lee's army to deliver a series of rousing speeches in support of the war to regiments from the state. Lee, Jeb Stuart, Richard S. Ewell, A. P. Hill, and other notables attended Vance's address to Junius Daniel's brigade, and a huge crowd heard the governor when he spoke later to Dodson Ramseur's regiments. "He had the whole assembly in an uproar in less than two minutes after he arose," stated one of Ramseur's admiring soldiers. "I was in a good place to hear every word that he said, and I don't think I ever listened to a more able speech of any kind in my life." Several generals gave brief comments following Vance's two-hour oration, after which the governor stepped forward to relate "two or three anecdotes relative to the Yankee characters and then retired amidst deafening 'Rebel Yells.'" James A. Graham of the 27th North Carolina of John R. Cooke's brigade estimated that "a *large majority* of the soldiers" agreed with Vance's sentiments, noting as well that the governor "does not mention Holden at all in his speeches." Another Tarheel wrote his sister that Vance's address was "very highly appreciated by a good portion" of Alfred M. Scales's brigade but was chagrined to admit "there are some here who prefer Holden."[20]

Antipathy toward Vice-President Stephens ran deeply through the ranks of the army. Col. James Conner of the 22nd North Carolina called Stephens's criticism of conscription and suspension of the writ of habeas corpus (offered in a speech delivered on March 16) "injudicious, illtimed, uncandid, and calculated to do much mischief." Alluding to W. W. Holden's pro-peace activities in North Carolina, Conner accused Stephens of attempting "to place Virginia side by side with the Holdenites." Artillerist William Meade Dame employed far harsher language: "I would like to see that scoundrel Alexander Stephens our dishonoured vice-president tarred and feathered and hung," he blustered, "miserable traitor he

Alexander H. Stephens. The Confederate vice-president, with Governor Joseph E. Brown of Georgia and W. W. Holden of North Carolina, alienated many soldiers in the Army of Northern Virginia during the winter and spring of 1864.
Robert Underwood Johnson and Clarence Clough Buel, eds., Battles and Leaders of the Civil War, *4 vols.* (New York: Century, 1887–88), 1:100

stayed away from Congress when the Laws were being passed and then disclaims against them." Dame added that he was pleased to see "the Georgia Soldiers denounce Gov Browns course 'in toto.'" Ordnance chief Josiah Gorgas, who kept a close eye on affairs in Lee's army from his post in Richmond, noted approvingly in late March that Stephens and Brown "excite much remark, and are looked upon with general disfavor."[21]

Evidence of wavering morale at home frustrated soldiers who prided themselves on their own firm allegiance to the Confederacy. News from North Carolina, which along with Georgia seemed to have a significant number of disgruntled civilians, prompted James A. Graham to rebuke residents of his home state. Four men had been executed recently—"a very sad sight"—because they had deserted after receiving letters from North Carolina. "Many a poor soldier has met with the same disgraceful death from the same cause. I wish the people at home," concluded Graham, "would keep in as good spirits as the soldiers in the army." South Carolinian Abram Hayne Young, a sergeant in Joseph B. Kershaw's brigade, poured out his feelings on this subject in a letter that made up in fervor what it lacked in polish. "This Armey hear is in as good Spirits as eny other part of the Confederte Armey, and there is non hoo have boore more of the hardships, and are still willing to endure them rather than Submit to Such men as are Seeking to destroy us and all we have," he affirmed. "I dont write this to disharte you but rather to encorage You to bare it with fermnance. . . . If the men at home and in Congress would doo their part the men in the field is Sufishent if fead well."[22]

Col. Clement A. Evans of the 31st Georgia confided to his diary a belief that a system of furloughs Lee instituted in January had a double benefit: "The soldier becomes satisfied and returns cheerfully to duty, and the people at home catch somewhat of the soldier's spirit of cheerfulness while he is at home." Most of the gloom in the Confederacy could be found among civilians, thought Evans, and some soldiers were happy to get back to their units because "at home, long faces, dolorous groans, and fearful apprehensions meet them at every turn." Dodson Ramseur agreed with Evans that the presence at home of men on furlough might operate for the good among the "weak kneed gentry." Ted Barclay of the Stonewall Brigade manifested impatience with homefolk who complained to soldiers at home and at the front that the war had altered their lives in unwanted ways. "I trust as our army, who have to stand the hardships of the war, are thus determined and consecrated to the cause," he wrote his sister, "that those at home will cheerfully bear the little inconveniences which must necessarily result from such a state of affairs and at least speak words of encouragement to the soldiers and not endeavor to shake their confidence in the cause of religious and civil liberty."[23]

Many of Lee's soldiers employed language suggesting a loyalty to the Confederacy that transcended attachments to state or locality. A quintet of Georgians illustrate this phenomenon. A sergeant in the 45th Georgia confessed to his wife that he longed to be with her and their son but could not enjoy time at home while still able to do duty. "Others would be fighting for their Country and My Country and home while I would be skulking my duty," he explained, "and it would render me miserable. I am happier just as it is while the war lasts." Daniel Pope took the occasion of his twenty-fourth birthday to muse about the fact that he had spent the most pleasant portion of his life in the army—a circumstance sad to contemplate. "But when we consider the great duty we owe our country in the struggle for independence," continued Pope, "I cannot be but content with my fate, although it may be, indeed, a cruel one. I am determined to do anything and everything I can for my country." If he fell in battle, Pope hoped his wife would believe that he had contributed his part to a struggle that would ensure her and their son "the great boon of freedom."

Pvt. Jesse M. Garrett of the 35th Georgia vowed to fight three more years and subsist on bread and water rather than submit to the abolitionist North. "I never thought of any thing else but that we will gain our independence," he stated. "Oh how I long to see the sun of peace and the banner of liberty float . . . triumphantly over the green fields of the Sunny South." Francis Marion Howard of the 18th Georgia used comparable phrases to make the same point. "I am willing to fight as long as we can keep an army together," he vowed, "I *do* hope to live to see the South gain her independence & be free of the tyranical yoke of abolitionists." Howard savored the thought of "telling the yankee wherever I may meet him that his people ware not able to subjugate the South." In a touching letter to his children, Isaac Domingos, a sergeant in the 51st Georgia, explained that he might fall "on the battle field fighting for my God and my country, liberty and our homes." [24]

Men in the army often seemed more willing than their counterparts at home to sacrifice a measure of freedom to achieve nationhood. In February Col. James Conner lauded Congress for passing legislation to restrict the currency, raise taxes, and expand conscription. These constituted "three very important Acts," he believed, "and severe as they unquestionably are, I think they will do good." Conner subsequently described the suspension of habeas corpus as "wise, just, and necessary, unless we meant to give up the army." Lt. Josiah Blair Patterson of the 14th Georgia took a similar view, affirming that Georgians in the field—unlike "villainous grumblers and croakers" behind the lines—would "spurn with contempt any term of settlement less than an independent nationality." Congress had acted correctly regarding conscription, the currency, and habeas corpus, he insisted—though these measures admittedly threatened the bulwarks of states' rights and individual privileges. Condemning the challenges to central authority mounted by Joseph E. Brown, Alexander H. Stephens, and others, Patterson claimed Confederates must "win and possess rights national state and individual before we vex our brain in settling discriminating lines of demarcation." [25]

Men such as Conner and Patterson followed the lead of R. E. Lee, who from the opening of the conflict had called for the subordination of all private concerns to the goal of achieving national independence. Throughout the late winter and spring the army's commander pressed officials in Richmond to tighten conscription. He deplored the actions of speculators and urged Quartermaster Gen. Alexander R. Lawton to impress leather for shoes if necessary. Aware of the potentially divisive effects of large-scale seizure of goods from civilians, Lee nonetheless advocated authorizing the government "to impress when necessary a certain proportion of everything produced in the country. . . . If it requires all the meat in the

Catherine Ann Devereux Edmondston. The wife of a planter in eastern North Carolina, Edmondston kept a diary that underscored Lee's importance to Confederate soldiers and civilians.
Capital Area Preservation at Mordecai Historic Park, Raleigh, N.C.

country to support the army, it should be had, and I believe this could be accomplished by not only showing its necessity, but that all equally contributed, and that it was faithfully applied." Proper oversight of impressment agents would limit civilian complaints, Lee stated, as would assurances that all impressed goods reached the men in the field. In mid-April Lee urged Secretary of War James A. Seddon to seize temporary control of the railroads to guarantee timely delivery of supplies to the army.[26]

A profound bond with Lee formed a vital ingredient in the recipe for high morale in the army. One veteran impressed Catherine Ann Devereux Edmondston with his great devotion to the general. "He says '*Marse Robert*,' as the men all call him, can carry them anywhere," recorded Edmondston in her revealing journal. "They think him as pure a patriot as Washington and a more able General . . . [and use] 'Marse Robert' . . . as a term of endearment and affection." A woman in Richmond, after speaking about Lee with groups of furloughed soldiers, commented, "It is delightful to see how they reverence him, and almost as much for his goodness as for his greatness."[27]

Clement Evans also summoned Washington's name in a perceptive evaluation of the relationship between Lee and his soldiers. "General Robt. E. Lee is regarded by his army as nearest approaching the character of the great & good Washington than any man living," wrote Evans in his diary. "He is the only man living in whom they would unreservedly trust all power for the preservation of their independence." Stonewall Jackson had inspired enthusiasm, but the "love and reverence for Lee is a far deeper and more general feeling." In a sentence that belies the notion that Lee's image of perfection was entirely a postwar construction, Evans remarked that "General Lee has no enemies, and all his actions are so exalted that mirth at his expense is never known." A private in the 12th Virginia Cavalry conveyed much the same impression of Lee in far fewer words: "No army ever had such a leader as General Lee." At army headquarters Walter H. Taylor, the young adjutant whose wartime letters expressed occasional unhappiness about Lee's penchant for running the army with minimal staff, exhibited utter confidence in his chief's military capacity: "If all our army is placed under G[enera]l Lee's control, I have no fear of the result."[28]

A memorable scene involving Lee and the soldiers of James Longstreet's First Corps highlighted the ties between the army commander and his men. Longstreet's two divisions had returned to Virginia in April after several months' service in Georgia and Tennessee, setting the stage for what artillerist Edward Porter Alexander later likened to "a military sacrament." On a clear and pleasant late April day Lee rode across a broad field where Longstreet's veterans were arrayed. Music and an artillery salute heralded his appearance, and when the soldiers caught sight of him on Traveller for the first time since the preceding summer, "a wild and prolonged cheer, fraught with a feeling that thrilled all hearts, ran along the lines and rose to the heavens." Men tossed their hats skyward, color-bearers shook their standards, and palpable emotion surged through the assemblage. Lee moved forward to acknowledge the greeting, triggering, according to one witness, "on all sides expressions such as: 'What a splendid figure!' 'What a noble face and head!' 'Our destiny is in his hands!' 'He is the best and greatest man on this continent!'" A soldier in the 15th South Carolina recorded that Lee and Longstreet "were enthusiastically cheered by [the troops] as long as they were in sight." Another proudly told his sister, "Yesterday we had a grand review by the Greatest of Generals: Gen'l R. E. Lee. . . . There was a grate many of the fair Sex out to see us. And after the review was over they all crowded around the old Gen'l to Shake handes with him. And some Said they had Shuck handes with the gratest general in the world."[29]

The arrival of the First Corps boosted confidence to another level among Lee's soldiers. Images bespeaking an organic conception of the army appeared in letters and diaries remarking on the event. One officer told Lt. Col. Franklin Gaillard of the 2nd South Carolina that he "felt as if the right arm of the army had been restored." Walter Taylor, who had longed for the presence of the First Corps for many weeks, recorded with unabashed delight that "a portion of *our family* has been returned to us. Old Pete Longstreet is with us and all seems propitious." A member of Cobb's Legion thought Longstreet's appearance foreshadowed hard fighting. "We have more men here now than we ever have had before," said Francis Marion Whelchel, "and they all are in high spirits. . . . I dont have any fears but what we will give the yanks the worst whiping they ever have got if they do attemed to take Richmond." As for Longstreet's troops, Thomas Goree described "pretty general rejoicing" among them. Although Goree thought a campaign into Kentucky by the First Corps might have yielded excellent results, he wrote his mother that "we ag[ain] constitute a part of the greatest of all armies under the leadership of the greatest living chieftain, and if we can succeed in inflicting on Grant a crushing defeat, it will do much towards bringing about a speedy peace."[30]

Goree's prediction of victory over Grant reflected a widespread impression that the North's champion would be no match for Lee. Some of the men took a sarcastic view of the new Federal commander. Activity in the Federal camps during late April led O. H. Steger of the 21st Virginia to observe drolly that the Federals seemed to be preparing for another campaign: "Mr. Grant I reckon is getting too popular for Lincoln and he wishes Gen Lee to take him down which I believe by the help of Providence will be done." F. Stanley Russell mocked Grant as that "*mighty* man of *valour*" charged with accomplishing a task that had sent George B. McClellan, Ambrose E. Burnside, and Joseph Hooker into oblivion. "Poor Grant," wrote Russell, "his doom is sealed; the glory of his former deeds will fast fade, in the failure of his latter undertakings." James Conner passed along to his mother a new nickname the Confederates had given their opponent: "The Yankees call him 'unconditional surrender Grant'; our men already have given him a name; 'Up the spout, Grant.'" A Georgian warned his parents in less clever but equally confident prose that a battle with the enemy would soon erupt. "All we want you to do is to be hopeful & continue to ask God for aid," he implored on behalf of his comrades, "& Gen Grant will go down like the rest of [the] yankey Gens, that have bin brought against this army."[31]

Conspicuous in his dismissal of Grant as a worthy opponent, Walter

Taylor may have conveyed the tenor of attitudes at Lee's headquarters. Speculating in March about whether Grant would finally be the Union general-in-chief or merely commander of the Army of the Potomac, Lee's adjutant professed not to fear him in either case. Overrated because of his victories against the inept Pemberton, Grant enjoyed a much inflated reputation. "He will find, I trust, that General Lee is a very different man to deal with," stated Taylor with more than a tinge of condescension toward the efforts of Confederate forces in the Western Theater, "& if I mistake not will shortly come to grief if he attempts to repeat the tactics in Virginia which proved so successful in Mississippi." [32]

Some men tempered their optimism with thoughts about impending carnage and the odds they faced. "Grant is evidently collecting a heavy force in our front, and a few short weeks will probably startle the country with the thunders of the most terrible battle of the war," Green Berry Samuels informed his wife. Satisfied that the army would fight desperately to defend their homes and families, Samuels bravely suggested that "with a decided success this summer, the enemy must forego all hopes of subjugating us." Brig. Gen. Wade Hampton noticed strong morale among his troopers and hoped "confidently for success" but at the same time suffered anxiety about "many thousand of the brave hearts, now eager for the strife," who would be dead at the conclusion of the next campaign. Yet more pessimistic was Henry Robinson Berkeley of the Hanover Artillery, who looked at a landscape covered with enemy tents on the Culpeper side of the Rapidan River on April 23 and exclaimed, "What a mighty host to keep back!" "Can we do it?" he pondered. "We will try. Who of us will be left when peace comes?"

Capt. Charles Minor Blackford, who served on Longstreet's staff, agreed with Samuels that "Grant is certainly collecting a large army against ours." A victory would break Union military strength, and Confederate officers and men were confident of triumph. "I am also," averred Blackford without much enthusiasm, "but sometimes I find my fears giving away to the force of numbers. . . . Grant can afford to have four men killed or wounded to kill or disable one of ours. That process will destroy us at last, by using up our material." The next ninety days would be decisive. "If we succeed," Blackford summed up with marginally more enthusiasm, "we will have peace in less than twelve months." [33]

Relatively few of Lee's soldiers seem to have shared Blackford's understanding of the respective strengths of the armies. Instead, a sense that the Federals lacked their usual preponderance of manpower fueled expectations of victory. Typical of this frame of mind, Chaplain James B. Sheeran of the 14th Louisiana believed Lee's "well disciplined army, approximating somewhat to the enemy in numbers . . . and with hearts glowing with the purest of patriotism and minds determined to conquer" would smite the Federals. Both Clement Evans and Walter Taylor placed Grant's strength at 75,000 to 80,000 (a considerable underestimate) and concurred that, as Evans put it, "We will be fully able to cope with them." Second Corps cartographer Jedediah Hotchkiss quoted Lee himself as saying on April 11 that "the enemy had not as large a force as they had last year,—though it was said they were coming with a large force in every direction." Even a good look at the enemy's extensive camps failed to impress Maj. Tully Francis Parker of the 26th Mississippi. From atop Clark's Mountain on May 4 he spied "many a Yank in our front, but from what I can see they don't have any advantage on us." The soldiers placed great trust in Lee and would fight desperately, he confirmed, predicting that if Grant advanced, "he will certainly meet with a bad defeat."[34]

Numbers aside, the notion of a demoralized enemy took root on the Confederate side of the Rapidan. At Second Corps headquarters Lt. Gen. Richard S. Ewell received encouraging intelligence about Federal morale: "They are said to be re-enlisting very rapidly, but after receiving the bounty, to be deserting as fast." A lieutenant in the 4th Virginia contrasted Lee's "noble army voluntarily reenlisting for the war" with "the Yankees offering enormous bounties and getting so few soldiers at that." Influenced by a "frenzy of despair at the prospect of their fast failing cause," believed this man, the Federals would mount one last gigantic campaign to salvage their war effort. Similarly, Clement Evans mentioned Federal deserters who spoke of their army as "demoralized & deserting in large droves." A Virginian in the Stonewall Brigade made a common inference that Confederate victories in Louisiana, North Carolina, and Tennessee had been "very discouraging to the enemy," who would get "pretty badly whipped" if they crossed the Rapidan to attack the Army of Northern Virginia.[35]

Shifting their lens from the Army of the Potomac to the northern home front, some Confederates detected a broader malaise. Political turmoil and rising gold prices ranked among the most often mentioned examples of looming crises that might undermine Union civilian morale. An artillery lieutenant read about a resolution in the U.S. Congress to expel Alexander Long of Ohio for making speeches in favor of peace—an indication that "opposition to the war is getting stronger and more fearless." A Confederate military victory could set loose the tongues of antiwar men such as Long and Mayor Fernando Wood of New York City against Lincoln and his party. In mid-April Surgeon Spencer Glasgow Welch of the 13th South Carolina—who thought northerners more susceptible than Confederates to discouragement because "their cause is not just"—celebrated the latest economic news from the North: "Gold is 179 in New York, but if we whip Grant we may send it up to 300 for them."[36]

At the Bureau of War in Richmond, diarist Robert Kean mirrored the attitude of many soldiers in Lee's army. Skyrocketing gold prices constituted just one of many "hopeful indications of a general breaking up in the United States, political as well as financial," he wrote on April 3. Angry disputes between Democrats and Republicans in Congress, Lincoln's "military usurpation," and jockeying for the presidential succession augured well for the Confederacy. Having laid out this background of potential chaos in northern society, Kean turned to the factor that would settle the fate of both nations: "Everything depends on the next battle in Virginia."[37]

Misconceptions about Federal numbers and morale joined pervasive confidence in Confederate prowess to inspire thoughts about another offensive across the Potomac. A captain in the 60th Georgia of John B. Gordon's brigade reported Lee's army fully ready to counter Grant's movements and then march northward. "The men are now very anxious to move forward," he told a cousin. "They are also anxious that Genl. Lee should carry them in to Penn. again." Sergeant Fitzpatrick of the 45th Georgia expected the campaign to open in May with Lee attacking Grant and then proceeding to Pennsylvania. A member of Micah Jenkins's brigade, with retribution in mind, set his sights a bit farther south: "Something tells me we shall be successful if we invade Md. once more," stated Stephen Elliott Welch. "War is a curse but I want the Yanks to realize its horrors in their own boundaries."[38]

Dodson Ramseur savored a scenario involving a raid across the Potomac that would send destructive tremors through northern society. Lee's army would "crush Meade—*before* crossing the Potomac," strike through Maryland into Pennsylvania, subsist for a while off the fat of the Pennsylvania countryside, and then withdraw to Virginia to await the next Federal move. "In the mean time the Yankee debt will go on piling up," asserted the young brigadier, who firmly believed that northerners cared more about their purses than anything else. "Gold will mount higher. Yanks will consider 'the job' bigger than they expected in which all con-

Brig. Gen. Stephen Dodson Ramseur (shown earlier in the war as a major of artillery). Ramseur's optimism about the spring 1864 military campaign reflected a common attitude among soldiers of all ranks in the Army of Northern Virginia.
Robert Underwood Johnson and Clarence Clough Buel, eds., Battles and Leaders of the Civil War, *4 vols. (New York: Century, 1887–88), 4:242*

cerned are apt to be hurt. Old Abe will be defeated for Pres't—& the people will be ready & anxious to sustain the peace policy of the new Pres't."[39]

A belief that victory would be impossible without God's blessing underlay virtually all of the speculation about the spring campaign. The army experienced a surge of religious activity during the winter and spring of 1864 that came to be called the "Great Revival." In describing this phenomenon in one part of the army, a South Carolinian noted approvingly that "a deep religious feeling pervades McLaws' Division. In three brigades there is preaching every night, with prayer and inquiry meetings . . . during the day." One historian places the number of converts at roughly 7,000 and estimates that the revivals touched at least thirty-two of the army's thirty-eight brigades of infantry. The specter of death in battle, hardships endured by soldiers and civilians alike, and uncertainties about the future all contributed to a milieu ripe for religious examination.[40]

Diaries and letters from Lee's army offer little evidence of fear that God had deserted the Confederacy—though many soldiers interpreted the war as God's punishment for their sins. J. M. Miller of the 14th South Carolina used typical language in making this point: "Now I believe the war was brought on us for our sins and whenever the people repent aright the war will end." Miller evinced no doubt that God would favor the Confederates over their enemies, however, commenting that in the next campaign Grant "will undoubtedly get whipped and I hope and believe the war will end." Virginian William L. Wilson echoed Miller's sentiments. "Though in the past three years He has suffered us to be sorely tormented and aliens to occupy our lands and strangers our houses," he wrote of God's hand in the war, "He never brought us so far in that struggle to turn us over to the tender mercies of the enemy." Wilson joined many other soldiers in hoping that "many humble fervent petitions of Christians throughout the Confederacy" would promote final success.[41]

Others identified God's blessings on a just cause and the continued devotion of the southern white populace as the keys to victory. "If God does add another to our list of victories," averred Walter Taylor, "we may confidently look for peace soon thereafter. This army is determined, always presupposing Heaven's help, to accomplish this." Lee's brilliance and the army's fine material condition should encourage hope, wrote Ted Barclay in early May, "But more than this, our cause we believe to be a just one and our God is certainly a just God, then why should we doubt." A third soldier could not "but think that if we are true to ourselves and do our whole duty that a just and almighty God will crown our efforts with success and peace." This man thought it wonderful that Confederates had begun to "rely solely on God and themselves for success—they have ceased to look to Europe, the outside world for support."[42]

John W. Watson of the 47th Virginia found the prospect of a summer's hard fighting discouraging. "But it wont do to be so low spirited," he added quickly. "I believ it is the best way to chear up, and trust in our great Captain who can give the victory to whom he sees propper to give it to." Lt. John W. Hosford of the 5th Florida would have agreed with Watson's implication that the Lord would decide victor and vanquished. He insisted that only God could extricate the Confederacy from its difficult trials. "I do not believe we have done our duty to Him," he confided to his sweetheart, "from no other source need we expect peace."[43]

R. E. Lee joined many of his men in believing a strict devotion to duty and the Almighty's favor would yield Confederate success. As the army grimly confronted hunger during the lean, cold days of January, he issued a general order that evoked the Christian sacrifice of the Revolutionary generation. "Continue to emulate in the future, as you have in the past, their valor in arms, their patient endurance of hardships, their high resolve to be free," he implored, "and be assured that the just God who crowned their efforts with success will, in His own good time, send down His blessings upon yours." Lee also subscribed to the idea that God would bless the side that most closely followed a Christian path. The failure of Dahlgren's raid against Richmond and subsequent revelations about assassination plots elicited a strong response. Lee spoke of the enemy's "unchristian & atrocious acts" and observed that Dahlgren's "plans were frustrated by a merciful Providence, his forces scattered, & he killed."[44]

Did the commanding general share the confidence of his officers and men as May 1864 drew near? Logistics vexed him greatly, as demonstrated by his persistent search for food, fodder, and other materials throughout late winter and spring. Rations and supplies of shoes and clothing improved with time, but Lee remained partially hamstrung by logistics in his effort to meet Federal offensives. Among other expedients, he dispersed portions of the army's cavalry and artillery to areas able to support their heavy demands for fodder. Always in favor of holding the strategic initiative, he suggested to Jefferson Davis and James Longstreet that Confederate attacks in the East or West (or in both theaters) could disrupt Grant's plans. "The great obstacle everywhere is scarcity of supplies," he told Longstreet. Shortages might force the Confederates to conform to Federal plans "and concentrate wherever they are going to attack us."[45]

On March 30 Lee informed Davis that the time approached when "I shall require all the troops belonging to this army." Six days later he had concluded that Virginia would be the target of Grant's largest effort and recommended that Longstreet's corps be summoned to Virginia. Braxton Bragg, installed as a bureaucrat in Richmond after his removal from command of the Army of Tennessee, heard from Lee on April 7. "I think every preparation should be made to meet the approaching storm, which will apparently burst in Virginia," read Lee's dispatch, "& unless its force can be diverted by an attack in the West, that troops should be collected to oppose it." Lee asked for the return of Robert F. Hoke's and Robert D. Johnston's brigades "& all the recruits that can be obtained," and urged the collection of supplies in Richmond. Interruption of railroads that fed into Richmond, warned Lee, would compel him to withdraw from Virginia.[46]

Lee's almost desperate requests for reinforcements stemmed from his knowledge that the Army of the Potomac would number at least 100,000 when it moved southward. Even with Longstreet's two divisions the Army of Northern Virginia would muster fewer than 65,000 men. The nearby presence of Ambrose E. Burnside's Federal corps—the objective of which Lee could only guess—and the rumored arrival of the Federal Eleventh and Twelfth Corps further tilted the odds against the Confederate defenders. Thus Lee scarcely could have shared the pervasive illusion that the armies would contend on fairly equal numerical terms (why Walter Taylor, who certainly must have been privy to the reports on which Lee based his estimates, indulged such an optimistic view in this regard is a mystery).[47]

Offensive thoughts and logistical doubts continued to dominate Lee's thinking through April. He told Bragg that the addition of Longstreet's troops and George E. Pickett's division (which had been detached from the First Corps after Gettysburg) would provide the manpower necessary to mount an offensive against Grant along the Rappahannock. In that way Lee could oblige the enemy to look to the safety of their capital and relinquish thoughts about menacing Richmond. But logistics tied his hands: "I cannot even draw to me the cavalry or artillery of the army, and the season has arrived when I may be attacked any day. The scarcity of our supplies gives me the greatest uneasiness." On May 4 Lee telegraphed Bragg that the Federals had struck tents and were en route to the Rapidan River's fords. "This army in motion toward Mine Run," he reported. "Can Pickett's division move toward Spotsylvania Court House?" Lee's request for Pickett's brigades underscored his continuing concern about numbers as the opening clash with Grant's host drew near. Any thoughts of a strategic offensive must have receded as he planned to block the Army of the Potomac's strike southward through the Wilderness.[48]

However troubled by his army's relative paucity of numbers and Grant's possessing the strategic initiative, Lee knew he led veterans who had delivered victories on many difficult fields. His soldiers strode toward battle on May 5 with an equally unshakable faith in their commander and an expectation of success. South Carolinian Alexander Cheves Haskell had caught the essence of their esprit in a pair of sentences penned near the end of March: "While I observe no boastfulness or effervescence in the courage of our men, the indications of spirit are of a better kind than I have ever seen them. Plenty of enthusiasm, but of a subdued and concentrated sort, that fully appreciates the dangers ahead and a determination to put an end, if possible, to the fighting this year."[49] The ensuing conflagration in Spotsylvania's grim Wilderness would fully justify the men's confidence in themselves and their chief—and would leave gaps in their ranks never to be filled with soldiers their equal.

NOTES

The author wishes to thank Keith S. Bohannon, Peter S. Carmichael, Robert E. L. Krick, and Robert K. Krick for their help in turning up testimony pertinent to Confederate morale in early 1864.

1. Bell I. Wiley, *The Road to Appomattox* (Memphis: Memphis State College Press, 1956), 67–68, 70; Richard E. Beringer, Herman Hattaway, Archer Jones, and William N. Still Jr., *Why the South Lost the Civil War* (Athens: University of Georgia Press, 1986), 425. In his influential study of the Georgia upcountry, Steven Hahn portrays a Confederate populace hugely disaffected from its government by the beginning of 1864 (Hahn, *The Roots of Southern Populism: Yeoman Farmers and the Transformation of the Georgia Upcountry, 1850–1890* [New York: Oxford University Press, 1983], esp. chapter 3). Other recent works that portray serious erosion of southern white commitment to the war by the end of 1863 include Malcolm C. McMillan's *The Disintegration of a Confederate State: Three Governors and Alabama's Wartime Home Front, 1861–1865* (Macon, Ga.: Mercer University Press, 1986), and Wayne K. Durrill's study of Washington County, North Carolina, *War of Another Kind: A Southern Community in the Great Rebellion* (New York: Oxford University Press, 1990). Hahn and Durrill emphasize class antagonism between yeomen and planters as a major factor in undermining civilian morale.

2. Edward A. Pollard, *Southern History of the War: The Last Year of the War* (New York: Charles B. Richardson, 1866), 13–14.

3. James B. Sheeran, *Confederate Chaplain: A War Journal of Rev. James B. Sheeran, c.ss.r., 14th Louisiana, C.S.A.*, ed. Joseph T. Durkin (Milwaukee: Bruce, 1960), 72 (entry for January 21, 1864); Dr. William Alexander Thom to J. Pembroke Thom, April 16, 1864, in Catherine Thom Bartlett, ed., *"My Dear Brother": A Confederate Chronicle* (Richmond, Va.: Dietz, 1952), 156.

4. Samuel D. Knight to Joseph E. Brown, February 22, 1864, in Mills Lane, ed., *Times That Prove People's Principles: Civil War in Georgia* (Savannah: Beehive Press, 1993), 137; Robert Garlick Hill Kean, *Inside the Confederate Government: The Diary of Robert Garlick Hill Kean*, ed. Edward Younger (New York: Oxford University Press, 1957), 140 (entry for March 13, 1864); Pauline DeCaradeuc Heyward, *A Confederate Lady Comes of Age: The Journal of Pauline DeCaradeuc Heyward, 1863–1888*, ed. Mary D. Robertson (Columbia: University of South Carolina Press, 1992), 38. On Brown, Stephens, Holden, and the controversies in which they played crucial roles, see Joseph H. Parks, *Joseph E. Brown of Georgia* (Baton Rouge: Louisiana State University Press, 1977); Thomas E. Schott, *Alexander Stephens of Georgia: A Biography* (Baton Rouge: Louisiana State University Press, 1988); and William C. Harris, *William Woods Holden: Firebrand of North Carolina Politics* (Baton Rouge: Louisiana State University Press, 1987). For a selection of documents that help illuminate the situation in North Carolina, see

W. Buck Yearns and John G. Barrett, eds., *North Carolina Civil War Documentary* (Chapel Hill: University of North Carolina Press, 1980).

5. Richmond *Dispatch*, January 9, 13, 1864; Charleston *Daily Courier*, January 14, 16, 1864; Richmond *Enquirer*, February 5, 1864.

6. Richmond *Dispatch*, March 24, 1864; Charleston *Daily Courier*, February 16, 1864.

7. Atlanta *Southern Confederacy*, March 31, 1864; article from the Montgomery *Advertiser* quoted in the Atlanta *Southern Confederacy*, March 24, 1864; Richmond *Enquirer*, February 6, 1864; Charleston *Daily Courier*, February 26, April 2, 1864.

8. Mary Jones to Mary S. Mallard, April 30, 1864, in Robert Manson Myers, ed., *The Children of Pride: A True Story of Georgia and the Civil War* (New Haven: Yale University Press, 1972), 1162–63; Belle Edmondson, *A Lost Heroine of the Confederacy: The Diaries and Letters of Belle Edmondson*, ed. William Galbraith and Loretta Galbraith (Jackson: University Press of Mississippi, 1990), 113, 124 (diary entries for April 14, May 6, 1864); Susan Emeline Jeffords Caldwell to Lycurgus Washington Caldwell, April 22, 1864, in J. Michael Welton, ed., *"My Heart Is So Rebellious": The Caldwell Letters, 1861–1865* (Warrenton, Va.: Fauquier National Bank, n.d.), 218.

9. [Judith W. McGuire], *Diary of a Southern Refugee during the War* (1867; reprint, Salem, N.H.: Ayer, 1986), 269–70.

10. (Macon) Georgia *Messenger & Journal*, March 30, 1864; Atlanta *Southern Confederacy*, March 27, 1864; Charleston *Daily Courier*, April 11, 1864; Richmond *Dispatch*, April 13, 1864.

11. Alexander Frederick Fleet to Benjamin Fleet, April 11, 1864, in Betsy Fleet and John D. P. Fuller, eds., *Green Mount: A Virginia Plantation Family during the Civil War, Being the Journal of Benjamin Robert Fleet and Letters of His Family* (Lexington: University of Kentucky Press, 1962), 320; Henry W. Barrow to John W. Fries, April 9, 1864, in Marian H. Blair, ed., "Civil War Letters of Henry W. Barrow to John W. Fries," *North Carolina Historical Review* 34 (January 1957): 81–82.

12. W. Johnson J. Webb to Dear Parents, April 22, 1864, Lewis Leigh Collection, United States Army Military History Institute, Carlisle, Pa.; Stephen Dodson Ramseur to Ellen Richmond Ramseur, April 24, May 3, 1864, Stephen Dodson Ramseur Papers, Southern Historical Collection, Wilson Library, University of North Carolina, Chapel Hill (repository hereafter cited as SHC).

13. Stephen Dodson Ramseur to David Schenck, January 28, 1864, Ramseur Papers, SHC; D. J. Hileman to Miss Kate McCutchan, January 18, 1864, Daniel J. Hileman Letters, James G. Leyburn Library, Washington and Lee University, Lexington, Va.

14. R. E. Lee to Jefferson Davis, January 2, April 12, 1864, in R. E. Lee, *The Wartime Papers of R. E. Lee*, ed. Clifford Dowdey and Louis H. Manarin (Boston: Little, Brown, 1961), 647, 698.

15. R. E. Lee to James A. Seddon, February 16, 1864, in ibid., 672; Thomas J. Goree to Sarah Williams Kittrell Goree, February 8, 1864, in Thomas J. Goree,

Longstreet's Aide: The Civil War Letters of Major Thomas J. Goree, ed. Thomas W. Cutrer (Charlottesville: University Press of Virginia, 1995), 117; Charles E. Denoon to [?], January 16, 1864, in Charles E. Denoon, *Charlie's Letters: The Civil War Correspondence of Charles E. Denoon*, ed. Richard T. Couture (Collingswood, N.J.: Civil War Historicals, 1989), 92; Burwell Thomas Cotton to My Dear Sister, April 30, 1864, in Michael W. Taylor, ed., *The Cry Is War, War, War: The Civil War Correspondence of Lts. Burwell Thomas Cotton and George Job Huntley, 34th Regiment North Carolina Troops* (Dayton, Ohio: Morningside, 1994), 172; J. E. B. Stuart to Flora Stuart, February 8, 1864, in James E. B. Stuart, *The Letters of Major General J. E. B. Stuart*, ed. Adele H. Mitchell ([Richmond, Va.]: Stuart-Mosby Historical Society, 1990), 370–71.

16. LeRoy S. Edwards to [?], January 10, 1864, in LeRoy S. Edwards, *Letters of LeRoy S. Edwards, Written during the War between the States*, ed. Joan K. Walton and Terry A. Walton (n.p., [1985]), letter no. 59 (unpaginated work with letters arranged chronologically); Benjamin H. Freeman to W. H. Freeman, February 19, 1864, in Benjamin H. Freeman, *The Confederate Letters of Benjamin H. Freeman*, ed. Stuart T. Wright (Hicksville, N.Y.: Exposition Press, 1974), 34; Thomas J. Barron to Ada, April 23, 1864, in Ray Mathis, ed., *In the Land of the Living: Wartime Letters by Confederates from the Chattahoochee Valley of Alabama and Georgia* (Troy, Ala.: Troy State University Press, 1981), 115.

17. "A Fire Side Defender" [probably William Judkins of the 22nd Georgia] to the Editor, February 17, 1864, Rome (Ga.) *Tri-Weekly Courier*, March 3, 1864; James Marion Garrett to Dear Mother, April 14, 1864, copy of original in private hands provided by Keith S. Bohannon; Tully F. Parker to My Dear Wife and Children, May 4, 1864, typescript, bound vol. 201, Fredericksburg and Spotsylvania National Military Park Library, Fredericksburg, Va. (repository cited hereafter as FSNMP); John Henry Stover Funk to his parents, March 5, 1864, typescript of original in private hands provided by Keith A. Bohannon.

18. Kate Cumming, *The Journal of a Confederate Nurse, 1862–1865*, ed. Richard Harwell (Savannah: Beehive Press, 1975), 177; Emma Holmes, *The Diary of Miss Emma Holmes, 1861–1866*, ed. John F. Marszalek (Baton Rouge: Louisiana State University Press, 1979), 339; Richmond *Enquirer*, January 30, 1864.

19. Charles Augustus Conn to Mary A. Brantley, March 18, 1864, in T. Conn Bryan, ed., "Letters of Two Confederate Officers: William Thomas Conn and Charles Augustus Conn," *Georgia Historical Quarterly* 46 (June 1962): 194; Stephen Dodson Ramseur to David Schenck, February 16, 1864, Ramseur Papers, SHC.

20. Walter Raleigh Battle to My dear Mother, March 29, 1864, typescript, bound vol. 85, FSNMP; James A. Graham to My Dear Mother, April 2, 1864, in James A. Graham, *The James A. Graham Papers, 1861–1884*, ed. H. M. Wagstaff (Chapel Hill: University of North Carolina Press, 1928), 184; Burwell Thomas Cotton to My Dear Sister, April 16, 1864, in Michael W. Taylor, *Cry Is War*, 170.

21. James Conner to My dear Mother, April 3, 1864, in James Conner, *The Letters of General James Conner, C.S.A.*, ed. Mary C. Moffet (Columbia, S.C.: State Co., 1933), 121; William Meade Dame to My own Dear Mother, April 29, 1864,

typescript, FSNMP; Josiah Gorgas, *The Civil War Diary of General Josiah Gorgas*, ed. Frank E. Vandiver (University: University of Alabama Press, 1947), 88 (entry for March 25).

22. James A. Graham to My Dear Mother, February 1, 1864, in Graham, *Papers*, 178; Abram Hayne Young to Dear Parents and Sisters, March 13, 1864, in Mary Wyche Burgess, ed., "Civil War Letters of Abram Hayne Young," *South Carolina Historical Magazine* 78 (January 1977): 63.

23. Clement A. Evans, *Intrepid Warrior: Clement Anselm Evans, Confederate General from Georgia, Life, Letters, and Diaries of the War Years*, ed. Robert Grier Stephens Jr. (Dayton, Ohio: Morningside, 1992), 341–42 (diary entry for January 18–28); Stephen Dodson Ramseur to David Schenck, February 16, 1864, Ramseur Papers, SHC; Ted Barclay to Dear Sister, March 21, 1864, in Ted Barclay, *Ted Barclay, Liberty Hall Volunteers: Letters from the Stonewall Brigade (1861–1864)*, ed. Charles W. Turner (Natural Bridge Station, Va.: Rockbridge, 1992), 134–35.

24. Marion Hill Fitzpatrick to Amanda Olive Elizabeth White Fitzpatrick, April 10, 1864, in Marion Hill Fitzpatrick, *Letters to Amanda, from Sergeant Major Marion Hill Fitzpatrick, Company K, 45th Georgia Regiment, Thomas' Brigade, Wilcox Division, Hill's Corps, CSA to His Wife Amanda Olive Elizabeth White Fitzpatrick, 1862–1865*, ed. Henry Mansel Hammock (Nashville: Champion Resources, 1982), 125; Daniel Pope to his wife, March 12, 1864, in Mills Lane, ed., *"Dear Mother: Don't grieve about me. If I get killed, I'll only be dead." Letters from Georgia Soldiers in the Civil War* (Savannah: Beehive Press, 1977), 282–83; Jesse M. Garrett to Dear Mother, April 14, 1864, typescript, FSNMP; Francis Marion Howard to Dear Brother, April 19, 1864, typescript, bound vol. 104, FSNMP; Isaac Domingos to My dear son Joseph & daughter, Tallulah, April 19, 1864, Confederate Miscellany, Ib, Special Collections, Emory University, Atlanta, Ga.

25. James Conner to My Dear Mother, February 19, April 3, 1864, in Conner, *Letters*, 115, 122; Josiah B. Patterson to My Dear Niece Lizzie, March 17, 1864, in Garland C. Bagley, *History of Forsythe County, Georgia* (Easley, S.C.: Southern Historical Press, 1985), 529–30.

26. R. E. Lee to Jefferson Davis, January 13, 19, 1864; Lee to Alexander R. Lawton, January 19, 1864; Lee to James L. Kemper, January 29, 1864; Lee to James A. Seddon, April 12, 1864, all in Lee, *Wartime Papers*, 650–51, 653, 654–55, 663 (quotation), 696.

27. Catherine Ann Devereux Edmondston, *"Journal of a Secesh Lady": The Diary of Catherine Ann Devereux Edmondston, 1860–1866*, ed. Beth Gilbert Crabtree and James W. Patton (Raleigh: North Carolina Division of Archives and History, 1979), 524 (entry for February 10); [McGuire], *Dairy*, 256 (entry for March 20).

28. Evans, *Intrepid Warrior*, 342–43 (diary entry for January 18–28); William Lyle Wilson to My Dearest Ma, March 24, 1864, in Festus P. Summers, ed., *A Borderland Confederate* (Pittsburgh: University of Pittsburgh Press, 1962), 78; Walter H. Taylor to Bettie Saunders, May 1, 1864, in Walter H. Taylor, *Lee's*

Adjutant: The Wartime Letters of Colonel Walter Herron Taylor, 1862–1865, ed. R. Lockwood Tower (Columbia: University of South Carolina Press, 1995), 158. In a rare dissent from the consensus that Lee was the ablest Confederate general, F. Stanley Russell of the 13th Virginia described Joseph E. Johnston as "the acknowledged strategist of the South" (F. Stanley Russell, *The Letters of F. Stanley Russell: The Movements of Company H, Thirteenth Virginia Regiment, Confederate States Army 1861–1864*, ed. Douglas Carroll [Baltimore: Paul M. Harrod, 1963], 58). For the unpersuasive argument that Lee's preeminence in the Confederate military pantheon was a postwar phenomenon, see Thomas L. Connelly, *The Marble Man: Robert E. Lee and His Image in American Society* (New York: Knopf, 1977).

29. Edward Porter Alexander, *Fighting for the Confederacy: The Personal Recollections of General Edward Porter Alexander*, ed. Gary W. Gallagher (Chapel Hill: University of North Carolina Press, 1989), 346; R. to the editor of the *Daily South Carolinian*, May 1, 1864, printed in the *Daily South Carolinian* (Columbia), May 10, 1864; David Crawford to Dear Mother, April 30, 1864, typescript, FSNMP; Abram Hayne Young to Ever Dear Sister, April 30, 1864, in Burgess, "Letters of Abram Hayne Young," 70.

30. Franklin Gaillard to Dear Maria, April 24, 1864, Gaillard Papers #3790, SHC; Walter Taylor to Bettie Saunders, April 24, 1864, in Walter H. Taylor, *Lee's Adjutant*, 155; Francis Marion Whelchel to Dear Sisters and Cousin Mary, April 26, 1864, typescript, bound vol. 81, FSNMP; Thomas J. Goree to Sarah Williams Kittrell Goree, April 26, 1864, in Goree, *Longstreet's Aide*, 122–23.

31. O. H. Steger to [?], April 23, 1864, typescript, FSNMP; F. Stanley Russell to Dear Papa, March 31, 1864, in Russell, *Letters*, 64–65; James Conner to My dear Mother, April 3, 1864, in Conner, *Letters*, 122; Charles O. Goodwyne to Dear Pa & Ma, March 10, 1864, typescript, FSNMP.

32. Walter H. Taylor to Bettie Saunders, March 20, 1864, in Walter H. Taylor, *Lee's Adjutant*, 139.

33. Green Berry Samuels to Kathleen Boone Samuels, April 3, 1864, in Carrie Esther Spencer, Bernard Samuels, and Walter Berry Samuels, eds., *A Civil War Marriage in Virginia: Reminiscences and Letters* (Boyce, Va.: Carr, 1956), 211; Wade Hampton to Mary Fisher Hampton, February 14, May 6, 1864, in Charles E. Cauthen, ed., *Family Letters of the Three Wade Hamptons* (Columbia: University of South Carolina Press, 1953), 103–4; Henry Robinson Berkeley, *Four Years in the Confederate Artillery: The Diary of Private Henry Robinson Berkeley*, ed. William H. Runge (Chapel Hill: University of North Carolina Press [for the Virginia Historical Society], 1961), 72; Charles Minor Blackford to Mrs. Blackford, May 3, 1864, in Charles Minor Blackford III, ed., *Letters from Lee's Army, Or, Memoirs of Life In and Out of the Army of Northern Virginia During the War Between the States* (New York: Scribner's, 1947), 242–43.

34. Sheeran, *Confederate Chaplain*, 85 (diary entry for April 26); Clement A. Evans to Dear Darling, April 20, 1864, in Evans, *Intrepid Warrior*, 373; Walter H. Taylor to Bettie Saunders, May 1, 1864, in Walter H. Taylor, *Lee's Adjutant*, 158; Jedediah Hotchkiss, *Make Me a Map of the Valley: The Civil War Journal*

of Stonewall Jackson's Topographer, ed. Archie P. McDonald (Dallas: Southern Methodist University Press, 1973), 198–99; Tully F. Parker to My Dear Wife and Children, May 4, 1864, typescript, FSNMP.

35. Richard S. Ewell to Benjamin S. Ewell, February 18, 1864, in Richard S. Ewell, *The Making of a Soldier: Letters of General R. S. Ewell,* ed. Percy Gatling Hamlin (Richmond, Va.: Whittet & Shepperson, 1935), 126; Ted Barclay to Dear Sister, February 22, March 21, 1864, in Barclay, *Ted Barclay,* 128; Clement A. Evans to My dearest Dearest, May 2, 1864, in Evans, *Intrepid Warrior,* 380; John Garibaldi to Dear Wife, April 22, 1864, typescript, bound vol. 172, FSNMP. This view of Federal morale also appeared in civilian letters and diaries. For example, Susan Emeline Jeffords Caldwell wrote in April that Grant "has a very large army but many are heartily sick of the war and say they do not intend to reenlist. Their time will be out in August and they are going home to stay—I hope they will be true to their word" (Caldwell to Lycurgus Washington Caldwell, April 22, 1864, in Welton, *Caldwell Letters,* 218).

36. William Beverley Pettit to Arabella Speairs Pettit, April 19, 1864, in Charles W. Turner, ed., *Civil War Letters of Arabella Speairs and William Beverley Pettit of Fluvanna County, Virginia, March 1862–March 1865,* 2 vols. (Roanoke, Va.: Virginia Lithography & Graphics, 1988–89), 2:25; Spencer Glasgow Welch to his wife, January 16, April 19, 1864, in Spencer Glasgow Welch, *A Confederate Surgeon's Letters to His Wife* (1911; reprint, Marietta, Ga.: Continental, 1954), 86, 90–91.

37. Kean, *Diary,* 443–44.

38. Benjamin F. Keller to My dear Cousin Annis, April 7, 1864, in *The Land and The People: Readings in Bulloch County History, Book 5* (Statesboro, Ga.: Bulloch County Historical Society, 1986), 55; Marion Hill Fitzpatrick to Amanda Olive Elizabeth White Fitzpatrick, April 14, 1864, in Fitzpatrick, *Letters to Amanda,* 127; Stephen Elliott Welch to Dear Mother, February 14, 1864, in Stephen Elliott Welch, *Stephen Elliot Welch of the Hampton Legion,* ed. John Michael Priest (Shippensburg, Pa.: Burd Street Press, 1994), 24.

39. Stephen Dodson Ramseur to David Schenck, March 13, 1864, Ramseur Papers, SHC.

40. R. to editor of the *Daily South Carolinian,* May 1, 1864, printed in the *Daily South Carolinian* (Columbia), May 10, 1864; Gardiner H. Shattuck Jr., *A Shield and a Hiding Place: The Religious Life of the Civil War Armies* (Macon, Ga.: Mercer University Press, 1987).

41. J. M. Miller to My dear Cousin, April 7, 1864, in [Dotsy Boineau, comp.], *Recollections and Reminiscences, 1861–1865 through World War I,* 6 vols. to date (n.p.: McNaughton & Gunn [for the South Carolina Division, United Daughters of the Confederacy], 1990–95), 5:374–75; William Lyne Wilson to My Dearest Mother, April 19, 1864, in Summers, *Borderland Confederate,* 78. For the argument that religion played a crucial role in bringing Confederate defeat, see Beringer and others, *Why the South Lost,* esp. chaps. 12 and 14.

42. Walter H. Taylor to Bettie Saunders, April 10, 1864, in Walter H. Taylor, *Lee's Adjutant,* 150; Ted Barclay to Dear Sister, May 2, 1864, in Barclay, *Ted*

Barclay, 143–44; F. Stanley Russell to Dear papa, March 14, 1864, in Russell, *Letters*, 62.

43. John W. Watson to My Dear Wife, April 19, 1864, typescript, FSNMP; John W. Hosford to Miss Laura, April 1, 1864, in Knox Mellon Jr., ed., "A Florida Soldier in the Army of Northern Virginia: The Hosford Letters," *Florida Historical Quarterly* 46 (January 1968): 269–70.

44. General Orders No. 7, dated January 22, 1864, in Lee, *Wartime Papers*, 659.

45. R. E. Lee to Jefferson Davis, March 25, 1864, and Lee to James Longstreet, March 28, 1864, in ibid., 682–85.

46. R. E. Lee to Jefferson Davis, March 30, April 5, 1864, and Lee to Braxton Bragg, April 7, 1864, in ibid., 690–93.

47. R. E. Lee to Braxton Bragg, April 13, 1864, in ibid., 698.

48. R. E. Lee to Braxton Bragg, April 16, May 4, 1864, in ibid., 701, 718.

49. Alexander Cheves Haskell to [?], March 27, 1864, in Louise Haskell Daly, *Alexander Cheves Haskell: The Portrait of a Man* (1934; reprint, Wilmington, N.C.: Broadfoot, 1989), 123.

JOHN J. HENNESSY

I Dread the Spring

THE ARMY OF THE POTOMAC PREPARES

FOR THE OVERLAND CAMPAIGN

O n the morning of November 30, 1863, the Army of the Potomac stood on the verge of what might have been the grandest, most dramatic, most horrific moment in its history. More than 30,000 veterans of places such as Manassas and Gettysburg prepared to go across nearly a mile of open ground, traversing Mine Run, into the teeth of bristling Confederate lines. "Of all hard looking places, that of Mine Run was the hardest I ever beheld," wrote a surgeon in the Sixth Corps. "All along the [opposite] heights could be seen battery upon battery . . . ready to belch their iron contents of grape and canister into the stiffened, freezing flesh of the best blood of America. As I looked out upon the task proposed to be executed, my heart died within me." Five miles of Yankee soldiers mused similarly that morning. "All now seemed to feel the magnitude of the task before them— the responsibility resting on each one, the grandeur of the charge if successful, the slaughter of our Army if defeated," remembered Col. Robert McAllister of the 11th New Jersey. "Stillness mingled with sadness pervaded our ranks."[1]

Through frigid minutes the Union army waited for the signal to advance. The artillery, scheduled to open at 7:00 A.M., fired only sporadically. The designated hour of 8:00 arrived and passed with only a smattering of shots in front. Artillery fire faded away. Soon whispers passed through the ranks: the attack was postponed. "The countenances of our men now began to brighten and the apparent sadness wore away," wrote McAllister. There would be no attack at Mine Run that November 30.[2]

For the Army of the Potomac and its commander George

G. Meade, the canceled assault at Mine Run was probably the most important nonevent in the army's history as well as something of a turning point. The men in the ranks saw in Meade that day a moral courage they had not often seen in their top leaders.

Soldiers in this army had watched and grumbled when George B. McClellan did not attack on September 18, 1862, in the aftermath of Antietam, and Lee eventually escaped disaster. One year before Mine Run, they had seen Ambrose E. Burnside stare down an impregnable position at Fredericksburg and then demonstrate a lack of both imagination and will by ordering attacks that left the army bloodied and contentious. At Chancellorsville they had seen "Fighting Joe" Hooker declare that Lee must "ingloriously fly" and then yield all the fruits of brilliant maneuver to wobbly nerves. And they had seen their current commander follow his uplifting victory at Gettysburg with what many in the army considered a pallid pursuit that allowed Lee to escape yet again.

An autumn's fruitless maneuvering had further damaged confidence in Meade, leaving him, on the eve of Mine Run, only marginally more popular with the men than Burnside had been. "This is strictly private," a New York officer confided to his parents, "but I assure you, nearly everyone in the army from the highest to the lowest, have lost all confidence in Gen. Meade as a fighting man, but all have the greatest confidence in his ability to keep us out of the way of the Rebels." A Second Corps staff officer lamented in the early fall, "It seems likely we shall be led in a plodding, ordinary sort of way, neither giving nor receiving any serious blows, a great pity." Marsena R. Patrick, the army's "fossilized" provost marshal general, likewise viewed Meade's pre–Mine Run efforts with skepticism: "I cannot make out his plans," Patrick wrote, "because he cannot make them out himself."[3]

But as the men of the army sat down to scribble their letters in the aftermath of Mine Run, their attitudes toward Meade had changed because of his decision not to fight on the banks of that chilly Virginia stream. "I tell you how it is, Louisa," wrote a Sixth Corps surgeon, "if Meade ever did a noble act in his life, it was when he concluded not to fight Lee." Staff officer Theodore Lyman marveled, "I shall always be astonished at the extraordinary moral courage of General Meade." Lyman noted that Meade "had the firmness to say, the blow has simply failed and we shall only add disaster to failure by persisting." To some eyes the nonattack elevated Meade to a level exceeding even that of the beloved McClellan. "His conduct in the last campaign has fastened his name firm in the hearts of those who compose this army," stated a Fifth Corps officer. "He is not Grant or Rosecrans," commented Charles Francis Adams from army headquarters, "but he is ten times Hooker and twice McClellan." Meade's newfound popularity in fact had something in common with McClellan's. Both showed determination to avoid needless bloodshed, and both seemed willing, as one man put it, to "not suffer himself to be influenced" by politicians and public opinion. The Army of the Potomac demonstrated great affinity for generals willing to defend it against outside influences (Pope, Hooker, and Burnside had been weak in that regard, McClellan had not been), and in December 1863 Meade reaped a windfall of goodwill on that account. One soldier summarized the basic thought of thousands: "Thank heaven that we are back to our old camping ground, and that I still live."[4]

It was perhaps fitting that George G. Meade distinguished himself by inaction, for he came from a tradition of conservatism (some might say mediocrity) in the high command of the Army of the Potomac. This was an army whose first, most influential, and most beloved commander abided faithfully to a concept of war that required him to determine the worst thing the enemy could do to him and then prepare to meet it. This was an army whose high command, in its first eighteen months, feverishly tried to shape Union war aims in a conservative mold. Its officers largely opposed emancipation, opposed interference with southern civilians, opposed confiscation, opposed the use of black troops—indeed opposed almost everything on the Radical Republican agenda. Meade agreed with most of these views, although, unlike many, he took pains to keep his expressions quiet. He reacted to the political game by trying to ignore it as much as possible, which constituted a subtle and effective form of political machination. He recognized that survival in the ever-more-radical political world around him required such discretion.[5]

George Gordon Meade rose to command of the army by virtue of workmanlike performances on many battlefields. At every level of his steady rise, he put his energy not into politics but into running his command, which he did in brusque, businesslike form. An Ohio correspondent said that Meade was "altogether a man who impresses you rather as a thoughtful student than as a dashing soldier." Another noted that Meade "did not care much for reviews, but believed greatly in reports and inspections. . . . As a rule he was a better listener than talker." Possessed of a temper that "on occasions, burst forth like a twelve-pounder spherical case," Meade ruled with directness and, occasionally, intimidation. Cavalry officer Charles Francis Adams called him "a man of high character; but he was irritable, petulant and dyspeptic." Assistant Secretary of War

Maj. Gen. George Gordon Meade.
Robert Underwood Johnson and
Clarence Clough Buel, eds., Battles
and Leaders of the Civil War, *4 vols.*
(New York: Century, 1887–88), 3:257

Charles Dana remembered he was "agreeable to talk with when his mind was free, but silent and indifferent to everybody when he was occupied." He was subject to fits of "nervous irritation," Dana continued, and "was totally lacking in cordiality toward those with whom he had business, and in consequence was generally disliked by his subordinates."[6]

Unlike predecessors who relied on physical form as an important part of their command presence, Meade did little to project the classic image of a soldier. Indeed, he was the only ugly commander the Army of the Potomac ever had. The best description of him comes from a New York newspaper correspondent: "His face is almost covered with beard, and his neck displays a leather stock that might have been used in the days of his ancestors. He is otherwise collarless, and his face is colorless, being of a ghastly pale, with thought, study, and anxiety marked upon his every lineament. . . . His nose is of the antique bend, [and] is the most prominent feature of the face." Second Corps staff officer Frank Haskell wrote of him, "His fibers are all of the long and sinewy kind. His habitual personal appearance is quite careless, and it would be difficult to make him look well dressed." Army command had weighed heavily on Meade, adding to his haggard look. John Sedgwick noted in November 1863, "Meade is twenty years older than when he took command" just five months before. All this added up to a largely uninspiring package. According to Josiah Favill of the Second Corps, "He has none of the dash and brilliancy which is necessary to popularity."[7]

So when the men of the Army of the Potomac withdrew from Mine Run on December 2, 1863, they did so with confidence in their commander's discretion, if not his fighting abilities; they did so with tolerance of his quirks and looks, if not outright affection for his being. In contrast to the retreats after Fredericksburg and Chancellorsville, the army moved back to its camps around Culpeper and Brandy Station cloaked not in melancholy but relief. In taking their places at new winter camps, the soldiers began the quietest and most uneventful epoch in the army's history. The four months prior to the Overland campaign would leave their morale and physical condition excellent in every respect. Given the defeats under indecisive leaders and unprecedented political turmoil of the two previous years, the recovery was remarkable. To understand the army's condition that winter requires some comparison with more tumultuous times under different guiding hands.

For its first eighteen months the Army of the Potomac experienced constant transformation. At the outset in August 1861 its men had wanted to be a simple tool to achieve military ends, and most of northern society supported that view. As the war ground along without decisive result, political agendas increasingly crept into military matters. The Union war effort changed from a straightforward attempt to put down rebellion into a crusade to transform American society. By the spring of 1863 the army —directed by a more progressive administration and Congress—had become a tool to achieve both political and military ends. Within the army and the country as a whole, that transformation had caused vociferous debate. Many of the Potomac army's most prominent officers, often with the warm support of their men, fiercely resisted radicalization and spent much of their energy in 1862 and early 1863 trying to define northern war aims. Letters from officers of the Army of the Potomac spilled onto the desks of newspaper editors, senators, congressmen, and governors and into the hands of friends and loved ones at home. Theirs was not an organized effort, but it attained considerable volume and hence influence. It simultaneously reflected and contributed to social divisions afflicting a nation caught up in a transforming conflict.[8]

The expressions by some of the army's hierarchy in 1862 constitute a vivid record of the nation's strains of discord. Gouverneur K. Warren, commander of the Fifth Corps during the Overland campaign, saw doom in the rising talk of abolition that swept the nation in the wake of defeat on the Peninsula: "The army has suffered enough in hardships to no longer act out any abolition programme," he wrote. "It [the army] is fighting for the Union, which is unattainable without allowing the Southern people their rights." The issuance of the preliminary Emancipation Proclamation in September 1862 prompted many officers to muse as did John Gibbon: "If this contest is going to end in an abolition war, I cannot remain in the service." Fitz John Porter, the army's greatest articulator of the conservative patriot's view, offered that "the proclamation was ridiculed by the army—caused disgust," and that radical steps "tend only to prolong the war by rousing the bitter feelings of the South, and causing unity of action among them." He avowed that the army "was tired of the war and wish to see it ended . . . by a restoration of the Union—not merely a suppression of the Rebellion, for there is a wide difference." In the midst of all this turmoil Alexander Webb went so far as to declare, "I have no hope left. Was there ever such a Government, such fools, such idiots? I hate and despise them more intensely than I do the Rebels!"[9]

The rank and file of the Army of the Potomac largely concurred with these views and sensed unrest between the high command and the government. "The principles that we have to fight for now are too black for anyone to come out for," wrote a man of the 3rd Michigan in February 1863. "We poor cuses do not want to stay out here in the field as targets & instruments for the Black Abolition party & that rotten congress."

But the soldiers of 1862 and early 1863 had more to grumble about than emancipation, war aims, and rotten politicians. And grumble loudly they did—about failure on the battlefield, food, lack of success at home, delayed paychecks, and general atrophy of the army's administration.[10] The chorus attained such volume that some mistook it for a fatal cancer and advocated the dissolution of the army. Charles Francis Adams, a keen observer, wrote pointedly on January 30, 1863, "I most earnestly hope [the government] will now break up the army, else some day it will have it marching on Washington."[11]

Adams's attitude of early 1863 contrasted with the mood of the men who settled into the camps at Brandy Station and Culpeper in the winter of 1863–64. The change was not embodied so much in gleeful expressions as in an absence of complaint. Judging by the lack of grousing found in letters of the period, the army of 1863–64 was content. "Never since we came out, has a better feeling existed in the army than now," wrote Surgeon Daniel Holt of the 121st New York. "If they only feed us well, pay us well, and use us well, we will do all the fighting the north can desire."[12]

What caused this dramatic change in outlook over a twelve-month period? The army had trudged through a year of campaigning punctuated by disappointment and stalemate, yet it emerged with a perspective on the war that would carry it through to Appomattox. The reasons for the change were many, and they reflect not just the evolution of an army's psyche but also the transformation of an entire nation's outlook on war and its government—a transformation with huge implications for the America that emerged from this conflict.

The most obvious reason for the army's positive outlook during the winter of 1863–64 was that its administration never had been better. Complaints about food, intermittent mails, delayed paychecks, and backbiting on the home front simply vanished from soldiers' letters of this period. "We have all got . . . warm and comfortable log houses with nice fire places and bunks," a New York soldier told his homefolk. "We have plenty of rations and have soda bread every day. Indeed we are as well of as an[y] soldiers . . . might wish to be." Life in the army had taken on a rhythmic, businesslike aspect. "The war seems to be now the one grat [sic] job on hand, a steady regular job, in a business reduced to science. . . . Men in the army are getting to look more upon it as a profession," wrote staff officer Uriah Parmelee.[13]

George Meade deserves great credit for the army's improved circumstances. The administrative decay begun under McClellan in 1862 and worsened by Burnside had been retrieved by Hooker in 1863, and Meade had sustained Hooker's improvements. But someone else had a great deal to do with the physical condition of the army that winter of 1863–64: Andrew Atkinson Humphreys—the best chief of staff the Army of the Potomac ever had.[14]

Contemporary opinions on Humphreys varied widely. A longtime topographical engineer, he had thus far in the war swayed between staff and line work and commanded divisions commendably at both Fredericksburg and Gettysburg. After Gettysburg he replaced the energetic but narrow-minded Daniel Butterfield as army chief of staff. Humphreys unintentionally had become one of the army's notable characters. He fussed over himself, "continually washing . . . and putting on paper dickeys," said staff officer Lyman. A civilian noted that he habitually rode with the wide brim of his hat turned down, "making him look like a Quaker." Another soldier wrote of his "keen blue eyes which, protected by gold-bow spectacles, beamed in a philosopher-like way." "There never was a nicer old gentleman," wrote Lyman, "and so boyish and peppery that I continually want to laugh in his face."[15]

Humphreys's image as a quirky professorial type vanished when he focussed on business. He ruled all around him with an unquavering hand, though his odd visage often belied an iron will. In battle he was fearless, a fact that endeared him to all who witnessed his displays. Less endearing were his vile outbursts, which became legendary. Brigade commander Regis de Trobriand recorded that Humphreys "was given to flaming outbreaks in which all the vigor known or unknown to the English language burst forth like a bomb." Lyman noted similarly, "When he does get wrathy, he sets his teeth and lets out a torrent of adjectives that must rather astonish those not used to" such outbursts. These displays no doubt were carefully calculated and certainly achieved the desired effect. Few dared to cross Humphreys—not even the crotchety provost marshal general of the army, Marsena R. Patrick. After long days of working with Humphreys, Patrick pronounced him a "very queer fellow." But the fact remains that under his eye—and with help from smart and experienced department heads such as Rufus Ingalls, Seth Williams, and Patrick—the army ran in a fashion previously unmatched in its history. The demeanor of the army attested to the success of Humphreys's labors. By meeting the most obvious needs of the soldiers, Humphreys helped remove a basic source of grumbling. His efforts were fundamental to the success of the Union war effort. Charles Dana called him simply "the great soldier of the Army of the Potomac."[16]

Diligent attention to the needs of 100,000 soldiers was just one of many reasons the army of 1863–64 differed so dramatically from that of 1862–63. Improved support from behind the lines also helped. During the winter of 1862–63, rampant civilian carping about the army, its efforts, and its commanders left soldiers and their officers frustrated and angry. The army's conservative predilections did not extend to the peace movement that swept parts of the North in the spring of 1863. To those looking northward from the front, Copperheads seemed to have invaded every corner of the Union, and the men acutely felt the apparent betrayal. In March 1863 a Pennsylvania soldier eloquently captured the army's resentment when he called peace agitators "mean low bred cowardly traitors and

*Maj. Gen. Andrew Atkinson
Humphreys (shown earlier in the war
as a brigadier general).
Robert Underwood Johnson and
Clarence Clough Buel, eds.,* Battles
and Leaders of the Civil War, *4 vols.
(New York: Century, 1887–88), 4:115*

scoundrels." Furthermore, he vowed that "when after this war is over . . .
we will take vengeance on those cowardly skunks." Another man wrote
that "it is hard to fight two battles at the same time—one in the front and
the other in the rear; but if necessary we can attend to both."[17]

In the wake of the fall 1863 elections the army rejoiced at the political
demise of the Copperhead factions. The results in New York—a state long
a source of political discontent for the army—were especially gratifying.
"I had no fear that but that the Union ticket would be elected," wrote a
Democratic New York officer. "Copperheads seem to be at a discount at
present . . . and every true Union *Man* is, and must be rejoiced that the
people have shown by their votes, that they mean to support the government." Another New Yorker rejoiced that his home state had "spoken in
louder and more fearful tones to the Southern Confederacy than all the
cannon of the Universe pouring death and destruction into [them]. The
Army is in a perfect frenzy of delight."[18]

Soldiers also applauded the government's willingness to enforce the draft. While veterans never embraced draftees (who retained second-class status until the end of the war), the army choked with anger over the prospect of northern men resisting conscription. When elements of the army went to New York City in July and August 1863 to quell the draft riots, the only lament on the Virginia front was that the entire army had not gone. "We would much rather have gone to New York," remembered one New York soldier, "and fought the accursed Copperheads at home than the rebels in Virginia." Another declared that the army should "force that draft in NY City or I would bury every inhabitant under its ruins." For others the simple fantasy of going to New York gave pleasure. Artilleryman William Wheeler noted, "There is a fine position for artillery on Broadway below Canal Street, commanding the street as high as Eleventh, and the balls would ricochet splendidly on the hard pavement." Whether a regiment delivered direct retribution on the "cowards" in New York or gloried in vicarious pleasure, most agreed on the virtue of enforcing conscription. "I believe in the North's being made to feel the war," wrote Wheeler, "which she has not yet done as a nation, and to really offer up something to win this great, almost infinite good."[19]

In declaiming the need for others to enlist, veterans could not avoid the question of their own continued employment in the war effort. Thousands of three-year enlistments would expire in 1864, and this was a hot fireside issue in the winter of 1863–64. Although many at first resisted, ultimately more than half of those eligible for reenlistment did so. That rate surely reflected the relatively high morale of the army as well as the considerable inducements the government offered in bounties and furloughs.[20]

A more tangible source of pleasure for men in the field, and a vivid demonstration of support from home, was the work in camp of the Christian Commission and the Sanitary Commission. Both organizations tended to the physical wants of the men. Indeed, the Sanitary Commission transformed both field hospital and camp during the war. The Christian Commission also looked to spiritual needs. More than any other civilian organization, it earned the affection of men in the camps around Brandy Station. The commission constructed a chapel for almost every brigade, and soldiers often crowded these makeshift structures, some of which held up to 300 men, for nightly meetings led by commission delegates. Vermont soldier Wilbur Fisk, whose letters are a wonderful source for the texture of everyday life in the army, explained the popularity of the meetings in a March 1864 letter:

Members of the U.S. Christian Commission in the field.
Alexander Gardner, Gardner's Photographic Sketch Book of the War, *2 vols.*
(Washington, D.C.: Philips and Solomons, 1866), vol. 2, plate 53

This large attendance is owing to two or three causes. One is because it is something new, for it has been a long time since we have enjoyed any religious privileges to speak of. Another is, because it is a very agreeable way to spend an hour—a pleasant change from the dull monotony of camp life, whether one cares particularly for the meeting or not. Cheerful sacred singing and speaking is pleasant always; but I believe a soldier enjoys them the best of anybody. It is very natural from his circumstances that he should. These reasons and the desire on the part of a great many to do good, has so far kept up a full attendance.

Fisk also described the meetings themselves:

The meetings commence at half past six and are held till the drum calls us to roll call at eight. One of the delegates preaches a short sermon, or rather makes a few practical remarks founded upon some text of Scripture, and then the time is occupied by any one who wishes to speak, sing or pray. Generally the time is fully occupied, and often two or more rise to speak at once. Many have risen at the invitation to manifest a desire for the others in their behalf, and some have spoken there that never spoke in meeting before. Besides these, a sort of Bible class is held every day in the Chapel, and where the boys that desire it may meet for studying the Scriptures, and for mutual improvement.... A good work is begun here, one which every Christian will rejoice to see prosper.[21]

The efforts of the Christian Commission spurred something of a revival in the army that winter. "I have never witnessed anything like it," wrote Col. Robert McAllister in April 1864. "When our regiment is not on picket, our church is crowded for preaching and prayer every night. After the regular meeting is over, a large number still remains for conversation and more prayer." Corporal Fisk declared that "no missionary in any field can receive a heartier welcome than the soldier is willing to accord the delegates of the Christian commission; and . . . no more can be accomplished anywhere else than can be accomplished here." Just as important as the efforts of the commissions in the field was the ultimate source of those efforts—the living rooms, sanitary fairs, churches, and charitable organizations at home. The collective efforts of the northern populace, as expressed through the work of the commissions, were a constant reminder of grassroots support for soldiers at the front. Wilbur Fisk probably voiced the feelings of thousands of soldiers that winter when he wrote, "We shall remember with gratitude what has been done for us here, and some will have all eternity to be grateful in. Probably no other army was ever cared for as ours has been."[22]

The army that huddled in winter camps after the debacle at Fredericksburg in December 1862 also had protested major political issues such as confiscation, emancipation, and the prospect of black troops taking the field. As vivid example, a New Jersey soldier had declared in February 1863, "If a Negro regiment were to come and camp near an old regiment out here, the men would kill half of them."[23] A year later the tumult had calmed. The great debate over war aims that racked this army for much of its existence had yielded to quiet acceptance. Chaplain John R. Adams of the 5th Maine reflected the prevailing (though sometimes grudgingly offered) opinion in February 1864: "There is a great change in the army and in the country on the subject of slavery. Its overthrow was a military necessity. We destroy tanneries, flour-mills, and other fixtures," Adams explained, "Why not then weaken and destroy the strong arm of slavery, which has been used to raise food for the army of the Confederates, or to dig rifle pits, and throw up earthworks?" Emancipation and the use of black troops had become, in short, a "military necessity."

Examination of hundreds of letters written during the winter of 1863–64 reveals almost no rekindling of the previous year's debate over emancipation. Even formerly ardent opponents remained silent on the subject. Many men of the Army of the Potomac still harbored fierce prejudices against black Americans, and especially against former slaves, but they largely had come to see that emancipation would help the Union war effort by diminishing the Confederacy's ability to resist.[24]

For the Army of the Potomac, the winter of 1863–64 also witnessed the emergence of the type of strong collective identity necessary to the health of any organization. This identity was not, as it once had been (and still was in the Confederate army), tied to the persona of the army's leader. Rather, the army identified strongly with itself as a mass. This had much to do with the recognition of a common past, a military heritage that helped bind the men together.

The victory at Gettysburg abetted growing solidarity. Robert G. Carter probably reflected the views of many in a letter to his family in April 1864. "Oh! . . . those are the proudest days of my life, in memory," he affirmed. "*I would not sell the honor of being a poor humble member of that brave band of men who fought the bloody battle, for all the gold that gilds the treasury.*" Carter then asked his family if they "ever pause and think what we saved you from, those three days of carnage?" Staff officer Morris Schaff stated that the army "had been smelted, so to speak, in those three trying days at Gettysburg. . . . And the result of this supreme test of courage was that the officers and the men of the Army of the Potomac felt that respect for one another and that pride in one another that only a battlefield can create." Indeed, most of the army viewed Gettysburg as a decisive turning point after two years of frustration. One soldier gloated in the battle's aftermath, "They are at our mercy now." Few in the army doubted the war's outcome.[25]

The army's growing sense of heritage also exhibited itself in other ways. Some of the first regimental histories appeared in 1864 (many were published in abridged form in local newspapers), and soldiers rushed to collect them. Upon publication of a history of his regiment, a man in the 57th New York claimed that "the boys were as eager to get hold of them, almost, as they would their discharge." A reading of the history prompted him to declare his belief that the regiment "would fight like heroes today to maintain its fair reputation." This period also witnessed the start of the

Third Corps Union, begun to provide funeral expenses for men but later important as a commemorative organization. It was also in the winter of 1863–64 that the army literally started the process of enshrining itself when the First Corps formed an association to raise funds for a monument to Maj. Gen. John F. Reynolds, killed at Gettysburg.[26]

None of this diminished the men's longing for home, but it tended to bolster their determination. "I hope this war will soon be over," wrote one of the army's signalmen in February 1864, "but as long as the reballs are not conquered I am willing to stay and fight." Reflecting on the hardships the army had endured, another soldier wrote that "never have men been known to fight as this army has fought, even when we knew we were out-generaled and defeated. Any man will fight when flushed with former victories, but it is only this shattered army that will face the enemy though defeat be certain."[27]

A last important reason for the army's calm that winter grew out of drastic changes among its leadership over the preceding fifteen months. Most of the officers who in 1862 and 1863 had flung themselves into the debate over defining Union war aims were either gone or silenced. McClellan, who had lectured the president on the war's scope in his Harrison's Landing Letter and privately muttered about marching with his army on Washington, was fast becoming a memory to the men in the ranks. Likewise gone (in fact court-martialed, though wrongly) was Fitz John Porter, McClellan's confidant and the army's most articulate advocate for a limited approach to war. William B. Franklin and William F. "Baldy" Smith —staunch conservatives, former friends of McClellan, and opponents of Burnside—also had been ushered out of the Eastern Theater. Many less prominent men of similar stripe had departed, too, including William T. H. Brooks and John Cochrane. Of those staunch conservatives who remained in the army, a few such as John Sedgwick and Winfield Scott Hancock survived by virtue of silence; John Newton, George Sykes, and others were disposed of in a major reorganization in March 1864 (more on that below).[28]

The removal or silencing of conservative officers represented one of the most important trends of the war. This transformation in the high command resulted from a concerted effort on the part of the government to quash debate in the army over war aims by reassigning the debaters. Systematic throughout 1862 and into 1863, the effort succeeded entirely and marked a turning point in American history. It confirmed civil government's control over the nation's army. Never again would there be talk of an American army marching on Washington. Only rarely would letters from dissenting officers appear in congressional offices and on editors' desks.

Those officers who remained in the upper echelons of the army during the winter of 1863–64 did not necessarily differ politically from their predecessors, but they had learned important lessons. They had seen Porter court-martialed, Charles P. Stone arrested, and McClellan relieved; they had heard the rumblings of the Committee on the Conduct of the War, whose sticky clutches could ruin a career in an instant. They understood that determining war aims lay beyond their sphere and that they were simply to carry forth the government's policies. They may have disagreed with the government on some issues, but now they tended to their jobs in the field and let politicians in Washington manage the war effort. A letter from Hancock to his wife in May 1863 suggests that conservative officers appreciated the need to segregate military and political matters. Hancock wrote that he had "been approached again in connection with the command of the Army of the Potomac," but he would not accept the command because "I do not belong to that class of generals whom the Republicans care to bolster up. I should be sacrificed." The crippling antagonism between Washington and the Army of the Potomac thus diminished, which produced a calm that enhanced army morale.[29]

The winter of 1863–64 produced few episodes of notice for the Union army, and that by itself was a welcome development. "It was the most pleasant experience in our army experience," wrote a Jersey man. Throughout December, soldiers perfected their camps. They built huts, company streets, chapels, bake ovens, officers' quarters, stables, and even dance halls. In the process they transformed much of Culpeper County — denuding forests, consuming fences, and fighting constant battles against mud and excrement. "A man's shoes must be well tied or he will leave them buried in this red clay mortar," recorded a Vermonter. "Go where you will, there is no relief; everywhere it is the same universal mud." By mid-January the camps spread across more than 100 square miles.[30]

Supplies by the trainload poured into Brandy Station, and virtual nineteenth-century shopping malls sprang up there. "Persons of almost any trade are improving the time by making money from the soldiers," wrote a New Yorker. "There you will see a sign over the door of a little board shanty, 'Oysters,' 'Fresh Fish,' 'Condensed Milk,' 'Beer,' and numberless other signs which tempt the pocketbook of the soldier." The daily arrival of newspapers at 3:00 P.M. added a sense of normality to the burgeoning military city in Culpeper County, as newsboys spread through the camps yelling the papers' names — "Herald," "Washington Chronicle,"

"Baltimore American." Library books, lecturers, concert bands (a division band in the Second Corps boasted thirty-two pieces, plus stringed instruments), and women also arrived to brighten the winter days. "There are perfect shoals of womenkind now in the army," wrote staff officer Lyman. An enlisted man noted wryly that their presence would "tend greatly to remove much of the 'dull monotony of camp life.'" Lonely men lavished affection on the women. "The ladies are in ecstasies, bewildered by the immense attention they received," a Second Corps staffer wrote. "Every officer is devoting himself, his horses, and his servants to their comfort." Some of the women even saw combat from a distance when they ascended Stony Mountain to watch the battle of Morton's Ford on February 6, 1864.[31]

Monotony and discomfort served as a backdrop for these happier aspects of the winter of 1863–64. The Army of the Potomac maintained more than fifty miles of perimeter pickets, and a soldier's life consisted of stretches of unpleasantness punctuated by cheery interludes. Even in the happiest moments, however, men suffered severely at the hands of cold and constant dampness. Part of the army failed to escape the ultimate horror of battle. A division of the Union Second Corps crossed the Rapidan at Morton's Ford and engaged Confederates in a sharp little battle on high ground beyond. The winter's only burst of serious combat, this action yielded no important results.[32]

Only two noteworthy events broke the winter's routine. The army underwent reorganization, and Ulysses S. Grant arrived in the Eastern Theater. Both occurred in March and had a huge effect on the Army of the Potomac.

On March 23, 1864, the War Department issued orders consolidating the Army of the Potomac's five infantry corps into three and reassigning numerous officers long associated with the army. The Second, Fifth, and Sixth Corps were reorganized into two divisions each. Abolished and redistributed among those corps were the old First Corps, once Irvin McDowell's and later John Reynolds's, and the Third Corps, home to a host of army anomalies, such as Daniel E. Sickles and David Bell Birney. The orders provided that men in the dismantled corps could retain their old corps badges—a slight salve for a painful disruption. Many detected the hand of the newly arrived Grant behind the reorganization; others saw it as an attempt to reconfigure the high command by political machinations. Neither explanation was correct. George G. Meade planned the reorganization, which had been in the works for months, and the reassignment of officers was driven not by politics but by seniority—the "Army List."[33]

Meade publicly gave only one reason for the reorganization (which he described as a "temporary" necessity but never took steps to undo). In his orders for the reshuffling, he explained that the "reduced strength of nearly all the regiments serving in this army" had "imperatively demanded" the "temporary reduction of the number of army corps to three." But a pair of unspoken factors also prompted the reorganization.[34] One was the desire shared by Meade and the administration to rid the army of less-than-stellar corps commanders John Newton of the First Corps and William H. French of the Third. By consolidating the five corps into three, Meade could retain only a trio of the most senior officers, and Newton and French would not be among them. The limitations of some of the corps commanders provoked constant whispers in camp that winter; indeed, Gouverneur K. Warren, who received a permanent corps command as part of the reorganization, actively advocated revamping the high command. "My efforts to have those men removed made them all enemies of me," Warren wrote in December 1863. "Gen. Meade acknowledges with bitter feeling now, the truth of what I told him would be the consequences of retaining these men." Warren reserved special condemnation for Newton and French, and the rest of the army mirrored his opinion.[35]

The least known of the army's long-term corps commanders, John Newton was a Virginian who had taken charge of the First Corps at Gettysburg. He had graduated from West Point in 1842 and was schooled in the political game by his father, a twenty-nine-year member of Congress. A newspaper correspondent called the forty-two-year-old general "a little gray, a trifle proud, very mercurial." A staff officer noted that Newton had "somewhat of that smart sort of swagger, that people are apt to suppose characterize soldiers." Oft-visited in the field by his wife, he reveled in niceties and insisted on having a "very gorgeous tent" and "a huge variety of liquids" at hand. He could not have presented a greater contrast to his predecessor John F. Reynolds. Charles Wainwright, the First Corps chief of artillery, noted that "General Newton differs very much from Reynolds in his love for the comforts of life, and for good eating. Baked beans and cayenne pepper will never satisfy him for a meal." More ominously, Wainwright lamented Newton's inattention to details and, by extension, his laziness. He lacked "snap," said Wainwright, and exhibited a willingness to "leave matters in the hands of anyone who would take all the trouble off his shoulders."[36]

Beyond these unproductive tendencies, Newton suffered removal for other reasons. A battlefield record devoid of real accomplishment was the most obvious and easiest to justify. He had been a mainstay of the Sixth

Corps until Gettysburg; but that unit did relatively little fighting in the war's first two years, and Newton had borne a pedestrian part in what action it did see. During the fall campaigning after Gettysburg, Newton had been little more than a spectator.

Perhaps more than anything else, Newton's political stripes and personal method doomed his tenure as corps commander. His Virginia ancestry spurred inevitable suspicion among the Washington elite. Since the war's earliest days, he had been identified with McClellan. They were alike politically, and McClellan (who thought Newton a man of "excellent ability, but . . . perhaps a better engineer than a comdr of troops") used his vast patronage within the Army of the Potomac of 1861–62 to secure his friend a command. Newton had been a consistent conservative advocate and had schemed openly against Burnside. In this he shared the cancer that afflicted the army in its early years. Not only did Newton express adverse opinions about his commanders, the government, and the nature of war, but he also tried to generate support for his views within the army. The surprise was that he remained in command of the First Corps so long. His exit removed the last of the traditional McClellan malcontents from the army.[37]

Newton's criticism of Meade also certainly hurt him. He openly chastised Meade for "failing in an emergency & fearing responsibility" at Mine Run and elsewhere. Meade never responded to these wailings (though he surely heard of them), expressing only polite regret at Newton's departure in March. The army largely joined in such expressions, and Newton, like French, refused a lesser command in the Army of the Potomac. He subsequently saw service in the Western Theater.[38]

William H. French of the Third Corps stood second on the roster of undesirable corps commanders. "Old Blinkey" was a former West Point classmate and friend of Sedgwick's, closely allied personally and politically. He had been with the army through most of its campaigning and had established a tolerably good record at brigade and division levels. His men had done some of the army's hardest fighting. Taking command of the Third Corps after Dan Sickles was wounded at Gettysburg, French led that body dubiously in post-Gettysburg maneuvers, especially at Mine Run.[39]

Intemperate drinking canceled most of French's professional qualifications and inspired considerable quotable and derisive verbiage within the Army of the Potomac. Henry Blake of the 11th Massachusetts, who wielded one of the sharper pens among postwar memoirists, noted that "habitual drunkenness had covered his face with frightful blotches, and destroyed his control over some of his muscles." One Third Corps soldier, John Haley of the 17th Maine, launched into repeated tirades about French in his diary: "He is so repulsive in appearance as to invite nausea at the sight of his bloated and discolored visage," Haley wrote. "He looks like a perfect old soaker, a devotee of lust and appetite. One eye has a habit of blinking, which makes it seem drunker than the rest of him." In another passage Haley likened French's physique to that of a bulldog, but, he wrote, "it wouldn't do to judge his intellect by this standard, as I am convinced that the dog would show points of superiority." Lyman described French as like a "plethoric French colonel" who looked so "red in the face, that one would suppose some one had tied a cord tightly around [his] neck."[40]

French's removal met with no opposition within the army or from Washington. Conventional wisdom in the ranks held that he had been woefully drunk at Mine Run and had performed badly there. French denied this (as did his good friend John Sedgwick, who rushed to his public defense) and tried fruitlessly to fashion a public rebuttal. Whether drunk or not, his performance had been one of the worst of any corps commander in any campaign of the war in Virginia. Republicans in Washington considered French yet another old-line McClellan man (he owed much to McClellan for his brigade command early in the war). His devotion to Sedgwick, the army's greatest bastion of lingering devotion to McClellan, did nothing to change anyone's mind. Lacking political support that might have forced Meade to keep him in command, French was doomed. He saw no more active service for the rest of the war.[41]

George Sykes represented a significant and lamented loser in the reorganization. Commander of the Fifth Corps for nearly a year, "Tardy George" was "a mild, steady man, and very polite," with a thick bush of hair that tended to stand straight, wrote Theodore Lyman. Meade apparently worked hard against his departure, and why Sykes suffered removal is not entirely clear. His reputation as reliable but plodding probably did little to recommend him in an army on the verge of a great campaign. Nor did his crusty manner or conservative outlook engender political support in Washington. Perhaps his failing health also contributed. Whatever the causes, his departure stimulated at least a mild dose of grieving in the Fifth Corps. Young Gouverneur Warren, long associated with the corps, ascended in Sykes's stead.[42]

No less important than the removal of Sykes, French, and Newton was the coincidental relief of the army's cavalry commander, Alfred Pleasonton. Meade claimed no credit for Pleasonton's removal (though he did not oppose it). Not engineered as part of the army's reorganization, Pleasonton's departure was the work of Secretary of War Edwin M. Stanton and Grant. Pleasonton was ripe for removal. One man called him "quite a nice little dandy" and noted that he carried an "unsteady eye, that looks slily [sic] at you, and then dodges." Another recorded, "I judge him to not be very intellectual, at least he has not the expression on his face." Pleasonton's claim to fame in the army derived not from battlefield deeds but from an obsession with self-promotion and the press. "He is pure and simple a newspaper humbug," wrote one of his officers. "You always see his name in the papers, but to us who have served under him and seen him under fire he is notorious as a bully and a toady. He does nothing save with a view to a newspaper paragraph." That implied not just cowardice but also inefficiency. "Pleasonton . . . has and does, unnecessarily, cost the Government 20,000 horses a year," the same officer recorded. Virtually no one in the army credited the improved cavalry to Alfred Pleasonton.[43]

Grant wanted aggressive and outstanding performance from the cavalry and determined that Pleasonton could not meet that standard. On March 25, 1864, the adjutant general's office in Washington issued orders relieving Pleasonton. Maj. Gen. Philip H. Sheridan henceforth would have charge of the army's cavalry column.[44]

Beyond the shake-up of top personnel, Meade likely had another reason to implement consolidation. He hoped to accomplish by organizational means the coordination of large bodies of troops in the field that had proved impossible by other measures. Thus far in the war Lee had managed several massive assaults of the type that win campaigns. He had launched upward of 50,000 men at Gaines's Mill and 25,000 at Second Manassas. The Army of the Potomac had never approached those numbers. Indeed, the army's major attacks thus far had been delivered piecemeal, with bloody results at Antietam, Fredericksburg, and elsewhere. By reconfiguring the army's infantry into three big elements, Meade surely hoped to make it easier to coordinate large-scale movements on the battlefield. The results would be checkered, but there is no denying that the Army of the Potomac tended to wage larger and often more effective operations after the consolidation.

That is not to say everyone viewed the consolidation favorably. In the dismembered First and Third Corps, grumbling was initially loud (though never pervasive or destructive). Some First Corps veterans expressed their displeasure by combining the badges of their old corps (a lozenge) with the Maltese Cross of the Fifth Corps and attaching them to the seat of their pants. John Haley of the 17th Maine wrote that the change "was a heavy blow to the veterans of the old Third Corps," but he noted that under French, "the Corps had a better than even chance of losing whatever reputation it has, while under Hancock there is no such contingency." The sting of the change, though acute, passed rather quickly. Some units eventually abandoned the diamond or lozenge of the old corps in favor of the new. Compared with the emotional upheaval the army had endured in previous years, consolidation provoked only a relatively minor uproar that in no way impaired the army's fighting ability. "There are no troops in the Army of the Potomac," wrote Haley, "who wouldn't feel proud to fight under Hancock, Warren or Sedgwick."[45]

Most of the generals left to lead the Army of the Potomac in 1864 possessed little personal flair and only moderate combat records. Indeed, the only universal praise bestowed on them reflected on their manners rather than their performance. "A more courteous set of men it would be hard to find," noted Theodore Lyman shortly after joining army headquarters in the fall of 1863. "I have yet to meet a single gruffy one. They are of all sorts, some well educated, some highly Bowery, but all entirely civil." Unquestioned as the army's preeminent field commander on the eve of the Overland campaign, Maj. Gen. Winfield Scott Hancock directed the Second Corps and did not fit the dominant mold of mediocrity. He achieved lofty reputation through a pleasing mix of presence, personality, and performance. Few officers in the army equaled Hancock's ability to command a battlefield. "He is magnificent in appearance, lordly, but cordial," wrote staff officer Josiah Favill. At six feet, one inch, Hancock was the tallest of the army's corps commanders. Lyman described him as a "tall, soldierly man, with light-brown hair and military heavy jaw; and he has the massive features and the heavy folds round the eye that often mark a man of ability." He always remained mounted during battle and, wrote Favill, differed "from other officers I have served with in being always in sight during action." Another man wrote that "if he were in citizen clothes and should give commands in the army to those who did not know him, he would be likely to be obeyed at once, and without any questions as to his right to command." Favill called him "the most popular corps commander by all odds."[46]

Hancock boasted more than mere physical presence. His personality combined warmth and fierceness in appealing proportion. One of his brigadiers, Regis de Trobriand, wrote that Hancock habitually wore an "engaging expression." "His manners are polite," added the French-born officer, "and his speech as agreeable as his looks." Lyman wrote that Hancock and Meade were "great friends" and that when together, "they talk, and talk,

Maj. Gen. Winfield Scott Hancock.
Francis Trevelyan Miller, ed., The
Photographic History of the Civil War,
10 vols. (New York: Review of Reviews,
1911), 10:179

and talk." "Hancock is a great and vehement talker," noted Lyman, "but always has something worth hearing." Staff officer Favill noted another of Hancock's endearing qualities: "He is remarkably generous, giving everyone ample credit for what he does and call[ing] by name almost every officer in his command. This is a rare faculty and adds much to his popularity."[47]

But in action or at drill, any hint of gentleness or warmth left Hancock's visage. One of his soldiers called him "tyranical to the 'Volunteer' troops of his Command" and noted that "in giving orders to his men on a march, on drill, on parade, and even upon the battlefield, he seldom did so without an oath of the most unpardonable nature." This soldier concluded that Hancock "got into such a habit of indulging in profane language to his troops, that addressing them, without taking God's name in vain, was next to an impossibility to him." On the battlefield, commented de Trobriand, Hancock's "dignity gives way to activity; his features become animated, his voice loud, his eyes are on fire, his blood kindles, and his bearing is that of a man carried away by passion." Yet for all his natural appeal, Hancock did not fail to tend to his public image. De Trobriand explained Hancock's popularity "firstly by the brilliancy of his service, and also by the particular care he always took to have it known," adding that the "correspondents of the principal journals yielded, like every one else, to his captivating bearing and manners."[48]

Hancock's presence and personality complemented a superior set of performances on the battlefield. An anomaly in the staid Army of the Potomac, he consistently had assumed the initiative in combat. He had won unbridled praise from McClellan at Williamsburg, then contributed solid performances on the Peninsula, at Antietam, and at Fredericksburg. He effectively conducted the rearguard defense during the army's retreat at Chancellorsville, and at Gettysburg he fought his way into the army's book of vivid memories with important service on all three days. His spectacular accomplishments at Gettysburg on July 2 might have been the best ever rendered by any of the army's corps commanders. Assistant Secretary of War Charles Dana aptly said that Hancock "had more of the aggressive spirit than almost anybody else in the army."[49]

That aggressive spirit had taken a toll. The freewheeling confidence characteristic of Hancock in 1862 and 1863 was harder to find in 1864. On the eve of the Overland campaign, he still suffered severely from a thigh wound received at Gettysburg. Henceforth on the march, Hancock rode in an ambulance until near the enemy, when he would mount and assume his customary posture in battle. But no one could foretell that after three years of hard service this forty-year-old general would suffer from something akin to tactical claustrophobia on the confined battlegrounds of the Overland campaign. Most still saw Hancock as the gilded knight of Williamsburg, Chancellorsville, and Gettysburg. More would be expected of him than of any other corps commander.[50]

Perhaps the most intriguing of Meade's corps commanders that spring, Gouverneur K. Warren also was the youngest. Few men in the army had been involved in so much. Warren began his tenure as lieutenant colonel of the 5th New York Infantry (Duryee's Zouaves), but because of his talents as a topographical engineer he had wielded influence in uncommon places. During the siege of Yorktown he had been a frequent adviser to McClellan. After commanding his regiment and brigade through butchery at Gaines's Mill and Second Manassas, he had ascended to chief topographical engineer of the army under Hooker. In this capacity he had played a major role in planning the Chancellorsville campaign and then, in his most famous of all days, had acted quickly to secure Little Round Top at Gettysburg on July 2. After that performance Meade quickly moved Warren off the staff and back to field command, first as commander of the Second Corps and then as the permanent commander of the Fifth Corps. His record as corps commander in late 1863 had been checkered. After good service at Bristoe Station, where he delivered the army an easy victory, he had, to many eyes (including Meade's), fumbled badly at Mine Run. He still had much to prove.[51]

Warren had begun the war with strong political views but learned to subdue his expressions and focus on the military task at hand. Indeed, few in the army apparently knew of (or at least recorded knowing of) Warren's views on slavery and war aims delineated in a July 1862 letter. "The army has suffered enough now in hardships and perils to no longer act out any Abolition programme," he had observed. "It is fighting for the Union, which is unattainable without allowing the Southern people their constitutional rights, for it is otherwise degrading them." Beyond this expression to his brother, Warren studiously had avoided the debate surrounding war aims that proved fatal to the careers of so many officers around him.[52]

Whereas Winfield Scott Hancock won admirers by force of his personality, Warren's persona sometimes had a deflating effect on his men and colleagues. "Warren left me with a sense of lightness," recorded cavalry officer Charles Francis Adams. Another man called Warren "decidedly a lightweight, although a good soldier and engineer officer, [he] lacks dignity and force of character." He possessed a "queer sense of humor" and loved limericks. "He would repeat them at almost every meal," wrote a Fifth Corps staff officer, "and, I think, with wonder that they did not seem nearly so amusing to others as they did to him." He also relished playing cards ("he was a great card player," remembered one man) and, apparently, consuming spirits. On at least one occasion soldiers accused Warren of having too much to drink on the eve of battle. But alcohol appears to have been only a moderate handicap; Warren had far greater flaws to overcome.[53]

Physically Warren inspired interest rather than admiration. Wrote Lyman, "Fancy a small, slender man, with a sun-burnt face, two piercing black eyes, and withal bearing a most ludicrous resemblance to cousin Mary Pratt!" Another staff officer noted that "his eyes were small and jet black also, one of them apparently a bit smaller than the other, giving a suggestion of cast in his look." The latter witness further observed that "the striking characteristic was an habitual and noticeably grave expression which harbored in his dusky, sallow face, and instead of lightening, deepened as he rose in fame and command." Others described Warren in similarly dark terms. "An odd figure," wrote one. "He is . . . evidently of a nervous temperament," wrote another. And concluded a third, "He was egotistical. His caution was excessive."[54]

This picky and fastidious man also could be hard nosed and by-the-book when necessary. Charles Wainwright recorded in April 1864, "He thinks that if soldiers can die without their wives coming to them, the rule should work the other way also." He tended to criticize superiors as well,

Maj. Gen.
Gouverneur Kemble Warren.
Library of Congress

a characteristic perhaps learned from Joe Hooker, Warren's booster and the army's preeminent backbiter. Warren regaled Meade with the woes of his fellow corps commanders, urging their removal for the good of the army. To his wife and friends he even criticized Meade.[55]

The tendency to denounce colleagues hinted at Warren's fatal flaw as a commander. His major successes at Gettysburg and Bristoe Station had come not in response to orders but to situations. Where his work involved literally obeying orders, Warren insisted on changing, questioning, or even ignoring instructions when he believed such action necessary. Warren was "a brilliant and ambitious soldier," suggested a staff officer, "and one who was always ready to set up his own judgement against that of his superiors." As the 1864 campaign unfolded, this trait drove Meade, Grant, and finally Sheridan to distraction. Meade expressed the frustration succinctly: "I am forced to conclude that this defect in Genl Warren is not controllable by him, and he cannot execute an order without modifying it. . . . Such a defect strikes at the root of all military subordination." Because of this trait, Warren played a major role as the army moved inexorably south toward the James River that summer.[56]

"Uncle John" Sedgwick of Cornwall Hollow, Connecticut, commanded Meade's Sixth Corps. That Sedgwick, as devoted a McClellan man as the army possessed, led the Sixth Corps was fitting, for that organization long had been home to vociferous Democrats and McClellan devotees such as William B. Franklin, John Newton, Baldy Smith, and W. T. H. Brooks. Although Sedgwick barely knew McClellan, he nonetheless was identified strongly both militarily and politically with the army's first commander. More than that, he owed his stature in the army in part to McClellan, who had appointed Sedgwick to command in the army's early days.[57]

Sedgwick expressed his loyalty to McClellan in part by harboring McClellan's brother on his staff, despite the protestations of some in Washington. He attempted a far more ambitious gesture in the early fall of 1863, floating the idea that the army ought to raise a "testimonial" for its old commander (and future presidential candidate). Sedgwick pledged $20,000 from his own corps. "I would like to show that he still retains the love and confidence of the Army of the Potomac," explained Sedgwick to his friend and fellow McClellan supporter William French. The idea gained momentum and money until it came to the notice of President Lincoln and Washington at large. The press labeled it a "political move," and politicians in Washington rushed to derail it. The intrusion by politicians drew outrage from the army and lament from Sedgwick. "The idea now seems to be that this army will be broken up," wrote Marsena Patrick, "that it is so thoroughly McClellan as to be dangerous." Sedgwick's $20,000 pledge placed him in the forefront of the testimonial's organizers, and until his death Radical Republicans in Washington viewed him as a dangerous man to be shuffled out of the army. Meade expended much energy during the winter fending off efforts to have Sedgwick relieved.[58]

Sedgwick's vulnerability to removal stemmed not just from politics but also from a pedestrian combat record. While in corps command, he had benefited greatly by superior performances from subordinates, such as David A. Russell's at Rappahannock Station that secured the army's most convincing victory to date. Prior to corps command, Sedgwick had compiled a decidedly checkered record as division commander. His most notable moment came at Antietam, where his division "flew blindly" into the West Woods to suffer utter disaster and lose 2,200 men in just forty minutes. Corps commander Edwin Sumner's presence allowed Sedgwick to avoid major blame for this fiasco, but he surely could have done something to prevent it. Perhaps it highlighted an irksome characteristic noted by Hooker: Sedgwick manifested an "utter deficiency in the topographical faculty, and consequently [exhibited] great distrust of himself in exercising on the field important commands."[59]

John Sedgwick was best known in the army for a manner often described as endearing. Charles Francis Adams called him "quiet, unassum-

Maj. Gen. John Sedgwick.
Robert Underwood Johnson and
Clarence Clough Buel, eds., Battles
and Leaders of the Civil War, *4 vols.*
(New York: Century, 1887–88), 4:92

ing" and detected in the Sixth Corps commander "no pretense, no posing
for effect, no stage tricks." Charles Dana said, "He was a very solid man;
no flummery about him. . . . He was not an ardent, impetuous soldier
like Hancock, but was steady and sure." He came across as punctilious to
some—a common affliction in the Army of the Potomac. Charles Whittier
of his staff recorded that he was "studious of every detail. I never knew
a commander who so studied, so analyzed and remembered the morning
reports. He would address a colonel frequently on the march, calling attention to the number of men reported on extra duty, and so not available
for combat." Sedgwick's men were devoted to him. Whittier remembered
the day the Vermont Brigade returned from a stint of costly detached
service and greeted Sedgwick with wild cheers: "These soldiers acted as
if they had come home out of the storm to a loving and careful father."
John Sedgwick would march into the Wilderness better known as a father
figure than as a fighter.[60]

Because the last of the army's corps commanders was new and anoma-
lous in almost every respect, he is less instructive in an examination of
the Army of the Potomac. Philip H. Sheridan rode into the Wilderness
at the head of the army's Cavalry Corps. Small, aggressive, prickly, explosive, and most importantly to this army, from the Western Theater,
Sheridan cut a wide swath after he reached Virginia. Since John Pope

had so ungracefully strode into the Eastern Theater in 1862, proclaiming that in the West "we have seen only the backs of our enemies," the Army of the Potomac had looked askance at intruders from western longitudes. In fact, after Pope's departure the Army of the Potomac remained a remarkably self-contained organization with no major figures who had seen service in the Western Theater. The soldiers and troopers looked suspiciously on Sheridan, who presented a vastly different picture than his predecessor Pleasonton. "He is, apparently, a very quiet and determined man," recorded Marsena Patrick after meeting him in early April 1864. Staff officer Morris Schaff affirmed that a "certain wild, natural intrepidity and brilliancy in action, came nearer the old type of the Middle Ages than any of the other distinguished officers of our day." But to Brig. Gen. J. Warren Keifer "he seemed restless, nervous, and petulant."[61]

Sheridan never had commanded cavalry in large numbers, but the strong ideas he voiced about the use of mounted troops clashed directly with Meade's plans. Meade saw cavalry as an adjunct to the infantry. Sheridan saw it as a strike force and wanted to take his command away from guarding trains and bridges and into the field against Confederate horsemen. When the army marched south on May 4, 1864, it did so with Meade's views holding sway. That would soon change. Less than a week into the campaign, Sheridan—"the beau ideal of a fighting Irish-American of the better sort"—was off after Stuart's cavalry en masse. So it would be for the remainder of the war.[62]

Of all the commanders the soldiers discussed in the spring of 1864, the one who most interested them had no official connection to the army at all: Lt. Gen. Ulysses S. Grant, the new general-in-chief of all Union armies. Grant arrived at Meade's headquarters on March 10, 1864, and for the next seven weeks shuttled regularly between Washington and the field. His arrival stimulated curiosity—though not necessarily enthusiasm—among the men to a degree not seen since McClellan's first days. In early April 1864 the army's corps assembled, ostensibly to allow Grant to see them. In fact, the men in the ranks did most of the reviewing (though at least one cavalryman remarked dismissively, "I saw General Grant yesterday, but I would have given more to see [Grant's wife] Julia"). Hundreds of soldiers wrote descriptions of Grant in letters to their homefolk. One of the more succinct and lyrical portraits came from artilleryman Charles Wainwright: "He is ... stumpy, unmilitary, slouchy, and Western-looking; very ordinary in fact."[63]

Further characterizations of Grant would be superfluous, but his reception by the soldiers is crucial to an understanding of the Army of the

Potomac on the eve of the Overland campaign. Two words effectively capture the army's perspective on Grant: cautious hope. Many saw Grant as a complement to Meade. Maj. Henry Abbott of the 20th Massachusetts thought Meade "a good combiner and maneuverer & . . . unquestionably a clever man intellectually." Grant he saw as possessing the "force, decision &c, [and] the character which isn't afraid to take the responsibility to the utmost." This combination of Meade and Grant, Abbott concluded, "may be the next thing to having a man of real genius at the head." But a Fifth Corps soldier scoffed at Grant's future: "The army has been turned and twisted over again and now we will see how quick the Army of the Potomac will kill the reputation of 'Unconditional Surrender.'" Some acknowledged Grant's reputation but predicted tough times for him against R. E. Lee. "He may lose his Military reputation," wrote one soldier, "for he has got a different style of Rebels and a different General to fight."[64]

Others took a more positive view. After the Second Corps review on April 22, Josiah Favill recorded in his diary the hope that "this is the beginning of the end." Another man averred in late April, "I feel confident of success. No such thing as failure this time." But perhaps cavalryman and presidential scion Charles Francis Adams caught the mood best: "The feeling about Grant is peculiar—a little jealousy, a little dislike, a little envy, a little want of confidence. . . . All, however, are willing to give him a full chance. . . . If he succeeds, the war is over."[65]

The opinion of Grant that mattered most belonged to George G. Meade, whose letters are very revealing on this subject. Nowhere did Meade criticize the new general-in-chief. Indeed, his assessments of Grant are among the most balanced:

Grant is not a striking man, is very reticent, has never mixed with the world, and has but little manner, indeed is somewhat ill at ease in the presence of strangers; hence a first impression is never favorable. His early education was undoubtedly very slight; in fact, I fancy his West Point course was pretty much all the education he ever had, as since graduation I don't believe he has read or studied any. At the same time, he has natural qualities of a high order, and is a man, whom, the more you see and know him, the better you like him.

Knowing as he did the difficulties of commanding an army in the field, Meade greatly appreciated Grant's accomplishments in the West. He told his wife just a week after meeting Grant, "You may rest assured he is not an ordinary man."[66]

But something about Grant's arrival did irk Meade. In March Meade fully expected that Grant would replace him with "his own man" (at that time presumed to be Baldy Smith). Meade offered to step aside, but Grant kept him, impressed, he said, with Meade's magnanimity. Despite this vote of confidence, Meade could not shake the feeling that Grant would receive credit for any success in the spring campaign. His letters frequently refer to the topic. "You may look now for the Army of the Potomac putting laurels on the brows of another rather than your husband," he wrote with some bitterness to his wife on March 14. But ten days later Meade conceded, "Cheerfully I give him all credit if he can bring the war to a close."[67]

Given this seed of resentment and anyone's normal reaction to the suddenly close supervision he would receive during the campaign, Meade's ability to coexist contentedly with Grant was a notable accomplishment. Grant deserves much of the credit, as Charles Francis Adams suggested after nearly a month of campaigning: Grant "has humored us, he has given some promotions, he has made no parade of his authority, he has given no orders except through Meade, and Meade he treats with the utmost confidence and deference. The result is that even from the most jealously disposed and indiscreet of Meade's staff, not a word is heard against Grant." But Meade deserves accolades as well. It is impossible to imagine his predecessors—especially McClellan or Hooker—submitting productively to such an arrangement. The result of this hard-won partnership between Meade and Grant was, wrote Adams, "of inestimable importance"—a testimony to their old-fashioned commitment to country and accomplishment.[68]

On the evening of May 3, 1864, units of the Army of the Potomac assembled for parade. This was no ordinary exercise. As the men stood at attention, their officers read orders for the morrow's march. They would head south toward the Rapidan River, R. E. Lee and the Army of Northern Virginia, and Richmond. As word of the march spread through the camps, rookie artilleryman Frank Wilkeson heard shouting: "To the right, to the left, in the distance before us, and far behind us, cheers arose." Batterymen, artillerymen, and cavalrymen hollered until they were hoarse that night. Although they sensed vividly the horrors that might await them, their cheers reflected profound confidence borne of refreshed bodies, refreshed minds, and a seemingly refreshed sense of national purpose (though there would be shaky moments on all three counts during the coming months). The following morning, soldiers stuffed away their traps and started toward the fords. They did so in excellent physical condition, with unspectacular leaders they knew well, with a stern new general watching over them, and with remarkable resolve given the army's past. A man of the 2nd Vermont expressed well the determination of the army as it swung out if its camps that May morning: "Never in a war before did the rank and file feel a more resolute earnestness for a just cause, and a more invincible determination to succeed, than in this war; and what the rank and file are determined to do everybody knows will surely be done. We mean to be thorough about it too. We are not going to destroy the military power of the dragon Confederacy and not destroy its fangs also."[69]

NOTES

1. Daniel M. Holt, *A Surgeon's Civil War: The Letters and Diary of Daniel M. Holt, M.D.*, ed. James M. Grenier, Janet L. Coryell, and James R. Smither (Kent, Ohio: Kent State University Press, 1994), 160; Robert McAllister, *The Civil War Letters of General Robert McAllister*, ed. James I. Robertson Jr. (New Brunswick, N.J.: Rutgers University Press, 1965), 368. See also A. M. Stewart, *Camp, March and Battlefield; or Three Years and a Half with the Army of the Potomac* (Philadelphia: Jas. B. Rodgers, 1865), 365. For a marvelous description of the situation that faced the Federals on the morning of November 30, see letter of "True Blue" to the Rochester *Evening Express*, December 16, 1863.

2. McAllister, *Letters*, 368–69. For overviews of the Mine Run campaign and the events of November 30, see Martin F. Graham and George F. Skoch, *Mine Run: A Campaign of Lost Opportunities* (Lynchburg, Va.: H. E. Howard, 1987), 75–79, and Jay Luvaas and Col. Wilbur S. Nye, "The Campaign that History Forgot," *Civil War Times Illustrated* 8 (November 1969): 11–37.

3. Robert S. Robertson to his parents, October 21, 1863, Robert S. Robertson Letters (typescripts), Fredericksburg and Spotsylvania National Military Park Library, Fredericksburg, Va. (hereafter cited as FSNMP); Josiah M. Favill, *The Diary of a Young Officer* (Chicago: Donnelley, 1909), 261; Marsena Rudolph Patrick, *Inside Lincoln's Army: The Diary of Marsena Rudolph Patrick*, ed. David S. Sparks (New York: Yoseloff, 1964), 310. See also Holt, *Surgeon's Civil War*, 152, and Charles W. Bardeen, *A Little War Fifer's Diary* (Syracuse, N.Y.: C. W. Bardeen, 1910), 282. Gauging the contemporary standing of an officer is problematical because dissenting commentary always can be found. In this case, however, the record seems clear on Meade's sinking popularity before Mine Run. For an alternative opinion on Meade prior to Mine Run, see Henry Lee (126th New York) to his mother, October 21, 1863, and Lee to "Mr. Davis," November 1, 1863, Henry Lee Manuscripts, Ontario County Historical Society, Canandaigua, N.Y. (repository hereafter cited as OCHS).

4. Holt, *Surgeon's Civil War*, 160–61; Theodore Lyman, *Meade's Headquarters, 1863–1865: Letters of Colonel Theodore Lyman from the Wilderness to Appomattox*, ed. George R. Agassiz (1922; reprint, Salem, N.H.: Ayer, 1987), 58–59, 61; Robert G. Carter, *Four Brothers in Blue; or, Sunshine and Shadow of the War of the Rebellion, a Story of the Great Civil War, from Bull Run to Appomattox* (1913;

reprint, Austin: University of Texas Press, 1978), 375, 378; Worthington Chauncey Ford, ed., *A Cycle of Adams Letters*, 2 vols. (Boston: Houghton Mifflin, 1920), 2:111; Henry Crofoot (57th New York) to his cousin, December 20, 1863, Civil War Times Illustrated Collection, U.S. Army Military History Institute, Carlisle, Pa. (repository hereafter cited as USAMHI). See also Margaret Greenleaf, ed., *Letters to Eliza from a Union Soldier, 1862–1865* (Chicago: Follett, 1970), 61; Henry Livermore Abbott, *Fallen Leaves: The Civil War Letters of Major Henry Livermore Abbott*, ed. Robert Garth Scott (Kent, Ohio: Kent State University Press, 1991), 235; Charles S. Wainwright, *A Diary of Battle: The Personal Journals of Colonel Charles S. Wainwright, 1861–1865*, ed. Allan Nevins (New York: Harcourt, Brace, & World, 1962), 308–9. Wainwright wrote, "His not fighting will do as much for him in gaining the confidence of the army as if he had won a victory."

5. Hints about Meade's political views are sprinkled throughout George Gordon Meade Jr., *The Life and Letters of George Gordon Meade*, 2 vols. (1913; reprint, Baltimore: Butternut and Blue, 1994). See, for example, 1:356 for his views on the use of black troops. For commentary on Meade's politics, see Charles Albert Whittier, "Memoir," 8, in the Whittier Papers, MS 20th, cab. 6.3, Boston Public Library. For the best of all expressions of the "conservative patriot's" view of war in 1862, see Fitz John Porter to Manton Marble, September 30, 1862, Manton Marble Papers, Library of Congress, Washington, D.C. (repository hereafter cited as LC), and McClellan's "Harrison's Landing Letter" of July 7, 1862, in George B. McClellan, *The Civil War Papers of George B. McClellan*, ed. Stephen W. Sears (New York: Ticknor & Fields, 1989), 344–45. For a broader discussion of the political inclinations of the subordinate command of the Army of the Potomac, see John Hennessy, "The Forgotten Legion: The Subordinate Command of the Army of the Potomac," unpublished paper at FSNMP.

6. James F. Rusling, *Men and Things I Saw in Civil War Days* (New York: Eaton & Mains, 1899), 72–73; Lyman, *Meade's Headquarters*, 57; Charles A. Dana, *Recollections of the Civil War* (1898; reprint, New York: Collier, 1963), 171–72; Charles Francis Adams, *Charles Francis Adams, 1835–1915: An Autobiography* (New York: Houghton Mifflin, 1916), 157. See also Joseph Warren Keifer, *Slavery and Four Years of War*, 2 vols. (New York: Putnam's, 1900), 2:24.

7. Frank L. Byrne and Andrew T. Weaver, eds., *Haskell of Gettysburg: His Life and Civil War Papers* (Madison: State Historical Society of Wisconsin, 1970), 132; Favill, *Diary*, 261; letter of an unknown correspondent in the Rondout (N.Y.) *Courier*, July 17, 1863; John Sedgwick, *Correspondence of John Sedgwick, Major General*, 2 vols. ([New York: De Vinne Press], 1902–3), 2:162. See also Alexander Webb to his Wife, January 24, 1864, Alexander Webb Papers, Yale University Library, New Haven, Conn. (repository hereafter cited as YU). Charles Wainwright—the best of all contemporary observers—described Meade in 1862 as "a fine, soldierly, somewhat stiff-looking man, and the most thoroughbred gentleman in manners I have yet met within the army" (Wainwright, *Diary of Battle*, 105).

8. The political views of the army's high command (beyond its various commanders) has not been the subject of a comprehensive study. The most vivid and thorough examination of the schism that developed between the generals and their government can be found in studies of Charles P. Stone and Fitz John Porter,

whose cases were fraught with political overtones. See Henry Gabler, "The Fitz John Porter Case: Politics and Military Justice" (Ph.D. dissertation, City University of New York, 1979), and Stephen W. Sears, "The Ordeal of General Stone," *Military History Quarterly* 7 (Winter 1995): 46–56. Mr. Sears kindly supplied an advance copy of his article for use in this essay. See also T. Harry Williams, *Lincoln and the Radicals* (Madison: University of Wisconsin Press, 1941).

9. Gouverneur K. Warren to his brother, July 20, 1862, Gouverneur K. Warren Papers, New York State Library, Albany, N.Y. (repository hereafter cited as NYSL); John Gibbon to his wife, November 21, 1862, John Gibbon Papers, Historical Society of Pennsylvania, Philadelphia, Pa. (repository hereafter cited as HSP); Fitz John Porter to Manton Marble, September 30, 1862, Marble Papers, LC; Alexander S. Webb to his father, August 14, 1862, Webb Papers, YU.

10. Charles H. Church, *The Civil War Letters of Charles H. Church* (Rose City, Mich.: Rose City Area Historical Society, 1987), 32–33. See also Francis Edwin Pierce, "Civil War Letters of Francis Edwin Pierce of the 108th New York Volunteer Infantry," in *The Rochester Historical Society Publications: Rochester in the Civil War*, ed. Blake McKelvey (Rochester, N.Y.: Rochester Historical Society, 1944), 166–67; [William D. Landon], "The Fourteenth Indiana Regiment, Peninsular Campaign to Chancellorsville; Letters to the Vincennes Western Sun: Prock's Letters from the Eastern Front," *Indiana Magazine of History* 30 (1934): 341; Samuel Fisher (4th New Jersey) to his sister, January 18, 1863, Lewis Leigh Collection, book 24, USAMHI; letter from "Chaplain of the 104th N.Y.S.V.," Rochester *Union and Advertiser*, January 22, 1863; Alfred Davenport (5th New York) to his parents, January 17, February 7, 1863, Alfred Davenport Papers, New-York Historical Society, New York, N.Y. (repository hereafter cited as NYHS).

11. Ford, *Cycle of Adams Letters*, 1:250. For similar expressions, see also Cornelius Moore, *Cornie: The Civil War Letters of Lt. Cornelius Moore*, ed. Gilbert C. Moore (n.p., 1989), 82, and letter of "W. C.," Rochester *Democrat and American*, February 26, 1863. A. Wilson Greene has suggested that although loud, the grumbling during early 1863 reflected a superficial condition and that the army still stood ready to do its part. See A. Wilson Greene, "Morale, Maneuver, and Mud: The Army of the Potomac, December 16, 1862–January 26, 1863," in *The Fredericksburg Campaign: Decision on the Rappahannock*, ed. Gary W. Gallagher (Chapel Hill: University of North Carolina Press, 1995), 177–79. For a primary example of commentary on this issue, see the letter of Chapl. David T. Morrill (26th New Jersey) quoted in Alan A. Siegel, *For the Glory of the Union: Myth, Reality, and the Media in Civil War New Jersey* (Rutherford, N.J.: Fairleigh Dickinson University Press, 1984), 133.

12. Holt, *Surgeon's Civil War*, 167. See also Sedgwick, *Correspondence*, 2:160; Robert S. Robertson to his parents, December 30, 1863, Robertson Letters, FSNMP; letter of Luther C. Furst, February 1, 1864, Luther C. Furst Letters, Harrisburg Civil War Round Table Collection, USAMHI; letter of Uriah Parmelee (of Caldwell's staff), December 11, 1863, Samuel, Spencer, and Uriah Parmelee Papers, William R. Perkins Library, Duke University, Durham, N.C. (repository hereafter cited as DU).

13. Letter of Charles Brandage (146th New York) to his father, December 25,

1863, bound volumes, Richmond National Battlefield Library, Richmond, Va.; letter of Uriah Parmelee, November 21, 1863, Parmelee Papers, DU. See also Morris Schaff, *The Battle of the Wilderness* (1910; reprint, Gaithersburg, Md.: Butternut Press, 1986), 27–28.

14. For a description of the condition of the army in 1862 and 1863 and Hooker's efforts to improve it, see John Hennessy, "We Shall Make Richmond Howl: The Army of the Potomac on the Eve of Chancellorsville," in *Chancellorsville: The Battle and Its Aftermath*, ed. Gary W. Gallagher (Chapel Hill: University of North Carolina Press, 1996), 1–35.

15. Lyman, *Meade's Headquarters*, 6, 78; Thomas L. Livermore, *Days and Events, 1860–1866* (Boston: Houghton Mifflin, 1920), 414. See also Regis de Trobriand, *Four Years with the Army of the Potomac* (1889; reprint, Gaithersburg, Md.: Ron R. Van Sickle Military Books, 1988), 687–88; letter of Charles Page, July 12, 1863, quoted in Emerson Clifford Taylor, *Gouverneur Kemble Warren: Life and Letters of an American Soldier* (1932; reprint, Gaithersburg, Md.: Ron R. Van Sickle Military Books, 1988), 141; Schaff, *Battle of the Wilderness*, 43–44; Bardeen, *Little War Fifer's Diary*, 216.

16. De Trobriand, *Four Years with the Army of the Potomac*, 688; Lyman, *Meade's Headquarters*, 73; Patrick, *Inside Lincoln's Army*, 353; Dana, *Recollections*, 173–74. See also Ruth Silliker, ed., *The Rebel Yell and Yankee Hurrah: The Civil War Journal of a Maine Volunteer* (Camden, Maine: Down East Books, 1985), 274.

17. James T. Miller to his parents, March 30, 1863, James T. Miller Papers, Schoff Collection, William L. Clements Library, University of Michigan, Ann Arbor (repository hereafter cited as CLUM); Holt, *Surgeon's Civil War*, 81. See also Wilbur Fisk, *Hard Marching Every Day: The Civil War Letters of Private Wilbur Fisk, 1861–1865*, ed. Emil Rosenblatt and Ruth Rosenblatt (Lawrence: University Press of Kansas, 1992), 68; letter of a member of Reynolds's Battery, Rochester *Democrat and American*, April 15, 1863; "An Appeal to the People of the State of New York," signed by twenty-five officers of the 44th New York, Rochester *Democrat and American*, March 18, 1863. Siegel, *For the Glory of the Union*, 149, also includes an appeal from the 26th New Jersey to the people at home.

18. Robert S. Robertson to his parents, November 4, 1863, Robertson Letters, FSNMP; Holt, *Surgeon's Civil War*, 152. See also Abbott, *Fallen Leaves*, 227.

19. Letter of William H. Dobbin (123rd New York), Greenwich (N.Y.) *People's Home Journal*, August 27, 1863; William Wheeler, *Letters of William Wheeler of the Class of 1855, Y.C.* (n.p., 1875), 282–83; Charles Harvey Brewster, *When This Cruel War Is Over: The Civil War Letters of Charles Harvey Brewster*, ed. David W. Blight (Amherst: University of Massachusetts Press, 1992), 245. See also unsigned letter from the 13th New York, Rochester *Democrat and American*, February 3, 1863; letter of "Trume," Rochester *Democrat and American*, July 25, 1863; letter from "a private," 122nd Pennsylvania, Lancaster *Daily Evening Express*, April 3, 1863; Church, *Letters*, 35; Ford, *Cycle of Adams Letters*, 2:53.

20. U.S. War Department, *The War of the Rebellion: A Compilation of the Official Records of the Union and Confederate Armies*, 127 vols., index, and atlas

(Washington, D.C.: GPO, 1880–1901), ser. 1, 33:629 (hereafter cited as *OR*). For a good summary of the reenlistment struggle, see Bruce Catton, *A Stillness at Appomattox* (Garden City, N.Y.: Doubleday, 1953), 34–35.

21. George T. Stevens, *Three Years in the Sixth Corps* (New York: Van Nostrand, 1867), 300; Fisk, *Hard Marching Every Day*, 200–201.

22. McAllister, *Letters*, 405, 400–401; Fisk, *Hard Marching Every Day*, 213. See also Lt. George Breck to the Rochester *Union and Advertiser*, April 18, 1864.

23. Hugh Roden to his parents, February 16, 1863, Schoff Collection, CLUM. See also Col. John D. Wilkins (3rd U.S. Infantry) to his wife, February 4, 1863, John D. Wilkins Papers, CLUM; Paul Fatout, ed., *Letters of a Civil War Surgeon* (Lafayette, Ind.: Purdue University Studies, 1961), 52; letter of Henry Lee (126th New York), undated but early 1863, Lee Manuscripts, OCHS. This is not to suggest that the army was uniformly opposed to the use of black troops in 1862–63, just that the debate was current and raging. For other opinions, see letter of "M. S. D.," *Herkimer County Journal* (Little Falls, N.Y.), February 11, 1863; Holt, *Surgeon's Civil War*, 47; Siegel, *For the Glory of the Union*, 140; Charles F. Morse, *Letters Written During the Civil War* (n.p., 1898), 119–20.

24. John Ripley Adams, *Memorial and Letters of John R. Adams, D.D.* ([Cambridge, Mass.: University Press], 1890), 142, 145. For testimony on the changing views of the army, see letter from a member of the 33rd New York, Rochester *Union and Advertiser*, December 5, 1862; James P. Brady, ed., *Hurrah for the Artillery! Knap's Independent Battery "E," Pennsylvania Light Artillery* (Gettysburg, Pa.: Thomas, 1992), 190; letter of Capt. W. H. Spera, Lancaster *Daily Evening Express*, March 27, 1863; letter of "M. H. B." (44th New York), *Herkimer County Journal* (Little Falls, N.Y.), September 10, 1863. See also Fisk, *Hard Marching Every Day*, 207. For an example of a formerly ardent opponent of abolition fallen silent, see the letters of Robert S. Robertson, FSNMP.

25. Carter, *Four Brothers in Blue*, 386; letter of M. R. Casler to the *Herkimer County Journal* (Little Falls, N.Y.), August 6, 1863; Schaff, *Battle of the Wilderness*, 28. See also Ford, *Cycle of Adams Letters*, 2:45, 51; James R. Woodworth to his wife Phebe, July 8, 1863, Woodworth Papers, Schoff Collection, CLUM; Farewell order of John Newton, March 25, 1864, in *OR* 33:735.

26. Moore, *Letters*, 164–65; McAllister, *Letters*, 381; Wainwright, *Diary of Battle*, 313–14. See also Robert S. Robertson to his parents, December 30, 1863, Robertson Letters, FSNMP.

27. Letter of Luther C. Furst (signalman), February 1, 1864, Furst Letters, Harrisburg Civil War Round Table Collection, USAMHI; undated diary entry of James R. Woodworth (44th New York), June 1863, Woodworth Papers, Schoff Collection, CLUM.

28. For a discussion of the machinations of Cochrane, Smith, and Franklin during the winter of 1862–63, see Greene, "Morale, Maneuver, and Mud," 183–89. For McClellan's relationship with his government, and especially the context of the Harrison's Landing Letter, see Stephen W. Sears, *George B. McClellan: The Young Napoleon* (New York: Ticknor & Fields, 1988), 227–29. For commentary on Brooks's departure, see John Gibbon to his Wife, May 10, 13, 21, 1863, Gibbon Papers, HSP.

29. Almira R. Hancock, *Reminiscences of Winfield Scott Hancock* (New York: Charles L. Webster, 1887), 94–95. See also Meade, *Life and Letters*, 2:162; George G. Meade to Winfield S. Hancock, November 6, 1863, W. S. Hancock Papers, DU. Evidence of the army's calm is found not in the expressions of soldiers, but in their lack of commentary on the issue.

30. Letters of "Trume" (108th New York), Rochester *Democrat and American*, January 27, February 7, 1864; letters of Lt. George Breck (Reynolds's Battery), Rochester *Union and Advertiser*, December 21, 1863, January 22, 1864; Fisk, *Hard Marching Every Day*, 181, 202–3. See also Livermore, *Days and Events*, 305–6. For an excellent summary of the army's physical arrangements that winter, see Clark B. Hall, "Season of Change: The Winter Encampment of the Army of the Potomac, December 1, 1863–May 4, 1864," *Blue & Gray Magazine* 8 (April 1991): 8–22, 48–62. The opening quote in this paragraph appears on p. 20. I am indebted to Mr. Hall for supplying important source material for this essay.

31. Letter of George Eaton (121st New York), *Herkimer County Journal* (Little Falls, N.Y.), March 3, 1864; Moore, *Letters*, 156; Favill, *Diary*, 276–78; Lyman, *Meade's Headquarters*, 74; Charles D. Page, *History of the Fourteenth Regiment, Connecticut Volunteer Infantry* (1906; reprint, Gaithersburg, Md.: Ron R. Van Sickle Military Books, 1987), 229; Peter Welsh, *Irish Green and Union Blue: The Civil War Letters of Peter Welsh*, ed. Lawrence F. Kohl (New York: Fordham University Press, 1986), 143; Abner Small, *The Road to Richmond: The Civil War Memoirs of Major Abner Small of the Sixteenth Maine Volunteers*, ed. Harold Adams Small (Berkeley: University of California Press, 1939), 123; letter of Uriah Parmelee, March 5, 1864, Parmelee Papers, DU.

32. Hall, "Season of Change," 54–55. The best primary source on Morton's Ford (and indeed on the winter encampment as a whole) is Page, *Fourteenth Connecticut*, 217–22. See also a letter from the 111th New York and a letter from "Trume" (108th New York), Rochester *Democrat and American*, February 16, 1864, and Moore, *Letters*, 163.

33. For the orders outlining the reorganization, see *OR* 33:717–18, 722–23. For evidence that the reorganization had been long in the making and was unrelated to Grant's arrival, see Sedgwick, *Correspondence*, 2:160, 173; Robert S. Robertson, *Diary of the War by Robt. S. Robertson, 93d N.Y. Vols.*, ed. Charles N. and Rosemary Walker (n.p., n.d.), 150; Meade, *Life and Letters*, 2:166; Wainwright, *Diary of Battle*, 314–15, 329–30; letter of Lt. George Breck, Rochester *Union and Advertiser*, February 26, 1864.

34. *OR* 33:725. Speaking of the "temporary" status of the consolidation, Charles Wainwright wrote perceptively, "Temporary will no doubt be permanent; the consolidating into divisions and retaining old badges is merely a way to let [the men] down easy" (Wainwright, *Diary of Battle*, 335).

35. Gouverneur K. Warren to his brother, December 5, 1864, Warren Papers, NYSL. See also Cyrus B. Comstock, *The Diary of Cyrus B. Comstock*, ed. Merlin E. Sumner (Dayton, Ohio: Morningside, 1987), 261. Comstock wrote on March 17, 1864, "Saw Meade in the morning who says one benefit of proposed reorganization will be getting rid of some of the corps generals."

36. Byrne and Weaver, *Haskell of Gettysburg*, 133; George A. Townsend, *Rus-*

tics in Rebellion: A Yankee Reporter on the Road to Richmond, 1861–1865 (Chapel Hill: University of North Carolina Press, 1950), 145; Wainwright, *Diary of Battle*, 268–69, 307, 310. See also Lyman, *Meade's Headquarters*, 9; Thomas Chamberlin, *History of the One Hundred and Fiftieth Regiment Pennsylvania Volunteers, Second Regiment, Bucktail Brigade* (1895; reprint, Baltimore: Butternut and Blue, 1986), 195, 197–98.

37. Manuscript notes by George McClellan relating to his officers, vol. D-9, reel 71, frames 730ff., George B. McClellan Papers, LC; Wainwright, *Diary of Battle*, 324. Newton was consistently allied with conservative officers such as William B. Franklin, Baldy Smith, and W. T. H. Brooks. See *OR* 32(2):468 for Hooker's commentary on this alliance.

38. Comstock, *Diary*, 261. For Meade's expressions, see Meade, *Life and Letters*, 2:184–85, 190. See also Wainwright, *Diary of Battle*, 336–37, and Small, *Road to Richmond*, 126.

39. No biographical sketches of French exist beyond those in standard sources. Applause for French followed his performances on the Peninsula, at Antietam, and at Fredericksburg. More interesting is Hooker's praise of French for his role in the Gettysburg campaign. In describing French's service in protecting the Union rear and separating Stuart's cavalry from Lee's army, Hooker wrote, "No one can estimate the value of [French's service] . . . on the results of that great battlefield." See Hooker to Samuel P. Bates, September 19, 1876, Bates Papers, Pennsylvania State Archives, Harrisburg, Pa. (repository hereafter cited as PSA). For criticism of his roles at Wappings Heights in July 1863 and at Mine Run, see de Trobriand, *Four Years with the Army of the Potomac*, 530, and Graham and Skoch, *Mine Run*, 50–54.

40. Henry N. Blake, *Three Years in the Army of the Potomac* (Boston: Lee and Shepard, 1865), 256–57; Silliker, *Rebel Yell and Yankee Hurrah*, 111–12, 275; Lyman, *Meade's Headquarters*, 10. See also de Trobriand, *Four Years with the Army of the Potomac*, 530–31.

41. John Sedgwick to William H. French, *New York Times*, January 17, 1864; Patrick, *Inside Lincoln's Army*, 320; de Trobriand, *Four Years with the Army of the Potomac*, 530–31.

42. Lyman, *Meade's Headquarters*, 9; Wainwright, *Diary of Battle*, 336–37; letter of "True Blue" (140th New York), Rochester *Evening Express*, March 31, 1864; Timothy J. Reese, *Sykes' Regular Infantry Division, 1861–1864* (Jefferson, N.C.: McFarland, 1990), 293–94. See also Meade, *Life and Letters*, 2:184–85.

43. Byrne and Weaver, *Haskell of Gettysburg*, 133–34; Ford, *Cycle of Adams Letters*, 2:8, 44; William Aughinbaugh Journal (5th Ohio), April 28, 1863, CLUM. For many months Meade shielded Pleasonton from Washington influences, preserving him as cavalry chief. But in December 1863 Pleasonton's name arose as a possible replacement for Meade, and the following March the cavalryman publicly criticized Meade. At that point Meade withdrew his protective shield, and Grant and Stanton relieved Pleasonton. For the rumor of Pleasonton as successor to Meade, see Patrick, *Inside Lincoln's Army*, 320, 323; John S. Willey (1st Massachusetts) to his wife, December 10, 1863, Norman Daniels Collection of Civil War

Papers, Harrisburg Civil War Round Table Collection, USAMHI. For Meade's reaction, see Meade, *Life and Letters*, 2:176, 182–85.

44. Ulysses S. Grant, *Personal Memoirs of U. S. Grant*, 2 vols. in 1 (New York: Charles L. Webster, 1894), 414; *OR* 33:732.

45. Carter, *Four Brothers in Blue*, 384; Silliker, *Rebel Yell and Yankee Hurrah*, 139; Keifer, *Slavery and Four Years of War*, 2:72; Henry Lee (126th New York) to Mrs. Davis, March 26, 1864, Lee Manuscripts, OCHS.

46. Henry L. Bingham, "Anecdotes concerning Gen. Hancock and other officers at Gettysburg and elsewhere," manuscript memoir (1874), Western Reserve Historical Society, Cleveland, Ohio; Byrne and Weaver, *Haskell of Gettysburg*, 101, 133; Favill, *Diary*, 283. See also Schaff, *Battle of the Wilderness*, 42; Charles Francis Adams, *Autobiography*, 157; Rufus Dawes, *Service with the Sixth Wisconsin Volunteers* (Marietta, Ohio: Alderman, 1890), 24. Bingham wrote of Hancock, "The photograph containing the figures of General Wm. F. Smith, General Jno. Newton, and General Hancock, gives a good representation of the latter's form & figure during the war. In that photograph he is shown on the left leaning against a tree."

47. Favill, *Diary*, 283; de Trobriand, *Four Years with the Army of the Potomac*, 596–97; Lyman, *Meade's Headquarters*, 189.

48. William McCarter, manuscript memoir, 36–38, FSNMP; Favill, *Diary*, 283; de Trobriand, *Four Years with the Army of the Potomac*, 596–97. Bingham, "Anecdotes," describes Hancock's demeanor on July 3, 1863, at Gettysburg. See also Edwin C. Mason, "Through the Wilderness to the Bloody Angle at Spotsylvania Court House," in *Glimpses of the Nation's Struggle*, 4th ser. (St. Paul, Minn.: H. L. Collins, 1893), 299, and letter of Uriah Parmelee, April 9, 1864, Parmelee Papers, DU.

49. Dana, *Recollections*, 172. For McClellan's praise of Hancock after Williamsburg, see McClellan, *Papers*, 256–57, 269. See also Erasmus D. Keyes, *Fifty Years Observation of Men and Events* (New York: Scribner's, 1884), 449, and William F. Smith, *Autobiography of Major General William F. Smith, 1861–1864*, ed. Herbert M. Schiller (Dayton, Ohio: Morningside, 1990), 37–38.

50. For a thorough description of the effect of Hancock's Gettysburg wound, see Bingham, "Anecdotes."

51. Favill, *Diary*, 274; Charles Francis Adams, *Autobiography*, 157. For Meade's praise of Warren for Bristoe Station, see Meade to Winfield S. Hancock, November 6, 1863, Hancock Papers, DU. For Meade's criticism of Warren at Mine Run, see Meade to John A. Rawlins, June 21, 1864, Meade Papers, HSP. See also letter of Alfred Davenport (5th New York), February 25, 1863, Davenport Papers, NYHS, and Hall, "Season of Change," 54.

52. Gouverneur K. Warren to his brother, July 20, 1862, box 1, folder 3, Warren Papers, NYSL.

53. Schaff, *Battle of the Wilderness*, 30; Favill, *Diary*, 274. For evidence of Warren's drinking, see Page, *Fourteenth Connecticut*, 219 (Page accused Warren of being "indisposed" at Morton's Ford), and letter of Alfred Davenport (5th New York), January 26, 1863, Davenport Papers, NYHS. Davenport wrote, "Genl. War-

ren & our col. & officers are getting to be regular Gin Heads. . . . They keep their skins full of Commissary Whiskey."

54. Lyman, *Meade's Headquarters*, 26; Schaff, *Battle of the Wilderness*, 30; Wainwright, *Diary of Battle*, 338–39; Small, *Road to Richmond*, 126; Sylvanus Cadwallader, *Three Years with Grant as Recalled by War Correspondent Sylvanus Cadwallader*, ed. Benjamin P. Thomas (New York: Knopf, 1955), 202. The lone biography of Warren, Taylor's *Gouverneur Kemble Warren*, is uncritical but contains useful excerpts from Warren's letters. The originals of those letters, in great volume, are in the Warren Papers, NYSL. The best modern assessment of Warren is sprinkled throughout Gordon C. Rhea, *The Battle of the Wilderness: May 5–6, 1864* (Baton Rouge: Louisiana State University Press, 1994).

55. Wainwright, *Diary of Battle*, 341; Gouverneur K. Warren to his brother, November 15, December 8, 1863, Warren Papers, NYSL.

56. George G. Meade to John A. Rawlins, June 21, 1864, Meade Papers, HSP. See also Livermore, *Days and Events*, 304.

57. Sedgwick wrote of McClellan in April 1862, "I mean to stand or fall with McClellan. He has been very kind to me, giving me a large command without my asking for it." In September 1863 Sedgwick again wrote of his relationship with McClellan: "I have never been intimate with the General—have never visited him socially; at the same time I have the greatest regard and admiration for him, and I would like to show that he still retains the love and confidence of the Army of the Potomac" (Sedgwick, *Correspondence*, 2:43–44, 155). See also George B. McClellan, *McClellan's Own Story* (New York: Charles L. Webster, 1887), 140, and Abbott, *Fallen Leaves*, 240.

58. Sedgwick, *Correspondence*, 2:155, 175; Patrick, *Inside Lincoln's Army*, 291. For the best discussion of the testimonial, see Wainwright, *Diary of Battle*, 282–84. For Meade's efforts to preserve Sedgwick in command, see John Gibbon, *Personal Recollections of the Civil War* (New York: Putnam's, 1928), 209–10, and Whittier, "Memoir," 8. See also Robertson, *Diary of the War*, 128–29.

59. Joseph Hooker to Samuel P. Bates, November 29, 1878, Bates Papers, PSA.

60. Charles Francis Adams, *Autobiography*, 157–58; Dana, *Recollections*, 172; Whittier, "Memoir," 6–7. See also Mason W. Tyler, *Recollections of the Civil War* (New York: Putnam's, 1912), 74, and Stevens, *Three Years in the Sixth Corps*, 186–87.

61. Patrick, *Inside Lincoln's Army*, 355; Schaff, *Battle of the Wilderness*, 281; Keifer, *Slavery and Four Years of War*, 2:104–5. See also Rusling, *Men and Things I Saw*, 124–25.

62. Philip H. Sheridan, *Civil War Memoirs* (1888; reprint, New York: Bantam, 1991), 146–48.

63. Richard J. Del Vecchio, "With the 1st New York Dragoons: From the Letters of Jared L. Ainsworth," 67, Harrisburg Civil War Round Table Collection, USAMHI; Wainwright, *Diary of Battle*, 338. The descriptions of Grant are so numerous and familiar that they need not be recounted here. One of the best is in Rusling, *Men and Things I Saw*, 135. See also Lyman, *Meade's Headquarters*, 80, 83, 156; letter of "U. B." (16th Maine), Lewiston (Maine) *Daily Evening Journal*, April 19, 1864; Robert Hunt Rhodes, *All for the Union: A History of the 2nd*

Rhode Island Volunteer Infantry (Lincoln, R.I.: Andrew Mowbray, 1985), 141–42; letter of Lt. George Breck (Reynolds's Battery), Rochester *Union and Advertiser*, April 4, 1864.

64. Abbott, *Fallen Leaves*, 243–44; Carter, *Four Brothers in Blue*, 383; Brewster, *Letters*, 280. See also Thomas W. Hyde, *Following the Greek Cross, Or Memories of the Sixth Army Corps* (Boston: Houghton Mifflin, 1894), 180; Henry Lee (126th New York) to Mr. Davis, March 26, 1864, Lee Manuscripts, OCHS; letter of "U. B." (16th Maine), Lewiston (Maine) *Daily Evening Journal*, April 19, 1864. For an assessment of Grant and Meade closely matching Abbott's, see Charles Francis Adams, *Autobiography*, 157.

65. Letter of Frasier Rosenkrantz, April 28, 1864, Civil War Miscellaneous Collection, USAMHI; Favill, *Diary*, 286; Ford, *Cycle of Adams Letters*, 2:128. See also letter of "Excelsior," Jamestown (N.Y.) *Journal*, April 1, 1864.

66. Meade, *Life and Letters*, 2:180, 191. For Sedgwick's confirmation of the good relations between Meade and Grant, see Sedgwick, *Correspondence*, 2:177. See also Ford, *Cycle of Adams Letters*, 2:134.

67. Meade, *Life and Letters*, 2:176, 178, 184–85.

68. Ford, *Cycle of Adams Letters*, 2:134.

69. Frank Wilkeson, *Recollections of a Private Soldier in the Army of the Potomac* (New York: Putnam's, 1887), 39–40; letter of Lt. George Breck, Rochester *Union and Advertiser*, May 7, 1864; Fisk, *Hard Marching Every Day*, 207. See also Meade, *Life and Letters*, 2:192–93, and Peter S. Michie, *The Life and Letters of Emory Upton* (New York: Appleton, 1885), 91.

GORDON C. RHEA

Union Cavalry in the Wilderness

THE EDUCATION OF PHILIP H. SHERIDAN

AND JAMES H. WILSON

he battle of the Wilderness witnessed the opening performances of premier Union cavalry commanders Maj. Gen.
Philip H. Sheridan and Brig. Gen. James H. Wilson. Sheridan would win renown as the Army of the Potomac's cavalry chief and for his exploits in the Shenandoah Valley.
Wilson's fame would come primarily from victories in the
Western Theater. The initial efforts of these two men in
the scrub forest below the Rapidan River proved bum-
bling and inept, particularly when measured against what
experienced cavalrymen might have accomplished. Their
misadventures suggested little of their future greatness.
The story, however, is worth recounting. It helps explain
why Grant failed to defeat Lee in their first encounter and
chronicles a painful episode in the evolution of the Federal
mounted arm.

Maj. Gen. Alfred Pleasonton, who had provided able if
uninspired leadership at Brandy Station and Gettysburg,
headed the Potomac army's Cavalry Corps during the winter of 1863–64. Brig. Gen. John Buford, openly acknowledged by his peers as the "best cavalry general we had,"
commanded Pleasonton's First Division. Brig. Gen. Judson
Kilpatrick—nicknamed "Kill-cavalry" as much for the destruction that he inflicted on his own men and mounts as
for the damage he caused the enemy—superintended the
Third Division. The heavily bearded Pennsylvanian, Brig.
Gen. David McM. Gregg, led the Second Division with a
sure and steady hand. But as spring neared, leadership of
the Cavalry Corps seemed to be unraveling. Buford died of
typhoid fever, Kilpatrick ventured a mounted raid against

Richmond that ended in disaster, and Pleasonton's standing with his superiors plummeted to a low point.[1]

Lt. Gen. Ulysses S. Grant's appointment as commander-in-chief of the Union armies on March 11, 1864, brought swift changes. Grant expressed concern over the Potomac army's cavalry in a meeting with President Abraham Lincoln and chief of staff Maj. Gen. Henry W. Halleck, suggesting that the Cavalry Corps might improve under a "thorough" leader. Halleck proposed Sheridan, who had served in the West under both himself and Grant. "The very man I want," Grant replied.[2]

That same day—March 23, 1864—Sheridan received orders to report to Washington. When he learned why, he was "staggered." He was "but slightly acquainted" with cavalry operations in Virginia and knew "not a soul in Washington except General Grant and General Halleck, and them but slightly, and no one in General Meade's army, from the commanding general down, except a few officers in the lower grades, hardly any of whom I had seen since graduating at the military academy." Considering the field of eligible commanders, Sheridan was an unusual choice. He graduated from West Point in 1853 in the lower third of his class, served eight years on the western frontier, then held undistinguished positions during the first year of the Civil War, including a brief stint heading the 2nd Michigan Cavalry. Appointed to an infantry command, his star had risen quickly, and his impulsive attack against Missionary Ridge in November 1863 had cemented his reputation. He had attracted little notice, however, in the East. When his new appointment was announced, several newspapers confused him with Maj. Gen. William T. Sherman.[3]

Thirty-three years old when he arrived in Washington on April 4, Sheridan was "thin almost to emaciation." He met with Lincoln, who later described him as a "brown, chunky little chap, with a long body, short legs, not enough neck to hang him, and such long arms that if his ankles itch he can scratch them without stooping." Proceeding to the army's camps around Brandy Station, the new cavalry chief visited Maj. Gen. George G. Meade's headquarters. An aide thought he looked "very like a Piedmontese," being a "small, broad-shouldered, squat man, with black hair and a square head." When someone opined that Sheridan was "rather a little fellow to handle your cavalry," Grant snapped back, "You will find him big enough for the purpose before we get through with him."[4]

The Army of the Potomac received Sheridan with skepticism. Western commanders were suspect in Virginia, particularly since Maj. Gen. John Pope's disastrous showing two years before. Doubts about Sheridan's competence with the mounted arm also existed within the Cavalry Corps.

"Prejudice that had always existed and will always exist among mounted troops against being placed under the orders of an officer whose experience has been obtained in other arms of the service," observed one officer, "affected to some extent [Sheridan's] reception by his new command." Sheridan, however, responded tactfully. One of Meade's aides wrote home that "Sheridan makes everywhere a favorable impression." The general also displayed commendable diplomacy in selecting his aides, importing from the West only Lt. T. W. C. Moore and Capt. James W. Forsyth, the latter a close friend with valuable eastern connections. Otherwise he retained Pleasonton's former staff. "Although they were all unknown to me when I decided on this course, yet I never had reason to regret it," Sheridan explained. It was a politic move that facilitated his transition.[5]

Kilpatrick's days were numbered, and Grant—apparently with Sheridan's concurrence—selected James H. Wilson as his replacement. A former aide of Grant who recently had completed a ten-week assignment running the Cavalry Bureau, Wilson had demonstrated formidable administrative talent but remained unproven as a manager of cavalry. Only twenty-seven years old, he had neither commanded troops in combat nor led a mounted force. The young man was smart—he had graduated third in his West Point class and had performed exemplary service by whipping the Cavalry Bureau into shape. An associate described him as "quick and impetuous." But it remained to be seen whether his desk savvy could translate into battlefield victories.[6]

A succession of problems got Wilson off to a rocky start after his appointment was announced on April 7. First was the thorny matter of what to do with Kilpatrick. A week after Wilson arrived, Sheridan complained that he was "very much embarrassed" by Kilpatrick's continued presence. "General Kilpatrick is anxious to be transferred to the west," Sheridan informed Grant. "Is it possible to do so?" On April 15 Sheridan referred to Kilpatrick's unresolved status when he alerted Meade's staff that "General Wilson has not yet been placed on duty, and no change has occurred." Not until April 17 was Wilson placed formally in command.[7]

Then there was the sticky issue of what to do about Kilpatrick's brigade commanders. George A. Custer and Henry E. Davies Jr. had received their brigadier general's stars a few months before Wilson, and army protocol prohibited their serving under him. Massive reshuffling ensued. Col. George H. Chapman and his brigade replaced Custer and his outfit. Davies's brigade was left in place; but Davies himself was assigned to a different unit, and Col. Timothy H. Bryan was put in his stead. Wilson's appointment "gave particular offense" to cavalry stalwarts and engendered "hard feelings and complications which were not without influence in the cavalry operations." Moreover, Wilson faced the difficult prospect of taking into combat two brigades led by colonels unaccustomed to the leadership styles of either Wilson or each other.[8]

As for the First Division, everyone viewed Brig. Gen. Wesley Merritt, who had commanded Buford's men since their popular general's death, as Buford's logical successor. To the army's surprise, Merritt was transferred to the Reserve Brigade of the corps, and on April 10 Brig. Gen. Alfred T. A. Torbert became the new head of the division. Although Torbert had amassed a solid combat record leading the New Jersey Brigade in the Sixth Corps, the reason for his cavalry appointment is not apparent. It probably stemmed from his friendship with Sheridan and Forsyth and the fact that he was overdue for promotion. He certainly looked the part of a cavalryman and was described by one acquaintance as "very handsome" and the "best-dressed officer in the army." Even Grant remarked that Torbert "rode a good horse." The shuffling necessitated by Wilson's appointment significantly affected the First Division. Custer and his all-Michigan brigade, nicknamed the "Wolverines," replaced Chapman and his brigade. Col. Thomas C. Devin—an experienced cavalryman and, at forty-two, the oldest brigade commander in the corps—headed Torbert's other brigade. Merritt's Reserve Brigade was placed under Torbert's authority.[9]

Sheridan's only experienced division commander was David Gregg, in charge of the Second Division. "Steady as a clock and as gallant as Murat," Wilson described him. "In discipline he was strict," a soldier reminisced, "but he knew how to take care of his men." Touted as the "best all-'round cavalry officer that ever commanded a division in either army," Gregg had been passed over as Pleasonton's replacement because of his "unusual modesty" and easygoing demeanor. One brigade was under Henry Davies, who had been shifted to Gregg's command after Wilson's arrival. A contemporary described this former New York lawyer turned cavalryman as "polished, genial, gallant." The other brigade was a predominantly Pennsylvania outfit under "steadfast" Col. J. Irvin Gregg.[10]

Grant acquired in Sheridan the "thorough" cavalry commander he wanted, and more. After arriving at Brandy Station, Sheridan reviewed his troopers and remarked on the haggard appearance of their mounts. His staffer Capt. Frederick C. Newhall fueled the general's concern. "In my opinion," Newhall reported after an inspection, "the troops are not in condition to perform active duty with credit, on account of the condition of their horses and in some cases inferior quality of firearms." Newhall

Union cavalry leaders. Left to right: *Brig. Gen. Wesley Merritt, Brig. Gen. David McMurtrie Gregg, Maj. Gen. Philip Henry Sheridan, Brig. Gen. Henry Eugene Davies, Brig. Gen. James Harrison Wilson, and Brig. Gen. Alfred Thomas Archimedes Torbert.*
Francis Trevelyan Miller, ed., The Photographic History of the Civil War, *10 vols. (New York: Review of Reviews, 1911), 10:94*

faulted "heavy outpost duty in all sort of weather" that had "worn down" men and mounts.[11]

Acting with characteristic bluntness, Sheridan requested in writing that the picket line "be at once diminished, so as to give rest to the horses and enable them to recuperate." Rather than requiring cavalry to police the army's entire sixty-mile perimeter, he proposed that his horsemen patrol only the fords, with infantry covering the rest of the line. "It is better to occasionally lose a cavalryman scouting or on outpost duty than to render so many horses so unserviceable by their hard labor," Sheridan suggested.[12]

Sheridan then confronted Meade in a wide-ranging debate over the proper function of cavalry. Only Sheridan's account survives, but in light of future developments, there is no reason to doubt its accuracy. Sheridan maintained that employing cavalry on picket duty was "both burdensome and wasteful." His horsemen "ought to be kept concentrated to fight the enemy's cavalry" instead of being subordinated to the needs of infantry. The proposition, Sheridan recounted, "seemed to stagger General Meade not a little." To Sheridan the army commander appeared governed by "prejudices that, from the beginning of the war, had pervaded the army regarding the importance and usefulness of cavalry."[13]

Meade responded by peppering Sheridan with pointed inquiries. Who would protect the army's wagon trains and artillery reserve? Who would cover the moving infantry columns? Who would protect the army's flanks? Sheridan had ready answers. If Meade would unleash him, he would make it too "lively" for the enemy to attack. Moreover, asserted Sheridan, infantry columns should police their own fronts. Then he revealed the centerpiece of his thinking. "I also told him," Sheridan related, "that it was my object to defeat the enemy's cavalry in a general combat, if possible, and by such a result establish such a feeling of confidence in my own troops that would enable us after a while to march where we pleased, for the purpose of breaking General Lee's communications and destroying the resources from which his army was supplied."[14]

Although Meade left no record of this stormy interview, the encounter must have fueled his growing resentment of the young upstart imposed on him by Grant. After only two weeks in the East, Sheridan claimed to hold the key to defeating Lee, a feat that had eluded Union commanders for three years. And he proposed doing so by relieving cavalry from its primary functions of screening and scouting. Sheridan reported that his suggestions were "contrary to Meade's convictions." Their disagreement over the appropriate role of cavalry seriously affected the course of the campaign.[15]

Sheridan's tirade produced at least one tangible result. Meade adopted his suggestion to reduce involvement of cavalry in picket duty. That change, along with reforms implemented by Wilson, accomplished Sheridan's objective. Men and mounts were soon rested, well fed, and in Wilson's words, "nearly ready as volunteer cavalry ever is."[16]

According to the Army of the Potomac's returns for April 30, 1864, Sheridan's Cavalry Corps contained 12,424 men "present for duty equipped." Torbert's First Division mustered 4,195; the Second Division under Gregg, 4,793; and Wilson's Third Division, 3,436. Capt. James M. Robertson's brigade of Horse Artillery—six batteries boasting thirty-two guns—completed the corps' compliment. Some troopers carried seven-shot carbines, which wonderfully magnified their firepower. How would this formidable mounted force fight under its new leaders? And what im-

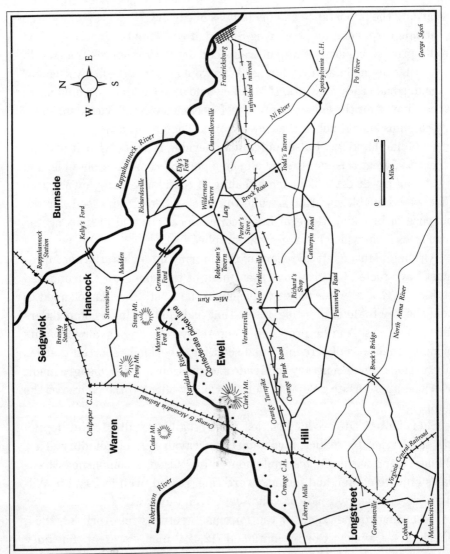

Theater of operations, May 2–7, 1864, showing corps placement on May 2.

pact would Meade's and Sheridan's rift have on its performance? Some answers lay but a few days ahead.[17]

By May 2 the Union commanders had decided on their plan of campaign. Gen. Robert E. Lee's Confederate Army of Northern Virginia stood firmly entrenched below the Rapidan River near Orange Court House. Rather than tackling the rebels head-on, Grant determined to cross east of Lee, then swing west, prying the Confederates from their Rapidan entrenchments and forcing a battle on ground favorable to the Federals. To facilitate the river crossing, the Union army was to split in two. The right wing, comprised of the Fifth and Sixth Corps, was to cross at Germanna Ford and proceed south to Wilderness Tavern. The Second Corps, meanwhile, was to splash across the river a few miles east at Ely's Ford, then drop south to Chancellorsville. Once the two segments reached their destinations, they would be about four miles apart but connected by a major east-west thoroughfare, the Orange Turnpike.

The army's route led directly into the Wilderness of Spotsylvania, a region of dense second-growth woods. Few clearings provided relief from the heavy foliage, and only a handful of narrow, twisting roads tunneled through the undergrowth. It was hard to imagine a worse place for cavalry.

Meade's scheme incorporated a conservative but judicious use of Sheridan's horsemen. Wilson would lead the army's right wing across Germanna Ford and scout ahead, taking particular care to patrol the roads that fanned west toward Lee's position. Gregg would precede the army's other wing across Ely's Ford, clear the way to Chancellorsville, then bivouac nearby at Alrich's farm to guard against rebel forays from Fredericksburg and protect the army's supply train. Torbert would remain behind and shield the army's rear, then cross at Germanna the next morning and join Wilson in posting the countryside toward Lee.[18]

On May 3 Sheridan briefed his subordinates. "Had a complete and definite understanding of the movement and what is expected of me," Wilson assured his diary.[19]

Shortly after midnight Wilson departed for Germanna Ford. George Chapman's brigade led, followed by Timothy Bryan's. The horsemen reached the ford around 4:00 A.M. and waited while Meade's engineers brought up mobile pontoon bridges. From the far bank a thin veneer of rebel pickets—probably from the 1st North Carolina Cavalry—fired at the interlopers. Chapman sent a regiment—either the 1st Vermont or the 3rd Indiana—splashing across the Rapidan. The rebels offered only token resistance, then scattered. By 6:00 Wilson's entire division was over. The

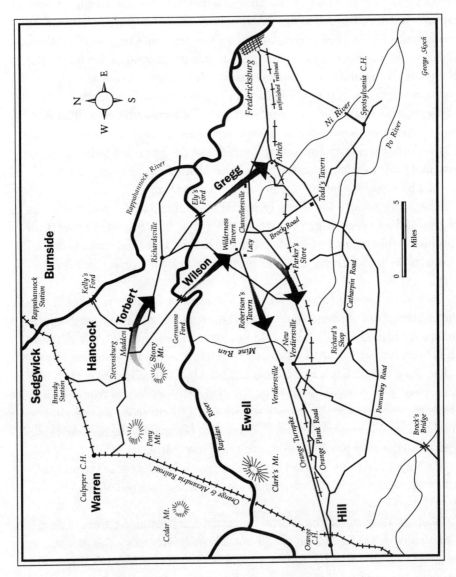

Union cavalry operations, May 4, 1864.

horsemen drew up on heights below the river and watched the engineers lay pontoon bridges. Soon the foremost elements of Maj. Gen. Gouverneur K. Warren's Fifth Corps were rumbling across.[20]

With the Germanna crossing secure, Wilson pursued the road south into the Wilderness. About four miles below the river his route intersected the Orange Turnpike. Nearby stood a rickety frame structure known as Wilderness Tavern. Wilson halted there before noon to wait for the infantry to catch up, meanwhile sending scouting parties out the roads threading south and west. Wilderness Tavern was the Fifth Corps's objective for the day, and Wilson's assignment was to make sure that it remained secure. "All well," he scrawled in his pocket diary.[21]

A few miles east, Gregg spearheaded the advance across Ely's Ford. The action there proved more exciting. The 1st New Jersey reached the crossing around 2:00 A.M., and a company waded across the chilly river, losing a few troopers to the swift current. The Federals tried to capture a Confederate outpost on the southern bank, but most of the rebels fled into the darkness. The rest of Gregg's division was soon over, and shortly after 9:00 a pontoon bridge spanned the Rapidan for Maj. Gen. Winfield S. Hancock's Second Corps. It was "intensely hot," but Gregg pressed south to Chancellorsville, where Hancock was to camp. Once the winded foot soldiers began arriving, Gregg continued two more miles to Alrich's, near the intersection of the Orange Plank Road and the Catharpin Road. His assignment was to safeguard Hancock's bivouac and protect the army's wagons, which were crossing nearby at Culpeper Mine Ford and parking near Chancellorsville. A squadron from the 16th Pennsylvania Cavalry skirmished with Confederates on the road to Fredericksburg. Otherwise all seemed quiet.[22]

While Gregg's riders fanned into Alrich's broad fields, Wilson's troopers prepared for the second phase of their assignment. Under Meade's master plan Warren was to proceed early on May 5 from Wilderness Tavern to Parker's Store on the Orange Plank Road. His route followed an obscure farm road that hugged high ground above Wilderness Run. Wilson was to reconnoiter to Parker's Store, then to "cover the infantry and give it timely notice of any movement of the enemy from his position beyond Mine Run."[23]

After the head of Warren's column reached Wilderness Tavern—around 11:00 A.M., according to Union dispatches—Wilson started out. At about 2:00 P.M. his horsemen reached Parker's Store. During the rest of the afternoon Wilson dispatched scouts south to the Catharpin Road and west to Mine Run. They found only small enemy squads.[24]

Before leaving Wilderness Tavern, Wilson had deployed a small force to probe west along the Orange Turnpike. Around 11:00 A.M. the troopers encountered rebels somewhere near Robertson's Tavern—about three miles out—and waged a heated little skirmish. Assuming that the Confederates were only pickets, the Federals withdrew. Before evening they rode south to join Wilson's main body at Parker's Store.[25]

Not long after the Federal horsemen had abandoned the Orange Turnpike, Lt. Gen. Richard S. Ewell's Confederate Second Corps hove into view. In an ironic episode that presaged the confused fighting to come, Ewell's men passed through Robertson's Tavern and bivouacked about two miles west of Warren's Wilderness Tavern encampment. Warren assumed that Wilson had posted the turnpike and made no effort to thrust pickets out the roadway. Wilson later explained that he "expected that the infantry would relieve our detachments on the various roads and throw out their own in turn, to cover and protect their flanks from the enemy." Consequently the stretch of turnpike between the two armies shimmered vacantly under the moonlight. Opposing troops bedded down a few miles apart, each blissfully ignorant of the other's proximity.[26]

Col. John Hammond probed west on the Orange Plank Road with his 5th New York Cavalry while Wilson's exhausted riders kindled their evening fires around Parker's Store. Hammond stirred up a few rebel cavalry squads near Mine Run but saw no indication of a significant Confederate movement in his direction. Around dusk he returned to the main encampment.[27]

At day's end Wilson informed his superiors of the situation as he understood it. He assured both Warren and Sheridan that he had the roads toward Lee well patrolled. In fact Wilson had stationed no pickets on the Orange Turnpike and none on the Orange Plank Road past Mine Run. Had he posted the roads as he represented, he would have known that Ewell was on the Union side of Robertson's Tavern and that Lt. Gen. Ambrose Powell Hill's Confederate Third Corps was shuffling into camp around New Verdiersville, only a short distance west of Mine Run on the Orange Plank Road. The Union commanders received unwelcome surprises at dawn when Lee's soldiers unexpectedly appeared, like apparitions in the morning mist, on both major east-west thoroughfares.[28]

Not only did Wilson neglect to determine Lee's position, but he apparently also unwittingly supplied the Confederates critical information about Grant's location and intentions. At 11:15 P.M. Confederate cavalry chief Maj. Gen. James E. B. "Jeb" Stuart reported to Lee that a civilian had overheard a courier alerting Wilson that he had advanced too far from the rest of Grant's command, which could proceed no farther than the "church" that night. Stuart correctly concluded that the Federals had stopped near Wilderness Church and hence were still in the Wilderness.[29]

What accounted for Wilson's dereliction? His orders had been to cover the army's flank and warn of Lee's approach. In his inexperience he had assumed that he was to investigate the roads leading toward Lee, then move on and leave the infantry commanders to patrol their flanks. The misunderstanding cost Grant dearly.

While Wilson's campfires illuminated Parker's Store and Gregg's men cooked their rations at Alrich's, Torbert's troopers bedded down above the Rapidan to guard the army's rear. Aside from minor skirmishes with roving rebel horsemen, their day had proved uneventful.[30]

According to Meade's plan Wilson was to continue south in the morning to the Catharpin Road; Torbert was to cross at Germanna and move to Wilson's support; and Gregg was to clear the way for Hancock's advance west along the Catharpin Road, taking care to cover the wagons. Sheridan, however, received intelligence that at least one Confederate cavalry division—a premier unit under Maj. Gen. Fitzhugh Lee, General Lee's nephew—lay camped below Fredericksburg at Hamilton's Crossing. The temptation proved too much. Here was Sheridan's chance to fight his cavalry en masse, precisely as he had been urging Meade. Again Sheridan made his case to Meade, and this time the army commander relented. The morrow's plans were redrawn. Torbert would proceed not to support Wilson but, rather, to join Gregg at Alrich's. From there the two divisions would advance to Hamilton's Crossing and defeat Fitzhugh Lee. The new arrangement left Wilson to his own devices, but Sheridan saw no reason for concern. After all, Wilson reported his sector quiescent.[31]

Thus did the Federals abandon their initial formula to concentrate the army's mounted force toward Lee. Instead nearly three-fourths of Sheridan's troopers were to ride off to Hamilton's Crossing, away from the Confederate army. Sheridan's most inexperienced general commanding his smallest division would be responsible for scouting the wooded countryside off the army's right flank. It was a foolish decision that threatened to imperil the entire campaign.

At 5:00 on the morning of May 5 Wilson started south toward the Catharpin Road. During the night Meade had issued new instructions reminding Wilson to "keep out parties" on the turnpike and the Plank Road as he moved south. Wilson later claimed that he never received Meade's directive and hence proceeded under the misapprehension that had governed his actions on May 4. He continued to leave the turnpike unposted and deployed only Hammond's 5th New York on the Orange Plank Road, with instructions to patrol the thoroughfare until relieved by Warren's infantry. Hammond's men began cooking breakfast at Parker's Store while Capt. William B. Cary explored west on the Plank Road with Company I.[32]

Cary's orders were to push out the roadway until he found the enemy, but not to become engaged. Riding west, he crossed a stream and started up a slight rise when he encountered Confederates. Driving the rebels back, Cary discovered that he was fighting infantry. He retired to the stream, dismounted his men, and sent for reinforcements. Soon embroiled in a sharp little brawl, he dropped back toward Parker's Store. From prisoners it became apparent that Hill's entire Confederate infantry corps was in front.[33]

Hammond instructed his troopers to erect fence-rail barricades and sent reinforcements to Cary, who was stubbornly contesting the enemy's advance. Warren's staff officer Washington A. Roebling soon pounded up. A Union infantry division under Brig. Gen. Samuel W. Crawford was forming on Chewning heights, a mile northeast of Parker's Store. Roebling asked Hammond how long he could hold. Fifteen minutes, the colonel answered. Roebling turned his mount and spurred back to Crawford.[34]

The advanced New York units retired to Parker's Store under irresistible pressure from Hill's veterans. A Federal recalled gray-clad forms "tumbling thru those Jack pines and persimmon trees in almost a solid battle line." Hammond ordered the horses rearward and formed his regiment behind the makeshift barricade, sternly directing his men to hold as long as possible. "Our seven-shooters worked sharp," a soldier reminisced, "and it was almost impossible not to hit our mark."[35]

As the engagement heated, Hammond was joined by Col. John B. McIntosh, who had been dispatched to command Colonel Bryan's brigade. Hill had blocked the way south, so McIntosh decided to stay with Hammond. He swiftly dispatched a courier to Meade with an urgent request. "We are now formed at the junction of the Parker's Store Road and [Orange Plank Road] without ammunition," he explained. "I understand General Crawford is on my right. He should extend his line at once across the Parker's Store Road." But McIntosh's plea came too late. In short order, Confederates streamed past both his flanks. A Federal explained that the southerners "made things buzz from all sides, and we were obliged to skip out for our horses." After retiring about a quarter-mile east, Hammond's men extended into a skirmish line and prepared for the next onslaught. "For God's sake, captain, hold this line!" McIntosh admonished.[36]

Hammond's evacuation of Parker's Store had important consequences. Wilson had continued south to the Catharpin Road and found himself severed from the rest of the Union army by Hill. Crawford's opportunity to block Hill also was fast disappearing. The danger to Grant's offensive was real. Three miles east, the Orange Plank Road intersected the Brock Road. If Hill occupied that intersection, Hancock's Union Second Corps, which was heading west on the Catharpin Road, also would be cut off.

For the rest of the morning Hammond's troopers waged a valiant delaying action, sparring with Hill's approaching infantry, then retiring to new positions. One of Hill's aides paid the regiment unintentional tribute. In front was a "heavy line" of "picked men," he remarked. Mutilated bodies along the roadside attested to the violence of combat at close quarters.[37]

By noon Hammond's fought-out regiment had been battered back to the Brock Road. But the time that it had bought helped save the day. Union infantry under Brig. Gen. George W. Getty stormed up just as Hill's advance elements arrived. One of Getty's officers recollected Hammond's horsemen strung out "like a flock of wild geese." Blue-clad soldiers occupied the intersection and continued to hold this important ground until the end of the battle.[38]

Hammond was not the only hard-pressed Union horseman that sweltering May morning. The rest of Wilson's division had reached the Catharpin Road and turned west, churning along the dusty thoroughfare in column of fours, Chapman's brigade first, Bryan's following. At about 7:30 Chapman reached a wooden structure called Craig's Meeting House, where he halted and ordered a Vermont battalion to scout ahead. In less than a mile the Vermonters encountered the 12th Virginia Cavalry and were "rapidly" driven back. Chapman dismounted his brigade and formed it near Craig's. Suspecting that a major fight was brewing, Wilson halted Bryan immediately above Robertson's Run, near where the Parker's Store Road joined the Catharpin Road.[39]

The thousand or so Confederates on the Catharpin Road belonged to Brig. Gen. Thomas L. Rosser, who coincidentally had been Wilson's contemporary at the military academy. After what Wilson described as a "very sharp fight and several handsome charges," Chapman managed to drive Rosser back about two miles. The 1st Vermont apparently bore the brunt of the combat. "Sharply engaged," a Vermonter recorded. Learning

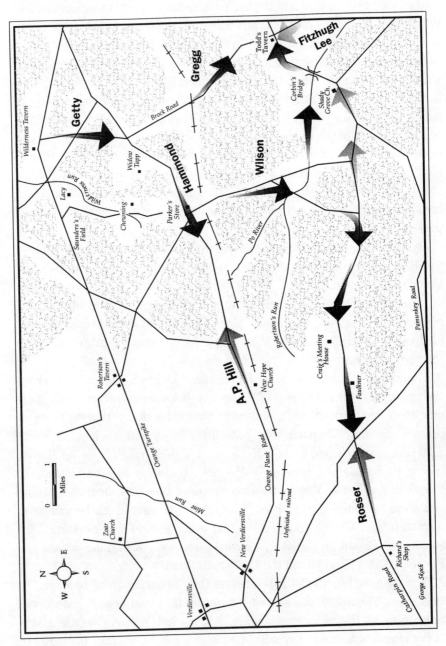

Union cavalry operations, May 5, 1864.

that Chapman was running low on ammunition and concerned that the impetuous brigadier had advanced too far, Wilson instructed him to halt and re-form. Chapman dismounted the 3rd Indiana along a ravine that crossed the road and massed the rest of his brigade a half-mile back. Wilson meanwhile advanced Bryan to Craig's Meeting House and positioned two horse artillery batteries nearby. The general himself established headquarters at the home of Mrs. Faulkner, a short distance west of Craig's.[40]

Around 1:00 in the afternoon Chapman ordered the 3rd Indiana back when he discovered Confederates edging around both its flanks. With the ravine now undefended, the road was open to Rosser, who sent his brigade thundering ahead. Chapman's brigade began tumbling rearward. "The confusion occasioned by getting a large number of led horses hastily back on one road was communicated to the men," Chapman admitted, "and caused the men to break badly, of which the enemy was not slow to take advantage."[41]

Firmly positioned near Craig's, Bryan opened his formation to let Chapman's fugitives through, then closed to meet the Confederate mounted charge. The two Federal batteries stationed by Faulkner's—twelve guns in all, under lieutenants Alexander C. M. Pennington Jr. and Charles L. Fitzhugh—opened on Rosser's flank as the rebels drove past. Chapman's troopers pitched in, and the fight commenced in earnest. "It was practically a head-on collision on a forest road in which both parties bore themselves gallantly, making all the noise they could," Wilson recounted. Then two Confederate pieces from Maj. Robert P. Chew's horse artillery appeared on the Faulkner clearing's western edge and began dueling with Pennington and Fitzhugh. The outgunned rebels got the worst of it. "Their shrapnel shot exploded all around and over us," a Confederate explained, "and the everlasting ping and thud of slugs, balls, and fragments and shell filled the air with horrid screams for an hour, and the death-dealing mixture tore and raked up the sod all around us like a raging storm of iron hail."[42]

In the confused charges and countercharges Wilson found himself and about fifty soldiers from the 8th Illinois isolated at the Faulkner house. As a ruse they charged the approaching Confederate column and scattered its head. Concluding that he was hopelessly outnumbered, Wilson ordered his men back to Robertson's Run.[43]

Wilson was in a tight spot. Hill's infantry filled the Orange Plank Road to his north, and Rosser's cavalry was arrayed along the Catharpin Road to his south. A short distance above Robertson's Run, Wilson discovered a wagon track that led east through the woods. He directed his division out the path, Chapman leading, Bryan following, and Lt. Col. William P. Brinton's 18th Pennsylvania protecting the rear. No sooner had the Federals begun, however, than Wilson discovered Rosser advancing parallel to him along the Catharpin Road. The Third Cavalry Division was in a race for survival.

After trotting some three miles east along the woods trail, Wilson's column turned south and entered the Catharpin Road, barely ahead of Rosser. His winded troopers streamed east, Rosser in hot pursuit. Colonel Brinton's regiment, which had been directed to "hold the ground at all hazards" in Wilson's rear, spilled into the Catharpin Road moments too late. "In our front, the Confederates were literally swarming," a Pennsylvanian recounted. "The right-hand road was crowded with them, while their batteries were belching hot shot into us on our left." More Confederates pressed Brinton's rear. Surrounded on three sides, Brinton's men darted into dense forest to their east. "Imagine, if you can, a cavalry regiment tearing through woods and underbrush, over logs, floundering through swamps, caps and cuss words flying in all directions, and you have a faint idea of our escape," a Pennsylvanian reminisced. The 1st Connecticut and an artillery section deployed across the Catharpin Road to stem the onslaught, but Rosser kept pounding. Elements from the 7th and 11th Virginia charged "like a solid shot into the ranks of the Federals, who now broke and ran," a Confederate explained. Any pretext of an orderly retreat evaporated as Wilson's troopers fled east along the Catharpin Road. "We were outflanked on both sides," a Connecticut man recounted, "and being under orders to hold the position at all hazards, were in immediate danger of being surrounded."[44]

While Hammond sought to delay Hill's inexorable advance and Wilson sparred with Rosser, the rest of Sheridan's Cavalry Corps idly marked time. Sheridan's plan to merge Gregg and Torbert in a steel-fisted assault against Fitzhugh Lee never got off the ground. For one thing, Torbert was horribly late. Although he started over the Rapidan at daylight, wagons and supplies packed the roads below Ely's Ford, and Torbert found himself threading through a monumental traffic jam. The general also suffered from a painful spinal abscess. By the time he reached Alrich's at noon, he was in excruciating pain and hobbled off to a hospital tent. Merritt replaced him heading the division. Then word arrived that the rebels had left Hamilton's Crossing the previous afternoon and had started toward the Wilderness. It was just as well that Torbert had been delayed. Otherwise Sheridan would have taken two divisions to Fredericksburg on a pointless expedition.[45]

Brig. Gen. Thomas Lafayette Rosser.
Francis Trevelyan Miller, ed., The
Photographic History of the Civil War,
10 vols. (New York: Review of Reviews,
1911), 4:73

Around noon Meade alerted Sheridan that Wilson had been cut off.
Sheridan directed Gregg to explore out the Catharpin Road to find Wilson and relieve him. Merritt remained behind to guard the wagons. At
2:30 P.M. Gregg's lead brigade under Davies reached Todd's Tavern,
where the Brock and Catharpin roads crossed. "General Wilson is falling
back to this point, followed by the enemy," Gregg informed Sheridan. "I
have my command here and will receive the enemy."[46]

Davies directed Col. John W. Kester to dispatch his 1st New Jersey
west on the Catharpin Road while the rest of the brigade formed in
support. Capt. James H. Hart pushed through Wilson's retreating horsemen with a company from Kester's regiment and slammed into the head
of Rosser's pursuing column. The Confederates recoiled in surprise, and
Kester began pumping in reinforcements. "With this skirmish line of two
hundred and fifty men we actually bore back the effective force of the
entire opposing brigade," the New Jersey regiment's historian reported.
Then Rosser, buttressed by Chew's pieces, countercharged, and it became the Jersey men's turn to fall back. They retired to where Davies had
formed his main line and were joined by the 1st Massachusetts, the 6th
Ohio, and perhaps the 10th New York.[47]

Amply reinforced, Davies turned on the Confederates, the 1st New
Jersey north of the road and the 1st Massachusetts below it. "Our skirmishers wheeled with one accord, and with a wild cheer the whole body
made a simultaneous and resistless charge," a Jersey man reported. According to Kester the regiment advanced "as steady as on parade, the
rebels endeavoring to check us by showers of canister, but to no avail."

After a vicious round of combat, the Federals drove Rosser back across Corbin's Bridge on the Po, halting only on orders from Davies.[48]

While Davies locked horns with Rosser, some of Fitzhugh Lee's Confederates appeared on the Brock Road below Todd's Tavern. Gregg responded by dispatching elements from the 1st Pennsylvania. About three miles below the tavern they encountered Lee's foremost brigade under Brig. Gen. Lunsford L. Lomax. The Pennsylvanians were hard pressed until men from the 1st Massachusetts and two artillery pieces arrived and shifted the balance. The rebels—primarily from the 6th and 15th Virginia Cavalry—retired to the southern edge of the fields around the Alsop house.[49]

By nightfall Gregg faced Confederates in two directions. Rosser's rebels held high ground west of the Po on the Catharpin Road, and Lomax —now reinforced by Fitzhugh Lee's other brigade under Brig. Gen. Williams C. Wickham—stood across the Brock Road near Alsop's. The southerners threw log and brush obstructions across the roads. Wilson's battered troopers bivouacked north and east of Todd's Tavern, where they passed the night in "intense anxiety." One piece of good news enlivened their camp. Long after Wilson had given them up as lost, Brinton's Pennsylvanians emerged from the forest, having lost one officer and thirty-nine men. That evening Wilson sent Brinton a bottle of wine with a note attached: "To the 18th Pa. Cav., which knows how to fight into and how to fight out of a very hard place." Before morning the entire Third Division fell back to Alrich's to replenish its men and mounts.[50]

At 6:00 P.M. Meade instructed Sheridan to "cover our left flank and protect the trains as much as possible." Perhaps to mollify the volatile cavalry chief, Meade added, "If you gain any information that leads you to conclude that you can take the offensive and harass the enemy without endangering the trains, you are at liberty to do so." Sheridan's response was predictable. "I cannot do anything with the cavalry, except to act on the defensive on account of the immense amount of material and trains here and on the road to Ely's Ford," he complained, concluding with his usual refrain: "Why cannot infantry be sent to guard the trains and let me take the offensive?"[51]

How had the Union mounted arm fared during its first fight under Sheridan? The Rapidan crossing had proceeded unopposed, and no rebels had threatened the wagons, although neither achievement was attributable to anything Sheridan had done. Most importantly, Sheridan had neglected to screen the army's critical western flank and had failed to discover two Confederate corps approaching on the major thoroughfares from Orange Court House. This dereliction enabled Lee to surprise Grant and to exploit the awkward Union deployments. The first encounter between Grant and Lee doubtless would have unfolded differently if Grant had been apprised of Lee's whereabouts during May 4. Rather than wasting May 5 reacting to rebel thrusts and scrambling to reassemble his army, Grant would have had opportunity to concentrate his forces and wage an offensive—and quite likely successful—battle. Moreover, by 8:00 on the morning of May 5, Confederates had interposed between Wilson and the Union army. Unable to communicate with Wilson, the Army of the Potomac was compelled to fight in ignorance of its foe's movements and dispositions.

Several years later Wilson claimed that he had "perfectly screened Grant's advance," engaging the enemy "wherever we encountered him and making good our hold on the important points of the field." In fact Wilson's cavalry screen had more fluff than substance and was demolished by a substantially smaller Confederate force. Although Wilson later boasted that he had fought three mounted Confederate brigades—those of Rosser, Lomax, and Brig. Gen. James B. Gordon—he in truth had faced only Rosser, whom he outnumbered by more than three to one.[52]

Wilson's inability to hold the Catharpin Road west of the Po River had serious repercussions. During May 5 Grant's lower infantry wing—Hancock's corps—had concentrated around the Orange Plank Road, with units extending south along the Brock Road to the Trigg farm. Hancock knew that Hill's infantry occupied the Plank Road. But with the Catharpin Road in Confederate hands, the Union commanders had no idea what surprises Lee contemplated off their left flank. That uncertainty compelled Hancock to hold a substantial force in reserve. These troops were sorely missed when combat resumed on May 6.

Sheridan's dispositions had been flawed from the outset. The greenhorn Wilson was the wrong choice for patrolling the army's sensitive flank —a mistake compounded by the subsequent decision not to reinforce Wilson with Torbert. Had Torbert joined Wilson as originally contemplated, he could have supported Hammond on the Orange Plank Road and perhaps delayed Hill at Parker's Store, giving Crawford opportunity to pitch in. If buttressed by elements from Torbert, Wilson certainly would have overwhelmed Rosser. The injection of more than 4,000 veteran troopers—Buford's former men—might well have tipped the battle's balance.

Blame for the Union army's misguided use of cavalry lay at all levels of command. Meade's almost compulsive concern about his wagons certainly played a part. He retained Torbert above the Rapidan on May 4 to protect the slow-moving procession of trains, thereby rendering him unavailable to assist Wilson. Moreover, Meade's acquiescence in reassigning Torbert to Sheridan's ill-conceived Hamilton's Crossing expedition doubtless stemmed from a perception that Fitzhugh Lee's rebels posed a threat to the Chancellorsville wagon park. Torn between the need to patrol his right flank and the safety of his wagons, Meade elected to leave Wilson to fend for himself. As for Sheridan, his lust for independent mounted forays blinded him to the importance of Wilson's sector. This was Wilson's first combat assignment, and Sheridan should have closely supervised his subordinate's dispositions. Meade's concern about protecting his supply trains and Sheridan's apparent indifference to the mundane tasks of screening and reconnoitering led them to ignore Wilson. Consequently the Union expeditionary force found itself fighting on a field of Lee's choosing without opportunity to prepare for the onslaught.

A few hopeful glimmers relieved this otherwise dismal picture. Some subordinate commanders—Hammond, Brinton, and Kester in particular—fought extremely well. Wilson showed commendable bravery and decisiveness, and Gregg displayed his usual gusto. Painfully absent, however, was judicious leadership at the corps level. Perhaps when combat resumed in the morning, Sheridan would justify the confidence that Grant had placed in him.

During the night Sheridan's horsemen wrapped a protective barrier around the Union army's lower flank. Gregg remained at Todd's Tavern, Wilson shifted Chapman's brigade north along the Brock Road toward Hancock, and Merritt camped at Catharine Furnace near Chancellorsville. Chapman's fought-out troopers were in no condition to defend the three-mile gap that separated Gregg from Hancock's lowermost infantry units at Trigg's farm, so Sheridan directed George Custer of Merritt's division to relieve them. Custer reached the Brock Road shortly after daylight, extending his right flank north toward Hancock and his left south toward Gregg. The mass of his brigade formed in woods east of the Brock Road, across from a broad field. Shortly afterward Thomas Devin started from Chancellorsville to join Custer, bringing with him a battery under Lt. Edward Heaton. His instructions were to form on Custer's right and consolidate the junction with Hancock.[53]

As morning advanced, Hancock found himself hard pressed by a counterattack from two Confederate divisions under Lt. Gen. James Longstreet. The whereabouts of two more rebel divisions remained a mystery, however, and Hancock became concerned that they were forming off his left flank in the void created by Wilson's precipitous retreat on May 5. Around 8:00 Custer received a curious order to take his and Devin's brigades and "move out on the Brock pike for the purposes of harassing Longstreet's corps." Longstreet, however, was nowhere near the Brock Road, as Custer well knew from his troopers along the pike. But Custer did not have long to puzzle over these instructions. Suddenly, from the field along the western side of the Brock Road, streamed Rosser's indomitable riders, led by the 35th Virginia Cavalry Battalion.[54]

Custer's pickets tumbled back, followed by Confederates emerging in droves from a farm track that meandered from the Catharpin Road. Realizing that intervening woods concealed his main force, Custer prepared to take the rebels by surprise. He struck a grand pose, resplendent in a black velvet jacket, blue shirt, red scarf, and slouch hat with a star aggressively pinned in front. "Strike up 'Yankee Doodle,'" Custer directed his brigade's band before ordering his men ahead. The 1st and 6th Michigan charged into the field and became inextricably mixed. Rosser accepted the challenge. In converging clouds of dust the two mounted forces drove to the field's center, where a deep ravine that diagonally traversed the clearing brought them up short. The antagonists fired from opposite sides of the swale while a few brave souls jumped in and crossed sabers like gladiators of old.[55]

Unable to break Custer with frontal attacks, the rebels began edging around his right. Custer dispatched his uncommitted units—the 5th and 6th Michigan—to block the turning movement. They shifted in the nick of time but soon found themselves heavily pressed. Just then Devin appeared. "The reinforcements came none too soon," the 6th Michigan's colonel later conceded. The Confederates retreated, encouraged in their flight by the arrival of Heaton's six guns and two more from Gregg.[56]

The affair deteriorated into an ugly artillery brawl with the Confederates suffering heavily. Some of Chew's rebel horse artillery pulled up and endured a galling barrage from the Union pieces, which had them in a deadly crossfire. "The batteries on both our flanks opened on us," a Confederate recounted, "their own shell crossing each other in mid-air, and spreading considerable alarm in our ranks." There was, he conceded, "nothing left for us but to retreat, and we came out hastily." Custer later claimed that Rosser was "driven from the field in great disorder, leaving his dead and many of his wounded upon the ground." The Confederates retired to a respectful distance.[57]

Custer had won a brilliant little engagement, but the victory did nothing to advance Union fortunes. Although Rosser had been thwarted, the Federals still had no idea of what lay behind the Confederate cavalry

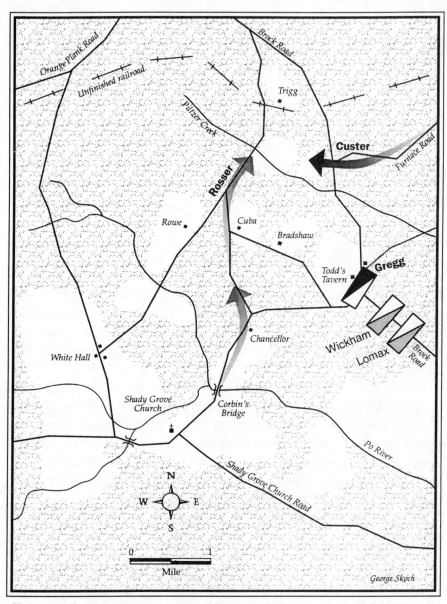

Union cavalry operations, morning, May 6, 1864.

screen. Hence Hancock continued to keep a substantial portion of his soldiers out of the combat raging along the Orange Plank Road. Taking advantage of the curtain that Stuart's mounted arm had drawn across the battlefield's lower sector, Longstreet maneuvered against Hancock's flank and drove the Union infantry back to the Brock Road. Hancock later complained that the absence of intelligence about Confederate activities below the Trigg farm "paralyzed a large number of my best troops, who would otherwise have gone into action at a decisive point on the morning of the 6th."[58]

While Custer and Rosser lobbed shells at each other, Col. J. Irvin Gregg's brigade from David Gregg's division sparred with Fitzhugh Lee's troopers below Todd's Tavern. Lee's goal was to thwart Union cavalry probes down the Brock Road, and he gave the assignment to Wickham. Positioned behind barricades, the Confederates effectively blocked the Federals. Gregg fed Davies's brigade into the fight around noon, but to no avail. Then the 1st, 2nd, 4th, and 8th Pennsylvania, along with the 10th New York, assaulted Wickham's barricade across the Brock Road but failed to break through. Wickham launched a "very stubborn" counterattack, a Union correspondent reported, which "looked for a time as though it would be successful." General Gregg—"the coolest man under trying circumstances I ever saw on the field"—threw in the 1st Maine and repelled the charge. "Cavalry skirmishing all day," a Pennsylvanian wrote in his diary.[59]

With Confederates pressing on two fronts, Sheridan hesitated to assume the offensive. He informed Meade at 11:40 A.M. that his troopers had "handled the enemy very handsomely in every attack that they have made." He recommended, however, against exploiting the advantage, "as the cavalry is now very far out from this place and I do not wish to give them any chance of getting at our trains." The suggestion that his wagons might be in jeopardy galvanized Meade. "General Hancock has been heavily pressed and his left turned," headquarters advised Sheridan at 1:00. "You had better draw in your cavalry so as to secure the protection of the trains." Around 2:30 P.M. Gregg received instructions to retire to Piney Branch Church. Custer and Devin were also to disengage and retrace their morning's route to Catharine Furnace.[60]

The decision to abandon Todd's Tavern was roundly criticized. Sheridan faulted Meade in his report and later in his memoirs. "The enemy took possession of the Furnaces, Todd's Tavern, and Piney Branch Church, the regaining which cost much fighting on the 6th and 7th, and very many gallant officers and men," he charged. Sheridan's rebuke was unfair. It was he, after all, who had suggested to Meade that the cavalry might be too far extended. Nor had he registered a word of protest against the order to withdraw.[61]

Union cavalry maneuvers on May 6—much like those of May 5—had been characterized by dogged local fighting and uninspired leadership from the top. Custer and Gregg had accomplished everything asked of them, but starkly absent was a firm hand imparting consistent purpose to the cavalry's operations. While Sheridan had successfully repelled Confederate forays, he had singularly failed to penetrate the wall erected by Stuart's horsemen. Sheridan's neglect in vigorously pursuing his primary assignment of scouting Lee's positions hamstrung Hancock's offensive along the Orange Plank Road. Failures of cavalry thus figured among the blunders and missed opportunities that contributed to the Wilderness stalemate.

But a new trend was evident in the casualty figures. Lincoln had asked Sheridan during their April meeting, "Who ever saw a dead cavalryman?" The implication was that cavalry shied from combat. There could be no doubt that Sheridan meant to fight. Wilson lost about 227 men on May 5, and Custer 53 on May 6. Together they put more than 150 of Rosser's Confederates out of service on May 5 and 120 on the sixth. As a student of Union cavalry operations later observed, anyone who wanted to see a dead cavalryman could have readily done so in the Wilderness.[62]

Meade's and Sheridan's rift had far-reaching consequences and culminated in an explosive conference on May 8. Sheridan stalked from Meade's tent in anger, and Meade reported the outburst to Grant, who solved the unpleasantness by granting Sheridan his independence. The next morning Sheridan took virtually his entire corps on an independent foray to destroy Stuart and threaten Richmond. The cost of acceding to Sheridan's vision proved high. With Sheridan off on a raid, Grant was deprived of his eyes and ears. Just as Lee had missed Stuart at Gettysburg, Grant was crippled at Spotsylvania by Sheridan's absence. The bloody Union assaults of May 10 and 12 might well have concluded differently had Sheridan been available to inform Grant about Lee's position and troop concentrations.

All of that lay in the future. As the Wilderness combat simmered to a close, a few questions posed at the fight's start had been answered. Union troopers could fight well, if not brilliantly, when led by men with the backbone of Hammond and Kester. It was not so clear, however, whether Sheridan and Wilson could supply the leadership that the mounted arm required. More evidence on that point would emerge a few days hence and several miles south, at a place called Yellow Tavern.

NOTES

1. Charles S. Wainwright, *A Diary of Battle: The Personal Journals of Colonel Charles S. Wainwright, 1861–1865*, ed. Allan Nevins (New York: Harcourt, Brace

and World, 1962), 309; Theodore Lyman to family, March 5, 1864, Theodore Lyman Collection, Massachusetts Historical Society, Boston, Mass. (repository hereafter cited as MHS). Pleasonton's difficulties are described in Stephen Z. Starr, *The Union Cavalry in the Civil War*, 3 vols. (Baton Rouge: Louisiana State University Press, 1981), 2:73–74.

2. Ulysses S. Grant, *Personal Memoirs of U. S. Grant*, 2 vols. (New York: Charles L. Webster, 1885), 2:133.

3. Philip H. Sheridan, *Personal Memoirs of P. H. Sheridan*, 2 vols. (New York: Charles L. Webster, 1888), 1:339–42; Edward P. Tobie, *History of the First Maine Cavalry, 1861–1865* (Boston: Emery and Hughes, 1887), 248.

4. Horace Porter, *Campaigning with Grant* (New York: Century, 1897), 24; Sheridan, *Personal Memoirs*, 1:346; U.S. War Department, *The War of the Rebellion: A Compilation of the Official Records of the Union and Confederate Armies*, 127 vols., index, and atlas (Washington: GPO, 1880–1901), ser. 1, 33:806 (hereafter cited as *OR*).

5. Henry E. Davies, *General Sheridan* (New York: Appleton, 1895), 93; Theodore Lyman to family, April 13, 1864, Lyman Collection, MHS. Assistant Secretary of War Charles A. Dana commented on Sheridan's popularity a few months later. "I was struck, in riding through the lines, by the universal demonstration of personal affection for Sheridan," he wrote. "Everybody seemed to be personally attached to him. He was like the most popular man after the election" (Charles A. Dana, *Recollections of the Civil War* [New York: Appleton, 1899], 249).

6. Theodore F. Rodenbough, "Sheridan's Richmond Raid," in *Battles and Leaders of the Civil War*, ed. Robert Underwood Johnson and Clarence Clough Buel, 4 vols. (1887–88; reprint, New York: Yoseloff, 1956), 4:188. Grant proposed to Halleck on March 28 that Wilson be relieved from the Cavalry Bureau as soon as possible but did not inform Halleck that he wished Wilson to command a cavalry division until April 6, after Sheridan had arrived. Sheridan later claimed that it was he, rather than Grant, who selected Wilson. See *OR* 33:753, 809; Sheridan, *Personal Memoirs*, 1:352.

7. *OR* 33:862, 872, 893.

8. James H. Wilson, *Under the Old Flag*, 2 vols. (New York: Appleton, 1912), 1:362, 365–67. The shift involving Davies, Chapman, and Custer was delayed until April 17, pending Wilson's formal assumption of command. See *OR* 33:893.

9. Thomas W. Hyde, *Following the Greek Cross, Or Memories of the Sixth Army Corps* (Boston: Houghton Mifflin, 1894), 180–81; Alanson A. Haines, *History of the Fifteenth Regiment New Jersey Volunteers* (New York: Jenkins and Thomas, 1883), 133–34; *OR* 33:830; George Alfred Townsend, *General Alfred T. A. Torbert Memorial* (n.p.: Historical Society of Delaware, 1922), 28–29. The most recent effort to explain Torbert's cavalry assignment appears in A. D. Slade, *A. T. A. Torbert: Southern Gentleman in Union Blue* (Dayton, Ohio: Morningside, 1992), 85–87.

10. Stanton P. Allen, *Down in Dixie: Life in a Cavalry Regiment in the War Days* (Boston: Lothrop, 1892), 214; Wilson, *Under the Old Flag*, 1:364; Milton V. Burgess, *David Gregg: Pennsylvania Cavalryman* (State College, Pa.: Nittany Valley Offset, 1984), 99; Rodenbough, "Sheridan's Richmond Raid," 188.

11. Sheridan, *Personal Memoirs*, 1:353; *OR* 33:891–92.

12. *OR* 33:909.

13. Sheridan, *Personal Memoirs*, 1:354–55; *OR* 36(1):787.

14. Sheridan, *Personal Memoirs*, 1:355–56.

15. Ibid., 356. When he wrote his official report of the Wilderness operations, Sheridan still rankled over Meade's rejection of his suggestions. See *OR* 36(1):787.

16. *OR* 36(1):923–24; Wilson, *Under the Old Flag*, 1:378.

17. Andrew A. Humphreys, *The Virginia Campaign of '64 and '65: The Army of the Potomac and the Army of the James* (New York: Scribner's, 1883), 14; *OR* 33:1036, 36(1):853, 875, 285. Sheridan reported that he began the campaign with 10,000 men. See *OR* 36(1):787. Custer's Michigan brigade and the 2nd and 5th New York were supplied with carbines, as were scattered companies from other regiments.

18. *OR* 36(2):331–34, 365–66.

19. James H. Wilson diary, May 3, 1864, James H. Wilson Collection, Library of Congress, Washington, D.C. (repository hereafter cited as LC).

20. Ibid., May 4, 1864; Charles Chapin diary, May 4, 1864, in Civil War Miscellaneous Collection, U.S. Army Military History Institute, Carlisle, Pa. (repository hereafter cited as USAMHI); Waldo J. Clark, "At the Wilderness," *National Tribune* (Washington, D.C.), October 23, 1890. Wilson recorded in his diary that his division set out "precisely at 12 o'clock midnight" (Wilson diary, May 4, 1864). In his report, which he wrote in February 1865, he placed his departure at 1:00 A.M., and in his memoirs he claimed to have started at 9:00 on the evening of May 3. See *OR* 36(1):875; Wilson, *Under the Old Flag*, 1:379. Similar discrepancies run throughout Wilson's accounts. This essay generally follows the times in his diary.

21. OR 36(1):876; Wilson diary, May 4, 1864.

22. Henry R. Pyne, *Ride to War: The History of the First New Jersey Cavalry* (New Brunswick, N.J.: Rutgers University Press, 1961), 183–85; Nathan B. Webb diary, May 4, 1864, Nathan B. Webb Collection, William L. Clements Library, University of Michigan, Ann Arbor; Isaac H. Ressler diary, May 4, 1864, Civil War Times Illustrated Collection, USAMHI.

23. *OR* 36(1):876.

24. *OR* 36(2):390.

25. Wilson diary, May 4, 1864; Morris Schaff, *The Battle of the Wilderness* (Boston: Houghton Mifflin, 1910), 93; *OR* 36(1):876, (2):389; Chapin diary, May 4, 1864.

26. Gouverneur K. Warren to Charles Porter, Gouverneur K. Warren Collection, New York State Library, Albany, N.Y. (repository hereafter cited as NYSL); Wilson, *Under the Old Flag*, 1:379.

27. *OR* 36(1):876.

28. *OR* 36(2):378, 390.

29. *OR* 51(2):886–87.

30. *OR* 36(1):803.

31. Humphreys, *Virginia Campaign of '64 and '65*, 21, 36; Cyrus B. Comstock diary, May 4, 1864, Cyrus B. Comstock Collection, LC; *OR* 36(1):787–88, (2):375, 389, 371.

32. *OR* 36(1):876, (2):371; William B. Cary, "Opening the Fight by the 5th New

York Cav. and the First Man to Fall There," *National Tribune* (Washington, D.C.), February 1, 1912.

33. Cary, "Opening the Fight"; Louis N. Beaudry, *Historic Records of the Fifth New York Cavalry, First Ira Harris Guard* (Albany, N.Y.: S. R. Gray, 1865), 122.

34. I. J. Lichtenberg, "The Wilderness: How the 5th N.Y. Cav. Had a Hand in Opening the Fight," *National Tribune* (Washington, D.C.), September 30, 1886; Washington A. Roebling's report, Warren Collection, NYSL.

35. D. H. Robbins, "Who Opened the Fight in the Wilderness?," *National Tribune* (Washington, D.C.), May 13, 1909.

36. *OR* 36(1):886; Robbins, "Who Opened the Fight in the Wilderness?"; *OR* 36(2):885; Cary, "Opening the Fight." McIntosh's note to headquarters bears the inscription "May 5, 1864 — 11 A.M."

37. William H. Palmer to William L. Royall, May 11, 1908, in William L. Royall, *Some Reminiscences* (New York: Neale, 1909), 28; Benjamin Justice to his wife, May 4-7, 1864, Benjamin Justice Collection, Emory University Library, Atlanta, Ga.

38. Hazard Stevens, "The Sixth Corps in the Wilderness," in *Papers of the Military Historical Society of Massachusetts,* 14 vols. (Boston: Military Historical Society of Massachusetts, 1881-1918), 4:189-90.

39. Wilson diary, May 5, 1864; *OR* 36(1):876-77, 896. Chapman placed the hour at 11:00 A.M., which is far too late. Wilson's diary has been used to fix the time.

40. *OR* 36(1):897, 902-3; James Wood diary, May 5, 1864, James Wood Collection, Virginia State Library, Richmond; G. G. Benedict, *Vermont in the Civil War: A History of the Part Taken by Vermont Soldiers and Sailors in the War for the Union, 1861-5,* 2 vols. (Burlington, Vt.: Free Press Association, 1888), 2:633-34.

41. *OR* 36(1):897. The fighting is detailed from Rosser's perspective in William N. McDonald, *A History of the Laurel Brigade: Originally the Ashby Cavalry of the Army of Northern Virginia and Chew's Battery* (Baltimore: Sun Job Printing Office, 1907), 225-27, and Frank M. Myers, *The Comanches: A History of White's Battalion Virginia Cavalry, Laurel Brigade, Hampton Division, A.N.V., C.S.A.* (Baltimore: Kelly, Piet, 1871), 258-63.

42. Wilson, *Under the Old Flag,* 1:381; Robert P. Chew's report, Lewis Leigh Collection, USAMHI; George M. Neese, *Three Years in the Confederate Horse Artillery* (New York: Neale, 1911), 259-60.

43. Wilson, *Under the Old Flag,* 1:382-83; *OR* 36(1):877.

44. W. A. Rodgers, "The 18th Pa. Cav. Had Lively Work in the Mine Run Fight," *National Tribune* (Washington, D.C.), May 27, 1897; McDonald, *History of the Laurel Brigade,* 226-27; Erastus Blakeslee's report, August 4, 1864, in *Annual Report of the Adjutant-General of the State of Connecticut for the Year Ending March 31, 1865* (New Haven: Carrington, Hotchkiss, 1865), 411; Adjutant General of Connecticut, *Record of Service of Connecticut Men in the Army and Navy of the United States During the War of the Rebellion* (Hartford: Case, Lockwood and Brainard, 1889), 57.

45. *OR* 36(1):803; Slade, *A. T. A. Torbert,* 95; Webb diary, May 5, 1864.

46. *OR* 36(1):788, (2):427, 429.

47. Pyne, *Ride to War,* 186; *OR* 36(1):860; N. D. Preston, *History of the Tenth*

Regiment of Cavalry, New York State Volunteers (New York: Appleton, 1892), 170–71.

48. *OR* 36(1):860; Pyne, *Ride to War*, 187–88; Well A. Bushnell, "Memoirs," 263, Palmer Regimental Papers, Western Reserve Historical Society, Cleveland, Ohio. A soldier in the 1st Pennsylvania Cavalry claimed that his regiment also participated in the countercharge and drove the Confederates "back across the Po River about three miles." See Thompson A. Snyder, "Recollections of Four Years with the Union Cavalry, 1861–1865," Fredericksburg and Spotsylvania National Military Park Library, Fredericksburg, Va.

49. William P. Lloyd, *History of the First Regiment Pennsylvania Reserve Cavalry* (Philadelphia: King and Baird, 1864), 90–91; Luther W. Hopkins, *From Bull Run to Appomattox* (Baltimore: Fleet-McGinley, 1914), 145–48; J. D. Ferguson, "Memoranda of the Itinerary and Operations of Major General Fitz Lee's Cavalry Division of the Army of Northern Virginia from May 4th 1864 to October 15th 1864, inclusive," Thomas T. Munford Collection, William R. Perkins Library, Duke University, Durham, N.C.; Fitzhugh Lee's report, Eleanor S. Brockenbrough Library, Museum of the Confederacy, Richmond, Va. A superb attempt to make sense of the fighting below Todd's Tavern is an unpublished manuscript by Bryce Suderow, "Todd's Tavern, Va., May 5–8, 1864: Sheridan vs. Stuart, the Opening Round," 2–3.

50. "The Second Virginia Cavalry in the Late Fights," Richmond *Sentinel*, May 21, 1864; William R. Carter diary, May 5, 1864, William R. Carter Collection, Hampden-Sydney College Library, Hampden-Sydney, Va.; Wilson, *Under the Old Flag*, 1:385; Rodgers, "18th Pa. Cav. Had Lively Work."

51. *OR* 36(2):428.

52. Wilson, *Under the Old Flag*, 1:384–85. Lomax was busy fighting Gregg on the Brock Road near Alsop's. Part of Gordon's brigade patrolled the Rapidan fords, but most of the unit did not reach the battlefield until May 6. See "Berringer's N.C. Brigade of Cavalry," Raleigh (N.C.) *Daily Confederate*, February 22, 1865. There is no question that Rosser's was the only Confederate brigade opposing Wilson. See Wade Hampton's report, Wade Hampton Collection, South Caroliniana Library, University of South Carolina, Columbia, and Theodore Sanford Garnett, *Riding with Stuart: Reminiscences of an Aide-de-Camp*, ed. Robert J. Trout (Shippensburg, Pa.: White Mane, 1994), 52–53.

53. *OR* 36(1):816, 877, 833. Chapman retired to Piney Branch Church, and Wilson's other division under Mcintosh camped at Alrich's. See *OR* 36(1):897, 877–78.

54. *OR* 36(1):816.

55. "The Great Cavalry Expedition Through Rebel Lines," *New York Herald*, May 17, 1864; James D. Rowe, "Reminiscences," Michigan Historical Collections, Bentley Historical Library, University of Michigan, Ann Arbor; James H. Kidd, *Personal Recollections of a Cavalryman with Custer's Michigan Cavalry Brigade in the Civil War* (Ionia, Mich.: Sentinel, 1908), 265–66.

56. *OR* 36(1):827, 833; Kidd, *Personal Recollections*, 269–71.

57. William Preston Chew's report, Leigh Collection, USAMHI; John J. Shoemaker, *Shoemaker's Battery: Stuart Horse Artillery, Pelham's Battalion, Army of Northern Virginia* (1908; reprint, Gaithersburg, Md.: Butternut Press, n.d.),

70–71; McDonald, *History of the Laurel Brigade*, 234–37; Garnett, *Riding with Stuart*, 54.

58. *OR* 36(1):325.

59. Ferguson, "Memoranda of the Itinerary and Operations"; Preston, *History of the Tenth Regiment*, 171; Snyder, "Recollections of Four Years"; *OR* 36(1):867; Tobie, *History of the First Maine Cavalry*, 242; Ressler diary, May 6, 1864.

60. *OR* 36(1):466–67, 470.

61. *OR* 36(1):788; Sheridan, *Personal Memoirs*, 1:362–63.

62. Sheridan, *Personal Memoirs*, 1:347; Starr, *Union Cavalry in the Civil War*, 2:82. For Wilson's casualties, see "Nominal List of Casualties in the 3d Division Cavalry Corps from May 4th to June 26th 1864," RG 94, entry 653, Office of the Adjutant General, Army Corps, Army, and Departmental Casualty Lists, Civil War, National Archives, Washington, D.C. Custer's casualties are in the 1st Brigade, 1st Division Casualty reports, RG 94, entry 652—Office of the Adjutant General, Regimental Casualty Lists, Civil War, box 12, National Archives. The James Wood diary, May 5, 1864, lists 173 of Rosser's men killed and wounded on the fifth; Rosser estimated his loss at 146 in the Philadelphia *Weekly Times*, April 19, 1884. For Rosser's losses on May 6, see *OR* 51:824.

PETER S. CARMICHAEL

Escaping the Shadow of Gettysburg

RICHARD S. EWELL AND AMBROSE POWELL HILL

AT THE WILDERNESS

T he reputations of Richard Stoddert Ewell and Ambrose Powell Hill have never recovered from Confederate defeat at Gettysburg. Many historians have argued that both men followed poor performances during their debuts in corps command at Gettysburg with a similar pattern of inept behavior for the remainder of the war.[1] Such an interpretation focuses too heavily on personality traits, minimizing the specific and unique circumstances surrounding the battles after July 1863 and turning Ewell and Hill into scapegoats for the Army of Northern Virginia's declining performance in the last two years of the war. Some of the harshest and least justified post-Gettysburg criticism of Ewell and Hill concerns their actions at the Wilderness. Both men rendered sound service on May 5–6, 1864, despite being hampered by questionable decisions and flawed instructions from army headquarters. R. E. Lee rather than his two subordinates should be the primary focus for those seeking to understand problems of Confederate high command during the first clash of the Overland campaign.

Secondary literature on the Wilderness generally portrays Lee as an officer who could not trust Hill and Ewell to carry out his wishes. According to this interpretation, their miscues during the battle reinforced misgivings Lee had entertained about both men since Gettysburg. With few exceptions, historians have criticized Hill for refusing to entrench his divisions on the evening of May 5, a costly mistake that almost resulted in destruction of the Confederate right flank the following morning. Scholars have been even less charitable to Richard Ewell at the Wilderness. They

Lt. Gen. Ambrose Powell Hill.
Robert Underwood Johnson and
Clarence Clough Buel, eds., Battles
and Leaders of the Civil War, *4 vols.*
(New York: Century, 1887–88), 2:626

charge him with squandering one of the greatest offensive opportunities ever presented to the Army of Northern Virginia. Instead of aggressively striking the enemy's exposed right flank on the morning of May 6, as his subordinate John B. Gordon had suggested, Ewell could not reach a decision. Only when Lee made a personal appeal, runs the common argument, did Ewell finally attack. Ewell's indecision wasted precious hours of daylight and prevented the Confederates from reaping the full rewards of the assault.

In reaching critical assessments of Hill on the evening of May 5 and of Ewell on May 6, most historians have embraced the memoirs of Henry Heth and John B. Gordon.[2] Both Heth and Gordon relied on their pens to protect their reputations at the expense of immediate superiors. Because of these false accounts many scholars have not fully appreciated that Hill and Ewell confronted difficult circumstances at the Wilderness arising from Lee's poor decisions from the onset of the campaign. Lee not only reacted slowly to the Federal advance across the Rapidan River on May 4, but he compounded this error by also issuing a series of ambiguous, often contradictory orders for the next two days. Ewell and Hill nevertheless displayed solid leadership in some of the most intense fighting the army ever witnessed. Neither officer deserves censure for his performance in the Wilderness.

Lt. Gen. Richard Stoddert Ewell.
Francis Trevelyan Miller, ed., The
Photographic History of the Civil War,
10 vols. (New York: Review of Reviews,
1911), 10:245

Lee's comments after the war have led historians to believe Ewell and Hill undermined his designs at the Wilderness. In his conversation with William Preston Johnston at Washington College in 1868, the general complained that "Ewell showed vacillation that prevented him from getting all out of his troops he might." "If Jackson had been alive and there," Lee believed "he would have crushed the enemy." Lee also wondered what could have been accomplished if the Third Corps had been prepared to resist the enemy on the morning of May 6. He claimed that the breakdown of Hill's troops dashed any chance to flank the enemy immediately with units from James Longstreet's First Corps. This incident, in fact, badly shook the commanding general's confidence in his men. Lee admitted to Johnston that "he always felt afraid when going to attack after" the Wilderness.[3] It is significant that only Gordon and Heth voiced similar complaints against Ewell and Hill, even though ex-Confederates typically entered any literary fray to help distance Lee from the supposed wrongdoing of his subordinates.[4]

The questionable character of Gordon's and Heth's accounts was lost on Douglas Southall Freeman, who relied on both narratives to condemn Ewell and Hill. In his popular and important history of the Army of Northern Virginia, Freeman suggested that Ewell vacillated on May 6 until Lee ordered the attack. The desperate pleas of Gordon, wrote Freeman, convinced the Confederate chieftain to dismiss the reservations of Ewell's subordinate Jubal A. Early and to demand that the Second Corps commander take the offensive. Freeman concluded that "Ewell's record in the

Maj. Gen. Henry Heth.
Francis Trevelyan Miller, ed., The
Photographic History of the Civil War,
10 vols. (New York: Review of Reviews,
1911), 10:109

Wilderness might have prompted the patient Lee to make the same criticism he subsequently passed on that officer's action at Gettysburg—that he could not get Ewell to act with decision." Hill fared no better in Freeman's narrative. Relying exclusively on Heth's memoirs, Freeman castigated Hill for allowing his exhausted soldiers to sleep the night of May 5 without entrenching, a decision that "might have been fatal." Freeman averred that Lee wanted Hill to take proper precautions "to protect the men from a sudden onslaught." In Freeman's analysis of the Wilderness, Ewell and Hill shoulder responsibility for these two Confederate debacles while Lee escapes unscathed.[5]

This interpretation has proved enduring and influential. In *Lee's Last Campaign: The Story of Lee and His Men against Grant, 1864,* Clifford Dowdey considered Ewell's behavior on May 6 "a curious re-enactment of the dusk scene on the first day at Gettysburg." Dowdey asserted that Ewell once again "had suffered paralysis of the will at the necessity of making a decision, and divorced his corps from the actions of the army."[6] Deviating from Freeman in one critical aspect, Dowdey exposed serious fallacies in Heth's memoirs. With the exception of James I. Robertson Jr. historians generally have overlooked this important contribution of *Lee's Last Campaign.* William Woods Hassler, Noah Andre Trudeau, Robert Garth Scott, and Gary W. Gallagher, among others, have constructed cases against Hill upon the foundation of Heth's memoirs.[7]

Although Dowdey absolved the Third Corps commander of responsibility for the near disaster on May 6, he refused to hold anyone else accountable for the confused state of Hill's troops that morning. In the Freeman tradition he failed to connect Lee to command breakdowns at the tactical level. "A curious blank exists about responsibility for the unpreparedness of Wilcox's and Heth's divisions for receiving attack," Dowdey observed. "With all the versions of and the apologies about leaving the men 'undisturbed' during the night, there is total silence regarding the failure to arouse them at first light."[8]

Most of the scholarship on Gordon's flank attack on May 6 also fails to implicate Lee. Ewell is the main culprit for Confederate blundering on the army's left. In one of the first monographs devoted to the Wilderness, Edward Steere suggested that if Ewell had "played a role in this affair similar to that of Longstreet in the flank movement on the Confederate right, the results, if Gordon's view of the situation is sound, would have been as spectacular as those achieved by Longstreet." Gary Gallagher offered a harsher critique of Ewell in a 1990 article on the high command of Lee's army. He asserted that Ewell "managed well enough on May 5, but on the sixth he experienced indecision reminiscent of July 1 at Gettysburg." Gallagher thought Lee correct in blaming "Ewell rather than Early for the failure to attack sooner—Early acted somewhat arrogantly, to be sure, but Ewell was the corps commander and held the final authority." In the most recent book on the Wilderness, Gordon C. Rhea maintains that "Ewell's orders for the sixth had been discretionary; he was to sever the Army of the Potomac from its base or support Hill. He failed to do either, and he deferred Gordon's proposed flanking movement until too late. Ewell lacked the aggressive spirit that Lee considered essential to success."[9]

In reaching this critical appraisal of Ewell, it should be noted that Steere, Trudeau, Gallagher, and Rhea use Gordon's *Reminiscences of the Civil War* with extreme caution. All of these historians basically agree that Ewell probably discussed the proposed attack on the afternoon of May 6 with Lee, and that Gordon's recommendations did not compel Lee to take action against the Second Corps commander. Rhea reflects the current consensus on this issue, writing that "in all likelihood, Gordon was not present" when Ewell discussed the flank attack with Lee. "In later years, the Georgian presumably embellished the story, inflating his own involvement and taking a slap at his professed antagonist, Early, by having Lee dramatically overrule Early's objections. Elsewhere in his

Brig. Gen. John Brown Gordon.
Robert Underwood Johnson and
Clarence Clough Buel, eds., Battles
and Leaders of the Civil War, *4 vols.*
(New York: Century, 1887–88), 4:525

Reminiscences, Gordon performed similar manipulations, building around a kernel of truth a dramatic story featuring himself as the hero."[10]

A number of factors unrelated to the Wilderness have made Ewell vulnerable to criticism and prevented historians from reaching a fair assessment of his actions on May 5–6, 1864. Ewell's replacing Stonewall Jackson as commander of the Second Corps led to inevitable comparisons between the two men. John B. Gordon, for example, believed that the "indisputable facts which made the situation at Gettysburg and in the Wilderness strikingly similar" conclusively proved that if Jackson rather than Ewell had been in control, the Confederacy would not have "died."[11] While it is true that Ewell never matched Stonewall's brilliance, such comparisons are invidious and counterproductive. During Jackson's tenure at the helm of the Second Corps, the Army of Northern Virginia fought at the pinnacle of its strength, morale, and leadership while facing Union generals of questionable ability. When Ewell held corps command, his troops were neither sufficient in number nor equal in quality to Jackson's. Confronting a formidable foe such as Grant under these conditions made the feats of 1862 and 1863 unattainable.

Ewell's peculiar appearance and eccentric behavior also have been used to prove he could not handle a crisis. Richard Taylor's classic description of him as a chirping woodcock captivated later writers who resisted examining Ewell as a complex person.[12] He has been portrayed in caricature—neurotic, highly excitable, and uninspiring in battle. In the most extreme example of this theme, Herman Hattaway and Archer Jones observed in *How the North Won* that "Ewell may have had severe mental problems. Legends persist that he sometimes hallucinated that he *was* a bird. For hours at a time he would sit in his tent softly chirping and, at mealtimes, he would accept only sunflower seeds or grains of wheat."[13]

Ewell's marriage to the widow Lizinka Brown marked a turning point in his military career. In the estimation of many contemporaries and even some historians, she was an intelligent, ambitious, outspoken woman who ruled her husband like a dictator. The general's staff sometimes wondered whom they actually served. Col. James Conner observed in the fall of 1863 that Lizinka "manages everything from the General's affairs down to the courier's, who carries his dispatches. All say they are under petticoat government." Division commander Robert E. Rodes once asked who commanded the Second Corps—the Widow Brown, Ewell, or chief of staff Sandie Pendleton. He hoped that it was Pendleton. Rodes's sarcasm reveals an assumption popularly held within the army, and especially among Ewell's subordinates, that a man married to a "strong-minded" woman would suddenly lose his aggressive edge in battle. Summing up the dominant opinion of the army, one officer in the Second Corps confided to his diary that "from a military point of view the addition of the wife did not compensate for the loss of the leg. We were of the opinion that Ewell was not the same soldier he had been when he was a whole man—and a single one."[14]

Just as Ewell's quirky behavior has made it difficult for historians to assess fairly his military abilities, so also have many historians made too much of Powell Hill's impetuous nature, high-strung personality, and repeated illnesses. One scholar recently has written that Hill's "strength had held while he headed a division, but elevation to corps command brought a rapid deterioration. The coincidence of Hill's physical decline and his unsuccessful struggle to master his new position suggested a psychological component to his malaise."[15] There is no doubt that Hill's weak constitution and his prickly personality interfered with his duties from time to time, but these factors did not define him as an officer.

In some instances Hill's record as a corps commander deservedly has come under fire. He rashly initiated the first day's fighting at Gettysburg and then essentially disappeared for the rest of the battle. Gary Gallagher surmises that "Lee's assignment of thousands of Hill's troops to Longstreet for the climactic assault strongly suggested a lack of confidence in 'Little Powell.'" Hill did not alleviate Lee's concerns when he launched a bloody attack the following October at Bristoe Station. According to Jedediah Hotchkiss, a bitter Lee "met Hill with [a] stern rebuke for his imprudence, then sadly directed him to gather his wounded and bury his dead." Most historians are in agreement with James I. Robertson Jr. that "Hill would never quite master that transition" to corps command.[16] Such an interpretation, however, overlooks Hill's growth as a senior officer. At the Wilderness and during the siege of Petersburg, he neither exhibited leadership similar to that at Gettysburg and Bristoe Station nor showed bad judgment because of declining health or an overdeveloped sense of honor.[17]

There is no question that Lee entertained doubts about Ewell and Hill as the Federals prepared for the spring offensive of 1864. Neither officer had demonstrated since Gettysburg that he was capable of corps command. Bristoe Station especially had damaged Hill's reputation. Ewell's declining health also troubled Lee, who hinted in the fall of 1863 that the Second Corps commander should consider a leave of absence.[18] Although the commanding general expressed doubts about both men and recognized they needed close supervision, he did not alter his supervisory style with either officer in the battles against Grant. From the inception of the campaign, Lee issued discretionary orders that muted the aggressive intentions of his original designs. He compounded this error by reacting slowly to the Federal movement toward the Rapidan River, a mistake that placed Ewell and Hill in a desperate situation on May 5.

It is difficult to explain why Lee was not better prepared at the opening of the Overland campaign. When he and his subordinates stood on Clark's Mountain on May 2 to observe Federal activity around Culpeper, the commanding general suggested "that the enemy would cross by some of the fords below us," probably Germanna or Ely's. He based his accurate prophecy on recent intelligence and a sound reading of Grant's dispositions. The addition of Ambrose E. Burnside's Ninth Corps to the Army of the Potomac on May 1 alerted the Confederate high command that the most serious Federal advance would emanate from Culpeper. Richmond was not in immediate danger.[19]

Even though Lee had decided at least tentatively by May 2 that Grant's opening move would be toward the Confederate right, he did not shift his army toward the endangered area of the Rapidan line until two days later. Allowing his troops to remain in their quarters on May 3 was one of Lee's greatest military blunders. That became the lost day for the

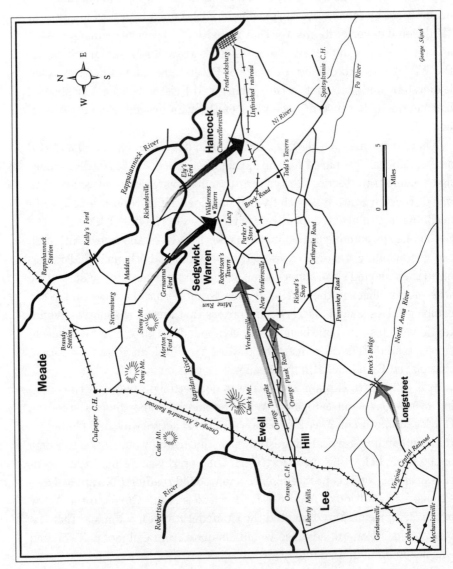

Movements toward the Wilderness battlefield, May 4–5, 1864.

Army of Northern Virginia, preventing the Confederates from exploiting the scattered condition of Grant's army on May 4–5. Longstreet's First Corps was encamped at Mechanicsville far behind the Confederate left, a full thirty-three miles from the battlefield by air and forty-three by the roads. At least a day's march stood between Lee's "Old War Horse" and the Rapidan River. If Hill and Ewell needed support, Longstreet's veterans would not be able to provide it quickly.[20]

The Confederacy's finest artillerist, Edward Porter Alexander of the First Corps, considered Lee's decision to keep Longstreet's men at Mechanicsville almost "fatal." In his personal memoirs Alexander could not understand why "Confederate history has heretofore passed over the matter in silence, as if it were one of no consequence." He "always believed it to have been one of those small matters upon which, finally, hung very great & important events." Lee might have been able to achieve decisive results on May 5 if all eight divisions had been on the field. Instead he greeted the Federals with only five. "The first day, naturally, offered us far the greatest chances," Alexander asserted. "Grant's army was not all in hand, & had no time to make breastworks. . . . We had here the one rare chance of the whole campaign to involve it in a panic such as ruined Hooker on the same ground."[21]

Lee opened the campaign cautiously because he wanted to protect the railhead at Gordonsville. Yet he could have nudged Longstreet's troops at least a few miles to the northeast on May 3. This oversight is simply unexplainable and inexcusable. Lee routinely had taken far greater risks. "Indeed in view of the great probabilities that Grant would move upon our right flank very early in May," Alexander opined, "it does not seem that there would have been any serious difficulty in having both Hill & Ewell out of their winter camps and extended a few miles in that direction & Longstreet's corps even as far down as Todd's Tavern." Once Lee received definite confirmation that Grant had crossed the Rapidan at Germanna and Ely's fords on May 4, he did not put his troops into motion until noon of that same day. It seems that the Confederate chieftain measured his response on the premise that Grant would move slowly through the Wilderness. "Of all the maneuvers Lee had made on the hazard of guessing the enemy's intention," reflected Clifford Dowdey, "he had never planned a movement when a wrong guess involved such finality."[22]

Lee wanted to trap the Federals in the Wilderness as he had a year earlier during the Chancellorsville campaign. The region's dense second growth effectively nullified the enemy's superior numbers and artillery. He could not allow the Federals to escape to the southeast, where high, open ground would enable Grant to dictate the terms of battle. Trapping the Union general in his favorite hunting grounds, however, posed a serious dilemma for Lee. If Grant mounted a rapid march through the Wilderness, the lead elements of the Army of the Potomac would safely exit the forests by May 5. Lee feared such a scenario but could not rush into a general engagement that day without imperiling his entire army. Only the Second Corps and two divisions of the Third were at hand, some 25,000 to 30,000 infantry (Richard H. Anderson's division of Hill's corps had been left behind at Orange Court House to guard the river). Longstreet remained a day's march away. The odds were stacked against Ewell and Hill, who had to contend with ten divisions of the Army of the Potomac.[23]

Lee's slow start had put his subordinates in a bad position that he never fully corrected. The commanding general rode with the Third Corps along the Orange Plank Road on the morning of May 5, probably issuing verbal instructions to Powell Hill. Written orders went to Ewell, whose Second Corps advanced along a parallel route to the north astride the Orange Turnpike. From the night of the fourth to the morning of the fifth, Ewell received a string of ambiguous, often contradictory instructions regarding terms for engaging the enemy. Never had Lee seemed so unsure about how to bring the Federals to bay. He vacillated between two courses of action: on one hand he wanted to seize the initiative and hit Grant's flank while the Federals were bogged down in the Wilderness, but on the other he did not want his scattered troops to be lured into a major engagement.

The two objectives were incompatible. How could Lee hope to bring Grant's columns to a halt in the Wilderness when he explicitly stated that he planned to retire to the Mine Run works if the Federals advanced westward? His instructions to Ewell on the evening of May 4 hinted at the conflicting goals for the first day's fighting: "If the enemy moves down the river, he [Lee] wishes to push on after him. If he comes this way, we will take our old line. The general's desire is to bring him to battle as soon now as possible." It seems that Ewell paid closest attention to the last sentence of Lee's directive. In a conversation with artillerist Robert Stiles, Ewell remarked that his orders were the kind he preferred—"to go right down the plank road and strike the enemy wherever I find him."[24]

By the early morning hours of May 5 the last thing Lee wanted was Ewell rushing down the turnpike to start a fight with Grant. Realization that Longstreet would not reach the battlefield before nightfall must have inspired this sudden caution. In one of the first dispatches of the day, Lee stressed that Ewell should "occupy lines at Mine Run" if pressed by Grant. Between 8:00 and 9:00 Ewell received similar instructions through his stepson and staff officer, Campbell Brown. In his meeting with Lee, Brown listened as the commanding general said that Ewell was "not to advance too fast, for fear of getting entangled with the enemy while still in advance & out of reach of Hill." Brown conveyed to Ewell Lee's desire to avoid "a general engagement" until "Longstreet *cd* come up (which *wd* hardly be much before night)." "If the enemy advanced & showed a willingness to fight," Brown believed that Lee "preferred falling back to our old position at Mine Run." "Above all," the staff officer added, "Gen. E. was not to get his troops entangled, so as to be unable to disengage them, in case the enemy were in force." At 11:00 Ewell's chief of staff, Alexander S. "Sandie" Pendleton, reported from Lee "substantially the same instructions as before."[25]

Prudence dictated that Lee follow such a course. He worried about the dispersed state of his army and the diverging paths of the Second and Third Corps. The turnpike and Plank Road moved away from each other as they entered the Wilderness, leaving a dangerous gap of almost three miles separating the two corps. Lee had not anticipated this troubling development, which rendered cooperation between the two wings of his army virtually impossible. In the end Lee wanted neither to launch an offensive movement nor to wage a defensive battle with the five divisions of Ewell and Hill on May 5. The Confederates on the turnpike and Plank Road were to perform a reconnaissance in force, avoiding battle if possible, until Longstreet arrived to launch a concentrated attack.[26]

The idea of a reconnaissance in force may have been sound, but Lee's repeated warnings to retire to the old Confederate works at Mine Run transmitted mixed signals to Ewell. Was the Second Corps commander to hold his ground and wait for Longstreet's arrival, or should he fall back to Mine Run if Grant made a quick offensive thrust? Ewell reasonably concluded that Lee was willing to abandon the Wilderness for the Mine Run line if the Federals suddenly became aggressive. Yet Lee later claimed that he had no intention of giving ground to Grant. Confusion over this issue resulted in the first Confederate crisis of the day.

It was close to 11:00 when Ewell's troops made contact with Federals near the Saunders's field. Ewell immediately halted so as not to outdistance Hill's column or provoke a major battle. John M. Jones's brigade covered the deployment of the rest of the corps while James A. Walker's Stonewall Brigade inspected the ground north of the turnpike along the Spotswood Road. Choosing not to deploy his entire corps in battle formation, Ewell pursued a cautious course that afforded maximum flexibility. Depending on circumstances, he could resume the advance quickly, hold his ground, or return to Mine Run. As his troops readied themselves for battle, he reminded his brigade commanders "not to allow themselves to become involved, but to fall back slowly if pressed." [27]

About 1:00 the Union Fifth Corps surprised Jones's regiments with a well-directed attack against the Confederate right flank. The Virginians panicked and collapsed upon Cullen A. Battle's brigade resting a few hundred yards to the rear. The ranks of both units became intermingled when an officer gave the order "Fall back to Mine Run." This added to the confusion as some of Battle's regiments pulled out of line and started to retire. Ewell's alert reaction averted disaster. He quickly stabilized the line with reinforcements, personally rallied stragglers, and exhorted his men to hold their positions. Lee later told Campbell Brown that he never intended for the Second Corps to fall back to the Mine Run trenches. His written dispatches undermine this assertion, however, and officers commanding at the brigade level assumed they were to retire westward in the face of Union pressure—a perception that nearly resulted in their undoing. Campbell Brown later wrote that "I don't believe these Brigades *wd* so easily have been broken had it not been for the general understanding that we were to retire to Mine Run if attacked in force." [28] Lee's inability to dictate a coherent course of action partially accounts for the turmoil among the Confederate troops at the Saunders's field.

For the remainder of the afternoon Ewell orchestrated a magnificent defense. He seemed to anticipate each Federal thrust, adeptly shifting his troops north of the turnpike to repel the final Union attacks of the day. Even though most of his approximately 14,000 men lacked time to build breastworks and fought without proper artillery support, they successfully overcame at least two-to-one odds in repulsing portions of the Union Fifth and Sixth Corps. Moreover, Ewell fought the battle in isolation from the rest of the army and his commanding general. Despite conflicting messages from headquarters, "Old Baldy" managed to fulfill Lee's wishes—he stood his ground without escalating the fighting by a reckless offensive act. Many of Ewell's contemporaries recognized his skillfulness on May 5, among them Porter Alexander, who wrote that "dear, glorious, old, one-legged Ewell, with his bald head, & his big bright eyes, & his long nose . . . , sat back & not only whipped everything that attacked him but he even sallied out on some rash ones & captured two guns & quite a lot of prisoners." The most recent study of the battle compliments Ewell as "the real hero" on the Confederate left who "executed his discretionary assignment to perfection." [29]

While Ewell's men spent a trying day on the turnpike, Hill's two divi-

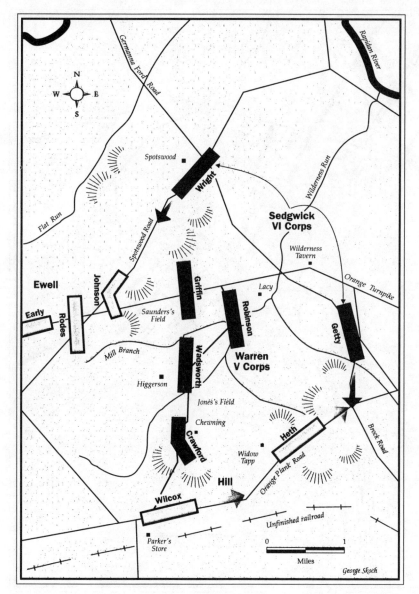

Ewell and Hill engage the Federals, May 5, 1864.

sions endured a far more serious crisis on the Plank Road. It is difficult to
determine what Lee proposed to Hill on the morning of May 5. He probably issued his instructions verbally. Written reports from Hill and Lee
for the Wilderness have never surfaced. Most likely Lee emphasized to
Hill, as he had to Ewell, the importance of avoiding a major battle until
Longstreet arrived. If Lee wanted Hill to act decisively on May 5, he could
have ordered his subordinate to secure the intersection of the Brock and

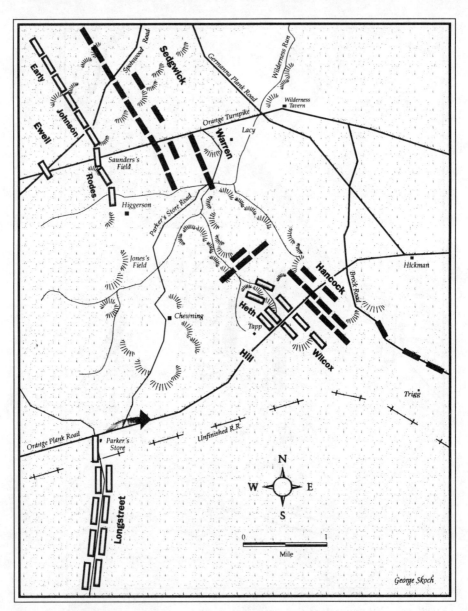

Ewell and Hill on May 6, 1864.

Plank roads. Hill's soldiers had reached Widow Tapp's field no later than 11:00 in the morning. An hour passed before Federals reached that critical juncture, and in the meantime Heth could have covered the mile to the Brock Road. Union infantry to the north and Federal cavalry to the east, however, dictated that Lee show restraint. A rapid movement toward the Brock Road might arouse the entire Army of the Potomac. Lee's failure to secure the important thoroughfare should be viewed as consistent with his sensible decision to avoid a general engagement on May 5 rather than as a missed Confederate opportunity.[30]

Just as Ewell's forced reconnaissance had evolved into a full-scale fight, Heth's division also was drawn into a fierce battle. His 6,500 men rested a few hundred yards west of the Brock Road, dangerously close to the enemy's lines. Before the Federals delivered their attack, Lee's right flank had been stretched to its virtual breaking point. The two- to three-mile gap that yawned between the two corps invited disaster the entire day. Lee directed Hill's other division, commanded by Cadmus M. Wilcox, to fill the Confederate center. While Wilcox's men marched north of the Plank Road to link with Ewell, some 17,000 soldiers, mostly from the Union Second Corps, pounded Heth's thin formations in a series of uncoordinated attacks that commenced at 3:00. Two hours later another pair of Union divisions entered the fray, giving the Federals 33,000 and odds of fifty to one against Heth's lone division.[31] Lee's permitting Longstreet to remain at Mechanicsville on May 3 had brought the Army of Northern Virginia to its greatest crisis since Antietam.

Lee realized that Heth could not hold for long. He recalled Wilcox, whose troops hurried to the Plank Road, where they delivered a fierce counterattack. This slowed the Federals temporarily, but they continued to drive Hill's soldiers back toward Widow Tapp's field. Only darkness saved the Confederates from destruction. Still, "Little Powell's" two divisions had fought sublimely. Few troops in the Army of Northern Virginia exhibited more resolve and determination. Shortly after the battle a North Carolinian wrote home that "Heth[']s & Wilcox Divisions were highly compliment[ed] for their unparalleled defense by every body day before yesterday. I heard one of Genl Lee's Staff say that such a defense was [never] recorded." Hill deserves the lion's share of the credit. Like Ewell, he made his presence felt among the troops and masterfully took advantage of the terrain while using his reserves to keep the Federals off balance. Hill's most recent biographer calls the first day's fighting in the Wilderness "his most brilliant as a corps commander."[32]

The night of May 5–6 ranks among the most controversial in the annals of the Army of Northern Virginia. That evening Hill's exhausted soldiers collapsed on the ground. Brigades, regiments, and companies lost any semblance of organization, leaving ragged Confederate battle lines disconnected and facing a variety directions. One of Hill's soldiers recalled that "none of the brigades seemed to be in line—some regiments isolated entirely from their brigades—in fact, no line at all, but just as they had fought."[33] If Hill's battered formations were not properly aligned by morning, the badly outnumbered Confederates would be doomed.

In his memoirs Heth contends that he pleaded with Hill on three different occasions to reform the troops into a cohesive, unified front. Sitting on a camp stool near his fire and hunched over with sickness, Hill initially assured his subordinate that "Longstreet will be up in a few hours. He will form in your front." Heth recalled that Hill promised that "your division" will not "do any fighting tomorrow, the men have been marching and fighting all day and are tired. I do not wish them disturbed." When Heth approached his superior to make his case the third and final time, Hill erupted: "D—— it, Heth, I don't want to hear any more about it; the men shall not be disturbed." "The only excuse I make for Hill," Heth wrote in subtle accusation, "is that he was sick." Undeterred, Heth claimed that he "hunted" for General Lee's headquarters for one hour "but could not find it."[34]

Evidently writing with intent to absolve himself and Lee of blame for the near rout of the Third Corps on May 6, Heth crafted an account that lacks credibility at crucial points. Why he could not locate Lee is a mystery. The commanding general's tent stood a few hundred yards behind Heth's own lines in Widow Tapp's field, and there seems to be no obvious explanation for his inability to make a case to Lee. Although Heth correctly claimed that he and Wilcox met with Hill to discuss the condition of their lines, he failed to mention that Lee believed Longstreet would reach the field by morning and ordered Hill to let the men rest. In fact Cadmus Wilcox's recollection of events contradicted Heth's story. Wilcox remembered going "to General Lee's tent" about 9:00 to suggest that "a skirmish line be left where the front then was, [and] the troops retired a short distance." Before Wilcox made his recommendation, Lee informed him that Anderson and "Longstreet will be up" and that Hill's two battered divisions "will be relieved before day." Once Lee had made these assurances, Wilcox thought it unnecessary to offer his suggestions.[35]

While on the surface it appears that Hill did not fulfill his duties energetically, he almost certainly was trying to abide by his commander's instructions. Hill privately disagreed with Lee's orders. Third Corps chief of staff William Palmer remembered that Hill agonized about the irregularity of his lines for most of the evening, finally deciding to search for Lee sometime after midnight. When he found the general and asked for permission to reorganize his troops, Lee reiterated his original orders to let the men rest. His intransigence made sleep impossible for Hill and his staff, recalled Palmer, "for we knew that at the first blush of the morning the turning attack on our right would open with overwhelming numbers, and, unsupported, the men must give way."[36]

Lee's refusal to rectify Hill's lines was a horrendous decision—maybe the worst of his career, considering he had learned shortly after 9:00 P.M. that Longstreet would arrive at sunrise rather than at the scheduled time of 1:00 A.M.[37] Simply retreating a few hundred yards to the west might have averted the rout of the Third Corps on the morning of May 6. Many of Hill's soldiers disobeyed orders and threw up a light set of works. But even construction of substantial works would have accomplished little because Union attackers stood poised to strike both of Hill's flanks. Only pulling back from its advanced position could have saved the Third Corps from disaster, and only Lee could have issued that order.

The dawn attack of the Union Second and Fifth Corps confirmed the fears of Hill and his subordinates. The Confederates offered slight resistance, not because they were whipped but because they were outflanked. A soldier in the 37th North Carolina believed that "the men were willing to fight, but had not the chance." Another man wrote that "our left flank and unformed line was rolled up as a sheet of paper would be rolled without the power of effective resistance." "If even a single brigade had changed front to the left before the enemy struck," he insisted, "they might have stemmed the tide and have stopped the rout." As the troops stampeded to the rear, they raced past some of Longstreet's soldiers, who asked Hill's veterans if they actually "belonged to General Lee's army" because they behaved "worse than Bragg's men."[38]

Although racked by illness, Hill showed tremendous resolve, frantically rallying his shattered divisions and even directing some of William T. Poague's artillerists to fire their cannon into the advancing Federals. His herculean efforts helped Lee buy time for Longstreet to reach the field. Once Longstreet stabilized the line, Hill remained ever vigilant. He organized the remnants of Wilcox's and Heth's commands, alertly moved them northward to fill the gap in Lee's center, and entrenched them on the high ground around the Chewning farm.[39] Hill had successfully united the flanks of Lee's army, one more impressive accomplishment the Third Corps could add to its Wilderness résumé.

On the Confederate left, Ewell handled his corps on May 6 competently but in less dramatic fashion than Powell Hill. The previous night Ewell had extended his troops farther north of the turnpike, sprinkled artillery along the entire line, and ordered the men to strengthen their earthworks. Even though Lee's written orders for May 6 do not survive, dispatches from the evening of May 5 provide insights into the commanding general's expectations. He wanted Ewell to sever the Federal right flank from the Germanna Ford if possible. If that could not be done, the Second Corps should support the Confederates on the Plank Road.[40]

Lee typically allowed his subordinates ample latitude. This style had worked with Jackson and Longstreet but not with Ewell, as Lee himself admitted after the war. In conversations with William Allan he expressed dissatisfaction with the "imperfect, halting way" that Ewell handled his corps during the Gettysburg campaign. If this were the case, Lee should have been more forceful with Ewell. Instead he issued unclear orders directing Ewell to cut the Federals off from Germanna Ford if it could "be done without too great a sacrifice." Such language gave the conservative Ewell just cause to maintain the defensive. When reflecting on Ewell's Wilderness record, Campbell Brown complained about the vagueness of Lee's orders. "I have frequently noticed before & have also since this occasion," he wrote, "that Gen. Lee's instructions to his Corps Comrs are of a very comprehensive & general description & frequently admit of several interpretations—in fact will allow them to do almost anything, provided only it be a *success*. They caution them particularly against failure & very frequently wind up with the injunction to 'attack whenever or wherever it can be done to advantage.'"[41]

Lee's discretionary orders for May 6 were not only too ambiguous for Ewell but also unrealistic. Ewell did not have the troops for a concentrated assault against Grant's right flank. Ordering an attack along Ewell's entire front would have been madness, requiring his soldiers to charge across rugged terrain in the face of entrenched Federals. As Grant had painfully discovered, the wasteland of the Wilderness made sustained infantry attacks virtually impossible. Also, frequent Union demonstrations pinned down the Second Corps so that Ewell could not shift units from the front to the far left flank. After the war Lee confided to William Allen that he had wanted Gordon's movement to be "a full attack in flank & intended to support it with all Ewell's corps and others if necessary, and to rout the enemy."[42]

Such a scenario borders on fantasy. Only when Robert D. Johnston's brigade arrived at 1:00 P.M. did Ewell have sufficient numbers to strike the enemy. Even then his force was too small to achieve decisive results. Lee must have known this. His high hopes might have been realized in 1862, when the army had plenty of reserves for bold maneuvering, but such an offensive stroke was not realistic in May 1864.

It is true that Ewell allowed Jubal Early to determine the course of the Second Corps on the final day of the battle. Shortly after 9:00 in the morning, when Gordon alerted Ewell to the exposed Union flank, Early had received intelligence that Burnside's Ninth Corps was moving between the river and the Confederate left flank. "Old Jube" feared a Union flanking maneuver and adamantly opposed any Confederate offensive. His men were outnumbered and had been bloodied by attacks earlier that morning. Although Ewell was intrigued by Gordon's scheme, "Early's strong personal appeals" persuaded him to call off the attack until he could examine the ground personally.[43] Ewell reasonably sided with his senior divisional commander over Gordon, who was only a brigadier. To override Early would have constituted a serious violation of military protocol, a step most officers in Ewell's position would have been unwilling to take. Prudence, not mental paralysis, characterized Ewell's decision making on May 6.

None of this is to say that the battle of the Wilderness redeems Ewell and Hill as corps commanders. Although on the whole they were mediocre lieutenant generals, the residue of defeat at Gettysburg, coupled with the self-serving words of Heth and Gordon, have made it difficult for scholars to take Ewell and Hill on their own terms. Instead of focusing on the range of choices that both officers faced at the Wilderness, armchair generals have judged Ewell and Hill by their own standards and scenarios. Because the two corps commanders miscarried these invented schemes, some historians have jumped to the conclusion that both men followed a leadership pattern reminiscent of Gettysburg. Underlying this problematic interpretation is a failure to show how Lee's command decisions largely defined his subordinates' actions at the Wilderness. Lee is even further removed from the battle's controversies because historians seldom have ascribed tactical breakdowns at the Wilderness or elsewhere in the Eastern Theater to him. In contrast, historians have excoriated Union commanders when their subordinates bungled well-laid plans, especially in the case of U. S. Grant, whose hand is seen behind every failure of the Army of the Potomac during the 1864 campaign.[44]

Ewell and Hill serve as convenient scapegoats for Confederate lost opportunities and near-disasters at the Wilderness. Not enough attention has been paid to the slow concentration of Lee's army at the beginning of the campaign that forced Ewell and Hill to fight against overwhelming numbers on May 5. Despite operating under that disadvantage, they mounted a stalwart defense and saved the Army of Northern Virginia from potential ruin. On the final day of the battle, Hill filled the critical gap in the Confederate center with his battered troops, while Ewell functioned within the parameters of Lee's instructions by keeping the Federals at bay without imperiling the army's left flank. Just as Ewell and Hill should not be turned into villains for Confederate defeat at Gettysburg, neither should they be blamed for the consequences of Lee's miscalculations and vague orders during the Wilderness campaign.

NOTES

1. On the Confederate debates surrounding Gettysburg and the Lost Cause interpretation of Richard S. Ewell and A. P. Hill in Pennsylvania, see J. William Jones and others, eds. *Southern Historical Society Papers*, 52 vols. (1876–1959; reprint with 2-vol. index, Millwood, N.Y.: Kraus, 1977–80), esp. vols. 4–6, and Thomas L. Connelly and Barbara L. Bellows, *God and General Longstreet: The Lost Cause and the Southern Mind* (Baton Rouge: Louisiana State University Press, 1982), 30–31. Ewell has particularly suffered at the hands of modern historians. For recent scholarship on Jackson that indicts Ewell for failing to seize Cemetery Hill, see Bevin Alexander, *Lost Victories: The Military Genius of Stonewall Jackson* (New York: Henry Holt, 1992), 330; Paul D. Casdorph, *Lee and Jackson: Confederate Chieftains* (New York: Paragon House, 1992), 396; and John Bowers, *Stonewall Jackson: Portrait of a Soldier* (New York: William Morrow, 1989), 356. For other critical assessments of Ewell, see Glenn Tucker, *High Tide at Gettysburg: The Campaign Pennsylvania* (Indianapolis: Bobbs-Merrill, 1958), 189; Douglas Southall Freeman, *Lee's Lieutenants: A Study in Command*, 3 vols. (New York: Scribner's, 1942–44), 3:93; and Clifford Dowdey, *Death of a Nation: The Story of Lee and His Men at Gettysburg* (New York: Knopf, 1958), 142. Critical assessments of Hill at Gettysburg include Freeman, *Lee's Lieutenants*, 3:170–71; Edwin B. Coddington, *The Gettysburg Campaign: A Study in Command* (New York: Scribner's, 1968), 273–74; Jennings C. Wise, *The Long Arm of Lee; or, The History of the Artillery of the Army of Northern Virginia, With a Brief Account of the Confederate Bureau of Ordnance*, 2 vols. (1915; reprint, Richmond, Va.: Owens, 1988), 2:615. Of late there has been a noticeable shift in the Gettysburg historiography toward Hill and Ewell, including Alan T. Nolan, "R. E. Lee and July 1 at Gettysburg," in *The First Day at Gettysburg: Essays on Confederate and Union Leadership*, ed. Gary W. Gallagher (Kent, Ohio: Kent State University Press, 1992), 22–29; Gary W. Gallagher, "Confederate Corps Leadership on the First Day at Gettysburg: A. P. Hill and Richard S. Ewell in a Difficult Debut," in Gallagher, *First Day at Gettysburg*, 30–56; and Harry W. Pfanz, *Gettysburg: Culp's Hill and Cemetery Hill* (Chapel Hill: University of North Carolina Press, 1993), 72.

2. Henry Heth, *The Memoirs of Henry Heth*, ed. James L. Morrison Jr. (Wesport, Conn.: Greenwood Press, 1974), 183–85; John B. Gordon, *Reminiscences of the Civil War* (New York: Scribner's, 1903), 243–61.

3. "Newly Found Record of Private Talks Shows . . . Lee Blamed Ewell and Longstreet for His Failure in the Wilderness," *Civil War Times Illustrated* 5 (April 1966): 5. Also see transcript of conversation between William Allan and

R. E. Lee, March 3, 1868, William Allan Papers, Southern Historical Collection, Wilson Library, University of North Carolina, Chapel Hill (repository hereafter cited as SHC).

4. On the deification of Robert E. Lee by ex-Confederates, see Thomas L. Connelly, *The Marble Man: Robert E. Lee and His Image in American Society* (New York: Knopf, 1977), and Gaines M. Foster, *Ghosts of the Confederacy: Defeat, the Lost Cause, and the Emergence of the New South* (New York: Oxford University Press, 1987).

5. Freeman, *Lee's Lieutenants*, 3:442.

6. Clifford Dowdey, *Lee's Last Campaign: The Story of Lee and His Men against Grant, 1864* (1960; reprint, New York: Barnes & Noble, 1994), 170.

7. Ibid., 127–30; William Woods Hassler, *A. P. Hill: Lee's Forgotten General* (Richmond, Va.: Garrett & Massie, 1962), 191–94; Noah Andre Trudeau, *Bloody Roads South: The Wilderness to Cold Harbor, May–June 1864* (Boston: Little, Brown, 1989), 76–77; Robert Garth Scott, *Into the Wilderness with the Army of the Potomac* (Bloomington: Indiana University Press, 1985), 105; Gary W. Gallagher, "The Army of Northern Virginia in May 1864: A Crisis of High Command," *Civil War History* 36 (June 1990): 115.

8. Dowdey, *Lee's Last Campaign*, 144.

9. Edward Steere, *The Wilderness Campaign* (New York: Bonanza, 1960), 448; Gallagher, "Army of Northern Virginia in May 1864," 113; Gordon C. Rhea, *The Battle of the Wilderness: May 5–6, 1864* (Baton Rouge: Louisiana State University Press, 1994), 444–45.

10. Rhea, *Battle of the Wilderness*, 416.

11. Gordon, *Reminiscences*, 260–61. On the importance of Jackson's legacy in the army, see Freeman, *Lee's Lieutenants*, 3:168–89.

12. Richard Taylor, *Destruction and Reconstruction: Personal Experiences of the Late War* (1879; reprint, New York: Longmans, Green, 1955), 36–37.

13. Herman Hattaway and Archer Jones, *How the North Won: A Military History of the Civil War* (Urbana: University of Illinois Press, 1983), 405.

14. James Conner, *The Letters of General James Conner, C.S.A.*, ed. Mary C. Moffet (Columbia, S.C.: State Co., 1933), 115; Randolph H. McKim, *A Soldier's Recollections; leaves from the diary of a young Confederate, with an oration on the motives and aims of the soldiers of the South* (New York: Longmans, Green, 1910), 134.

15. Rhea, *Battle of the Wilderness*, 17. For a similar interpretation, see James I. Robertson Jr., *General A. P. Hill: The Story of a Confederate Warrior* (New York: Random House, 1987).

16. Gallagher, "Army of Northern Virginia in May 1864," 106; Jedediah Hotchkiss, *Virginia* (Atlanta: Confederate Pub. Co., 1899), 426; Robertson, *General A. P. Hill*, 194.

17. Hill acquitted himself well during operations along the Weldon Railroad that included battles at Jerusalem Plank Road (June 23, 1864), Globe Tavern (August 18–19, 21, 1864), and Reams Station (August 25, 1864) and during the opening battles of Grant's Fifth Offensive near Popular Spring Church (September 20–October 2, 1864). In both campaigns he showed initiative without the

reckless aggressiveness that typified Gettysburg and Bristoe Station. See John Horn, *The Destruction of the Weldon Railroad: Deep Bottom, Globe Tavern, and Reams Station, August 14–25, 1864* (Lynchburg, Va.: H. E. Howard, 1991), and Richard J. Sommers, *Richmond Redeemed: The Siege at Petersburg* (Garden City, N.Y.: Doubleday, 1981).

18. Freeman, *Lee's Lieutenants*, 3:330.

19. U.S. War Department, *The War of the Rebellion: A Compilation of the Official Records of the Union and Confederate Armies*, 127 vols., index, and atlas (Washington, D.C.: GPO, 1880–1901), ser. 1, 36(1):1070, (2):940 (hereafter cited as *OR*).

20. Edward Porter Alexander, *Fighting for the Confederacy: The Personal Recollections of General Edward Porter Alexander*, ed. Gary W. Gallagher (Chapel Hill: University of North Carolina Press, 1989), 348–49. On Longstreet's role in the Wilderness, see Jeffry D. Wert, *General James Longstreet, the Confederacy's Most Controversial Soldier: A Biography* (New York: Simon and Schuster, 1993), 378–90, and William Garrett Piston, *Lee's Tarnished Lieutenant: James Longstreet and His Place in Southern History* (Athens: University of Georgia Press, 1987), 87–89. For less favorable critiques of Longstreet, see Freeman, *Lee's Lieutenants*, 3:355–68, and H. J. Eckenrode and Bryan Conrad, *James Longstreet: Lee's War Horse* (Chapel Hill: University of North Carolina Press, 1936), 295–318.

21. Alexander, *Fighting for the Confederacy*, 348.

22. Ibid.; Dowdey, *Lee's Last Campaign*, 54.

23. Rhea, *Battle of the Wilderness*, 87.

24. *OR* 36(2):948, 952; Robert Stiles, *Four Years under Marse Robert* (1903; reprint, Dayton, Ohio: Morningside, 1977), 245.

25. Richard S. Ewell Letter Book, box 2, folder 2, Campbell Brown–Richard S. Ewell Papers, Tennessee State Library, Nashville, Tenn. (repository hereafter cited as TSL); *OR* 36(1):1070.

26. Douglas Southall Freeman, *R. E. Lee: A Biography*, 4 vols. (New York: Scribner's, 1934–35), 3:278; Steere, *Wilderness Campaign*, 85–86.

27. *OR* 36(1):1070.

28. Cullen A. Battle, "The Third Alabama Regiment," Regimental Collection, Alabama Department of Archives and History, Montgomery; Ewell Letter Book, box 2, folder 2, TSL; *OR* 36(1):1070.

29. Alexander, *Fighting for the Confederacy*, 353; Rhea, *Battle of the Wilderness*, 252.

30. On Hill's movements to the battlefield, see Rhea, *Battle of the Wilderness*, 126–29.

31. Ibid., 194, 208.

32. Samuel Finley Harper to his father, May 6, 1864, Samuel Finley Harper Letters, North Carolina Department of Archives and History, Raleigh; Robertson, *General A. P. Hill*, 260.

33. Walter Clark, comp., *Histories of the Several Regiments and Battalions from North Carolina in the Great War, 1861-'65*, 5 vols. (1901; reprint, Wendell, N.C.: Broadfoot, 1982), 2:665 (hereafter cited as Clark, *N.C. Regiments*).

34. Heth, *Memoirs*, 184.

35. Cadmus M. Wilcox, "Lee and Grant in the Wilderness," in [A. K. McClure, ed.], *The Annals of the War Written by Leading Participants North and South. Originally Published in the Philadelphia Weekly Times* (Philadelphia: Times Pub. Co., 1879), 494–95.

36. William L. Royall, *Some Reminiscences* (New York: Neale, 1909), 30–31.

37. Rhea, *Battle of the Wilderness*, 278.

38. Clark, *N.C. Regiments*, 2:665, 1:595.

39. Rhea, *Battle of the Wilderness*, 315–16.

40. *OR* 36(2):952–53.

41. Conversation between William Allan and R. E. Lee, March 3, 1868, Allan Papers, SHC; Ewell Letter Book, box 2, folder 2, TSL.

42. Conversation between William Allan and R. E. Lee, March 3, 1868, Allan Papers, SHC.

43. Steere, *Wilderness Campaign*, 432–35; Jubal A. Early, *Lieutenant General Jubal Anderson Early, C.S.A.: Autobiographical Sketch and Narrative of the War between the States* (1912; reprint, Wilmington, N.C.: Broadfoot, 1989), 346–51.

44. The secondary literature on the battle of the Crater (July 30, 1864) reflects the historiographical trend that connects Grant to Union blundering at the tactical level. Grant and Meade's decision to rearrange the alignment of the black troops before the battle, many historians have pointed out, sealed the fate of the Union mission. Although Grant was partially to blame for the fiasco and should be criticized, rarely does Lee come under the same scrutiny. As the secondary literature on the Wilderness demonstrates, when matters went badly for the Confederates, the trickle-down effect of Lee's command decisions cannot be traced. On Grant's role at the Crater, see Bruce Catton, *A Stillness at Appomattox* (Garden City, N.Y.: Doubleday, 1953), 238–39; Freeman Cleaves, *Meade of Gettysburg* (Norman: University of Oklahoma Press, 1960), 279–83; William S. McFeely, *Grant: A Biography* (New York: Norton, 1981), 179; William Marvel, *Burnside* (Chapel Hill: University of North Carolina Press, 1991), 415–16; Noah Andre Trudeau, *The Last Citadel: Petersburg, Virginia, June 1864–April 1865* (Boston: Little, Brown, 1991), 123–27; and John Horn, *The Petersburg Campaign, June 1864–April 1865* (Conshohocken, Pa.: Combined Books, 1993), 118–19.

"Lee to the Rear,"
the Texans Cried

o back, General Lee, go back," the men of the famous Texas Brigade of the Army of Northern Virginia shouted on the morning of May 6, 1864. "We won't go forward unless you go back." The general eventually bowed to their entreaties, and his veteran soldiers lived up to their promise by advancing boldly and retrieving the army's desperate fortunes. More than one-half of them were shot within a quarter-hour while redeeming their pledge to go forward. The dramatic incident unfolded at a moment of deadly crisis in a fashion larger than life. In the aftermath the incident inevitably took on hues and dimensions even more passionate than those of that critical May dawn. After more than a century and a quarter, the "Lee-to-the-Rear" story remains one of the most notable human episodes of the war in Virginia.

The battle of the Wilderness raged for two days on two distinct fronts. Confederates thrusting eastward into the right flank of the Federal Army of the Potomac traveled on two east-west corridors, the Orange Turnpike and the Orange Plank Road. The dense thickets that gave the Wilderness its name segregated the fighting into discrete halves. Efforts by both sides to bridge the gap between the two sectors never succeeded for long. Gen. R. E. Lee spent most of his time on the southern half of the battlefield, the portion centered on the Plank Road. The general made his headquarters in the sole clearing along that road, a rundown forty-acre field where stood the rude cabin home of a widow named Catharine Tapp.

Soon after he reached the Tapp clearing on May 5, Lee had perhaps his closest personal brush with capture of the war. He and Gens. A. P. Hill, J. E. B. Stuart, and William Nelson Pendleton were comparing notes near the Tapp cabin when, without any warning at all, a line of blue-clad skirmishers materialized at the edge of the woods and emerged into the field at close range. Nearby Confederate infantry-men shouted at Lee, "Get out of here; you will get killed!" The general quietly called for his adjutant. Hill did not move. Stuart characteristically strode toward the threat and faced it squarely. Fortunately the Federals recoiled from the mutual surprise and turned back into the woods. Gen. E. L. Thomas's Georgia brigade chased them out of range. The startling, if bloodless, encounter might have been a sinister omen of crises to come in Widow Tapp's field.[1]

Later on May 5 Lee rallied a routed brigade from Gen. Henry Heth's division near the Tapp field in another foreshadowing of what would happen the next morning. In the face of "terrific" fire the general rode through the panicky troops and in his familiar dignified mien urged them to "go back, boys. . . . We want you in front now." Lee ignored protes-tations from staff members about his exposure to danger as he used his immense influence with the army's rank and file to mend the ominous gap that had opened. Success in stalling enemy advances left Lee "in fine spirits" that afternoon, one of Stuart's staff wrote.[2]

The Army of Northern Virginia held its own on both ends of the battle-field on May 5. It would be outnumbered about two to one when all of each army's units reached the field, but on the fifth Lee was missing fully one-third of his strength. As a result of that imbalance, and of hard fighting by Federals ably led by Gen. Winfield Scott Hancock, Confederate posi-tions east of the Tapp field at nightfall were in dreadful disarray. The line should have been perpendicular to the road, the flanks of its component units firmly knitted together. Instead Generals Heth and Cadmus M. Wil-cox said in front of Hill's chief of staff that "their lines in the woods were like a worm fence, at every angle." A North Carolinian in the smoky woods recalled that "none of the brigades seemed to be in line—some regiments isolated entirely from brigades—in fact, no line at all, but just as they had fought."[3]

The vagaries of battle had left Heth's division, generally left (north) of the road, even more disjointed than Wilcox's division on the right. Wil-cox had managed to maintain marginal tactical unity, "tho the line," the general admitted, "was irregular." Weary Confederates "all knew the two divisions would give way, if attacked," an artillerist wrote, "and all knew they would be attacked."[4]

Disorganized detachments of both armies strewn through the thickets brushed against one another (and against unidentified friends) through the night. Their desultory exchanges of fire punctuated a night thick with tension for southern leaders. Not long before dawn Lt. Col. William T. Poague undertook recovery of a piece of artillery lost by his battalion on May 5. Poague led eight volunteers to the Plank Road and eastward toward the abandoned gun. Both the cannon and the recovery crew belonged to the Madison Light Artillery, a Mississippi company. The artillerists were startled to find friendly infantry fast asleep, their muskets stacked in random piles. One of the Mississippians wrote that the Confederate front line "was lying flat on the ground with faces black from perspiration and powder." No sign of alignment could be seen, or even a cursory picket post. Nonetheless, when a line of enemy soldiers briefly threatened the retrieval party, Confederate muskets quickly obliterated the Federals with a devastating volley. The recovered Napoleon would be part of Poague's defensive cluster a few hours later near Catharine Tapp's cabin.[5]

Questions about responsibility for the lack of preparation overnight continue to provoke historical inquiry. The two division commanders insisted that corps commander Hill had assured them that Gen. James Longstreet's troops would be up before morning to relieve them. In a famous, though often impugned, postwar memoir, Harry Heth described telling Hill of "the almost inextricable mixing up" of his troops, which were "lying at every conceivable angle." Lieutenant General Hill, who was sick and soon would relinquish command as a result, was adamant that the weary troops should be allowed to rest. On his third desperate visit, Heth said, Hill exploded: "D—— it, Heth, I don't want to hear any more about it; the men shall not be disturbed." The rebuffed Heth then "walked the road all night" anxiously awaiting the first signs of Longstreet's arrival.[6]

Cadmus Wilcox left three accounts of that stressful night. In each he made clear, in the passive and noncontroversial style he always maintained, that he "had been told" that relief would come before dawn. At the end of the fighting on May 5, Wilcox noted, one of his brigades wound up parallel to the Plank Road—ninety degrees from its optimum axis. In a manuscript report prepared during the war, Wilcox stated, "But for the impression that other and fresh troops would be up and in position before day, the line would have been withdrawn for a few hundred yards and rectified." Wilcox's accounts do not identify Hill as the source of his instructions, but the inference is implicit.[7]

Where was Lee during this impasse, and what did he have to do with it? There is adequate evidence that the commanding general was in or near the Tapp field overnight. His chief of artillery, in a contemporary letter, wrote of bivouacking beside Poague's guns in the field's western edge with Lee "very near." The best postwar authority on Wilderness sites, who knew the Tapp descendants and other locals well, placed Lee's headquarters there. Wilcox himself saw the Confederate leader's tent in the field "at 9 P.M." and noted Lee there again "so early in the morning [of May 6]."[8]

A. P. Hill's chief of staff, writing forty-five years after the battle, declared that the orders "to let the men rest as they were" came from General Lee. He also, however, reported in apparent error that Hill and Wilcox each rode back to Parker's Store—far west of the Tapp field—to find Lee. Heth claimed to have spent an hour seeking Lee without finding him. Months later Heth attempted to explain to Lee (with whom he was on close personal terms) what had happened, but he met with a rebuff. Whatever its overnight relationship with the army commander, Hill's corps headquarters passed a sleepless night.[9]

There seems to be ample blame to spread around. The division commanders clearly were as uneasy as they should have been. Heth reported Lee's subsequent rebuke as this inarguable tenet: "A division commander should always have his division prepared to receive an attack." The division commander's predictable rejoinder, that "he must also obey the positive order of his superior," overlooked the need to achieve the best possible local tactical arrangements within the broad strictures put upon him. William Poague's artillery outing came across infantry officers unaware of enemy positions and "very indifferent and not at all concerned about the situation." Heth and Wilcox ought to have done what they could about that lassitude, even if proscribed from moving units around.[10]

The rest of Lee's seasoned army, accustomed to success, marveled at the confusion and the resultant route. A perceptive member of Longstreet's staff called the business "strange." General Hill drew considerable criticism. A colonel in his own corps wrote savagely that Hill "was guilty of . . . folly." He attributed the result in part to the corps commander being "disabled by illness." The critical colonel declared that "Hill was excused—or relieved from duty after his criminal negligence."[11]

The nightlong quandary for Heth and Wilcox ended with a crushing onslaught capably marshaled against them at dawn by General Hancock. As a last-minute hedge against inundation, Wilcox sent pioneer troops forward to fell trees to make a rudimentary abatis. Federals sprawled in the brush at very short range easily put an end to the effort, and Hancock's attack rolled over an extremely vulnerable southern position.[12]

Meanwhile the anxiously awaited First Corps of James Longstreet at last was approaching the field. Longstreet's arrival, unquestionably later than Lee had hoped it would be, is the most widely discussed of the three components that resulted in the early morning disaster on the Plank Road. The other two elements—Hancock's skilled and determined assault and Hill's unpreparedness to receive it—do not spring so readily to mind as does the notion of Longstreet being late again.

In fact, the sometimes uncooperative corps commander deserves far less blame on the large-scale question of timing than does the army commander. Much has been made of Lee's justly famous prescience in divining what his enemies would do. On the eve of the Wilderness he gathered most, but not all, of his army in ideal position to respond to Grant's onset. The exception was Longstreet's First Corps, newly returned to the army and perhaps not fully reintegrated into its machinery. Longstreet's one-third of Lee's infantry remained around Mechanicsville, a country locale near Boswell's Tavern some miles south of Gordonsville. From there Longstreet could not reach any prospective battlefront in good time. Lee doubtless was sensitive about the vital railroad junction at Gordonsville under the basic premise of assuming one's enemy would do what he *should* do. In the event, Grant spent the next year blithely ignoring Gordonsville (and Hanover Junction, too), seconded by his protégé Philip H. Sheridan, concentrating instead on less important railroad targets. During May's first week, however, Longstreet surely ought to have screened Gordonsville across an arc north of the place rather than remaining so far away from the Rapidan River line.[13]

James Longstreet's dangerously tardy arrival at the Wilderness has generated the same volume of inquiry that attends so many of his endeavors. Legitimate critiques of the march—once begun from unnecessarily far away—cannot extend to its actual execution. The pace was as vigorous as ought to have been expected and in fact far prompter and more rapid than Longstreet's metabolism usually preferred (albeit not at the level of a determined T. J. Jackson maneuver). Orders to begin reached the troops around Mechanicsville about noon on May 4, and they began moving within hours. Most of them marched without stopping until human endurance failed, and they wearily collapsed beside the road between 5:00 and 10:00 P.M. the next day. All of them had gone without rest for twenty-four hours. Some had stayed on the road longer than that.[14]

Exhausted Confederates benefited from only an abbreviated chance to recuperate. By 3:00 A.M., if not earlier, they had been routed out of bed and put back in motion toward the smoldering Wilderness. The average night's rest cannot have exceeded five hours. Haversacks had been emptied during the fifth. Confederates arriving hungry at the battlefield near 6:00 A.M. had been on the road for about thirty-five of the past forty hours—and had a full day of intense combat ahead of them.[15]

Some regiments awoke in the early dark of May 6 to the familiar, unsettling rattle of the long roll. Those close to Micah Jenkins's headquarters heard a band serenading the general at "that inopportune hour." One officer later wondered if the band was operating under "a presentiment that it would be the last time they would ever have the chance." The bandsmen, who came from the Palmetto Sharpshooters, were playing both reveille and requiem for Micah Jenkins.[16]

The march through dark fields and byways west of the Wilderness moved steadily from the start and rapidly soon thereafter. A South Carolinian in the column recalled, "We walked fast and double quick as much as we could." Another soldier described the hurried pace as "a turkey trot." For the final two miles the entire First Corps loped along at the double-quick step. Gen. Charles W. Field's division struck out across country to reach the Plank Road simultaneously with Kershaw's division, which was using a lateral road.[17]

Hurrying Confederates who converged on the Plank Road near Parker's Store, about two miles west of Widow Tapp's field, quickly reached an emergency accommodation: they would dash eastward on the road two divisions abreast. Participants never saw that unprecedented expedient again during the war. Side by side, Kershaw's men and Field's marched toward the "grand roars of musketry & quick thunders of artillery." An Alabamian listening to "the continued roll of musketry" noticed the sun, "blood red," rising directly in front of them above the Plank Road. His mates predicted "a hot time . . . today, for there is blood in the sun." Gen. John Gregg, at the head of the Texas Brigade destined for renewed fame in the Tapp field, harkened back to a classic bit of military history when he said to his staff, "There is the sun of Austerlitz."[18]

Before they reached the battle zone, Longstreet's First Corps troops had to breast a human tide sweeping against them and threatening to retard their progress. Men already wounded in the dawn Federal attack were seeking succor, and not a few able-bodied soldiers joined them in heading for the rear. As they passed a hospital, a colonel admitted, its "hideous sights, fractured limbs and bloody clothing, did not add much to our courage." The First Corps nonetheless, in a magnificent display of discipline and bravery, maintained its poise—and its all-important tactical alignment. "Those splendid troops came on," a brigadier general wrote proudly, "regardless of the confusion on every side, pushing their steady way onward." One of the men recalled, "I never before or after witnessed such excitement and confusion, it was perfectly appalling." The vital reinforcements sprinted through the chaos, determined if not oblivious. Men discarded playing cards, as usual on the brink of battle, and tore up love letters they could not bear to imagine falling into Yankee hands. Many units did not pause even a moment before wheeling into the fight. Others stopped long enough to load their muskets but did not take time to form a new line. A wounded Georgian admiring the arriving First Corps tossed his cartridge box to a man who had none. The man caught it and kept moving without a lost step.[19]

The time neared 6:00 A.M. (an hour after sunrise) when Longstreet reached the field ahead of his advance. His men had marched thirty-five to forty miles within forty hours, including the brief overnight rest. In his relentlessly disingenuous memoir, the general declared that his troops arrived "just as" the Federal attack opened, a reckoning that is awry by about one hour. The chief of A. P. Hill's staff, who knew Longstreet well, grasped his hand and said frankly, "Ah, General, we have been looking for you since 12 o'clock last night."[20]

Two well-informed Confederate officers criticized Longstreet (others less qualified did so as well) over the march of May 4–5. Gen. George Washington Custis Lee recorded the gist of an 1865 conversation with his father, R. E. Lee, in which the army commander allegedly regretted that Longstreet had brusquely rejected a young officer sent to guide him. This supposedly led to confusion on the march that contributed to the delayed arrival. Although Custis's tale does not match exactly, he may have been referring to an episode involving Henry B. McClellan, a bright twenty-three-year-old major on J. E. B. Stuart's staff. McClellan rode southwestward from the Wilderness during the night of May 5–6 with orders from R. E. Lee "to order Field's Division of Longstreet's Corps to move immediately to reinforce Wilcox and Heth. . . . Urgent need existed for speedy help." After a high-speed gallop, the major found Field, who received him in "somewhat cold and formal" style and dismissed him with word that he proposed to move at 1:00 A.M. Field later called McClellan back in and said he had a new order from Longstreet reaffirming 1:00 A.M. for the march. To McClellan's expostulations about Lee's order having preeminence and about the dire situation along the Plank Road, Field answered, "I prefer to obey General Longstreet's order." Major McClellan reported this result to Lee.[21]

Charles S. Venable of Lee's staff also visited Longstreet overnight on May 5–6. Venable recalled that his message from an "anxious" Lee was that Longstreet "was to try [to] reach Genl Lee's position as soon as practicable . . . 'by daybreak' was the order as I remember it." McClellan's account gains some credence from Venable's independent assertion that Stuart promised Lee—apparently after Venable's own return—to get further word to Longstreet "about the condition of things and the importance of getting up to us at the earliest possible hour."[22] What all of this portends about genuine intentions and real events is beyond knowing with certainty at this late date. Lee surely was disappointed that the First Corps did not arrive sooner.

While the sturdy infantrymen of the First Corps hurried eastward to the sound of the guns, their comrades of Heth's and Wilcox's divisions recoiled in desperation before Hancock's mighty assault. In calmer postwar days many of the retreating men, especially the officers, looked back on the near-disaster and smoothed off its rough edges. On the morning of May 6 things looked bleak indeed. The Third Corps troops, Porter Alexander wrote, "appreciating that their position was no longer tenable . . . came pouring down the road past the [Tapp] field." An approaching Texan described the rout as "a scene of utter, and apparently irremediable confusion, such as we had never witnessed before in Lee's army." General Field saw Confederates "in confusion" as they "came hurrying by us." The Federals who had triggered this disaster pushed forward with "dangerous vehemence," a South Carolinian acknowledged. Another First Corps man gauged the Union advance by listening for the distinctive Yankee cheers drawing near—a measured huzzah "which no one who ever listened to its sneaking apprehensive utterance, could mistake for one of our enthusiastic Confederate yells."[23]

In the inevitable style of proud soldiers and storied units, the First Corps men sneered at their retreating friends. An Alabamian admitted to having "chafed most unmercifully [our] retreating comrades." A withdrawing North Carolinian wrote that the reinforcements "wanted to know if we belonged to General Lee's army. . . . 'We were worse than Bragg's men.'"[24]

General Wilcox reported officially that his line originally stood "within less than three hundred yards" of the artillery gathered at the western edge of the Tapp field. Moving back that modest distance seemed to him to be little more than a realignment. Hill's chief of staff insisted, unreasonably, that the troops fell back "slowly and in order"—except along the road where they stood firm. Wounded men filtering west from the field answered First Corps inquiries with varying degrees of optimism. "If it was a private who was questioned he would say: 'They are sorter driving us back.' If it was an officer he would say: 'Well it's about a stand on both sides.'"[25]

Other Third Corps soldiers bluntly acknowledged their disarray. "Too bad boys they are driving us," a retiring Confederate admitted to one of the advancing Texans. Most units received orders to retire. "In effect," an artillerist wrote, "the men were ordered to run, and the signs are they obeyed, with all the means which God and nature had put into their feet." The commander of the 18th North Carolina admitted that when his troops reached the appointed rallying point, they kept right on going rearward. Gen. E. P. Alexander overheard an excited staff officer, attempting in vain to rally some of the fleeing masses, shout, "God damn 'em! They are running!"[26]

The most widely cited episode of this retreat involved Lee and the veteran brigade that had been Maxcy Gregg's and now followed Gen. Samuel McGowan. The commanding general rode up and said, "My God! Gen. McGowan is this splendid brigade of yours running like a flock of geese?" The brigadier's calm rejoinder—"They just want a place to form and they are ready to fight as well as ever"—reflected the poise of a seasoned army accustomed to landing on its feet. The brigade's acclaimed historian felt that "Lee's regrettable words" were based on a misunderstanding of the circumstances. The captain of McGowan's sharpshooter battalion, however, wrote candidly of "confusion" on the field during which the Carolinians were "rolled up" by the enemy line.[27]

The first order imposed on the rampant chaos came not in the Tapp field but to its right across the Plank Road. There Longstreet's leading units dashed into the thickets, somehow formed a line, and checked the Federal momentum. They were barely in time; enemy riflemen had penetrated the woods to a point nearly opposite Poague's guns. The First Corps's feat in forming in the face of an assault in progress was made more remarkable by the swarms of disordered friends who kept rupturing their formations. Some officers pushed their approach march off the Plank Road into the thickets in an attempt to maintain order there, rather than in the face of soldiers determinedly moving the wrong way. "The discipline of the command was sorely tried," Gen. Goode Bryan reported, as his "line was constantly broken through by men hurrying to the rear."[28]

Circumstances facing Longstreet's arriving van cried out for creation of a new front. Behind that new line, with a bit of time and space in hand, thoughts might then turn to the possibility of seizing the initiative. One of Kershaw's men reported the result in that context: "These regiments suffered severely, but they maintained their ground until the remainder of the division could be got into some sort of line." A staff officer serving General Field described the need to buy time for the First Corps's alignment—not realignment of the routed Third Corps: "Longstreet's corps as it then stood in one mingled mass . . . could not be thrown in, and time must be allowed for it to reform, and place itself in line of battle."[29]

Kershaw's division took on the vital task. The general's old brigade, now under Col. John W. Henagan (a forty-one-year-old former sheriff of Marlboro County, South Carolina), angled obliquely to the right of the road. The exigencies of the moment turned tactics into a company-level affair, "changing front forward" by turns and "each company engaging . . . the advancing foe as [it] came into line." The Carolinians eventually anchored their left on the Plank Road and established a firing line that lashed the woods in their front. The 2nd South Carolina remained on the road near the western end of Widow Tapp's farm. The Mississippi brigade of the division, next in the column, hurried to Henagan's assistance. The rest of the division, a Georgian wrote, "filed to the right, by brigades . . . as the head of the column arrived."[30]

The noise of the stout resistance by Kershaw's men inspired Confederates and served notice on their enemies that the morning's easy success had ended. With both sides firing steadily, the furious noise seemed to an artillerist near Parker's to make "what we had been hearing before seem like pop-crackers." Kershaw's success was less dramatic than most offensive displays—and than the episode about to unfold in the Tapp field—but it was a stellar achievement under the circumstances. "Nothing finer was ever done on a battlefield," Colonel Palmer of Hill's staff thought. "It was an inspiring homecoming for the First Corps." Moxley Sorrel of Longstreet's staff reflected proudly on the accomplishment: "I have always thought that in its entire splendid history the simple act of forming line in that dense undergrowth, under heavy fire and with the Third Corps men pushing to the rear through the ranks, was perhaps its greatest performance for steadiness and inflexible courage and discipline." Sorrel credited Longstreet's tenacity for the result. Relieved Third Corps soldiers, obviously agreeing, cheered Longstreet when he swept past.[31]

Meanwhile the front of Field's division was reaching the same vicinity on the Plank Road and filing left, northward, to assume responsibility for restoring the line there. While Kershaw's men coped with thick brush, just opposite them north of the road there opened a substantial clearing— the only open space of any size near the road for a long distance in either direction. Dozens of familiar descriptions of the Wilderness recount the density and impenetrability of its thickets: a "peculiar tangled forest of stunted oak, chinquapin or dwarf chesnut &c." A cavalry staff officer saw "for many miles not a house, and not an open field. Nothing but a Wilderness of trees and underbrush and marsh—and perfectly flat."[32]

The sole exception was Widow Tapp's field. Like much of Virginia's agricultural acreage, the Tapp farm had fallen on hard times. Most of it had not been cultivated for three years, and the neglect showed. A Texan who hurried into the field that morning thought it had been "long since abandoned." Grass and old grain had grown wild, and, in Virginia's custom, saplings were shooting up eagerly. The result was what several observers called simply an "old field." Despite being choked with "small pines & broom grass," the welcome open space looked like "a sort of broom-straw *oasis* in this Wilderness of black-jacks, willow-oaks and stunted pines."[33]

The rectangular open space, its long axis parallel to the Plank Road, covered about thirty acres. Two earlike projections of the field at its northeast and northwest corners brought the cleared area to about forty-five acres. A narrow band of thin growth on the road's north shoulder complicated the view a bit at the southwest edge of the field. Most of the field, especially near the road, was essentially level. Its northern reaches, however, dropped off toward the site of Catharine Tapp's dwelling. General Wilcox described the western edge of the field as "a gentle swell of the surface, in front [northeast, not due east] descending and open for several hundred yards." Men who focused on fighting that paralleled the Plank Road hardly were aware of the gradual dropoff to the north. One Texan wrote, "If there was any hill there I did not notice it."[34]

A crude log cabin, one story with a loft, stood on the northern edge of the field near a spring. No one would have any notion what the Tapp home looked like had not George Leo Frankenstein (1825–1911), an artist and veteran of service in the Union commissary corps, visited soon after the war and painted a watercolor of the building. Frankenstein produced thirty-three paintings of Civil War sites, eight on the battlefields around Fredericksburg. His likeness of the Tapp cabin, the only known graphic depiction of the place, came perilously near destruction in 1972 but survives to illustrate the historic landmark.[35]

A modest orchard containing plum, cherry, and apple trees straggled around the little house. Two meager outbuildings had sheltered four milk cows and seven pigs in 1860, with a total value of $90; the war had quite likely caused the loss of those animals. Catharine Tapp's net worth in 1860 had been merely $120 of personal property. The widow owned no real estate. Her little farm belonged to J. Horace Lacy of "Ellwood" and

Widow Tapp's house (watercolor by George Leo Frankenstein, ca. 1869). Fredericksburg and Spotsylvania National Military Park, Fredericksburg, Va.

"Chatham" (both of much renown during the war); she either rented it or operated on a sharecropper system. The fancy new Orange Plank Road, an incorporated toll route, was only eleven years old in 1864 and ought to have brought modest prosperity to the Tapps. It had proved, however, to be an abject failure as a substitute for the railroad that local people had feared and rejected.[36]

Catharine Tapp was fifty-nine years old in 1864. In 1860 she shared the cabin with three daughters, a son, a granddaughter, and a twenty-five-year-old white laborer named Jackson Lewis. All of the children were illiterate, she told the census enumerator. The destruction of Virginia's economy by the war probably had sent the laborer elsewhere. Some of Tapp's children, who would have been ages twenty-one to twenty-eight by 1864, may have been in the Wilderness in 1864; her four-year-old grand-daughter certainly was living there when the battle erupted.[37]

Little "Phenie" Tapp, as she was known (the census called her Eliza), remembered hearing the approach of a mighty spring thunderstorm of the sort she knew well. Then impressive men in gray clothes—her family later told her it was A. P. Hill with his staff—directed the civilians away from the center of what of course was in reality a terrible manmade storm of gunfire. Phenie "gathered . . . that a lot of very bad men in blue were going to get a whipping," she told interested visitors in later years. The tot presumed the villains had been throwing pebbles in the spring; that's what she always got a whipping for. As Phenie and her family hurried westward on the Plank Road, the storm broke over them. "Large drops hit the road and dust spurted up the way it does when the first raindrops fall, before the ground gets wet." None of the civilians were struck by the bullets dropping near them. They spent the two days of battle at the Pulliam place near Parker's. Meanwhile the dirt farm where they had scratched out a miserable subsistence became a famous place in American military legend.[38]

Control of Catharine Tapp's field depended for a time on W. T. Poague's battalion of artillery. It was the only instance on the brush-choked battlefield in which artillery played a pivotal role. Poague's four batteries totaled sixteen pieces of artillery sited roughly perpendicular to the road and facing east: Madison Light Artillery (Mississippi), Capt. Thomas J. Richards; Capt. Arthur B. Williams's North Carolina Battery; Albemarle Artillery (Virginia), Capt. James W. Wyatt; and Brooke Artillery (Virginia), Capt. Addison W. Utterback. An ordnance return later in the year reported these weapons in the battalion: nine Napoleons, two 10-pounder Parrott rifles, and two 3-inch rifles. The May 6 configuration probably reflected that ratio at full strength, with two smoothbores for each rifle. With a canister-range fight looming, the smoothbores were preferable to rifles.[39]

Poague's artillerists stood to their guns in the open, near the western edge of the field. One gun was in the Plank Road. Catharine Tapp's clearing stretched directly in front of the artillery for several hundred yards. As was customary by this stage of the war, the men improved their position for defense by throwing up breastworks overnight. In this instance the works had been improvised from convenient fence rails. A few rudimentary pits scraped out behind the rail piles completed the preparations, without any real expectation of close-range fighting. Men were attempting to strengthen the breastworks when the Texas Brigade reached that point, and some retreating infantry had rallied under their scant shelter.[40]

Pressure from in front, across the open field, did not develop promptly or in daunting force. There was simply too much naked ground for advancing Federals to negotiate. When Wilcox defended the withdrawal of his division, he cited proudly the fact that the enemy did not cross the field toward Poague. Some Confederate rearguard detachments, pursued by blue-clad skirmishers, fell back into the Tapp clearing after their friends had scampered away through the woods. General Pendleton and Colonel Poague moved among the cannoneers, encouraging them to stand their ground and "sweep back the enemy with canister" once friendly infantry was out of the way. Pendleton, of whom most artillerists thought little, made a second trip to each piece. All sixteen cannon were charged with canister—probably double-shotted—in preparation for the impending crisis.[41]

Trouble mounted much more ominously to Poague's right, across the Plank Road. No enemy forces were visible through the foliage, but the sound of firing drew steadily nearer. The gun in the road, a piece from Williams's Battery under Lt. Abdon Alexander, fired toward the right shoulder in its front. Infantry rounds coming back from the woods soon silenced the gun. A. P. Hill sent an urgent request for steady artillery fire against invisible targets in the woods—even if retreating friends interdicted the line of fire! The battery on Poague's right responded and "contributed materially towards arresting their advance." Soon more of the battalion turned obliquely to fire in that direction, but hostile riflemen had reached a point directly opposite Poague's right flank by the time Kershaw's infantry threw itself across the Federals' path.[42]

When Poague finally could turn loose all four batteries, unrestrained by concern for retreating friends, their canister scything across the field and into the woods threw a curtain of iron in front of the First Corps reinforcements just then arriving. The canister made the Plank Road untenable, thus denying the Federals use of the only real corridor in the area. The reliable C. R. Dudley estimated that each gun in the battalion fired "about three rounds"—a modest total of perhaps fifty rounds. If all were double-shotted with canister, however, they sent nearly 3,000 iron balls whistling at short range into an enemy flank. Kershaw's men in the woods south of the road ducked as the storm swept past their front and even over their heads. A captain in Kershaw's division later told his brother, who fought in Richards's Battery, "how near he came to losing his head from a cannon shot." The infantrymen, nonetheless, were not complaining. Poague was not far out of line when he estimated that "but for the artillery getting a position in that clearing a serious disaster would have overtaken the 3d Corps." Poague's guns fell silent not because of Kershaw's men to their right but because the Texas Brigade had come crowding up around them, straining to get into the clearing.[43]

The Texans (and Arkansans, who must have been disgusted at the universal designation of their brigade as simply Texan) had actually come up second in General Field's column, the division commander recalled. He reported that G. T. Anderson's brigade had been in front but dropped into a blocking position on the right of the road. The Texas Brigade forged leftward into the "dense thicket of underbrush," moving swiftly "over ditches, in water and out of it." Stray bullets whistled past, knocking off twigs and

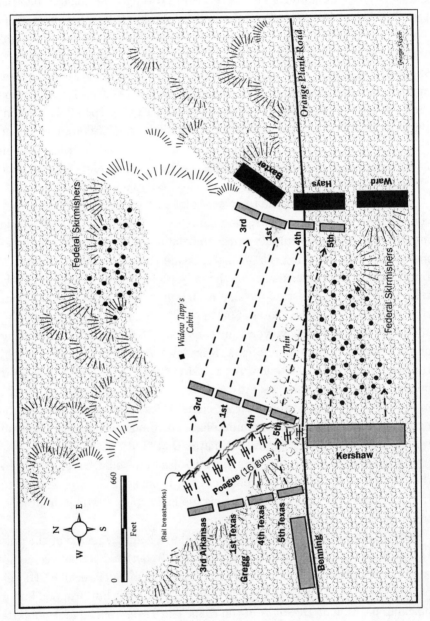

The Texas Brigade in Widow Tapp's field, May 6, 1864.

foliage—and occasionally knocking over men, too. Officers shouted orders to halt and "load and cap your pieces, men." The "jingle of the hundreds of iron ramrods up and down the line denoted that something horrible was soon to take place. . . . Every old soldier knew . . . what was in store for him."[44]

The tactical evolution that swung the Texans into position perpendicular to their line of march on the Plank Road and left them facing east, ready for action, included a good bit of confusion. One Texan described the alignment, under fire, as "a gradual right wheel." Another identified it as the more likely, albeit opposite, "half wheel to the left." The head of the column likely turned north and, when far enough in that direction, everyone faced right (only if the tail of the column had pulled the rest north would a right wheel be involved.) A member of the 1st Texas, which wound up as the left-center regiment, described simply what obviously happened: "[After] going north a short distance . . . we faced to the right and were now formed in line of battle." The rampant confusion and limited visibility left much of the line to knit itself together, as an officer said, "without order." Longstreet sought to help establish order in person, riding through the woods and enjoining those who could see and hear him to "keep cool, men, we will straighten this out in a short time—keep cool."[45]

As they approached action, the four regiments of Gregg's brigade were configured with the 3rd Arkansas on the left and the three Texas regiments in ascending numerical order to its right: 1st Texas, then 4th Texas, then 5th Texas. Despite the excitement and chaos of the moment, regimental officers followed tactical dogma by throwing out skirmishers from each regiment, some of whom were promptly shot. The left of the line (3rd Arkansas) leaned forward a bit, and the right (5th Texas) was refused a bit to the rear, perhaps retarded by the thin band of shrubs near the road. That alignment would affect the later stages of the advance, eventually throwing the right of the brigade south of the road. At the outset the 5th Texas anchored its right on the Plank Road.[46]

Gregg's brigade completed its hurried shift into battle line at the edge of the woods "immediately in rear of" Poague's guns. The brigade's first challenge was to move through the artillery without completely losing tactical cohesion. The veteran infantry made the move in "splendid style," cheering "lustily" as they "swept across" the artillery position. Those whose position put them directly athwart one of the breastworks "leaped over" them, shouting as they did so. One of the gunners described the passing foot soldiers as "rushing over our artillery and on to the fray."

The skirmishers quickly fell back to their places in the main line. Poague's guns, of course, had ceased firing as friendly troops swept past. The two pieces farthest right managed to stay in action to their right front for awhile longer, firing diagonally past the right of the 5th Texas and across the left front of Kershaw's troops beyond the road.[47]

R. E. Lee rode behind, in front of, beside, or between all four regiments at the four stages of their preparations: as the Texans formed up at the edge of the woods, swept through Poague's artillery, halted and composed themselves for the assault, and then launched their attack eastward. What came to be known as the Lee-to-the-Rear episode actually unfolded in those four stages and finally reached a crescendo east of the artillery position. Lee's movements and appearance are described in enough primary accounts to establish his location at many points in sequence. The effect is not contradictory, as at first it seems, but rather constitutes a cumulative and consecutive tapestry. The description that follows will examine by turns these details within the four sequential episodes: what Lee did, what Lee said, what the Texans said, and how the Texans turned Lee back.

The commanding general's first close interaction with his line of infantry that morning came in attempts to rally disorganized Third Corps units, before the First Corps arrived. Lee "dashed amid the fugitives," Walter Taylor of his staff wrote, and "personally called upon the men to rally." An artillery staffer watching Heth's and Wilcox's men "saw General Lee among them, the bullets were flying by, and it seemed to me to be a very critical moment." A Georgia lieutenant encountered the general, "mixed up among us and . . . talking to the men that came out. He said 'Go back men, you can beat those people.'"[48]

Several witnesses place Lee just behind Poague's guns and near the Plank Road during the morning's opening phases. From there he made forays into the disorderly mass on the road, sometimes mounted and sometimes afoot. A gunner with Poague saw Lee "just off the plank road and about twenty steps in rear of our battery."[49] There he met the anxiously awaited First Corps commander, who had ridden ahead of his troops. Longstreet met Lee "some 15 yards to the left of the road" and grasped his chief's hand. "I never was so glad to see you," Lee said. "Hancock has broken my line." The two men rode slowly together "talking earnestly" and "in close consultation."[50]

At this crisis Lee displayed more emotion than observers had seen before. A South Carolina soldier noticed that the general "had a white handkerchief in [his] hand, and once in a while, would wipe his eyes as if in trouble." One of Field's staff wrote, "I have often seen Gen. Lee, but never did I see him so excited, so disturbed—never did anxiety or care manifest itself before so plainly upon his countenance. If I mistake not he was almost moved to tears."[51] The answer to Lee's desperate need was marching rapidly toward him in the form of Gregg's brigade. The result would be a release of Lee's intense feelings in a dramatic episode that elicited even more emotion from the usually poised general.

Lee rode among the Texans as they formed up behind Poague. He bestrode his familiar war horse, Traveller, and wore his customary "ordinary field uniform and his old army sword." At this first of the four stages of the Lee-to-the-Rear encounter, the general asked the troops their identity, and some of them began to suggest that he retire to a safer place (see below for discussion of the various verbal exchanges). He paused at the left of the 1st Texas—and probably next to each of the forming units. Lee took off his hat and, atypically, waved it and "hurrahed for the Texas Brigade." The response, needless to say, was a mighty cheer from everyone who could see the scene. "I never heard such a shout," declared the major of the 1st Texas, "as when we saw General Lee, mounted upon his splendid horse, appearing a warrior where every god had set the seal."[52]

Lee sat mounted next to an artillery piece when Gregg's regiments began to advance through Poague's guns. As the infantry passed, the general pulled Traveller's head around and rode along. Everyone in the brigade saw him there, of course, and the sight occasioned more yelling. Lee again took off his hat in acknowledgment and tribute. He was by now, Colonel Poague wrote, "perfectly composed, but his face expressed a kind of grim determination." Traveller sensed the intensity loose in the field, "as indicated by his raised head with ears pointing to the front."[53]

Their formation unhinged a bit by passing through the guns, the Texans paused on the threshold of their major duty of assaulting across the field. Lee remained near the line at this third stage of the encounter. Field reported him at the center of the brigade, saying aloud that he would lead it. General Pendleton placed Lee near the left of the line and said that he also heard the army commander exhorting the troops. A member of the 4th Texas, on the left center, wrote that he saw "the fire of battle in [Lee's] eye, and his form quivered with emotions."[54]

The climactic finale of Lee's interaction with the Texas Brigade came when, realigned and ready to advance, the troops began to move purposefully across Catharine Tapp's field. The whole affair happened rapidly and without design, far more simply than any historical description— necessarily encumbered by multiple sources—can readily convey. One of

Poague's cannoneers thought that "less than a minute" transpired after they ceased firing before Lee attempted to lead the infantry forward. Texan J. B. Polley placed the general "in front of us, as if intending to lead us." Capt. A. C. Jones of the 3rd Arkansas described Lee at this point "wheeling his horse in front and uncovering his head" and verbally offering to lead the brigade. Both Polley and Jones, who was wounded in the right arm during the battle, probably recalled the incident behind the guns, moments before the troops advanced through them. General Heth, on the field but apparently not in the immediate vicinity, is the only source claiming that Lee seized a battle flag in preparation for leading the charge. The flag incident certainly is apocryphal.[55]

The best evidence about Lee's final, most dramatic contact with the Texans makes evident the fact that he followed *behind* the advancing line and that the men only became aware of him after they had moved some distance. A Texan officer wrote that Lee "had passed with the men some distance in the charge before he was discovered." Colonel Venable's eyewitness account moved the battle line some distance before cries for the general to turn back broke out. Another account noted that "the men did not perceive that he was going with them until they had advanced some distance in the charge." E. P. Alexander, wonderfully well informed but apparently not right at the scene, reported that "the old man, with the light of battle in his eyes . . . rode up behind their line, following them in the charge." Then, at the end of several encounters with the brigade and well in front of Poague's guns, the Texans turned Lee to the rear by means of shouted injunctions and physical interference with his horse.[56]

John Gregg—the other general involved in the Lee-to-the-Rear episode, came to the Wilderness with his brigade as a stranger to Lee's army. His predecessor, Jerome B. Robertson, had been one of the generals selected as scapegoats by Longstreet for his egregious failure at Knoxville and in East Tennessee. Gregg had been badly wounded in the neck at Chickamauga and sported a round patch in the collar of his brigadier's jacket covering the bullet hole. When Gregg and Lee met near Poague's guns, the army commander enjoined his new subordinate "to give those [northern] men the cold steel—they will stand and fire all day, and never move unless you charge them."[57]

Gregg also made a brief, stirring speech over the roar of gunfire to those of his men within hearing as they prepared to launch themselves across the field. Versions about Gregg's words vary, of course, but almost all include in virtually identical language the sentence "The eyes of General Lee are upon you." Most accounts open with something like "Atten-

General Lee at the battle of the Wilderness. "Lee to the Rear."
Frank Leslie's Popular Magazine, *October 1896, 385*

tion Texans" and end with the injunction "Forward!" When Lee followed
the troops Gregg had just inspired, the brigadier turned his horse toward
him and "remonstrated with him."[58]

Lee's verbal exchanges with Gregg's men were recorded by about two
dozen contemporaries. The accounts, of course, do not conform precisely;
they would be suspect if they did. It is hard to escape the conclusion that
later accounts include some echoing of earlier ones. Even so, there is broad
concurrence available on three separate times when Lee talked to the
men. When the Texans first arrived, he inquired loudly who they were,
and they answered. Thereafter, probably during the formation interval
behind Poague's guns, Lee expressed confidence in the brigade and lauded
its record. Then, before the charge began, he either encouraged the men
to charge, announced that he would lead them in person, or both. That
also likely occurred behind the line of artillery, so all of Lee's comments
date from the first two of the four episodes.

General Pendleton watched Lee approach the first few dozen gray-clad
infantry who started to form behind the guns and heard him call out, "Who
are you, my boys?" When they hollered back, "Texas boys," Pendleton
said, Lee exuberantly waved his hat and exclaimed, "Hurrah for Texas!

Hurrah for Texas!" Others heard the exchange similarly. Some thought Lee directed his query to General Gregg.[59]

The identity of the desperately needed reinforcements established, Lee applauded the exemplary record of the Texans and Arkansans in words that made everyone who heard them proud. The brigade had been among the handful of units most distinguished in the entire army, and its soldiers knew it. Hearing their revered leader say so in a moment of crisis elevated the stakes. Lee's plaudits generally were repeated in this vein: "The Texas Brigade has always driven the enemy back, and I expect them to do it again today." An early account of the same message in terser language probably is closer to the original: *"Texans always move them"* is how a division staff officer remembered Lee's prompting. Other participants in the tableau spoke of Lee's expression of confidence in general terms. Some styled the comments as addressed directly to John Gregg, who responded with the exhortation cited above.[60]

In a letter written at the time and again eight years later, Pendleton said that Lee used the word "Charge" in spurring the Texans forward. The soldiers being exhorted generally remembered Lee adding aloud that he intended to lead them. Arkansan Cpl. W. G. Lockhart wrote that the words were "I want to lead the Texas Brigade in this charge." Pvt. J. G. Wheeler of the 4th Texas, who lost an arm that morning, recorded similar wording. Capt. A. C. Jones of the 3rd quoted Lee saying, "I will lead you, men." Other contemporaries cited similar phrasing or alluded to Lee's voiced intentions without attempting to re-create the words.[61] Since much of the brigade did not at first notice Lee following when the attack actually rolled forward, this episode obviously took place during the interval behind the guns.

Seeing the South's legendary leader at short range gave the Texans the chance to observe him closely. Some of them thought that he was moved to tears by the emotional episode. The general's son said that Lee admitted as much to him.[62]

On most major battlefields, exchanges between individuals could not have been heard by more than a handful of men, and at very short range, except during brief moments of reduced fire. The peculiar phenomenon of nearly quiet intervals, a few seconds in length, was remarked on many fields. The Wilderness raged as loudly as any battle in Virginia, but it also featured unusually long lulls. The confusion inherent in fighting blindly in thickets may have been responsible. A member of J. E. B. Stuart's staff jotted a note early on May 6 that began, "What a din, what an uproar! The very heavens seem filled with sound." Later in the day he revised his report: "At intervals there is a perfect calm and you might imagine all over when suddenly the whole heavens reverberate with the clamor." That afternoon he concluded that the musketry had not been "as continuous" as he at first thought it would be.[63] One such interlude must have coincided with Lee's voice being heard by so many of Gregg's men.

The Texans' responses to Lee became more famous than his remarks to them. They answered his query about their identity, of course, as the first troops reached the edge of the woods. Gregg and others then exchanged comments with Lee as the brigade neared battle. The shouts of a few men near the army commander urging him to retire, which soon spread through most of the brigade, gave the incident its familiar name: Lee to the Rear.

At least thirty-eight witnesses described the shouts with which the Texas Brigade turned Lee back. Most of them belonged to the brigade or to a nearby unit or to a general's staff, although not all of the thirty-eight actually had a direct eyewitness vantage. A few are secondhand but decidedly contemporary accounts (for instance, the perspicacious Porter Alexander and a 12th Virginia soldier reporting a contemporary conversation with a Texan). Seven of the thirty-eight allude to the nature of the shouts directed at Lee, without providing direct language within quote marks.[64]

The majority of direct quotes include two primary themes: that Lee must go to the rear, and that the men would not go forward until the general went back (usually adding that they had fixed such problems before and would do so again). All but four of the thirty-one quotes include the words "Go back, go back," or a close approximation. Twenty of the thirty-one use the famous phrase "Lee to the rear" or at least something that includes "rear." Not one of the thirty-eight quotes or allusions deviates markedly from the familiar image of Texans imploring Lee to retire.

A battle scene involving hundreds of men, framed at a moment of monumental crisis, simply does not lend itself to crisply limned vignettes to be preserved in amber. Dozens—perhaps hundreds—of infantrymen shouted hoarse entreaties at General Lee. The ample evidence available makes it clear that a dominant chord was "Go back, General Lee, go back. We won't go forward until you go back." Some in the keyed-up, desperate crowd doubtless yelled, "Lee to the rear" as part of the refrain. That snappy rubric understandably caught on in historical writing.

Many another drawled entreaty disappeared from the record as soon as it was spoken, the author and his auditors meeting bullets moments later and scant yards away. Other exhortations fell on illiterate ears, leaving no discernible trace. A few of the shouts reported by contemporaries included deviations from the standard account by means of humor, profanity, or special emotion. A Texan officer said that the yells included, "If you'll go back we'll drive them to hell." John T. Allison of the 5th Texas heard a man shout that the country could not afford to lose Lee. In a contemporary note, Sam Blessing of the 1st Texas declared that some unsophisticated fellows "hollowed" quaintly, "You will get killed dad[d]y."[65]

Two enlisted men among the best candidates for grasping Traveller's reins and turning him to the rear were quoted by contemporaries in some detail. A staff officer heard Leonard Groce Gee of the 5th Texas, with "tears coursing down his cheeks and yells issuing from his throat, exclaim . . . 'I would charge hell itself for that old man.'" A comrade quoted Groce Lawrence of the 4th Texas, who was killed a few minutes later, as saying, "Go back, General Lee, go back! We have whipped them before, and damn 'em, we can whip 'em again!" As the general turned back, Lawrence kicked a foot toward Traveller and said wryly, "Get out of the Wilderness with General Lee, you old loony."[66]

Using the same criteria for proximity applied to sources for the shouts at Lee, at least twenty-nine witnesses report in some manner on the identity of those who turned Traveller to the rear. Twelve describe a generic enlisted man (or two at most); five credit an unnamed officer. Eight accounts speak of a group grabbing the horse; numbers in the group range from four to twenty but often are not precisely estimated. Four credible accounts specify an individual enlisted man as central to the scene; three identify an officer by name.[67]

Charles Venable, among the best situated and most reliable witnesses, in an early letter identified the first man pulling on Traveller's harness as "a sergeant (I remember distinctly)." Venable repeated the rank in a later article. Two decades later a reunion speech delivered before veterans of the brigade—an audience likely to be prickly about details of their great moment—also called the man a sergeant. Rank aside, eyewitnesses described a "stalwart" man (an easy adjective to defend under the circumstances) "of swarthy complexion and earnest expression." General Pendleton remembered the fellow as tall and gray-bearded. A contemporary description by a London newspaperman described "a grim and ragged soldier of the line."[68]

Unnamed officers seen as the motive force in turning Lee about were thought to be "several members of his staff" or "two of his staff." In fact Venable was the only official staff member at hand, but mounted men attending the army commander all fit that vague description. General Alexander heard that "a major took his horse by the bridle." Moxley Sorrel wrote that Lee "was almost forcibly stopped by his officers."[69]

Several individual names circulated as those first to get a hand on Traveller's leather furniture. The likeliest candidates for that distinction, if in fact any individual loomed above a crowd action, were the brigade adjutant, Capt. John William Kerr, and Leonard Groce Gee of Company E (the "Dixie Blues"), 5th Texas. Gee's role is validated by his selection by artist Harry A. McArdle, who painted the scene right after the war on the basis of extensive research with participants.[70]

The best accounts of Traveller's manhandling conclude that many men surged around his flanks at once. A Texan who claimed to have caught the bridle rein admitted that "six or eight men . . . rushed to General Lee . . . but all could not get hands on him. They formed a living barrier to stop his further progress." A member of Field's staff reported that "five or six . . . would gather around him, seize him, his arms, his horse's reins, but he shook them off. . . . Thus did he continue." In other words, more than one group of several men reached for Traveller by turns. Joseph Polley of the 4th Texas did not claim to be among the "twenty or more [who] sprang forward," but "like any other man in the brigade I would have done so" given the chance. Polley aptly concluded, "Exactly what occurred, not even those nearest Lee can tell." Ben Fitzgerald of the 5th Texas summarized the matter cogently. He had "heard as many different stories, as men asked. No two tell the same. . . . In a battle I know that the same thing will make different impressions upon the minds of men."[71]

Lee clearly rode near, perhaps even entirely around, each of the brigade's four regiments at some point, but the climactic episode as the assault rolled forward occurred toward the unit's right or right-center. The three good accounts by witnesses present with the 3rd Arkansas, which occupied the brigade's far left, make little or no claim of being at center stage. Given the egocentricity of humans, that is powerful evidence that events were nearer the Plank Road. Capt. William G. Lockhart—who called the unit "the Texas Brigade" despite being an Arkansan—guessed that the episode was nearest the 1st Texas. Alexander Jones, another Arkansas captain, wrote that "some Texas soldiers seized the reins of [Lee's] horse and forced him to the rear." An account by a member of the 3rd Arkansas, never before cited in connection with this event, claims a brief stint tugging at the reins for an Arkansas soldier but adds that Lee later rode among the Texans and it was there that the cries to go back began.[72]

As the rosy glow of the Lost Cause took a grip on recollections later in life, some veterans launched claims that the famous incident involved Gen.

The Wilderness. "Lee to the Rear" (sketch by Alfred R. Waud).
Angelina V. W. Winkler, The Confederate Capital and Hood's Texas Brigade
(Austin, Tex.: Eugene Von Boeckmann, 1894), opposite p. 160

Nathaniel H. Harris's Mississippi brigade or Georgians under Edward L. Thomas or George T. Anderson. An episode six days later at Spotsylvania between Lee and the Mississippians probably accounts for the first; the Georgian connection is pure myth.[73]

As he turned away from the Texans and left them to their deadly task, Lee rode toward General Longstreet, who had been busy aligning fresh troops on the right of the road and accordingly saw nothing of the famous episode. Solicitous officers steered Lee toward his highest-ranking subordinate. Capt. Erasmus Taylor of Longstreet's staff heard Lee say, "Can't I too, die for my country?" At Colonel Venable's prompting, Longstreet reassured his chief about the condition of the stabilizing lines during a brief meeting at the southwest corner of the field.[74]

The army commander soon had occasion to encourage more arriving troops, although in less stressful circumstances. To Law's arriving brigade Lee called out, "Go on, my brave Alabamians, and drive them back." Capt. J. J. Hatcher of the 15th Alabama—"a corpulent . . . old hero"—had lagged behind and was catching up at a sluggish trot when he passed Lee. "Go on, my brave Alabama captain," Lee exhorted him, "and drive them back!" The general then turned his attention toward the broader-gauge duties of an army commander. One of Stuart's staff reached him with a detailed report, and the two men studied a map as they sat under one of Catharine Tapp's apple trees. After a short ride toward the gap around the Chewning farm, Lee returned to near the Tapp field. As musket balls dropped around him there, Lee "muttered to himself, 'Those balls keep coming this way.'" His worry was about the direction of the shots. The Confederate flank attack Lee was expecting from the southeast would take care of that fire, he knew, if only it would get started.[75]

Gregg's Texans, meanwhile, had redeemed their pledge to Lee at high cost in blood. Their advance across the field soon degenerated into a deadly firefight—"a terrific crash, mingled with wild yells, which settled down into a steady roar of musketry." Federal lead "killed or wounded many of our best and bravest before they had fired a shot," a Texan lamented. The alignment that had thrown the left a bit forward of the right resulted in an advance that slanted across the open space. By the time the attack ground to a halt at the field's eastern edge, all of the 5th and part of the 4th Texas had crossed the Plank Road into the thickets on its southern shoulder. There, intermixed with Kershaw's advance and facing new enemy resistance, the last momentum dissipated. Gregg ordered the survivors to retreat. The brigadier somehow survived unscathed when his horse fell with five mortal wounds.[76]

The headlong lunge into the teeth of the enemy threat accomplished its goal. A Confederate brigadier just behind Gregg's Brigade said of his comrades, "They had delivered a staggering blow and broken the force of the Federal advance." One of Lee's staff wrote succinctly, "The Federal advance was checked, and the Confederate lines reestablished." Having done more than anyone should have expected, the Texans fell sullenly back whence they had come. A captain in the 5th Texas lay in the field with a leg hit so hard that he thought it had been shattered. When his friends fell back past him, though, and Yankees came into view, the captain "concluded just to try my leg, and by gar . . . for four hundred yards, I run like a deer."[77]

Hundreds of Texans strewn across the broom sedge were in no condition to get away, no matter what the impetus. Their desperate quarter-hour had cost the four regiments appreciably more than one-half of their strength. A standard reckoning, oft-repeated, is that the brigade carried in 800 men and lost about 500. A contemporary account reported with apparent precision that the morning strength was 715, of whom 452 were killed, wounded, and missing (about 75 in the first category and 20 in the last). A few years after the war someone computed the strength/loss totals as 811 and 565. A 4th Texas veteran declared that in his regiment the numbers were 207 and 130. The best source extant for losses, because it is a precise enumeration, is a nominal list of losses in the 5th Texas. The names tabulate to 13 killed or mortally wounded, 96 wounded, and 1 missing. Extrapolating from the two regimental totals yields about the same conclusion as the brigade estimates: 700 or 800 men crossed the Tapp field, and about one-third came back. A Texan who survived paraphrased a woeful military maxim as he contemplated the results: "Nothing, except a battle lost, can be half so melancholy as a battle won."[78]

The story of Lee's dramatic actions, and of the Texans' reactions, swept through the army, producing a predictable mixture of admiration and worry. Gen. Bryan Grimes wrote home to North Carolina that same day to pass on a terse description. A soldier in the 15th Georgia, which arrived after the Texans, told his wife in a May 6 letter that "General Lee was among the thick flying balls on the front lines, waving his hat and encouraging the men." Within weeks newspapers all over the South reported the event, often with editorial comment about the foolhardiness of risking what a South Carolina journal called "a life so important and precious to . . . all friends of liberty throughout the world."[79]

The exigencies of battle that spring of 1864, as his accustomed control of events grew elusive, would drive Lee to engage in a series of actions similar to what he did in Catharine Tapp's field. Three more incidents within the next six days, all at Spotsylvania, stand out: rallying troops when the line was penetrated at Doles's Salient on May 10, encouraging the Mississippians of Harris's brigade on May 12 as they approached a dreadful ordeal at what came to be known as the Bloody Angle, and riding near the front of troops under Gen. John B. Gordon facing a desperate counterattack, also on May 12. The last of these came closest to resembling—but by no means equaled for drama and impact—the May 6 encounter with the Texans.[80]

When the first (Texans) and last (Gordon) of the four incidents became garbled in the public press in 1865, author John T. Mason wrote to Lee and asked him to write an accurate version. Mason included his own synopsis, reasonably close to what happened on May 6, but he was uncertain about whether it happened at the Wilderness or Spotsylvania and whether it co-starred Gregg or Gordon. Lee characteristically refused to write a first-hand narrative. Also typically, he completely sidestepped questions about the actions of others, saying vaguely that Mason's account was "substantially correct." Lee admitted recalling something of the sort at Spotsylvania involving Gordon.[81]

The first, Texan-centered, Lee-to-the-Rear episode overshadowed the

"Lee at the Wilderness" (painting by H. A. McArdle).
Harold B. Simpson Confederate Research Center, Hillsboro, Tex.

other three recurrences in 1864 and still does so today. It quickly became the theme of perfervid poetry. The longest of several poetic creations about the brigade is by Mollie Evelyn Moore Davis (1844–1909); it runs to seventy-eight stanzas of four to sixteen lines each. The best-known, and probably best, poem about the event is "Lee at the Wilderness," by the well-known southern poet John Reuben Thompson (1823–1873): "But the fame of that wilderness fight abides / And down into history grandly rides / Calm and unmoved as in battle he sat / The grey-bearded man in the black slouched hat."[82]

Artistic depictions of Lee and the Texans became popular illustrations in war books. The largest and most carefully done graphic image was the appropriately famous "Lee at the Wilderness" by Harry Arthur McArdle. The artist, who also painted large-scale canvases about the Alamo and San Jacinto, had served for a time with the 21st Virginia Infantry. McArdle's careful research among veterans, conducted not long after the event, survives as important documentation. Unfortunately the painting does not; it burned with the Texas State Capitol in 1881.[83]

The first memorial at the site was the product of doleful necessity. Comrades gathered most of the brigade's four score dead and buried them next to the Plank Road at the southeast edge of the Tapp field. A

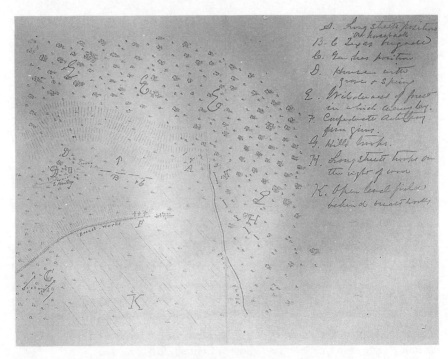

Map of the area where the Lee-to-the-Rear episode occurred, drawn by
H. A. McArdle while doing research for his painting.
Harold B. Simpson Confederate Research Center, Hillsboro, Tex.

single large excavation received all of the corpses, then a board crudely carved with the man's name was stuck in the ground opposite the head of each grave. A Texan who returned eighteen days after the battle to pay homage saw, "nailed to a tree nearer the road . . . another board on which were carved the simple but eloquent words, 'Texas Dead.'" To reach the spot, he had to brave the larval consequences of carnage: "The road and all the pathways leading into it were alive with worms, and above them swarmed myriads of flies." The Tapp field in mid-May 1864 had little of poetry or art about it.[84]

After the war the Texan dead—or at least those who could readily be found—were moved into Fredericksburg's Confederate Cemetery; some bodies must certainly remain beneath the Tapp field sod today. Maj. J. Horace Lacy marked the original grave location with a large, plain, rough quartz rock. It lies today next to some excavations from which Texan bodies were removed, although originally it was propped in vertical position by smaller stones. In 1903 Lacy's son-in-law James Power Smith, a veteran of Stonewall Jackson's staff, erected a more formal monument right next to the road. It says simply, "Lee to the Rear, the Texans Cried, May 6, 1864." Sixty years later the state of Texas added an elaborate red-granite marker nearby, full of officers' names, unit numbers, and statistics.[85]

To one of a literary bent, the most effective memorial to what the Texans and Arkansans did on May 6, 1864, is a vivid, moving fictional account from the pen of John W. Thomason Jr. Colonel Thomason, the grandson of a member of Longstreet's staff and the great-nephew of a Texan shot in the Tapp field, grew up as an admirer and intimate of John W. Stevens, a veteran of the brigade. In his spectacular characterization of Confederate fighting men, *Lone Star Preacher*, Thomason painted an unmatched word picture of the Lee-to-the-Rear episode and illustrated it with striking ink sketches. No one has ever evoked more movingly the moment when, under Lee's eye, the Texans moved "over the trampled rows of the Widow Tapp's kitchen garden, under the trees of her lean orchard, and across her worn-out fields, where the dead of Heth and Wilcox lay in the broom sage." To complete the story, Thomason added a postwar encounter in which his protagonist groused that he had heard 40,000 men claim, "each of them, personally, that he was the fellow who grabbed Traveller's bits and turned General Lee around."[86]

The Texas Brigade accomplished a great deal tactically in its headlong charge on the morning of May 6, 1864. By any objective standard, however, it did little if anything more than Kershaw's troops achieved across the Plank Road. The brigade's own earlier desperate daring at Gaines's Mill and on the slopes of Little Round Top counted more significantly in a purely military sense. The combination of immediate battlefield necessity and personal leadership extended by Lee at personal risk elevated May 6 in the eyes of participants and observers alike. The Texans and Lee had experienced an unparalleled military epiphany.

The terms of engagement in Virginia had changed. Without Jackson, with a dwindling supply of manpower, with Federals springing from the earth apparently inexhaustibly, the Army of Northern Virginia's certainties of 1862 and 1863 stood challenged. Among Lee's responses, generated by conscious duty and even more by visceral reaction, was to throw his person into battlefield situations that he earlier had mastered by other means. A newspaper correspondent writing twelve days after the Tapp field affair marveled and wondered. The incident, he wrote, "has given history a striking proof of the attachment of his troops to his person. The world did not, however, want any evidence of his own devotion; and can hardly fail to pronounce judgment against his course on that occasion as one of rashness. His exposure during the present campaign has been so unusual . . . as to have impressed his troops with profound concern."[87]

By the time that worried analysis was written, the Lee-to-the-Rear phenomenon had ended. The Confederate commander had adjusted to military realities beyond his power to affect by personal bravery.

NOTES

1. W[illiam] F[erguson] Smith, "Longstreet to the Rescue of Thomas' Brigade," Atlanta *Journal*, September 21, 1901; William H. Palmer in William L. Royall, *Some Reminiscences* (New York: Neale, 1909), 28; Theodore Sanford Garnett, *Riding with Stuart: Reminiscences of an Aide-de-Camp*, ed. Robert J. Trout (Shippensburg, Pa.: White Mane, 1994), 52. A remarkably similar episode involving Hill again, but not Lee, took place at the Chewning farm. It is sometimes confused with the event at Tapp's. The best account is from Palmer in Royall, *Reminiscences*, 33.

2. Garnett, *Riding with Stuart*, 53; P. H. Powers to his wife, May 4–6, 1864, typescript at Fredericksburg and Spotsylvania National Military Park Library, Fredericksburg, Va. (repository hereafter cited as FSNMP).

3. Palmer in Royall, *Reminiscences*, 30; Walter Clark, comp., *Histories of the Several Regiments and Battalions from North Carolina in the Great War, 1861–'65*, 5 vols. (Goldsboro, N.C: Nash Brothers, 1901), 2:665.

4. Cadmus M. Wilcox to E. Porter Alexander, March 10, 1869, Edward Porter Alexander Papers, Southern Historical Collection, Wilson Library, University of North Carolina, Chapel Hill (repository hereafter cited as SHC); Leigh Robinson, *The South Before and at the Battle of the Wilderness* (Richmond, Va.: James E. Goode, 1878), 74.

5. Susan P. Lee, ed., *Memoirs of William Nelson Pendleton* (Philadelphia: Lippincott, 1893), 325; William T. Poague, *Gunner with Stonewall*, ed. Monroe F. Cockrell (Jackson, Tenn.: McCowat-Mercer Press, 1957), 88; Charles R. Dudley letter, June 12, 1896, Confederate Veteran Papers, William R. Perkins Library, Duke University, Durham, N.C. (repository hereafter cited as DU). Dudley's long letter about the experience of the Madison Light Artillery at the Wilderness, which opens with neither addressee nor salutation, is an important source and seems reliable. He called the recovered piece a Napoleon; Poague said it was "a beautiful 3-inch rifle." Confirmation that the battery had four Napoleons is in Dunbar Rowland, *The Official and Statistical Register of the State of Mississippi* (Nashville: Brandon, 1908), 522.

6. Henry Heth, *The Memoirs of Henry Heth*, ed. James L. Morrison Jr. (Westport, Conn.: Greenwood Press, 1974), 184.

7. Cadmus M. Wilcox, "Lee and Grant in the Wilderness," in [A. K. McClure, ed.], *The Annals of the War Written by Leading Participants North and South. Originally Published in the Philadelphia Weekly Times* (Philadelphia: Times Pub. Co., 1879), 485–501; Cadmus M. Wilcox to E. P. Alexander, March 10, 1869, Alexander Papers, SHC; Wilcox's manuscript report of operations, Wilderness through

Cold Harbor, Lee Headquarters Papers, Virginia Historical Society, Richmond. The *Annals* account is the longest and best known, but the unpublished official report, submitted in November 1864, is the earliest and most important Wilcox version; the quote in the text is taken from the report.

8. Lee, *Pendleton*, 325; untitled 1922 Fred W. Cross memoir of a visit to Wilderness, FSNMP; Wilcox, "Lee and Grant in the Wilderness," 496.

9. Palmer in Royall, *Reminiscences*, 30–31; Heth, *Memoirs*, 184–85; Robinson, *The South*, 73.

10. Heth, *Memoirs*, 185; Poague, *Gunner with Stonewall*, 88–89.

11. G. Moxley Sorrel, *Recollections of a Confederate Staff Officer* (New York: Neale, 1905), 239–40; manuscript marginalia by Col. Samuel H. Walkup, 48th North Carolina, in his copy of John Esten Cooke's biography of Lee, in possession of Walkup's great-great-granddaughter. Walkup's mention of punitive removal is neither documented elsewhere nor generally credible. That he believed it, however, is an important revelation of army attitudes.

12. Wilcox's manuscript report; Robinson, *The South*, 73.

13. Lee's recognition of the crucial importance of Gordonsville also affected his broad arrangements at the beginning of the Chancellorsville campaign. Another reason to station Longstreet near Gordonsville was "to have the advantage of the two railroads intersecting there, in order . . . [to] be gotten into the best possible condition for the next campaign," Lee later told his son Custis Lee (G. W. C. Lee to Fitzhugh Lee, February 11, 1896, transcript from a Joseph Rubinfine manuscript sale catalog, ca. 1980).

14. For the departure from Mechanicsville, see an 1879 letter by E. P. Alexander in James Longstreet, *From Manassas to Appomattox: Memoirs of the Civil War in America* (Philadelphia: Lippincott, 1896), 570. Alexander timed the halt of his artillery on May 5 at "about five P.M." A member of Gen. John Gregg's staff wrote that his infantry went into camp "about 7 or 8 P.M." (R. C., "Gen. Lee at the 'Wilderness,'" *Land We Love* 5 [October 1868]: 482). The colonel of the 4th Alabama wrote, "We halted about 10 P.M." (Pinckney D. Bowles, "Battle of the Wilderness," Philadelphia *Weekly Times*, October 4, 1884).

15. Most primary accounts report arising at 1:00, 2:00, or 3:00 A.M. See H. Russell Wright, "Longstreet at Gettysburg," in [Dotsy Boineau, comp.], *Recollections and Reminiscences, 1861-1865 through World War I*, 6 vols. to date (n.p.: McNaughton & Gunn [for the South Carolina Division, United Daughters of the Confederacy], 1990–95), 1:37 (1:00 A.M.); J. B. Kershaw's official report (1:00 A.M.), in U.S. War Department, *The War of the Rebellion: A Compilation of the Official Records of the Union and Confederate Armies*, 127 vols., index, and atlas (Washington, D.C.: GPO, 1880–1901), ser. 1, 36(1):1061 (hereafter cited as *OR*); Sorrel, *Recollections*, 240 (1:00 A.M.); Robert T. Cole, "History of the 4th Alabama," Alabama Department of Archives and History, Montgomery (2:00 A.M.); Joseph B. Polley, *A Soldier's Letters to Charming Nellie* (New York: Neale, 1908), 231 (2:00 A.M.); Bowles, "Battle of the Wilderness" (2:00 A.M.); S. T. Blessing, "The First Month of the Virginia Campaign," Galveston *Weekly News*, July 27, 1864 (3:00 A.M.); R. C., "Lee at the 'Wilderness,'" 482 (3:00 A.M.); Joseph Prior Fuller diary, May 6, 1864, Fuller Papers, SHC (3:30 A.M.). Longstreet's

official report declared, with customary exaggeration, that the march began at 12:30 A.M. (*OR* 36[1]:1054).

16. R. C., "Lee at the 'Wilderness,'" 482, mentions the long roll; Bowles, "Battle of the Wilderness," recounts the serenading of Jenkins.

17. James B. Rawls, "Veteran's Sketch of Life from Battle of Chickamauga to Arrival at Home," *United Daughters of the Confederacy Magazine* 52 (June 1989): 17; Wright, "Longstreet at Gettysburg," 37; William Meade Dame, *From the Rapidan to Richmond and the Spotsylvania Campaign: A Sketch in Personal Narrative of Scenes a Soldier Saw* (Baltimore: Green-Lucas, 1920), 84; "Kershaw's Brigade," *Carolina Spartan* (Spartanburg, S.C.), May 26, 1864; Charles W. Field, "Campaign of 1864 and 1865," in *Southern Historical Society Papers*, ed. J. William Jones and others, 52 vols. (Richmond, Va.: Southern Historical Society, 1876–1959), 14:543 (hereafter cited as *SHSP*).

18. Edward Porter Alexander, *Fighting for the Confederacy: The Personal Recollections of General Edward Porter Alexander*, ed. Gary W. Gallagher (Chapel Hill: University of North Carolina Press, 1989), 356; Cole, "4th Alabama," 8; R. C., "Lee at the 'Wilderness,'" 482–83.

19. Evander M. Law, "From the Wilderness to Cold Harbor," in *Battles and Leaders of the Civil War*, ed. Robert Underwood Johnson and Clarence Clough Buel, 4 vols. (New York: Century, 1887–88), 4:124; Bowles, "Battle of the Wilderness"; Cole, "4th Alabama," 8; D. H. Hamilton, *History of Company M, First Texas Volunteer Infantry* (Waco, Tex.: W. M. Morrison, 1962), 57–58; "Benning's Brigade in the Virginia Battles," Augusta *Chronicle & Sentinel*, June 1, 1864; W. F. Smith, "Longstreet to the Rescue."

20. Robinson, *The South*, 74; Fuller diary, May 6, 1864; Longstreet, *Manassas to Appomattox*, 560; Palmer in Royall, *Reminiscences*, 31. Sunrise at Richmond that morning came at 5:07 (*The Confederate States Almanac . . .* [Mobile: H. C. Clarke, (1863)]).

21. G. W. C. Lee to Fitzhugh Lee, February 11, 1896, transcript from Rubinfine catalog; Henry B. McClellan, "The Wilderness Fight," Philadelphia *Weekly Times*, January 26, 1878. Field's own narrative ("Campaign of 1864 and 1865," 543) says blandly, "At midnight I received orders to move immediately."

22. Venable's account deserves special attention because it is in a friendly letter to Longstreet himself dated July 25, 1879 (Longstreet Papers, DU). Longstreet printed an innocuous snippet from the letter in his *Manassas to Appomattox*, 571. He characteristically omitted all of the content covering Lee's anxiety over the First Corps's arrival and about the multiple messengers.

23. Edward Porter Alexander, *Military Memoirs of a Confederate: A Critical Narrative* (New York: Scribner's, 1907), 503; Joseph B. Polley, *Hood's Texas Brigade* (New York: Neale, 1910), 230–31; Field, "Campaign of 1864 and 1865," 543; Fuller diary, May 6, 1864; "Kershaw's Brigade," *Carolina Spartan* (Spartanburg, S.C.), May 26, 1864; J. M. (probably James M. Goggin), "The Battle of the Wilderness," unidentified 1867 newspaper clipping in Alexander Papers, SHC.

24. Cole, "4th Alabama," 9; Clark, *Regiments and Battalions from North Carolina*, 2:665.

25. Wilcox's manuscript report; Palmer in Royall, *Reminiscences*, 31; Bowles, "Battle of the Wilderness."

26. Miles V. Smith, *Reminiscences of the Civil War* (n.p., n.d.), 49; Robinson, *The South*, 74; official report of Lt. Col. John W. McGill, 18th North Carolina, James H. Lane Papers, Auburn University, Auburn, Ala.; W. F. Smith, "Longstreet to the Rescue"; Edward Porter Alexander, *Fighting for the Confederacy*, 357; Edward Porter Alexander, *Military Memoirs*, 503. The swearing staffer appears in both Alexander accounts. The quote in the text is from the first citation (that in *Military Memoirs* is bowdlerized), omitting without ellipses a connective phrase not part of the quote.

27. Edward Porter Alexander, *Fighting for the Confederacy*, 357; J. F. J. Caldwell, "Reminiscences of the War of Secession," in *History of South Carolina*, ed. Yates Snowden, 5 vols. (Chicago: Lewis, 1920), 2:828; William S. Dunlop, *Lee's Sharpshooters; or, The Forefront of Battle. A Story of Southern Valor that Never Has Been Told* (Little Rock, Ark.: Tunnah & Pittard, 1899), 32.

28. Edward Porter Alexander, *Military Memoirs*, 503; *OR* 36(1):1063.

29. Peter Wellington Alexander, "From General Lee's Army," *Daily South Carolinian* (Columbia), May 28, 1864; R. C., "Lee at the 'Wilderness,'" 484.

30. Kershaw's report, *OR* 36(1):1061; Law, "Wilderness to Cold Harbor," 4:124; John W. Wofford, "A Gallant Company, Company K, Third South Carolina," in *History of the Wofford Family*, by Jane W. Wait, John W. Wofford, and Carrie W. Floyd (Spartanburg, S.C.: Band & White, 1928), 206; "Wofford's Georgia Brigade," *Southern Confederacy* (Atlanta), June 15, 1864. For Henagan, see Robert K. Krick, *Lee's Colonels: A Biographical Register of the Field Officers of the Army of Northern Virginia* (Dayton, Ohio: Morningside, 1992), 189.

31. Dame, *Rapidan to Richmond*, 84–86; Palmer in Royall, *Reminiscences*, 32–33; Sorrel, *Recollections*, 240.

32. William Nelson Pendleton to Henry A. McArdle, December 10, 1872, in Dayton Kelley, *General Lee and Hood's Texas Brigade at the Battle of the Wilderness* (Hillsboro, Tex.: Hill Junior College Press, 1969), 45; P. H. Powers to wife, May 4–6, 1864, FSNMP. Kelley's slender but well-done monograph also appeared in part in "The Texas Brigade at the Wilderness," *Texana* 11 (1973): 103–23.

33. Angelina V. W. Winkler, *The Confederate Capital and Hood's Texas Brigade* (Austin, Tex.: Eugene Von Boeckmann, 1894), 167; Wilcox, "Lee and Grant in the Wilderness," 496; Pendleton to McArdle, December 10, 1872, and George W. Clampitt to Henry A. McArdle, August 18, 1872, in Kelley, *Lee and Hood's Texas Brigade*, 45, 47; Garnett, *Riding with Stuart*, 52; Edward Porter Alexander, *Fighting for the Confederacy*, 357. Wilcox, Pendleton, and Clampitt each use the phrase "old field." The same description is familiar for other late-war battle sites (such as the Landrum farm of Bloody Angle fame six days after the Tapp field fight) in Virginia on fields once cultivated but by 1864 just a deteriorating "old field."

34. Wilcox, "Lee and Grant in the Wilderness," 496; Clampitt to McArdle, August 18, 1872, in Kelley, *Lee and Hood's Texas Brigade*, 47. The thin band of brush near the road is marked on a detailed survey done soon after the war by a visiting Federal engineer. Just how it looked in 1864 is unknowable. The C. R. Dudley

letter, June 12, 1896, DU, always reliable where susceptible to checking, thought the field covered "about forty acres."

35. Annabel S. Boyce, *The Artists Frankenstein* (Bryn Mawr, Pa.: Privately printed, 1981). The near-destruction of the original watercolor, which at that time had not been photographed, came about when the police officer placed in charge of historic preservation at FSNMP by the National Park Service took a fancy to the painting and kept it in his desk in a hold file full of law-enforcement dockets. The fragile watercolor survived by being pulled out of a waste bin after the policeman's transfer.

36. Morris Schaff, *The Battle of the Wilderness* (Boston: Houghton Mifflin, 1910), 171; 1860 Population Schedules of the Census of the United States, Spotsylvania County, St. George's Parish, 75, and 1860 Agricultural Census, 456, RG 29, National Archives, Washington, D.C.; file on location of the cabin site, including recollections of old residents, FSNMP; detailed diagram of "Tugg" homestead, unidentified map copy, FSNMP; Spotsylvania County Deed Book AL, 17, county courthouse, Spotsylvania Court House, Va. Garnett, *Riding with Stuart*, 56, adds apples to Schaff's plums and cherries. For the opening of the Plank Road, see Fredericksburg *Weekly Advertiser*, July 9, 1853.

37. 1860 Population Schedules of the Census of the United States, Spotsylvania County, St. George's Parish (dwelling #588, family #583), 75. That corner of the county was recorded in July.

38. Ralph Happel, " 'Phenie' Tapp Dies at 84; Saw Battle of Wilderness," Fredericksburg *Free Lance-Star*, June 3, 1944; "Mrs. Phenie Tapp Dies at Wilderness," Fredericksburg *Free Lance-Star*, June 2, 1944. This account is paraphrased and quoted in part, without citation or attribution, in Stephen W. Sylvia and Michael J. O'Donnell, *The Illustrated History of American Civil War Relics* (Orange, Va.: By the authors, 1978), 179–80. Phenie still lived on the Tapp field when she died, having supported herself at times by brewing moonshine; she was raided in desultory fashion by revenuers. Dr. Douglas Southall Freeman attempted to buy the farm to preserve it during the late 1930s but found Phenie eccentric, the title clouded, and funds hard to raise. This last member of the Tapp line in the region went by "Mrs. Phenie Tapp," the third generation named Tapp. Local lore insists that the origin of Phenie Tapp with one of Catharine's daughters was landlord Lacy. In 1944 Phenie was living in the third simple Tapp dwelling on the field. The approximate configurations of the field were restored by a 1987 clearing project. The site of the 1864 cabin was identified and then uncovered in 1989 by documentary research, followed by remote sensing and then by archaeology. Foundation stones of the second and third buildings were simply hauled away about 1970 by National Park Service crews weary of having to mow around them.

39. *OR* 36(1):1038, 1054; Palmer in Royall, *Reminiscences*, 31; C. R. Dudley letter, June 12, 1896, DU; William T. Poague to John Warwick Daniel, March 29, 1904, box 23, folder 1904, John Warwick Daniel Papers, University of Virginia, Charlottesville (repository hereafter cited as UVA). A 1st Texas soldier, moving past the guns in a feverish moment, recalled only "a few pieces of cannon" (O. T. Hanks, *History of . . . Benton's Company, Hood's Texas Brigade, 1861–1865* [Austin, Tex.: Privately printed, 1964], 28). An artillery return by William Nelson Pendleton,

purporting to show 1864 campaign strengths but dated February 28, 1865 (*OR* 36[1]:1038), reports twelve guns for Poague. Dudley, Palmer, and Poague as cited above, however, all record sixteen guns in action.

40. Palmer in Royall, *Reminiscences*, 32, mentions the one gun in the road. Porter Alexander (*Fighting for the Confederacy*, 357) said, "Poague's guns . . . were among the small pines," but he probably referred to the "thin" strip closest to the road or the scattered saplings springing up in mid-field; those same imprecise boundaries must have affected other accounts as well. Poague (*Gunner with Stonewall*, 88) described the location as "about midway of the field" but still estimated 300 yards open to the east. Pendleton (to McArdle, December 10, 1872, in Kelley, *Lee and Hood's Texas Brigade*, 45) wrote, "Near the border of this old field were . . . cannon ready for action," and the fine C. R. Dudley letter (June 12, 1896, DU) declared that the field "was directly in front of our guns." The rail works are mentioned in Winkler, *Confederate Capital*, 164; Charles S. Venable, "The Campaign from the Wilderness to Petersburg," *SHSP*, 14:525; Samuel H. Emerson, *History of the War of the Confederacy* (Malvern, Ark.: Privately printed, 1918), 62. Only Venable mentioned artillery pits; he did so twice. R. C., "Lee at the 'Wilderness,'" 483, is authority for the continuing work on the pits and for the infantry rallying in them.

41. Wilcox, "Lee and Grant in the Wilderness," 496; Dunlop, *Lee's Sharpshooters*, 33; Pendleton to McArdle, December 10, 1872, in Kelley, *Lee and Hood's Texas Brigade*, 45; Lee, *Pendleton*, 326.

42. Palmer in Royall, *Reminiscences*, 31–32; Poague, *Gunner with Stonewall*, 89–90; C. R. Dudley letter, June 12, 1896, DU; Poague to Daniel, March 29, 1904, Daniel Papers, UVA; Wilcox, "Lee and Grant in the Wilderness," 496.

43. Dunlop, *Lee's Sharpshooters*, 33; Palmer in Royall, *Reminiscences*, 31; Hanks, *Benton's Company*, 28; C. R. Dudley letter, June 12, 1896, DU; Poague to Daniel, March 29, 1904, Daniel Papers, UVA.

44. Field, "Campaign of 1864 and 1865," 543; Alexander Carson Jones, "Lee in the Wilderness," Philadelphia *Weekly Times*, May 8, 1880 (the account by Jones, who was an officer in the 3rd Arkansas, also appeared in the Lexington [Va.] *Gazette*, May 20, 1880); Emerson, *History of the War*, 62; Winkler, *Confederate Capital*, 166; Hanks, *Benton's Company*, 28; Polley, *Hood's Texas Brigade*, 231.

45. Polley, *Charming Nellie*, 231; Polley, *Hood's Texas Brigade*, 231; Winkler, *Confederate Capital*, 164; Hanks, *Benton's Company*, 28; Palmer in Royall, *Reminiscences*, 32.

46. The regimental alignment is established well in Kelley, *Lee and Hood's Texas Brigade*, 16–18. There is no reason to revise Kelley's skillful construction. Among the useful bits of primary evidence is Clampitt to McArdle, August 18, 1872, in Kelley, *Lee and Hood's Texas Brigade*, 47, which reports that Clampitt's 5th Texas "reached the plank road," and E. J. Parrent, "General Lee to the Rear," *Confederate Veteran* 2 (January 1894): 14, which places the 4th Texas "on the left, center of the brigade." Emerson, *History of the War*, 62, is authority for the skirmishers. For the right being tied to the road, see Field, "Campaign of 1864 and 1865," 543, and Poague, *Gunner with Stonewall*, 90.

47. Polley, *Hood's Texas Brigade*, 231; John T. Allison, 5th Texas, in Mamie

Yeary, comp., *Reminiscences of the Boys in Gray* (Dallas: Smith & Lamar, 1912), 13; Winkler, *Confederate Capital*, 170; Venable to McArdle, September 20, 1872, in Kelley, *Lee and Hood's Texas Brigade*, 49; C. R. Dudley letter, June 12, 1896, DU; Emerson, *History of the War*, 62; Poague, *Gunner with Stonewall*, 90.

48. Walter H. Taylor, *Four Years with General Lee* (New York: Appleton, 1877), 127; William W. Chamberlaine, *Memoirs of the Civil War* (Washington, D.C.: Byron S. Adams, 1912), 94; Alfred Zachry, "Four Shots for the Cause," *Civil War Times Illustrated* 33 (November–December 1994): 101.

49. Pendleton to McArdle, December 10, 1872, in Kelley, *Lee and Hood's Texas Brigade*, 46; Venable, "Wilderness to Petersburg," 525; Vivian Minor Fleming, *The Wilderness Campaign* (Richmond: W. C. Hill, 1922), 11; Edward Porter Alexander, *Fighting for the Confederacy*, 357; Law, "Wilderness to Cold Harbor," 4:124; C. R. Dudley letter, June 12, 1896, DU.

50. Cadmus M. Wilcox to E. P. Alexander, March 10, 1869, Alexander Papers, SHC; Wright, "Longstreet at Gettysburg," 37; LeGrand James Wilson, *The Confederate Soldier* (Fayetteville, Ark.: M'Roy Printing Co., 1902), 153; R. C., "Lee at the 'Wilderness,'" 484.

51. Rawls, "Veteran's Sketch," 17; R. C., "Lee at the 'Wilderness,'" 483.

52. W. L. Goldsmith, "Gen. Lee About to Enter Battle," *Confederate Veteran* 2 (February 1894): 36; Venable to McArdle, September 20, 1872, and Pendleton to McArdle, December 10, 1872, in Kelley, *Lee and Hood's Texas Brigade*, 49, 46; B. L. Aycock, *A Sketch of the Lone Star Guards* (n.p., n.d.), 12; R. J. Harding, "Lee to the Rear," in *Unveiling and Dedication of Monument to Hood's Texas Brigade*, comp. F. B. Chilton (Houston: F. B. Chilton), 174–75; Allison in Yeary, *Boys in Gray*, 13; Parrent, "General Lee to the Rear," 14.

53. The best of the many accounts of Lee during the passage through the guns are Palmer in Royall, *Reminiscences*, 32; Poague to Daniel, March 29, 1904, Daniel Papers, UVA; Law, "Wilderness to Cold Harbor," 4:124; Robinson, *The South*, 75; Venable to McArdle, September 20, 1872, in Kelley, *Lee and Hood's Texas Brigade*, 49; and Poague, *Gunner with Stonewall*, 90.

54. Field, "Campaign of 1864 and 1865," 544; Lee, *Pendleton*, 326; Winkler, *Confederate Capital*, 167.

55. C. R. Dudley letter, June 12, 1896, DU; Polley, *Hood's Texas Brigade*, 231; Jones, "Lee in the Wilderness"; Heth, *Memoirs*, 185.

56. Chilton, *Unveiling and Dedication*, 222 (this account appeared first in the Galveston *News*, May 7, 1874); Venable to McArdle, September 20, 1872, in Kelley, *Lee and Hood's Texas Brigade*, 50; Winkler, *Confederate Capital*, 170; Edward Porter Alexander, *Fighting for the Confederacy*, 358.

57. The extent of Gregg's Chickamauga wound is attested by Julia Morgan, *How It Was, Four Years Among the Rebels* (Nashville: Publishing House, Methodist Episcopal Church, South, 1892), 59. Morgan saw Gregg in Marietta with "his face and head bandaged" and apparently "in great pain." Venable to McArdle, September 20, 1872, in Kelley, *Lee and Hood's Texas Brigade*, 50, reported the bullet hole. The conversation with Lee is from R. C., "Lee at the 'Wilderness,'" 484.

58. Leonard Groce Gee, "The Texan Who Held Gen. R. E. Lee's Horse," *Confederate Veteran* 12 (October 1904): 478; Emerson, *History of the War*, 62 (which

has Gregg waving his hat, too); Winkler, *Confederate Capital*, 164; Aycock, *Lone Star Guards*, 12; R. C., "Lee at the 'Wilderness,'" 485; Polley, *Charming Nellie*, 232; Chilton, *Unveiling and Dedication*, 174; Venable, "Wilderness to Petersburg," 526. Most accounts include some variables, but—as proved to be the case with most of the elements of this affair—a pervasive general conformity does exist.

59. Lee, *Pendleton*, 326; Gee, "Texan Who Held Lee's Horse," 478; Hanks, *Benton's Company*, 28; Blessing, "First Month"; Miles V. Smith, *Reminiscences*, 49.

60. Chilton, *Unveiling and Dedication*, 174; Winkler, *Confederate Capital*, 164; Polley, *Charming Nellie*, 231; Miles V. Smith, *Reminiscences*, 49; Blessing, "First Month"; R. C., "Lee at the 'Wilderness,'" 485; Gee, "Texan Who Held Lee's Horse," 478.

61. Lee, *Pendleton*, 326; Pendleton to McArdle, December 10, 1872, in Kelley, *Lee and Hood's Texas Brigade*, 46; William G. Lockhart, "Lee at Orange C. H.," *Confederate Veteran* 11 (June 1903): 268; John Gill Wheeler, "Lee to the Rear," *Confederate Veteran* 11 (March 1903): 116; Jones, "Lee in the Wilderness"; Field, "Campaign of 1864 and 1865," 544; Hanks, *Benton's Company*, 28–29; Robinson, *The South*, 75.

62. John F. Sale (12th Virginia Infantry) diary, May 31, 1864 (based on a conversation with a Texan eyewitness), copy in bound vol. 3, FSNMP; James T. Hall in Yeary, *Boys in Gray*, 297; Col. R. J. Harding, citing conversation with Lee's son, in Chilton, *Unveiling and Dedication*, 175; Wilson, *Confederate Soldier*, 154.

63. P. H. Powers to wife, May 4–6, 1864, FSNMP.

64. Each of the thirty-eight sources is cited in other notes, most of them repeatedly. To enumerate them again here would require a full page—and constitute misplaced pedantry. The summary of their content in the text in succeeding paragraphs includes notes citing only the few unusual variants.

65. "Did Gen. Lee Offer to Lead Two Brigades?," *Our Living and Our Dead* 2 (March 1875): 48; Allison in Yeary, *Boys in Gray*, 13; Blessing, "First Month." In a much later account Blessing quoted his mates as saying, "Go back, Daddy, we will go without you" (in Yeary, *Boys in Gray*, 61). Another witness recounted a conversation during which a lieutenant tried to convince Lee that his presence posed an obstacle to the Texans' counterattack: "You are about to spoil everything; the Texas brigade will not charge with you in front; they will not see you killed" (W. D. Wood, comp., *A Partial Roster of the Officers and Men Raised in Leon County, Texas* [n.p., 1899], 14–15).

66. R. C., "Lee at the 'Wilderness,'" 485; Val C. Giles, *Rags and Hope: The Recollections of Val C. Giles, Four Years with Hood's Brigade, Fourth Texas Infantry, 1861–1865*, ed. Mary Lasswell (New York: Coward-McCann, 1961), 107.

67. Each of the twenty-nine sources is cited in other notes. As with attribution of the troops' exhortations to Lee (n. 64, above), there is no point in repeating them in a block. Succeeding notes cite descriptions that make specific points. The categories in the text add up to thirty-two, not twenty-nine. The difference arises from individuals specified in accounts that also speak of group action.

68. Venable to McArdle, September 20, 1872, in Kelley, *Lee and Hood's Texas Brigade*, 50; Venable, "Wilderness to Petersburg," 526; James W. Throckmorton,

Speech of Hon. James W. Throckmorton . . . at a Soldiers' Re-union at Waco, Texas (McKinney, Tex.: Examiner Book and Job Printing House, 1889), 7; Walter H. Taylor, *General Lee: His Campaigns in Virginia, 1861–1865* (Norfolk: Nusbaum, 1906), 234; Aycock, *Lone Star Guards*, 13; Lee, *Pendleton*, 326; "Battle of the Wilderness," letter dated May 18, 1864, by correspondent of the London *Herald*, in Augusta (Ga.) *Daily Constitutionalist*, May 31, 1864.

69. Poague, *Gunner with Stonewall*, 90; Samuel F. Harper (22nd North Carolina, detailed as courier to A. P. Hill) to father, May 6, 1864, North Carolina Department of Archives and History, Raleigh; Edward Porter Alexander, *Fighting for the Confederacy*, 358; Sorrel in John R. Turner, *The Battle of the Wilderness!: The Part Taken by Mahone's Brigade. An Address Delivered by . . .* (Petersburg, Va.: Fenn & Owen, [1892]), 3.

70. An efficient summary of the known claimants (several identified by second parties, rather than autobiographically) is in Kelley, *Lee and Hood's Texas Brigade*, 11–19. Kelley's conclusion that Gee is the likeliest candidate is hard to dispute. The only individual claimant whom I have found that Kelley missed was Lewis P. Butler of Company I, 3rd Arkansas (Emerson, *History of the War*, 63). The account citing Butler, however, admits that Lee subsequently moved on well to the right into a crowd of Texans, so it is doubtless referring to a portion of the earlier encounters between Lee and the troops. Adjutant Kerr, a Virginia Military Institute man, suffered a peculiar fate for a participant in the famous Lee tableau: he died in Brooklyn in 1903.

71. R. J. Harding in Chilton, *Unveiling and Dedication*, 175; R. C., "Lee at the 'Wilderness,'" 485; Polley, *Hood's Texas Brigade*, 231; Parrent, "General Lee to the Rear"; B. S. Fitzgerald to H. A. McArdle, December 4, 1872, in Kelley, *Lee and Hood's Texas Brigade*, 51–52.

72. Lockhart, "Lee at Orange C.H."; Jones, "Lee in the Wilderness"; Emerson, *History of the War*, 63.

73. Examples of the confused versions are A. E. Graves (45th Georgia), "Led Lee to the Rear," unidentified newspaper account in clippings folder, Charles Edgeworth Jones Papers, DU, and Travis Hudson, ". . . History of the 59th Georgia . . . ," *Atlanta Historical Journal* 26 (Winter 1982–83): 21. The latter cites a manuscript at Georgia Department of Archives and History that actually describes an undated incident. Neither of two excellent accounts of the Wilderness by General Harris so much as mentions Lee (Harris to William Mahone, August 2, 1866, Virginia State Archives, Richmond, and Harris to Charles J. Lewis, March 22, 1899, copy in possession of the author). A convincing account of the battle by a First Corps staff officer—evidently James M. Goggin—states accurately that "Harris's Mississippi brigade had no part or lot in it. . . . It was not on the ground" (J. M., "The Battle of the Wilderness," unidentified 1867 newspaper clipping in the Alexander Papers, SHC).

74. Pendleton to McArdle, December 10, 1872, in Kelley, *Lee and Hood's Texas Brigade*, 46; Edward Porter Alexander, *Fighting for the Confederacy*, 358; Law, "Wilderness to Cold Harbor," 4:125; Winkler, *Confederate Capital*, 168; Erasmus Taylor memoir, Orange County Historical Society, Orange, Va.; Longstreet, *Manassas to Appomattox*, 560–61.

75. Garnett, *Riding with Stuart*, 56; Cole, "4th Alabama," 10; Bowles, "Battle of the Wilderness"; Poague to Daniel, March 29, 1904, Daniel Papers, UVA; Chamberlaine, *Memoirs*, 95.

76. Edward Porter Alexander, *Military Memoirs*, 504 (which makes the point that losses left of the road, in the open, were heavier than on the right); Law, "Wilderness to Cold Harbor," 4:125; Polley, *Hood's Texas Brigade*, 232; Polley, *Charming Nellie*, 232 (which specifies an advance of 200 more yards after crossing the road); C. R. Dudley letter, June 12, 1896, DU; Winkler, *Confederate Capital*, 164; Clampitt to McArdle, August 18, 1872, in Kelley, *Lee and Hood's Texas Brigade*, 47. For Gregg and his horse, see R. C., "Lee at the 'Wilderness,'" 486, and Emerson, *History of the War*, 63.

77. Taylor, *Four Years*, 128; Law, "Wilderness to Cold Harbor," 4:125; *Land We Love* 4 (February 1868): 349.

78. Venable, "Wilderness to Petersburg," 526 (800 strong/lost "half"); R. J. Harding in Chilton, *Unveiling and Dedication*, 175 (800/500); Field, "Campaign of 1864 and 1865," 544 (two-thirds lost); Blessing, "First Month" (715/452); Galveston *News*, May 7, 1874, in Chilton, *Unveiling and Dedication*, 222 (811/565); Polley, *Hood's Texas Brigade*, 232 (207/130 in 4th); manuscript letters cited by Harold B. Simpson, *Gaines' Mill to Appomattox* (Waco, Tex.: Texian Press, 1963), 201 (800 strong); *Hood's Brigade Historical Papers* (n.p., n.d.), 13–14 (110 loss in 5th). The last source, which is unrecorded, apparently dates from 1870–1880. The melancholy quote (from Polley, *Charming Nellie*, 233) may derive from Wellington's "There is nothing so dreadful as a great victory—except a great defeat."

79. Bryan Grimes, *Extracts of Letters of Major-General Bryan Grimes to His Wife*, ed. Pulaski Cowper (Raleigh, N.C.: Alfred Williams, 1884), 51; Edgeworth Bird and Sallie Bird, *The Granite Farm Letters*, ed. John Rozier (Athens: University of Georgia Press, 1988), 164; "Interesting Incidents," Columbus (Ga.) *Enquirer*, June 4, 1864; Peter Wellington Alexander, "From General Lee's Army."

80. These later affairs are acceptably summarized in the standard secondary literature on the army (see, for instance, Douglas Southall Freeman, *R. E. Lee: A Biography*, 4 vols. [New York: Scribner's, 1934–35], 3:313–21) but deserve more careful examination both as dramatic events and as keys to Lee's changing behavior at a time when demands on him increased.

81. Lee's letter, dated December 7, 1865, is in Emily V. Mason, *Popular Life of Gen. Robert Edward Lee* (Baltimore: John Murphy, 1872), 245–46. A portion of its contents reached print three years later in *Our Living and Our Dead* 2 (March 1875): 46–51. Subsequent authorities have cited the later, partial version. Despite its superficial-sounding title, Mason's book contains primary material of this sort and information garnered through her friendship with Mrs. Lee that is not available elsewhere.

82. Mollie E. M. Davis, *Minding the Gap and Other Poems* (Houston: Cushing and Cane, 1867); Chilton, *Unveiling and Dedication*, 363–64. The Wilderness incident looms large in Texan lore discussed in Harold B. Simpson, *Hood's Texas Brigade in Poetry and Song* (Hillsboro, Tex.: Hill Junior College Press, 1968).

83. McArdle's traces and the painting's origins are thoroughly explored in Kelley, *Lee and Hood's Texas Brigade*.

84. Polley, *Hood's Texas Brigade*, 233–34.

85. "On Historic Spots," *SHSP*, 36:204; James Power Smith, "Spotsylvania Markers," *SHSP*, 39:100–101; untitled 1922 Fred W. Cross memoir of a visit to Wilderness, FSNMP; "The Texas Brigade," Richmond *Times*, September 22, 1891; Harold B. Simpson, *Red Granite for Gray Heroes* (Hillsboro, Tex.: Hill Junior College Press, 1969). The 1960s monument is of the same design and material used for brigade markers at Antietam and Gettysburg. Former park historian Thomas J. Harrison has seen an old photo of the field showing the plain Lacy rock in an upright position, but that view has been lost.

86. John W. Thomason Jr., *Lone Star Preacher* (New York: Scribner's, 1941), 246–49, 266–73. Thomason's magnificent book ranks as perhaps the best Civil War novel ever written despite—or perhaps even because of—having nothing to do with Bowdoin College memoirists.

87. "Battle of the Wilderness," letter dated May 18, 1864, by the correspondent of the London *Herald* in Augusta (Ga.) *Daily Constitutionalist*, May 31, 1864.

CAROL REARDON

The Other Grant

LEWIS A. GRANT AND THE VERMONT BRIGADE

IN THE BATTLE OF THE WILDERNESS

"**I**n some respects the battle of the Wilderness was the most remarkable of the civil war," wrote General Grant in 1897.[1] Not Ulysses S. Grant, who faced Robert E. Lee for the first time in the tangled undergrowth west of Fredericksburg, but "the other Grant" penned these words. Newly promoted Brig. Gen. Lewis A. Grant, a Vermont lawyer turned soldier who commanded the 2nd Brigade of Brig. Gen. George W. Getty's Second Division of Maj. Gen. John Sedgwick's Sixth Corps, had every reason to believe the essential truth of his assessment. His command, best known as the 1st Vermont Brigade—one of thirty-two Union brigades that crossed the Rapidan River in early May 1864—suffered one-tenth of the northern casualties and the greatest loss of its four years of service in just a few hours at the Wilderness.

Brig. Gen. William F. Smith broke from usual practice in the fall of 1861 when he organized the Vermont Brigade of five regiments from a single state. Army leaders generally acted on the idea that brigades could absorb and rebound from great losses more easily if the casualties were distributed over commands from several states. They argued as well that "rivalry between regiments of different States in the same brigade would conduce to the efficiency of all."[2] The Vermonters disproved the validity of these notions. New Jersey, New York, and Pennsylvania formed similar brigades, and in the spring of 1864 the original five Vermont regiments still served together as well.

The 2nd Vermont, the state's first three-year regiment, went to the front in time to take part in the first battle of Bull Run. They marched to war clad in Vermont-made uni-

Brig. Gen. Lewis Addison Grant.
Francis Trevelyan Miller, ed., The
Photographic History of the Civil War,
10 vols. (New York: Review of Reviews,
1911), 10:125

forms of gray faced with green to honor the Green Mountain Boys. Among
the most notable characters in the regiment was Pvt. George Flagg, a
farmboy turned wrestler who beat all comers in competitions throughout the Champlain Valley before the war; now he reigned as the wrestling
champion of the Army of the Potomac. Pvt. Peter Chase of Company I,
a typical Vermont company, left a condensed descriptive role of his comrades: of the 198 men who served in his company during the war, 133 were
native Vermonters, 33 came from other states, 13 were from Canada, 7
were from Ireland, 3 were from Scotland, and 1 was from England. They
ranged in height from 5'2" to 6'3", with the average at 5'8". At least 140
had blue eyes. Their average age was 24. They represented 21 occupa-
tions, with the 117 farmers being the most numerous. In May 1864 25-
year-old Col. Newton Stone, a Bennington lawyer when he became a first
lieutenant back in 1861, had commanded the 2nd Vermont for just more
than one month. The largest regiment in the brigade with a strength of
800, the 2nd marched into the Wilderness with 700 men in the ranks.[3]

The 3rd Vermont, raised in July 1861, also had begun service in uniforms of gray trimmed in green. The unit had been manhandled at Lee's

Mill on the Peninsula in April 1862, where one of the early war's popular figures, the sleeping sentinel William Scott, redeemed with his life his pledge to Abraham Lincoln to do his duty faithfully. As about 570 of the 3rd Vermont's 600 men entered the Wilderness, Col. Thomas O. Seaver rode at their head.[4]

The 4th Vermont, sent forward in September 1861 in standard Union blue, counted Capt. Daniel Lillie among its officers. The first three-year volunteer to step forward and raise a company in the little town of Barnard, Vermont, won from his men the interesting nickname "Tiger." In May 1864 Tiger Lillie's men would follow him anywhere. Col. George P. Foster commanded the 600 soldiers of the 4th Vermont.[5]

The 5th Vermont likewise mustered in during September 1861. It learned of war the hard way. Its first serious fight, a twenty-minute contest at Savage Station, cost Company E alone 25 of its 59 men killed or mortally wounded. Lewis Grant had headed the 5th Vermont; now his second-in-command, Lt. Col. John R. Lewis, led the regiment, about 500 strong, across the Rapidan River.[6]

The 6th Vermont, mustered in October 1861, carried about 450 of its nearly 550 men into action in the Wilderness. Col. Elisha R. Barney had been a merchant in Swanton before the war. Commissioned a captain in 1861 and seriously wounded in the temple at Crampton's Gap in September 1862, Barney "was a man of high Christian character, brave to a fault, a faithful and respected commander, a good disciplinarian, and a gallant leader." Vermonters followed the adventures of this regiment through the colorful reports of Lt. Albert A. Crane, a part-time correspondent for the Rutland *Herald*.[7]

"To say that the Sixth fought with desperate bravery, and suffered fearfully in the battles of the Wilderness, is the same as saying that it was a regiment of the old First [Vermont] Brigade," a postwar scribe wrote. Indeed, as a brigade the five Vermont regiments together had already won praise throughout the army for their steadiness. They believed their actions had saved the Sixth Corps from destruction during its withdrawal from Salem Church across Banks Ford during the Chancellorsville campaign, when "it was the Green Mountain boys against the chivalry of Louisiana." After that fight, Lieutenant Crane had written, most of the Vermont officers "wear [captured] rebel swords." Their corps commander so completely admired their fighting capacity that, by tradition, on the way to Gettysburg a few months later, "Uncle John" Sedgwick had ordered, "Put the Vermonters in front, and keep the column well closed up."[8]

The winter encampment preceding the Wilderness campaign restored the fighting spirit of the Vermont Brigade. A substantial number of new recruits, substitutes, and conscripts arrived to fill depleted ranks. Religious meetings flourished in camp. Pvt. Jerome Cutler of the 2nd Vermont worshiped with a congregation "composed of representatives of different evangelical churches" where "no sectarianism exists, no doctrinal points of difference arise to mar our worship." Pvt. Wilbur Fisk appreciated that "nobody inquired of another if he was a Methodist, a Baptist, or an Episcopalian. . . . If a man was a Christian, it was enough." Only rarely did excitement break the welcome respite from active campaigning. A late March snowfall triggered a huge snowball fight, and Sgt. Charles Morey of the 2nd Vermont recalled that his unit was "victorious, drove the sixth into the camp, and took possession of their commissary tent." On April 18 the Vermonters passed in review for new general-in-chief U. S. Grant, with Pvt. Luther B. Harris of the 4th Vermont telling a friend at home that the 35,000 parading troops "would make some show in Sutton but not much here."[9]

Amid the calm of winter quarters, one issue stirred great contentiousness: reenlistment. Many of the recruits of 1861 signed on for a second tour, lured in part by the promise of a furlough back home as "veteran volunteers." Not all had agreed to a second hitch, however, and "the great topic of discussion and interest just now among some of the 'old' boys, who have not re-enlisted, is as to when their time of service will expire," Private Fisk wrote. Some believed the magic day to be June 1—cited by Vermont state authorities—while others argued for June 20, the day of their acceptance into Federal service.[10] With active campaigning and the likelihood of battle on the horizon, the matter became no idle concern for soldiers who had already endured nearly three years of hard service.

By early May 1864, well before those who had not reenlisted could go home, the pace of life in the Vermont camps picked up tremendously. Sutlers had already been ordered to leave camp by April 15, a sure sign of impending movement. Representatives of the Christian Commission left too, and Private Fisk regretted the departure of these "faithful, earnest men—men who appeared anxious only for the soldier's good." Morning reports on May 1 showed 3,308 officers and men present for duty. Finally, on May 3, the men of the Vermont Brigade learned they would march the next day. Many wrote quick letters home. Pvt. Peter M. Abbott of the 2nd Vermont anticipated action soon: "We have got orders to march tomorrow morning at 4 o'clock with 50 rounds of cartridges and six days of rations." Sergeant Morey sent the same information home to his mother, along with ten recent photographs and the prayer that the new Union commander "will not meet with disaster." Still, he reaffirmed his willingness to trust "the event in[to] the hands of Him who rules the raging battle as well as the quiet sunshine" and hoped that "this campaign may end this Hydra headed rebellion and cause the people of the south to see the error of their ways." [11]

The route of march for May 4 took the Vermont Brigade from the division camps around Brandy Station to Germanna Ford on the Rapidan River. A final roll call just before the brigade stepped off, one that excluded detached soldiers and those sick in camp who could not accompany the column, counted 2,880 men in line. After crossing the river, they went into camp for the night in fields about two miles south on the Germanna Plank Road. [12]

At 7:00 A.M. on May 5 the Vermonters marched to the Old Wilderness Tavern, where they no doubt noted with interest the detritus of the Chancellorsville battle the year previous. Here they awaited orders. As other elements of the Sixth Corps moved off to support the growing fight along the Orange Turnpike, the Vermonters and the rest of Getty's division remained in place. Private Harris recalled, "It was whispered about among the men that they had been selected as a reserve for the army, for it was felt that a great battle was to be fought. The honor of being on the reserve and the possibility of not being called upon to take part in the fight, put the men in good spirits." [13] That good mood quickly evaporated.

About noon General Getty received orders from Meade to hurry the three brigades still with him—one had been detached earlier—to the junction of the Orange Court House and Germanna Plank roads to support the Union cavalry then being driven back from Parker's Store, several miles west. After reaching the assigned position, Getty's 6,000 men pressed on a bit farther west of the Germanna Plank Road to take a position at the intersection of the Brock Road and the Orange Plank Road. [14]

It was a smart move. Getty had reached the key crossroads on that part of the field. As the general explained, "That point was of vital importance to us, and its falling into the hands of the enemy would have cut our army in two, separating the Second Corps from the Fifth and Sixth, and would have exposed to capture the Artillery Reserve, then moving up from Chancellorsville on the Orange plank road." Moreover, Getty's men constituted the only available infantry in the immediate vicinity capable of countering any substantial force of Confederates coming up the Plank Road toward the crucial junction. The fight along the Orange Turnpike consumed the troops of the Fifth Corps; the rest of the Sixth Corps had gone to their aid; the Second Corps was too far south to backtrack to the threatened position in time; and Burnside's Ninth Corps had not yet arrived.[15]

In later years Vermonters saw real purpose, not mere default or necessity, in the selection of Getty's division for this mission. To secure this vital point, one Vermonter claimed, "The force thus sent, we may be sure, was selected with care." It was "the division of the army which in the opinion of its commanders would be surest to reach the key-point in time, and to hold it against all comers." Additionally, he argued, "there is some reason to suppose that the selection was made to some extent due to the fact that the Vermont brigade was part of that division."[16] Such boastfulness contrasted sharply with more typical Vermont stoicism.

The arrival of Getty's division could not have been timed more propitiously. Grant wrote later, "We were not a minute too soon." As Union cavalrymen retired to the rear of the yet-undeployed infantry, North Carolina skirmishers from Brig. Gen. John R. Cooke's brigade of Henry Heth's division in A. P. Hill's Third Corps opened fire on Getty's men. To give his soldiers time to form into line of battle, Getty and his staff rode out into the crossroads itself to suggest the presence of an organized force. The ruse worked. "The presence of my small retinue, consisting of my staff and orderlies, standing firmly at the point in dispute, although under fire, served to delay their advance for a few minutes," the general reported. A quick volley by Brig. Gen. Frank Wheaton's men, the first of Getty's troops to deploy, helped too. As Heth later reported, "From the resistance made by the enemy at this point, it was evident that he was here in considerable force." Union troops later found some of Heth's dead and wounded "within 30 yards of the cross-roads, so nearly had they obtained possession of it." With pride Getty explained that "in wresting the possession of the crossing of the Orange Court-House and Brock roads from Hill's corps, when already occupied by his skirmishers, it is not claiming too much to say, that the Second Division saved the army from disastrous defeat."[17]

The southern advance had indeed stalled, and during this brief respite Getty completed his deployment. He formed the three brigades then under his command into two lines at right angles to the Orange Plank Road. Wheaton's men continued to straddle the roadway, while Brig. Gen. Henry L. Eustis's troops took position on Wheaton's right, in the woods extending north up the Brock Road. The Vermont Brigade held the left of the line, south of the Plank Road.

From the ranks of the 2nd Vermont, Private Fisk forged a first impression of the battleground that captured both its military importance and its potential for horror: "Here was a high point of land where the roads cross at right angles, and it is in the midst of an endless wilderness— 'a wilderness of woe,' as the boys call it." Nonetheless, the Vermonters set about their business; they "massed here in considerable numbers, and after some moments got into working order." Private Harris recalled that those first moments were full of "hurley burley" that was "so great and so general that no orders were given to load even." Grant sent out as skirmishers two companies of the 5th Vermont under Capt. C. J. Ormsbee. The rest of the brigade deployed in two lines. The 4th Vermont was in the first line, on the right of the brigade. The 3rd Vermont fell in on its left. Left to right, the 6th Vermont and 2nd Vermont made up the second line. For now, the 5th Vermont served as the brigade reserve.[18]

Except for the fire of the ubiquitous skirmishers, quiet reigned for nearly two hours. The Vermonters threw up rude breastworks, which, as Grant later admitted, "subsequently proved of great value." The skirmishers sent a few prisoners to the rear. But little else transpired. The Vermonters listened intently while the southerners "were evidently getting into position and forming their lines."[19]

About 3:30 P.M. Hancock's Second Corps approached Getty's line from the south and began to deploy on his left flank. The arrival of Hancock's men allowed Getty to shorten his line a bit. Wheaton moved his regiments south of the Plank Road northward to join Eustis's men in the woods along the Brock Road, and the Vermonters filed into Wheaton's old position until their right flank rested on the Plank Road. Sometime between 3:00 and 4:00 P.M. both Hancock and Getty received orders to advance west along the Plank Road, Getty's instructions specifying that he should begin his attack immediately, with or without the Second Corps.[20]

Years later Lewis Grant remained convinced of Meade's belief that Hancock could have supported Getty's efforts immediately if needed. Meade could not have known, however, that Hancock's corps artillery had so clogged the narrow Brock Road that it slowed the arrival of his infantry. Even Hancock admitted that when the order arrived, "the formation I had directed to be made before carrying out my instructions to advance was not yet completed." Lewis Grant—who accompanied Getty at the time—realized that "a crisis was upon us." For Getty's small force to attack without Hancock's close support "was almost a forlorn hope. But the order was imperative, and left no discretion." Only after the battle, Grant admitted, did he learn the truth behind Meade's urgency. Confederate pressure against the Fifth Corps on the Orange Turnpike and the

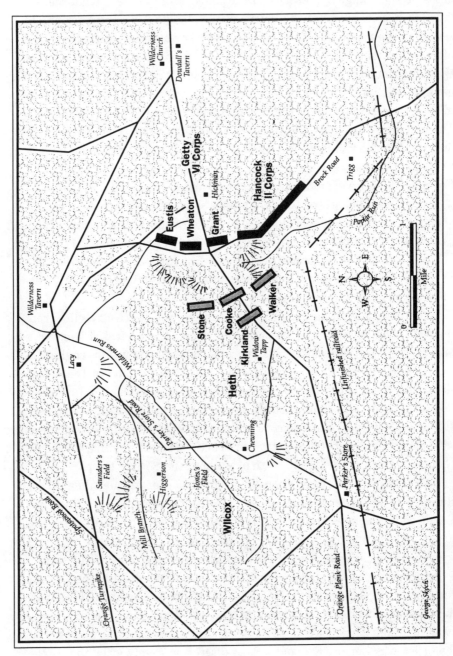

Grant's brigade, 4:30 P.M., May 5, 1864.

George Skoch

appearance of potentially fatal gaps in the Union line north of the Plank Road required a relief effort that only the immediate advance of Getty's division could provide.[21]

For the next two hours Getty's division, and especially the Vermont Brigade, underwent the severest test of fire it had ever faced. Their advance started off badly. With Captain Ormsbee attending to duties at the right of his line near the Plank Road, much of the left half of his skirmish line did not hear the order to move. Colonel Seaver of the 3rd Vermont, noting that the 4th Vermont on his right was advancing, ordered his own men forward, passing over the prone skirmishers along his front. Seaver felt uncomfortable about taking such action, knowing that an unprotected advance into such terrain courted disaster. As he later reported, however, the skirmishers "were not under my control."[22]

Advancing blind into the Wilderness, the men of the 3rd and 4th Vermont worked their way through the thickets and brush. Grant put the best possible face on it when he later wrote that "as good a line as possible was preserved." Pvt. Henry Houghton, one of Seaver's soldiers, more honestly admitted that maintaining alignment quickly frustrated them: "We could not keep any formation."[23]

Grant's men no doubt expected to meet a skirmish line before they hit the strongest Confederate resistance. They did not know that the southern skirmishers already had drawn back to their main line. Therefore, wrote one soldier, "the first we knew of the enemy we received a volley from a line of battle within a stone's throw." The Vermonters had run into Cooke's North Carolinians again. The fight was on. "There was nothing of brilliancy or maneuver in it," wrote Private Harris. "The contending forces could not see each other until within a few paces."[24]

Where this occurred is a matter of contention. Seaver was certain that his men advanced 200 yards before they first took fire. Any measurements of distance in the Wilderness, especially those delineated in after-action reports, must be taken with healthy skepticism. Lieutenant Colonel Pingree of the 4th Vermont thought his men took fire after advancing not 200 yards but only 25 yards beyond Wheaton's initial line. But Pingree's men found themselves as surprised as Seaver's men had been. They, too, "were met by a terrible fire from a concealed foe at a distance of less than 75 yards."[25]

Whatever the distances, those first volleys devastated the Vermonters. Seaver reported that he "lost many valuable lives." Private Houghton recalled that in those initial moments, "One man at my left fell dead, and a bullet went so near the face of the man in my rear that it took an eye out."

Lewis A. Grant and the Vermont Brigade • *209*

Among the first to fall was twenty-four-year-old Capt. Dennie W. Farr of the 4th Vermont, who had enlisted as a private in August 1861. He took a bullet through the head and died instantly, "a willing sacrifice to his country." In the same regiment and about the same time, Capt. J. W. D. Carpenter, who "was as usual at this post of duty at the head of his company urging his men" forward, died instantly from a bullet just above the heart. Capt. William Tracy received the first of a reported twenty-four bullets that hit him over the next two days.[26]

In the confusion of the Wilderness, soldiers soon wandered around almost aimlessly, without organization, precise direction, or recognizable formation. Lewis Grant recalled later that all the men could do was aim "at the wall of fire and smoke in our front. This distance between the two lines was so short that under ordinary conditions we could have charged upon the enemy with the bayonet before giving time to reload." Private Harris wrote that "stones could have been used as missels." "A bayonet charge was impossible," Grant admitted. In the Wilderness a "line could advance only slowly and with great difficulty even when unopposed. Anything like a dash upon the enemy was simply out of the question."[27]

The woods made accurate post-battle accounts of the progress of the fight nearly impossible. Grant's brigade report stated that the 3rd Vermont obliqued somewhat to the left to engage in a tough firefight. Colonel Seaver, the regimental commander, remembered no such movement. After absorbing that first volley, he remembered only that he ordered a charge, conceding "that the nature of the ground and the heavy fire of the enemy rendered it impossible for me to move my men forward in such shape as to give any hope of dislodging him." His inability to coordinate assaults with the 4th Vermont next to him also troubled Seaver. All that could be done, according to Grant, was to attempt to advance at those points where the enemy fire abated, but "each attempt was met by increased firing and great loss of life."[28] Even worse for the 3rd Vermont, Confederates began to lap around its flanks, and Seaver had to counter simultaneous fire from several directions.

When it seemed the situation could get no worse, Union artillery opened, and the engagement became general along the front of Getty's entire division. Although only two guns from Capt. R. Bruce Ricketts's Battery F, 1st Pennsylvania Artillery, could find room to deploy at the crossroads, they added new horrors to the already terrible fight. Gunners could not see targets clearly even when the pieces advanced down the road to provide close support for the infantry. As the artillerymen fired blindly into the woods, some of their rounds claimed victims among the

Vermonters. A shell fragment hit Sgt. H. E. Taylor of the 4th Vermont in the small of the back and came to rest near his spine; it would remain there for four months before surgeons extracted it. Private Harris, who disliked Lewis Grant for some unexplained reason, asserted years later that "our Brigade Commander directed the fire" and expressed his dismay that "the first shot killed eight men on the left of my co[mpany]." Harris complained that a common soldier guilty of a trifle always paid a high price for his transgression, but "a brigade commander [who] chose to stay in the rear and practice as a gunner and kill two score of his own command" received no punishment and could "write a glowing account of the battle, in his report, and commend himself."[29]

The men of the 3rd and 4th Vermont did what came naturally to veterans. They fell to the ground, seeking shelter behind trees and in folds of earth. Such protection quickly proved insufficient. Private Houghton later discovered that "two bullets went through my haversack and one through my canteen and another passed so near my neck that it burned the skin then entered my blanket." When he unrolled the blanket, he found nineteen holes in it. Private Harris watched gaps open in the 4th Vermont's line, but, he wrote with postwar bravado, "when there was lack of men to take the places of the dead, the soldiers would maintain their front by increased bravery."[30]

The two Vermont regiments in the first line held for as long as possible. "The men's faces became powder-grimed, and their mouths black from biting cartridges," wrote a Vermonter later. "The musketry silenced all other sounds; and the air in the woods was hot and heavy with sulphurous vapor. The tops of the bushes were cut away by the leaden showers which swept through them; and when the smoke lifted occasional glimpses could be got of gray forms crouching under the battle-cloud which hung low upon the slope in front." They gave as good as they got. James A. Graham, one of Cooke's North Carolinians, described the fight as "hot and heavy." He even believed the Vermonters had begun to outflank the southern line when elements of Brig. Gen. Henry H. Walker's Brigade of Virginians and Tennesseans came to Cooke's aid.[31]

Help finally came for the 3rd and 4th Vermont as well. While the 5th Vermont remained in reserve, the 2nd Vermont marched to the support of the 4th, and the 6th Vermont advanced to the aid of the 3rd. It was just as well they moved forward. Private Fisk of the 2nd Vermont had found no special protection while waiting in the second line: "We followed close to them [the first line], and were equally exposed." They did not fire as they advanced; they could not separate friend from foe. As Pvt.

Peter Chase took his place in the firing line, he noted that "the brush was so thick that we were unable to see the enemy, even while standing at so close a range." The men of the 6th Vermont felt much the same. Lt. Edward Holton wrote home that when they advanced, "the 1st thing we knew a perfect storm of bullets was poured into us and threw the Regt. into confusion." Still, the "great exertion of the officers and sergts." soon rallied the men and "we held our own."[32]

Like the first line, the second quickly hugged the ground for cover. Years later, with obvious pride that masked the fear wrought by battle, Private Chase admitted that "we had been taught the art of fighting, but how to run at such times was not so easily learned by Vermonters. We held our ground until 35 [of 63] of us had fallen, killed or wounded." Private Fisk admitted that "the rebels gave us a warm reception. They poured their bullets into us so fast that we had to lie down to load and fire." Grant still did not consider their position a good one: "The rebels had the advantage of position, inasmuch as their line was partially protected by a slight swell of ground, while ours was on nearly level ground."[33]

It seemed the Vermonters could best assure their safety by wresting that slight rise from the Confederate infantry. Small groups of northern soldiers repeatedly rose to storm the position. Each time, Grant reported, "the rapid and constant fire of musketry cut them down with such slaughter that it was found impracticable to do more than maintain our then present position." As a Confederate volley crashed into the ranks of the 2nd Vermont's Company I, Private Chase went down with three bullets, one in the neck and one through each leg. Pvt. Henry B. Brush took two bullets that knocked him senseless. Nearby, Pvt. Daniel Schofield was hit in the head and thigh almost simultaneously. Some of the men of the 6th Vermont also tried a bayonet attack. Lieutenant Holton wrote home that "just before it occurred we lost David" (Holton's brother). "The last word he spoke was 'Forward,'" when a bullet killed him instantly. The bayonet charge allowed the 6th Vermont to advance about forty rods. There they "found a pile of dead Rebs," but that was as far as they got. Before the lieutenant could see to his brother, he also was wounded, in the leg two inches below the knee.[34]

Not satisfied with merely absorbing the punishing fire, some of the Vermonters went after Heth's Confederates in less dramatic fashion. As Grant phrased it, a part of the 2nd Vermont "crept forward" to draw even with the 4th Vermont, and together they edged toward the southern position, pouring "a constant and destructive fire into the enemy's line." But the Confederate fire proved equally destructive. To stop a perceived flanking movement around the 2nd Vermont, Lt. Col. John S. Tyler ordered sixteen men under Cpl. Albert A. May to deploy against it. May was wounded, and all the men with him were killed or wounded before they could complete the maneuver.[35] Advance or retreat in the Wilderness must have been measured by feet or yards.

The Vermonters probably could have done little more in any case. Although Lee is supposed to have attacked Grant in the Wilderness to cancel the Federal preponderance of numbers, on this front the troops under Heth and the newly arriving division of Cadmus M. Wilcox for a brief time clearly outnumbered Getty's 6,000 men. While discussing their wartime experiences in a lull after the surrender at Appomattox, Getty and Wilcox discovered that their commands fought each other along the Plank Road on May 5. Wilcox admitted that Getty's attack "was so vigorous and persistent that all they could do was to hold their line until dark." Getty asked Wilcox how large a force he led and was stunned at the southerner's reply that he and Heth advanced with a combined force of 14,000 to 15,000 men. Grant's brigade apparently had faced the brunt of the attack. "Our force was almost all placed on our right and your left of the Plank road," Wilcox had told Getty. "Indeed," the Union general replied, "I had only my little Vermont brigade on that side of the road." Wilcox could offer no excuse for his troops' inability to oust the smaller force: "Well, the brush was so thick we couldn't see anything."[36]

To attempt to impose any further semblance of order on the Vermonters' fight in the Wilderness is folly. In later years Private Harris of the 4th Vermont wrote that the battle was "more obscure tha[n] most battles and all battles are obscure, and a description of the Wilderness by one of its participants, will read like another field to one engaged in another part of the same army corps." Another Vermonter observed that the Wilderness was "perhaps the least understood and most insufficiently described of the battles of the Army of the Potomac." The tangled growth "has seemed to envelop the battle in mystery, and description of many of its details has been and will always be impossible." Indeed, one of the Vermonters' favorite bits of testimony about the intensity of the fighting along the Plank Road came from Robert E. Lee: "General Lee was not given to the use of strong adjectives in his reports, and when he calls the fighting 'most desperate,' we may be sure it was so."[37]

One of the few clear things about this most impressionistic battle was the men's awareness that conduct of the fighting rested heavily on individual soldiers. These veteran Vermonters, fortunately, needed little direction in a struggle marked by "unseen movements of troops, terrific volleys of musketry bursting at close range from the thickets; charges through woods so dense that a field officer could scarce see more than the line of a company; sudden appearances and disappearances of bodies of troops through the smoke and jungle; regiments on each side hugging the ground for shelter, not daring to rise for either advance or retreat, yet keeping up incessant fusillades; an almost Indian warfare in the forest."[38]

The self-reliance of the enlisted men became increasingly important as commissioned officers fell in great numbers. With their gold braid, shiny buttons, and swords that picked up what little light penetrated the smoke and shadows, officers often provided the most visible targets. Shortly after the 2nd Vermont reached the front lines, Colonel Stone received a bullet in the fleshy part of the leg and retired to seek medical help. As soon as the wound was dressed, he came back. Silencing his men's cheers, he reminded them that "I have done as I told you I wished you to do, not to leave for a slight wound, but to remain just as long as you can do any good. I am here to stay as long as I can do any good."[39]

The effectiveness of the Confederate fire challenged the Vermonters' descriptive abilities. As Private Fisk saw it, "Just a little to the rear of where our line was formed, where the bullets swept close to the ground, every bush and twig was cut and splintered by the leaden balls. . . . I doubt if a single tree could have been found that had not been pierced several times with bullets, and all were hit about breast high. Had the rebels fired a little lower, they would have annihilated the whole line; they nearly did it as it was." Perhaps Lieutenant Colonel Lewis summed it up best: "Now came the holocaust."[40]

The raw recitation of numbers provided only one measure of the human cost of the fight. Vermonters watched as their comrades-in-arms for nearly three years began to fall in great profusion. Captain Ormsbee of the 5th Vermont, who had tried his best to lead a skirmish line into the clutching undergrowth, fell dead. Private Flagg of the 2nd Vermont, the army's wrestling champion, also went down. In the sad aftermath of the fight, George T. Stevens, a sympathetic Sixth Corps surgeon from New York, commented that "our friends, the Vermonters, fought with that gallantry which always characterized the sons of the Green Mountain State. Their noblest men were falling thickly, yet they held the road."[41]

Clearly feeling the pressure all along his front, Lewis Grant reported his situation to division commander Getty. Sitting with Getty was Maj. Gen. David B. Birney, commanding a division in the Second Corps, who expressed a willingness to support the Vermonters' fight and directed to their aid three of his closest regiments: the 20th Indiana, the 141st Pennsylvania, and the 40th New York of Brig. Gen. W. H. H. Ward's brigade.[42] The Pennsylvanians, at least, advanced immediately.

About the same time, Lewis Grant noted that the enemy line facing his reserve 5th Vermont—posted to the rear and slightly to the left of his other regiments—seemed less protected than it was in front of the rest of the brigade. To relieve the pressure on his four fighting units, he prepared to send in his last uncommitted troops. Nearly as soon as he gave the order for the 5th Vermont to advance, Colonel Lewis fell severely wounded and had to be taken from the field. Grant then asked Maj. Charles P. Dudley, the senior unwounded officer present, if his men could break the southern line if Birney's other two fresh regiments helped them. As Grant reported it, "'I think I can,' was the reply of the gallant major." Likewise, when Grant asked the soldiers of the 20th Indiana and the 40th New York to go to the aid of his Vermonters, "The men rose and with a cheer answered, 'We will.'"[43]

This new push did not break the stalemate along the Plank Road. The underbrush threw the Hoosiers and New Yorkers into confusion. The 5th Vermont advanced alone. After covering forty or fifty yards, Capt. Eugene Hamilton reported what by now had become common experience: "We found ourselves . . . wholly unsupported and exposed, not only to a front fire of unprecedented severity, but also to a raking fire on both flanks of the most galling description." Major Dudley, discovering his men alone and increasingly vulnerable to fire from both flanks, ordered them to fall to the ground. The 20th Indiana (and perhaps some of the New Yorkers) finally came up, and they enjoyed one of the Union's small victories that day. As they pressed the Confederate line, the Hoosiers captured the flag of the 55th Virginia from Color Sgt. William Richardson. Shortly thereafter, however, the 55th rallied and, along with the 47th Virginia, repulsed the Union attackers yet again. Getty, with decided understatement, noted that "the fighting was very heavy."[44]

Help finally came in the form of still more troops from Ward's brigade of Birney's division and from Brig. Gen. S. S. Carroll's and Brig. Gen. Joshua T. Owen's brigades of Brig. Gen. John Gibbon's division of the Second Corps. They timed their arrival perfectly. As Lewis Grant reported, the Vermonters' ammunition was "well nigh exhausted." The regiments on the right—the 4th and the 6th Vermont—retired first. But the Confederates did not let them go unmolested. Almost at the moment the 2nd and 3rd Vermont regiments received their orders to retire, the southerners attacked. Before he pulled out, Sgt. Fred Fish stopped to fasten a strap around the leg of Private Chase to stop the flow of blood. He could do no more. He told Chase to "keep a stiff upper lip" and headed for the rear just ahead of the onrushing southerners, still firing his rifle and uttering with each discharge "pet names" that "would not read well in print."[45]

In this final withdrawal to the Brock Road, the 2nd Vermont's second-in-command, Lt. Col. John S. Tyler, was wounded in the thigh. Some of his men came out to help the twenty-one-year-old officer, but he ordered them back into ranks; their muskets were needed there more. When Sgt. Carlos Rich of Company D, 4th Vermont, reached the Brock Road, he realized that all his officers were down. He learned that Capt. Abial Fisher had been wounded in the head and evacuated to a field hospital. Lt. Winfield Scott Wooster was dead. Rich ran back through the musketry to find Lt. Edward W. Carter, lying facedown on the ground and shot through the abdomen. As Rich wrote later, "I didn't dare to lift him to a standing position for fear that his entire intestine would all come out." Rich returned to the Brock Road, found Cpl. Albert Carter, the fallen officer's brother, and returned to the field. Together they dragged the lieutenant to safety through a "heavy fire from the enemy and also from our own troops who were laying down and firing close to the ground."[46]

The 5th Vermont, the last of the brigade to advance, also retired last. The southern attack broke so suddenly that Lt. Horace French of Grant's staff, carrying the 5th Vermont's orders to retire, became a prisoner. The exhausted regiment, finding itself pressed hard on both flanks, "judiciously retired" without orders.[47]

The action did not end when the troops reached the Brock Road. "Very heavy fighting . . . without either gaining or losing ground, was kept up until after dark," Getty recalled. Finally, after nightfall, the tired and battered Vermonters, along with the other exhausted men of Getty's division, were withdrawn east of the Brock Road and replaced by still more fresh troops from Hancock's Second Corps. As Private Fisk reported, "We all had our hairbreadth escapes to tell of."[48]

In later years, Sixth Corps veterans of Getty's division would nurse a bit of a grudge against the Second Corps. Even in the press coverage right after the battle, correspondents gave greater attention to the efforts of Hancock's soldiers, overshadowing — sometimes ignoring entirely — the hard work of Getty's division. Vermont survivors of May 5 may well have laughed ironically at *New York Herald* reporter Finley Anderson's comments: "General Getty's division was already formed in line awaiting [Hancock's] arrival; for he was not strong enough to make the attack alone." They no doubt could have pointed out the graves of many of their comrades who died while, as Anderson wrote, Hancock's "different divisions were formed as speedily as possible in three lines of battle." The *New York Times* likewise reported that "Gen. HANCOCK, with the assistance of GETTY's division of the Sixth Corps, held his position under musket fire of two and a half hours' duration, in which his command suffered severely, inflicting much injury upon the rebels." Even Confederate general Heth would write in his report that "the attacking force was Hancock's Corps numbering probably 25,000 men." The Vermonters could take only a little satisfaction in this telling bit of Heth's testimony: "The enemy's dead marked his line of battle so well, and were in such numbers that, if living, they would have formed a most formidable line. This was especially the case in Cooke's and Davis' front." The Vermonters had fought Cooke's brigade.[49]

The misperception secured a place in much of the history of the battle. George G. Benedict, leading author about Vermont troops in the war, dismissed all claims to glory for Hancock's men: "The facts are that the assault was opened and sustained for hours by Getty alone, with 7,000 men, being three-fourths of his division. Other troops of the Second corps supported Getty at a later stage of the battle; but the entire loss of the Second corps on the 5th of May was not equal to that of the Vermont brigade in killed and wounded—a fact which indicates distinctly what troops did the fighting." Benedict had a point: the 141st Pennsylvania that moved to the support of the Vermonters late in the day suffered only one killed and eighteen wounded on May 5.[50]

Lewis Grant certainly believed that Hancock's report was "somewhat indefinite as to who made and maintained this attack" along the Plank Road on May 5. Indeed, Hancock—while admitting that Getty's division attacked first and before the Second Corps was ready to advance—also made it seem as if no more than fifteen to thirty minutes passed until his own men were fully engaged alongside those of Getty. Grant ultimately decided to write about the Vermont Brigade's efforts on May 5 because "I simply want for Gen. Getty and his command, and for myself and my command, what belongs to us."[51]

But the fight for the history books lay in the future. The horrors of the night of May 5 immediately impressed the Vermonters. Private Harris remembered that "the heat, the physical and mental exercise had developed a great thirst in the men and the only supply of water they had was what by accident was in their canteens." No one went out to search for water, he wrote, because after the hard work of the day, "they expected a retreat," and "of course, a march in any direction would take them to a creek or some water." Soldiers separated from their commands during

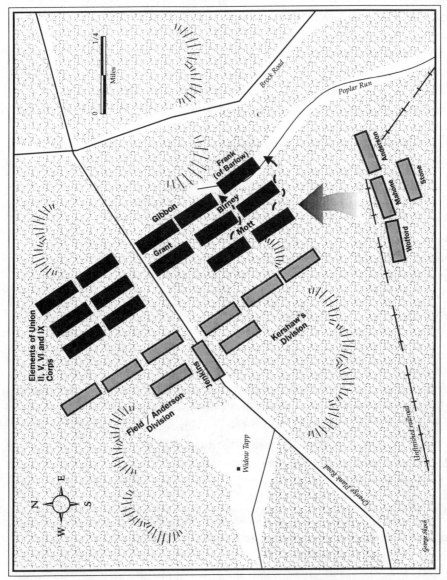

Longstreet's flank attack, 11:00 A.M., May 6, 1864. Grant's brigade holds as Mott and Birney collapse.

the day came in that night. A pair of new recruits in the 4th Vermont had slipped away early in the fight and now came looking for their two closest friends. Both lay dead on the field. The older of the two, stricken by conscience, "said why could not I have died with them" and vowed "we will never leave the ranks again."[52]

Grant recalled that the most horrific moments of the night came when soldiers tried to rest among the wounded and the dead or went out to search for lost friends. Until at least 2:00 A.M. occasional volleys "lit up the dark woods with flame," making such rescue efforts dangerous. The wounded Peter Chase of the 2nd Vermont still lay between the lines, and after dark Cpl. E. W. Prior and three friends went out to find him. Prior lit a small candle, but, as Chase observed, "as soon as the rebels saw the light they began to fire on it. The balls whistled so near us it made us feel rather uncomfortable, and he was obliged to conceal the light under his coat. They soon had me out on the plank road," where they put him in an ambulance. Although Chase did not know it, one of the next ambulances picked up Chase's company mate, Dan Schofield. When both soldiers were unloaded at a rear-area aid station, Chase recognized Schofield's "dreadful" cries; he would not have known him merely to see him, since his hair and face were covered with dried blood. "The next day, all battle-stained and battle-torn, on [a] southern field," mourned Chase, Schofield "the patriot died," and "his friends know not his resting place."[53]

Among others retrieved that night was Col. Newton Stone of the 2nd Vermont, who had returned to his command after having his leg wound treated. Following his speech encouraging his men to ignore slight wounds, a bullet hit him in the head and killed him instantly. Some of Captain Carpenter's soldiers in the 4th Vermont brought in his body about 11:00 P.M. His saber and belt had been stolen, but his personal effects remained untouched. As his family learned, "He was buried at midnight in the same grave with Capt. Farr" of the 4th.[54] Hundreds of soldiers performed similar acts of personal courage in those woods that night. With skittish pickets firing at every light or sound that pierced the darkness, however, many of the dead and dying simply could not be removed.

The Vermonters found little time to mourn their losses. Early on May 6 Lewis Grant received orders to advance at first light with the Second Corps troops in an attack west along the Orange Plank Road. "To me, personally," Grant wrote years later, "the order came like a death-warrant. If the struggle of the day before was to [be] repeated, it evidently meant death to many of us. I felt as I never felt at any other time." Grant even had a presentiment of his own death so strong he left his personal belongings with noncombatants with directions for their disposition in the event he did not survive. Private Fisk of the 2nd Vermont noted that "there were pale and anxious faces in our regiment when that order was given. . . . But the order was forward, and I do not know that a single man failed to take his place." Not all recalled the orders so glumly. Private Harris recalled that when the men received the order to renew the fight at daylight, they were pleased because the idea "was new to them." After so many retreats, it came as a distinct pleasure to know that "a man of iron had taken the command of the army." While they still dreaded battle, they "saw that it was best to wear the enemy out and that there was but one way to do it and that was to fight."[55]

For this dawn attack Birney's division of Hancock's Second Corps led off; Getty's division of the Sixth Corps made up the second line. The Vermont Brigade now straddled the Plank Road, two regiments north of it and three south. The advance went much better this day. Heth's exhausted troops had been permitted to rest in place at the end of the previous day's fighting—a poor decision that later became a matter of contention among senior southern commanders—and the disorganized Confederates crumbled in the face of the onrushing Union advance. "We of the rear line didn't get a shot or a sight of them," recalled Grant, "and we were in no danger except from the bullets and shells that came to the rear, and these were not many, as the most of them were stopped by the intervening trees." The arrival of Maj. Gen. James Wadsworth's Fifth Corps division, which came sweeping in from the right, hurried the dissolution of the southern resistance. To make room for Wadsworth's force, Union troops along the Plank Road sidled a bit to the south; the Vermont Brigade soon found itself again united, all on the south side of the road.[56]

It was a promising start but no more. The northern advance progressed steadily until it broke into open ground near Widow Tapp's farm, where southern artillery took it under fire. The arrival of elements of James Longstreet's First Corps at the right time and place destroyed much of the attack's remaining momentum. Pressed in front and on the flanks, Birney's division finally broke. Hancock attempted to restore order south of the Plank Road "by throwing back my left, in order to hold my advanced position along that road and on its right."[57] Although he did not give them credit, in attempting to execute this movement Hancock had left much of his second line, including the Vermonters, at the most vulnerable part of that advanced position.

For the second consecutive day the Vermonters found themselves in difficult circumstances. Colonel Seaver suddenly discovered his 3rd Vermont, which began the advance in the third line, "in front, with the Second Vermont Regiment on my left, and a regiment on my right, the designation of which I do not know." Seaver's men put up as much of a fight as they could, until the 6th Vermont rushed to their aid. The remnant of the 5th Vermont, which also had started in the third line of battle that morning, now found itself in the front lines as well.[58]

The Vermonters fought with the rest of Getty's division to stem the flight of the Second Corps and stabilize the Union line. It was tough going. Getty left the field with a shoulder wound. Still, his men did all they could to prevent the withdrawal from degenerating into a rout. The Vermonters fell in line at a former Confederate position marked by "two irregular lines of old logs and decayed timber" on a slight elevation, most likely part of the ground they had tried to capture the previous day. "We necessarily took possession of the wrong side" of the works, Grant admitted, "but improved what time we had in adjusting them to our own use." As Private Fisk saw it, "We were in the point of the letter V, and the rebels were fast closing up the sides."[59]

The experience of the veteran troops told. "Each man felt it incumbent upon himself to see that his front was protected." As Birney's shattered forces filed through the temporary line, the Vermonters received the charging Confederates "with a bold front and galling fire," checking their advance and throwing them back in confusion. This stout defense slowed the southerners for a little while. Again and again the Confederates charged the entire Union line. "The attack was many times repeated, and as many times repulsed," Lewis Grant later wrote, adding with pride that "the repulse, however, was complete only in front of this brigade."[60]

As happened so many times on this field, the Vermonters soon felt isolated, even if they were not quite as alone as it seemed. The Confederate forces made progress against both flanks of the Union line. Hancock admitted that the effort to restore his left, south of the Plank Road, failed, "owing to the partial disorganization of the troops, which was to be attributed to their having been engaged for many hours in a dense forest, under a heavy and murderous musketry fire, when the formation was partially lost." The Vermonters initially grew more nervous as "the Union troops gradually gave way, especially upon the right." The 4th Vermont changed front from west to north to fire on Confederates advancing against the brigade from that direction. Frank Wheaton, now the acting division commander, sent a brigade to protect the right and rear of the Vermonters, and the line continued to hold. Until this moment, "Perhaps the valor of Vermont troops and the steadiness and unbroken front of those noble

Union battle line along the Orange Plank Road,
May 6, 1864 (sketch by Alfred R. Waud).
Library of Congress

regiments were never more signally displayed," Lewis Grant wrote after the battle. "They stood out in the very midst of the enemy, unyieldingly, dealing death and slaughter in front and flank. Only the day before one-third of their number and many of their beloved leaders had fallen, but not disheartened the brave men living seemed determined to avenge the fallen."[61]

In praising his own men Grant never criticized Union troops on his flanks who left his men in that exposed position. He was wise to forbear. Plenty of Union units from the Second Corps and from Wadsworth's division of the Fifth Corps fought on, especially north of the road, albeit in disjointed small-unit actions. Still, he believed it necessary to explain why his men, above all others, held on so long. As he wrote in retrospect, "We not only had the advantage of position, but we were well protected by the temporary works. The troops on my right and left did not have the protection my brigade had." Even in 1897 it seemed important to upholding the good name of his Vermonters to make clear that "it had fallen to them twice to hold the key of the region, and they held it to the end." Grant might as easily have turned to James Longstreet for further validation: his First Corps troops, Longstreet wrote in his after-action report, had pressed back the Union forces in confusion "over half a mile to a line of temporary works, where they were re-enforced by reserves."[62] It proved to be sufficiently tough resistance that Longstreet embraced the opportunity to launch a flank attack from a railroad cut to break the Union line rather than continue frontal assaults alone.

But the Vermonters' stand extracted still more of the unit's lifeblood. While Private Fisk hugged the ground, "a comrade, less timid than myself, had raised himself up, and was loading and firing as fast as possible," when a "ball struck near his heart. He exclaimed, 'I am killed,' and attempted to step to the rear, but fell on me and immediately died." Sergeant Morey noted that in addition to the nineteen members of his company killed and wounded on May 5, another eight fell on May 6 when "the rebels broke the 2nd corps on our left and came in our rear and we were obliged to fall back." Morey watched as his captain, Orville Bixby, was hit in the back of the head, a mortal wound he survived by only a few hours. Also among the mortally wounded was the 4th Vermont's Capt. Tiger Lillie. The regiment's two shirkers of the previous day who vowed to stay in line after their friends died both survived.[63]

The Vermonters gave up the position only when Longstreet's flank attack crumpled the Union left a quarter-mile away. Grant tried to face two regiments to the south to slow the southern assault and prevent further buckling of the Union defense. Colonel Seaver simultaneously took the initiative to make the same move; however, the Vermonters had used up their stock of luck. As Seaver admitted, "The left of the line had broken in confusion, and in order to save my command from capture, I was obliged to retire" to the Brock Road entrenchments. Confederates pouring through a gap in the Union line to the south placed the rear of the Vermonters' position under a heavy musketry fire. Seaver later complained that "if two or three regiments could have been formed at a point near where [Longstreet's flank] attack was made, running at right angles with the main line of battle, the attack of the enemy would have been repulsed." But this was no time for wishful thinking. Lewis Grant realized that further resistance short of the Brock Road line was "worse than useless."[64]

The Vermonters finally retired to the trenches along the Brock Road. They arrived to discover that "all organization and control seemed to have been lost" on this part of the line. Nonetheless, reported Grant, "out of that disorder the Vermont brigade quietly and deliberately took its position in the front works on the Brock road, and awaited the enemy's advance." The general must be excused for his wartime hyperbole. His soldiers admitted that they had lost cohesion and felt just as confused as the Second Corps troops who reached the road before them. "I was shame-

Confederate assault against works along the Brock Road,
late afternoon, May 6, 1864 (sketch by Alfred R. Waud).
Library of Congress

lessly demoralized," acknowledged the stalwart Private Fisk. "I didn't know where my regiment had gone to, and to be candid about it, I didn't care. I was tired almost to death, and as hungry as a wolf. . . . My patriotism was well nigh used up, and so was I, till I had some refreshments." Years later Grant gave in a little, admitting that all three of Getty's (now Wheaton's) brigades—and not just his Vermonters—fell into line at the crossroads.[65]

About 4:00 P.M. the Confederates made a final push against the Union line along the Brock Road. As Grant noted, the "heaviest part fell upon the troops on our immediate left, but a portion of it fell upon this brigade." While Hancock's men broke the final southern attack, the Vermonters watched in horror as the forest floor and the log breastworks caught fire. As Hancock described it, the works became "a mass of flames which it was impossible at that time to subdue." The "intense heat and the smoke, which was driven by the wind directly into the faces of the men, prevented them on portions of the line from firing over the parapet, and at some points compelled them to abandon the line." The flames consumed all in their path, including the dead and the unreachable wounded. Few who witnessed the scene ever forgot it. Years later Private Harris still mourned that "many wounded ones were killed that could have lived but for the fire."[66]

The Vermonters hoped that their stalwart fighting on May 6 had not gone unnoticed. "It is, perhaps, a fact worthy of note," Grant suggested, "that the key-point to all the movements of that portion of the army was on the plank road, which position the Vermont brigade held during the entire engagement." He expressed dismay years later upon discovering that Hancock made even less mention in his report of the work of Getty's three brigades on May 6 than he had about their efforts of the previous day. Indeed, Hancock dismissed the contribution of the Sixth Corps troops from the latter phases of the May 6 fight, asserting they had lost heavily earlier that day. "In point of fact," Grant complained, "Getty's brigades had not lost heavily nor been engaged 'earlier in the morning,' and they were not relieved" by any Second Corps troops. His Vermonters "occupied the extreme front to the very last, and were the last to leave the front." He offered one seemingly plausible explanation for Hancock's misconception. Hancock had found them in line of battle along the Brock Road before his own shattered troops took up their positions on Getty's left. Because the Second Corps soldiers, who had just retired in disorder, were not yet in line, Grant argued, "it was very natural for him [Hancock] to suppose that they [the Vermont Brigade] had been relieved from the front [earlier] and formed there." Still, if further evidence of the fighting prowess of the Vermont Brigade were required, the survivors pointed out, Hancock himself provided it. While the other brigades of Getty's division had been ordered to rejoin the Sixth Corps on the evening of May 6, the Vermont Brigade was ordered to stay in place: "General Hancock declared that he could not spare the Vermont brigade, and it stayed and held its position."[67]

The last formal action on the Plank Road sector of the Wilderness battlefield also fell to the badly battered Vermont Brigade. After a night of sending out parties to collect the wounded and bury their dead comrades, Grant on the morning of May 7 deployed skirmishers from the 6th Vermont west along the Orange Plank Road to ascertain the Confederate position and intentions. They met only light resistance. The main southern force had disengaged. A second skirmish line from the 5th Vermont went out a bit later to help cover parties of soldiers collecting discarded rifles from the battlefield. Finally, during the afternoon of May 7, the Vermont Brigade received orders to rejoin its comrades in the Sixth Corps on the army's right.[68]

Within the week, in his first official comment on the fight at the Wilderness, Grant wrote that "it is with a certain pride that I assure you there are no dishonorable graves." He expressed satisfaction that "the flag of each regiment, though pierced and tattered, still flaunts in the face of the foe, and noble bands of veterans with thinned ranks, and but few officers to command, still stand by them; and they seem determined to stand so long as there is a man to bear their flag aloft or an enemy in the field." [69]

Glory had been purchased at heavy cost. When he explored the field shortly after the battle, Grant reflected, "In view of the evidence there, the wonder was not that more than one-third of the command was killed and wounded, but how so many escaped. How men could remain there during the battle and still live seemed unaccountable." Grant probably can be excused for asking a sharply worded question: "One thousand brave officers and men of the Vermont brigade fell on that bloody field. Was the result commensurate to the sacrifice?" [70]

The losses had indeed been huge. On the morning of May 7 at least 191 Vermont Brigade soldiers lay dead. In a postwar statistical study of Civil War casualties, a register of Union regiments at the Wilderness ranked by battle deaths listed the five Vermont units among the first seven. The cost could be measured in other ways, too. The small town of Salisbury sent fifteen of its sons into Company F, 5th Vermont; at the Wilderness four of them died, and two more were wounded. As Surgeon Stevens of New York commented, "The Vermont brigade has lost many of its brightest ornaments." [71]

At least 947 more Vermonters received wounds that required some kind of medical attention. The devastation wrought in the brigade's ranks, made even worse in the next week by the fighting at Spotsylvania, caused the Vermont surgeon general to send additional volunteer physicians to Virginia to care for the state's wounded. When the first contingent of six new doctors arrived at Fredericksburg, they discovered wounded Vermonters scattered throughout the city, "stretched upon the floors of churches, deserted houses, stores and shops, with nothing underneath them except their tattered and blood-stiffened garments, with amputated stumps, shattered limbs and ugly flesh wounds which had not been dressed for four or five days." Dr. A. T. Woodward found 55 Vermonters among the 300 wounded men assigned to his charge; he had so little in the way of medical supplies that the treatment of all but the slightest injuries "taxed our strength to dress, and our ingenuity to devize means for the relief of the suffering though patient soldier." [72]

The doctors were especially infuriated because many men had to find their own way to the hospitals, often with less severely wounded com-

*Wounded Union soldiers from the battles of the Wilderness and
Spotsylvania in Fredericksburg, Va., May 1864.*
Francis Trevelyan Miller, ed., The Photographic History of the Civil War,
10 vols. (New York: Review of Reviews, 1911), 7:268

rades rendering the only assistance. There had not been enough wagons and ambulances to transport all the wounded in timely fashion. Pvt.
Robert Rogers of the 4th Vermont, lightly wounded in the arm on May 5,
found a ride to Fredericksburg but died of loss of blood before the doctors could get to him. Private Chase, who kept his leg after the bullet was
removed at a temporary medical facility near the battlefield on May 7,
had to wait nearly untended until May 12 for a ride to the general hospitals in Fredericksburg. Rank brought few benefits. It took Lieutenant
Colonel Lewis of the 5th Vermont about forty-six hours to travel a dozen
miles, and he, like Chase, began his journey only after he had already suffered through an operation—an exsection of the humerus—at a behind-
the-lines aid station. Lewis was lucky; his wife came to Fredericksburg
to supervise his recuperation.[73]

The newly arrived Vermont doctors hoped that their presence would convince wounded soldiers of "the consideration and sympathy of the State" for their welfare. The physicians were impressed that even the badly injured "did not utter a word of complaint—not a murmur escaped their lips—but with patience and heroic endurance bore their sufferings and privation in a manner worthy of the good cause in which they have suffered." The volunteer physicians arrived in time to assist army surgeons entirely overwhelmed with work. Some of the exhausted doctors seemed to take out their frustrations on the wounded men they were there to help. "The worst treatment I received in all of my army service was from the brute that called himself an army surgeon," Private Chase averred. "He appeared to be void of all feeling for humanity and seemed to delight in torturing wounded men as much as a savage." Mostly, however, the surgeons were physically and mentally spent. Chase saw Dr. William J. Sawing of the 2nd Vermont in Fredericksburg. The weary physician told him, "This is not my place in this room. I am very tired. I have amputated one hundred limbs today." Despite the best efforts of army and civilian doctors alike, 151 of the 947 Vermonters wounded in the Wilderness died. Among them was Capt. Erastus Buck of the 3rd Vermont, who succumbed on May 22 just after assuring his wife that she need not worry about him.[74]

Slowly, one by one, a procession of caskets headed back to Vermont. The body of the 2nd Vermont's Colonel Stone traveled to Bennington for burial. Lewis Grant eulogized the twenty-five-year-old dead colonel: "He was beloved by his command, and by all who knew him." Lieutenant Colonel Tyler, Stone's successor, set out for Vermont, too, to allow his severe thigh wound to heal. His wound became infected, and he died at the Metropolitan Hotel in New York City on May 23. Capt. Tiger Lillie also went home; interment in his hometown cemetery quickly became known as "the largest funeral ever held in Barnard." The 6th Vermont's Colonel Barney was dead, too. Surgeon Stevens mourned him as "the highest type of man; a christian gentleman." His remains were interred at Swanton with great solemnity; nearly 2,000 people attended, businesses closed, and on his coffin was laid the sword of the Louisiana colonel who had surrendered to him at Salem Church. Lieutenant Crane, the soldier/correspondent who wrote about the capture of the Confederate swords, could not cover the funeral; he lay dead in the Wilderness. The Masonic Lodge of Island Pond, Vermont, issued a resolution to mourn the loss of their brother, Captain Buck, who "loved the stars and stripes" and "discharged his duties as becomes a Patriot and a Mason." Captain Carpenter's remains would be disinterred in time and returned home to St.

Johnsbury for formal burial in June 1865. Then, the Reverend E. C. Cummings told how the captain fell at a place where "the Prince of Darkness seemed to shroud himself in the sombre and deadly thickets and to defy the zeal and devotion of our brave troops," but the cause for which they fought did not deserve to be remembered as "a destiny for pity."[75]

Not all of Vermont's dead returned home. Even in 1888 Private Chase still mourned Orric R. Ward, Joseph E. Butterfield, John Sweeney, and Parker Swazey, who "met a soldier's fate, dying in the face of the foe. No monument marks their resting-place; that honor, so justly their due, they never received." The 4th Vermont's Pvt. John Esdon, born in Scotland and drafted into service in August 1863, died in a Fredericksburg hospital on May 18 of a wound through both knees received in his baptism of fire on May 5. Pvt. Ephraim Hartshorn of the same regiment, a new recruit of December 1863 who likewise was wounded in his first exposure to combat on May 5, died the same day as Esdon. They were "buried by strangers." Many of the brigade's ninety-six missing men no doubt lay in the Wilderness in nameless graves. Some few more would die in Andersonville and other southern prisoner-of-war camps. In the wake of the events of May 5–6, people in Vermont could understand a wounded soldier's statement that appeared in the Rutland *Daily Herald*: "All previous battles, not excepting Savage's Station and Gettysburg, were mere skirmishes compared with the Battle of the Wilderness."[76]

There were a few happy endings. Private Flagg, the wrestler, recovered from his wound and returned to the 2nd Vermont; he enjoyed quite a reputation in national sports affairs after the war and always attributed his success to being "brought up on salt pork, corned beef, boiled potatoes and maple sugar and seasoned by four years service in the Civil War." Henry Brush, hit by two bullets, declared dead by the physicians, and laid out for interment, regained consciousness when the burial party arrived to pick him up the next day; he lived, too. Private Cutler, who could not wait for his enlistment to end, survived to go home safely. Sergeant Morey found himself able to write to his parents, "I don't know what to say first but will say praise God for his goodness in spearing my life while so many of our brave comrads have fallen victims to the enemy's shots." After the Wilderness, however, he tried to improve his odds a bit; at Spotsylvania, he told his fiancée, "if I keep a pretty good lookout and well to the rear I guess I shall not get shot."[77]

Lieutenant Holton, who had watched his brother die before he was wounded in an abortive bayonet attack, also survived. Lt. Edward Carter, the gutshot lieutenant of the 4th Vermont whom Sergeant Rich saved, overcame his severe wounds; for his heroism, Rich won the Medal of Honor, the only Vermont Brigade soldier so honored for actions at the Wilderness. But some of those happy endings were only temporary. Capt. William Tracy, who amazingly survived his twenty-four wounds from the Wilderness, died instantly a few months later at Reams Station, the victim of a single bullet.[78]

The men who fought and bled so freely under the flags of the Vermont Brigade at the Wilderness represented some of the best mettle of the American citizen-soldier. They did not fight for personal glory or for state pride. When Brig. Gen. George J. Stannard's 2nd Vermont Brigade helped turn the tide of war at Gettysburg, where they crushed the right flank of Pickett's Charge, the state legislature immediately honored them with a resolution of thanks. At the same time, a resolution to salute the 1st Vermont Brigade, which "had long been fighting battles without results" and "remained in the field, fighting on and doing its duty" after Stannard's nine-month troops mustered out, was tabled. "Yet the First Brigade felt no jealousy of the Second," one veteran wrote. "Why should they?" he asked, since the 2nd Brigade's senior officers were "all, with one exception, soldiers taken from the Old Brigade."[79]

What did they fight for, then? In 1872 Colonel Pingree tried to explain why his men absorbed the punishment they took in May 1864: "Too little has been understood and appreciated by those who were not of them, of this ruling spirit which animated that noble body of American soldiers,— their steadfastness for the sovereignty of their cardinal principle, the indissoluble unity of the States, their fealty to that principle through adversity and suffering and in the shadow of death, attested by a faith in its ultimate vindication, as sublime amid reverse as in the hour of triumph— a faith by which they sometimes fought, as in the tangled copse of the Wilderness, more than by sight, and which guided and sustained them throughout the varying fortunes of their four years of military life."[80]

To Colonel Lewis it was something more personal: "These were not brave soldiers of the nation only, who fell on those fields," he wrote. "Long years of peril incurred together, of labors shared, of duties divided, of kindness reciprocated, of love and friendship bestowed, had made them our devoted comrades, our dearest friends, our beloved brothers. These were noble souls, whose bloody death made many, many hearts to bleed. Their names recall, each one, the noblest characteristics of human nature. The smiling, kind and gentle Barney, the prompt and urbane Stone, the cool and chivalrous Tyler, the ready and impetuous Dudley, and all that galaxy of stars, noble hearts that went down amid the fire and smoke, roar and crash, death and carnage of those dreadful battlefields."[81]

Now, perhaps, it is easier to understand why Lewis Grant, at this stage of the war when veteran soldiers rarely gave in to hyperbole, could conclude his official report of the battle with this commentary: "It was a terrible struggle—a time which truly 'tried men's souls.' The memory of those who fell will be sacredly cherished among the true and tried patriots of Vermont; and those who survive, well may proudly say, 'I, too, was in the battles of the Wilderness.'"[82]

NOTES

1. Gen. L. A. Grant, "In the Wilderness," *National Tribune* (Washington, D.C.), January 28, 1897.

2. G. G. Benedict, *Vermont in the Civil War: A History of the Part Taken by Vermont Soldiers and Sailors in the War for the Union, 1861-5*, 2 vols. (Burlington, Vt.: Free Press Association, 1886), 1:235.

3. Howard Coffin, *Full Duty: Vermonters in the Civil War* (Woodstock, Vt.: Countryman Press, 1993), 236; Peter S. Chase, *Reunion Greeting, Together with an Historical Sketch and a Complete Descriptive List of the Members of Co. I, 2d Regt., Vt. Vols., in the War for the Union . . .* (Brattleboro, Vt.: Phoenix, 1891), 40–41; Benedict, *Vermont in the Civil War*, 1:112, 115, 414.

4. Benedict, *Vermont in the Civil War*, 1:145, 414.

5. William Monroe Newton, *History of Barnard, Vermont, with Family Genealogies, 1761-1927*, 2 vols. ([Montpelier, Vt.]: Vermont Historical Society, 1928), 1:105; Benedict, *Vermont in the Civil War*, 1:168. Benedict initially places the unit strength at 600 but later asserts that the regiment numbered 680. See *Vermont in the Civil War*, 1:414.

6. Benedict, *Vermont in the Civil War*, 1:414, gives 510 as the unit's official strength when it crossed the Rapidan River, very close to the figure of 500 cited earlier.

7. Ibid., 1:414, 223–24; Donald Wickman to Robert K. Krick, July 24, 1991, copy in bound vol. 75, Fredericksburg and Spotsylvania National Military Park Library, Fredericksburg, Va. (repository hereafter cited as FSNMP).

8. Benedict, *Vermont in the Civil War*, 1:223; Lt. Albert A. Crane to Editor, Rutland *Herald*, May 7, 1863, printed in Rutland *Herald*, May 23, 1863; Crane to Editor, Rutland *Herald*, May 14, 1863, copy in vol. 193, FSNMP. Sedgwick quoted in Rowland E. Robinson, *Vermont: A Study in Independence* (Boston: Houghton Mifflin, 1899), 346.

9. Jerome Cutler to Emily, April 13, 1864, in Jerome Cutler, *Letters of Jerome Cutler, Waterville, Vermont, during His Enlistment in the Union Army 2nd Regiment Vermont Volunteers, 1861-1864* (Bennington, Vt.: Privately printed, 1990), not paginated; Wilbur Fisk letter, April 26, 1864, in Wilbur Fisk, *Anti-Rebel: The*

Civil War Letters of Wilbur Fisk, ed. Emil Rosenblatt (Croton-on-Hudson, N.Y.: Privately printed, 1983), 212; Charles C. Morey Diary, March 23, 1864, Stuart Goldman Collection, U.S. Army Military History Institute, Carlisle, Pa. (repository hereafter cited as USAMHI); Luther B. Harris to "Friend Olive," April 19, 1864, copy in bound vol. 117, FSNMP. Sergeant Morey also noted the review in his diary entry for April 18, 1864, and in a letter to his mother, April 22, 1864, Goldman Collection, USAMHI.

10. Wilbur Fisk letter, April 15, 1864, in Fisk, *Anti-Rebel*, 209.

11. Morey diary, April 8, May 3, 1864, and Charles C. Morey to his mother, May 3, 1864, Goldman Collection, USAMHI; Wilbur Fisk letter, April 26, 1864, in Fisk, *Anti-Rebel*, 211; Coffin, *Full Duty*, 233.

12. U.S. War Department, *The War of the Rebellion: A Compilation of the Official Records of the Union and Confederate Armies*, 127 vols., index, and atlas (Washington: GPO, 1880–1901), ser. 1, 36(1):696 (hereafter cited as *OR*).

13. Luther B. Harris, "The Wilderness," manuscript dated 1888, in bound vol. 117, FSNMP.

14. *OR* 36(1):676.

15. *OR* 36(1):678; Grant, "In the Wilderness," January 28, 1897.

16. Address of G. G. Benedict, November 2, 1882, in *Proceedings of the Reunion Society of Vermont Officers, 1864–1884, with Addresses Delivered at its Meetings . . .* (Burlington, Vt.: Free Press Association, 1885), 396–97 (hereafter cited as Benedict, "1882 Address"); Benedict, *Vermont in the Civil War*, 1:422. In a footnote Benedict mentioned the assertion of Surgeon S. J. Allen of the 4th Vermont, who was with Getty when the order to march arrived. According to Allen the order to Getty "was accompanied by a special direction that he should take the Vermont brigade, with two other brigades of his division."

17. Grant, "In the Wilderness," January 28, 1897; unpublished after-action report of Henry Heth, covering operations "from the 4th of May 1864 to the present date," December 7, 1864, copy in bound vol. 178, FSNMP; *OR* 36(1):676, 678.

18. Wilbur Fisk letter, May 9, 1864, in Fisk, *Anti-Rebel*, 215; Harris, "The Wilderness"; *OR* 36(1):711, 696, 709.

19. *OR* 36(1):696, 676.

20. *OR* 36(1):677.

21. *OR* 36(1):320; Grant, "In the Wilderness," January 28, 1897.

22. *OR* 36(1):696–97, 709–10.

23. Grant, "In the Wilderness," January 28, 1897; Henry Houghton, "The Ordeal of Civil War: A Recollection," *Vermont History* 41 (Winter 1973): 46.

24. Grant, "In the Wilderness," January 28, 1897; Coffin, *Full Duty*, 236; Heth's report, FSNMP; Harris, "The Wilderness."

25. *OR* 36(1):711.

26. Houghton, "Ordeal of Civil War," 46; Otis F. R. Waite, *Vermont in the Great Rebellion* (Claremont, N.H.: Tracy, Chase, 1869), 271; E. D. Redington to Sarah, May 16, 1864, copy in bound vol. 149, FSNMP; Harris, "A Prison Story," in Sgt. Luther B. Harris Memoirs, Civil War Miscellaneous Collection, USAMHI.

27. Harris, "The Wilderness"; Grant, "In the Wilderness," January 28, 1897.

28. *OR* 36(1):710; Grant, "In the Wilderness," January 28, 1897.

29. *OR* 36(1):697, 320 (when Ricketts's men exhausted their ammunition, the guns were replaced by a section from Dow's 6th Maine Battery); Benedict, *Vermont in the Civil War*, 1:435n. The similarity of Taylor's spinal wound to that suffered by assassinated President James Garfield drew Benedict's special attention. Taylor stood out because his case "has been cited as a very rare one of recovery from such an injury" (Harris, "The Wilderness").

30. Houghton, "Ordeal of Civil War," 46; Harris, "The Wilderness."

31. Benedict, *Vermont in the Civil War*, 1:425; James A. Graham, *The James A. Graham Papers, 1861–1884*, ed. H. M. Wagstaff (Chapel Hill: University of North Carolina Press, 1928), 191; Heth's report, FSNMP.

32. Wilbur Fisk letter, May 9, 1864, in Fisk, *Anti-Rebel*, 215; Chase, *Reunion Greeting*, 51; Edward A. Holton to Katie, May 6, 1864, copy in bound vol. 87, FSNMP.

33. Chase, *Reunion Greeting*, 43; Wilbur Fisk letter, May 9, 1864, in Fisk, *Anti-Rebel*, 215; *OR* 36(1):697.

34. *OR* 36(1):697; Chase, *Reunion Greeting*, 43–45, 51; Edward A. Holton to Katie, May 6, 10, 1864, copies in bound vol. 87, FSNMP.

35. *OR* 36(1):697; Chase, *Reunion Greeting*, 51.

36. Grant, "In the Wilderness," February 4, 1897. See also *Proceedings of the Reunion Society of Vermont Officers*, 261–62.

37. Harris, "The Wilderness"; Benedict, "1882 Address," 395–97.

38. Benedict, "1882 Address," 398.

39. Waite, *Vermont in the Great Rebellion*, 277.

40. Wilbur Fisk letter, May 9, 1864, in Fisk, *Anti-Rebel*, 215; Address of Lt. Col. John R. Lewis, January 8, 1880, in *Proceedings of the Reunion Society of Vermont Officers*, 314.

41. Coffin, *Full Duty*, 236; George T. Stevens, *Three Years in the Sixth Corps* (New York: Van Nostrand, 1870), 311.

42. See *OR* 36(1):473 for a brief mention of the 40th New York's participation in this specific action. The identification of the other two regiments is taken from Gordon C. Rhea, *The Battle of the Wilderness: May 5–6, 1864* (Baton Rouge: Louisiana State University Press, 1994), 197.

43. *OR* 36(1):714, 697.

44. *OR* 36(1):714; Richard O'Sullivan, *55th Virginia Infantry* (Lynchburg, Va.: H. E. Howard, 1989), 68; Homer D. Musselman, *47th Virginia Infantry* (Lynchburg, Va.: H. E. Howard, 1991), 69; *OR* 36(1):677.

45. *OR* 36(1):320; Chase, *Reunion Greeting*, 43, 51.

46. Benedict, *Vermont in the Civil War*, 1:113–14; "Case of Carlos H. Rich, late first sergeant, Company D, Fourth Vermont Veteran Volunteers. Application for a medal of honor," Records and Pensions Office doc. no. 402,755, copy in vol. 198, FSNMP.

47. *OR* 36(1):697, 700.

48. *OR* 36(1):677; Wilbur Fisk letter, May 9, 1864, in Fisk, *Anti-Rebel*, 215.

49. "Hancock in the Wilderness," *New York Herald*, May 14, 1864; *New York Times*, May 8, 1864; Heth's report, FSNMP.

50. Benedict, *Vermont in the Civil War*, 1:427; David Craft, *History of the One*

Hundred Forty-First Regiment Pennsylvania Volunteers, 1862–1865 (Towanda, Pa.: Reporter-Journal, 1885), 178.

51. *OR* 36(1):320; Grant, "In the Wilderness," January 28, 1897. Grant elaborated very specifically on his good opinion of Hancock in the continuation of "In the Wilderness," February 4, 1897.

52. Harris, "The Wilderness."

53. Benedict, *Vermont in the Civil War*, 1:428; Chase, *Reunion Greeting*, 44–45. The three other soldiers who helped Prior carry Chase to safety—Pvts. Elmer G. Holmes, George A. French, and Ira D. Clark—were all killed in action at Spotsylvania the next week. Chase never saw his "noble, brave, loving friends" again.

54. E. D. Redington to Sarah, May 16, 1864, copy in bound vol. 149, FSNMP.

55. Grant, "In the Wilderness," February 4, 1897; Wilbur Fisk letter, May 9, 1864, in Fisk, *Anti-Rebel*, 216; Harris, "The Wilderness."

56. *OR* 36(1):677, 698; Grant, "In the Wilderness," February 4, 1897.

57. *OR* 36(1):323.

58. *OR* 36(1):710, 714.

59. *OR* 36(1):678; Wilbur Fisk letter, May 9, 1864, in Fisk, *Anti-Rebel*, 216.

60. Grant, "In the Wilderness," February 4, 1897; *OR* 36(1):699.

61. *OR* 36(1):323, 699.

62. Grant, "In the Wilderness," February 4, 1897; Benedict, "1882 Address," 399; *OR* 36(1):1055.

63. Wilbur Fisk letter, May 9, 1864, in Fisk, *Anti-Rebel*, 216; Morey diary, May 5, 6, 1864, and Morey to parents, June 7, 1864, Goldman Collection, USAMHI; Newton, *History of Barnard, Vermont*, 1:115; Harris, "The Wilderness." These two unnamed soldiers allegedly died at Spotsylvania a few days later. Harris ended his story thus: "The wavering timid recruit of the morning of May 5th became the hero of May 9th."

64. *OR* 36(1):710, 699.

65. *OR* 36(1):699; Wilbur Fisk letter, May 9, 1864, in Fisk, *Anti-Rebel*, 217; Grant, "In the Wilderness," February 4, 1897.

66. *OR* 36(1):699, 324; Harris, "The Wilderness."

67. Grant, "In the Wilderness," February 4, 1897; Benedict, "1882 Address," 400.

68. *OR* 36(1):678, 700.

69. *OR* 36(1):696.

70. Grant, "In the Wilderness," February 4, 1897; *OR* 36(1):698.

71. William F. Fox, *Regimental Losses in the American Civil War* (Albany, N.Y.: Albany Pub. Co., 1889), 445; James E. Peterson, ". . . This Thing Will Never Be Settled . . ." *Vermont History News* 40 (March/April 1989): 41; Stevens, *Three Years in the Sixth Corps*, 323. Fox lists the seven Union regiments that suffered the most battle deaths at the Wilderness in this order: 2nd Vermont, 4th Vermont, 93rd New York, 5th Vermont, 57th Massachusetts, 3rd Vermont, and 6th Vermont.

72. Surgeon General's Report, October 1, 1864, in *Message of the Governor to the General Assembly of Vermont. October Session 1864.* (Montpelier, Vt.: Walton's Steam Press, 1864), 29.

73. E. E. Rollins, *The Memorial Record of the Soldiers Who Enlisted from*

Greensboro, Vermont, to Aid in Subduing the Great Rebellion of 1861–5 . . . (Montpelier, Vt.: Freeman Printing House, 1868), 38; Chase, *Reunion Greeting*, 45; Benedict, *Vermont in the Civil War*, 1:196.

74. Surgeon General's Report, October 1, 1864, 26–27, 29; Chase, *Reunion Greeting*, 46; John E. Balzer, ed., *Buck's Book: A View of the 3rd Vermont Infantry Regiment* (Bolingbrook, Ill.: Balzer and Assoc., 1993), 81.

75. Coffin, *Full Duty*, 236; Waite, *Vermont in the Great Rebellion*, 264; Newton, *History of Barnard, Vermont*, 1:105; Stevens, *Three Years in the Sixth Corps*, 323; Benedict, *Vermont in the Civil War*, 1:224; resolution printed in Balzer, *Buck's Book*, 81; "At the Funeral of Capt. Carpenter. (North Church, St. Johnsbury, June 25th, 1865, Rev. E. C. Cummings)," typescript in vol. 149, FSNMP.

76. Peter Chase, "In the Wilderness," *Vermont Phoenix*, May 4, 1888, reprinted in Chase, *Reunion Greeting*, 52; Rollins, *Memorial Record of the Soldiers Who Enlisted from Greensboro, Vermont*, 23, 27–28; Coffin, *Full Duty*, 242.

77. Coffin, *Full Duty*, 236; Chase, "In the Wilderness," 52; Charles C. Morey to parents, May 13, 1864, Goldman Collection, USAMHI; Jerome Cutler to "My dear Emily," May 19, 1864, in Cutler, *Letters*, no pagination.

78. "Case of Carlos H. Rich, late first sergeant, Company D, Fourth Vermont Veterans Volunteers. Application for a medal of honor"; Harris, "A Prison Story."

79. Unattributed reunion comments, November 15, 1876, in *Proceedings of the Reunion Society of Vermont Officers*, 261.

80. Address of Lt. Col. S. E. Pingree, November 7, 1872, in ibid., 195.

81. Address of Col. John R. Lewis, January 8, 1880, in ibid., 314.

82. *OR* 36(1):701.

ROBERT E. L. KRICK

Like a Duck on a June Bug

JAMES LONGSTREET'S FLANK ATTACK,

MAY 6, 1864

hen military historians define the place of an army in the annals of warfare, they frequently point to some unique characteristic or maneuver as a trademark. Hannibal and his Carthaginians are inextricably associated with envelopment tactics, and it is difficult to separate the German army of World War II from the term "blitzkrieg." Although many generals employed turning maneuvers long before the Civil War, none perfected them so well as Robert E. Lee and his Army of Northern Virginia. Flank attacks were their specialty.

By May 1864 the army had launched so many flanking operations—both strategically and tactically—that an end-around had become its preferred option. Under Lee's tutelage Thomas J. "Stonewall" Jackson turned McClellan's right flank during the Seven Days campaign in June 1862. Two months later Jackson marched his men into position behind John Pope's Federal army near Manassas. At Chancellorsville Jackson brought about arguably the most memorable moment in the army's history when he flanked O. O. Howard's Eleventh Corps on the second day of the battle. Unanticipated enemy movement had aborted other efforts at Gaines's Mill and Mine Run. The necessary dangers of dividing the army had proved well worth the risk, as Lee's finest victories "were won under a blade suspended by a hair." This record of overwhelming success enhanced the well-known self-confidence and aggressive spirit of Lee's army.[1]

The morning of May 6, 1864, found that army in desperate need of relief. The entire Third Corps, having been placed in unfortunate circumstances overnight, retreated in chaos westward before the rolling masses of the Union Second Corps. The arrival of James Longstreet's First Corps and the subsequent Lee-to-the-Rear episode merely restored order along the Orange Plank Road. The battle had not been decided, nor was it yet certain that Lee could even repel the renewed Federal attacks brewing in the woods on either side of the road.

The presence of Longstreet's corps allowed Lee to extend the Confederate line to the left, reaching toward Richard S. Ewell's Second Corps on the Orange Turnpike. A. P. Hill's hastily repaired divisions moved northward onto the Jones and Chewning farms. Their belligerent presence proved sufficient to scare away parts of Ambrose E. Burnside's Union Ninth Corps and secure the gap between the two isolated Confederate wings. With a nearly intact front at last, Lee could begin to ponder offensive operations.

Sporadic fighting continued in mid-morning on the Plank Road. While Lee awaited the arrival of Richard H. Anderson with the last fresh Confederate division, the Federal army lurched into a final disjointed attack on both sides of the road. Brig. Gen. James S. Wadsworth's Fifth Corps division assaulted on the north, while a miscellaneous collection of troops from Hancock's Second Corps moved through the woods south of the road. The resultant fighting struck Union officer Charles H. Banes as "the most unsatisfactory and objectless . . . of any campaign through which we had passed." These Union attacks pushed against Maj. Gen. Charles W. Field's division north of the Plank Road and Brig. Gen. Joseph B. Kershaw's brigades south of it.[2]

The unaccustomed mildness of Hancock's attack can be traced to the confused situation at his headquarters. Prisoners taken in earlier fighting confirmed that both Field and Kershaw had arrived on the scene. That left Longstreet's other division—the Virginians of George E. Pickett—unaccounted for. Noisy musketry and vague reports of massed men south of the battlefield near Todd's Tavern played on Hancock's nerves. Fearing for his left flank, he extended it by posting several fresh brigades on the Brock Road to guard against Confederate incursions from the south. These dispositions, reported Hancock, "prevented me from pushing my success . . . on the plank road."[3]

That imaginary danger along the Brock Road helped open the way for a more substantial threat closer to the front. Hancock had carefully secured the left wing of the army but in the excitement had neglected the southern edge of his own front line. That flank, composed mostly of men from Brig. Gen. Gershom Mott's division, dangled helplessly in the dense woods below the Plank Road, only yards from the inquisitive pickets of Kershaw's division.

While the action sputtered on both sides of the road, the Confederate high command searched for an opportunity to strike. After enduring agonizing suspense, Lee finally had his entire army at hand, with Grant still temporarily ensnared in the Wilderness. Ewell already had orders to look for chances to attack on the northern end of the field. Now Lee hoped for an opening near the Plank Road. To that end he sent the army's chief engineer to James Longstreet with instructions to probe the woods for a weakness in Hancock's line. Maj. Gen. Martin Luther Smith had joined the army in April 1864 after distinguished service in western operations, and he remained a little-known figure to most of the Virginia army's officers. One observer noted that Smith "rides his horse as erect as a ramrod." General Longstreet remembered Smith as "a splendid tactician as well as a skilful engineer, and gallant withal." Otherwise the new import from the West seems to have made little impression on his peers.[4]

Smith returned to General Longstreet by 10:00 A.M. His expedition had found that the southern flank of Hancock's battle line certainly lay exposed in the woods. Furthermore, a perfect avenue of approach existed for moving a sizable body of attackers into position perpendicular to that flank. This was the uncompleted bed of the Fredericksburg and Gordonsville Railroad.[5]

The ambitious attempt at linking Fredericksburg and Gordonsville by railroad had commenced (like so many other transportation projects in Virginia) in the 1850s. Engineers had graded portions of the route by the time work stopped in 1861. They had not laid any rails, and the unfinished bed ran from Fredericksburg to Orange Court House rather than to Gordonsville. From the start it competed with the adjacent Orange Plank Road, which also dated from the mid-1850s. The two avenues ran through the Wilderness on a nearly parallel course, separated by less than one mile in some places.[6]

One of the chief antebellum figures in the development of the Wilderness's transportation corridors was William Mahone—destined to be a prominent figure in the 1864 battle. Mahone became chief engineer in 1852 for the Orange Plank Road, which he and others constructed during that decade. Surviving plans for the Fredericksburg and Gordonsville Railroad indicate that it originally was planned for ground that Mahone's Orange Plank Road ultimately traversed. Crowded out by the Plank Road, the railroad moved a short distance south when construction began.[7]

Section of the Orange Plank Road near the Wilderness and Chancellorsville battlefields. The planking, which covered just the eastbound lane of the road, can be seen above the fallen tree in the lower right corner.
Francis Trevelyan Miller, ed., The Photographic History of the Civil War, *10 vols. (New York: Review of Reviews, 1911), 9:62*

The presence of the unfinished railroad could not have been a surprise to any senior officer of either army on the southern end of the battlefield. That same railroad had figured prominently in the battle of Chancellorsville. More recently both armies had maneuvered through its cuts and fills as part of the Mine Run operations in November and December 1863. During that campaign some of Hancock's Second Corps had taken an overnight position astride the unfinished railroad at a point just west of what would become the Wilderness battlefield. Parts of that same corps even had marched back and forth across the bed of the railroad at its intersection with the Brock Road on the morning of May 6. No one has adequately explained why Hancock did not use such a natural avenue for offensive operations of his own, or why he did not at least attempt to secure it from Confederate use.[8]

"After a brief consultation," Lee and Longstreet agreed on the merits of a flank attack based on Smith's intelligence. They then sought to piece together a strike force from among the scattered divisions at hand. The four brigades finally chosen to participate originated with four different divisions of the army and were picked more because of geographic convenience than special merit. Brig. Gen. William T. Wofford's brigade of Georgians came from Kershaw's division; Brig. Gen. George T. Anderson's Georgians originated in Field's division; Brig. Gen. William Mahone's Virginia brigade was freshly arrived with Anderson's division; and the remnants of Brig. Gen. Joseph R. Davis's mixed brigade came from Henry Heth's division.[9]

Wofford was a natural choice to participate in offensive operations. The balding brigadier had served in Hood's Texas Brigade earlier in the war and absorbed most of its superb aggressive qualities. His combat record as both a field officer and a general had established him as one of the most dependable mid-level leaders in the army. Wofford's six regiments extended the southern flank of the army nearly to the unfinished railroad; some accounts credit Wofford rather than Smith with discovering the advantages of that corridor through the woods. A brigade correspondent writing to one of the Atlanta newspapers after the battle identified Wofford as the hero of the tale, declaring that "seeing the immense advantage" of the railroad bed, Wofford asked permission to make a flank attack, to which Longstreet "immediately acceded." A diarist in the 16th Georgia confirmed the claim: "Gen Wofford went to Gen Longstreet [and] asked permission to manuver his Brigade[;] permission [was] granted." General Kershaw wrote officially that Wofford suggested the movement, while Longstreet noted that Wofford "volunteered."[10]

George T. Anderson brought five more Georgia regiments to the assault. Eighty percent of this brigade consisted of low-numbered regiments that had crafted outstanding records as early as First Manassas. Many of Georgia's finest young men had joined the 7th, 8th, 9th, and 11th Georgia immediately on the eruption of war. Most were dead or wounded by May 1864, but enough remained to sustain the pride of Anderson's brigade. An unpolished member of the brigade summed it up in a May 5 letter to his mother: "We air now verry Near in to afight we may get in to it before the Sun goes Down. . . . I am joust as willing to go in it as I will

Brig. Gen. William Mahone.
Francis Trevelyan Miller, ed., The
Photographic History of the Civil War,
10 vols. (New York: Review of Reviews,
1911), 3:191

ever bee and if the good Lord Sees Proper to take me from this world you
will Pleas take Care of what I have got at home."[11]

The least weary troops on the field came from William Mahone's brigade of Virginians. Not only had Mahone's brigade missed all the Wilderness fighting so far, but in the larger picture they had somehow escaped
on the fringe of many of the war's most serious contests. It had been fully
one year since the five Virginia regiments had last seen sustained action.
They reached the field as part of Richard H. Anderson's division, which
on its arrival had immediately been cannibalized to restore weak sec-
tions of the lines. Despite his trademark frailness, Mahone stood large in
battle, where he was "a dangerous man," according to a colleague. As the
flanking party gathered, Mahone's men already occupied a convenient slot
adjacent to the Plank Road, ideally placed to join the initial southward
leg of the movement. After the battle the story circulated in the proud
brigade that "Genl. Longstreet asked Genl. Lee to let him have Mahone's
Brigade" for the attack.[12]

The final cluster of Confederates to participate in the flank attack came
from Joseph R. Davis's brigade, commanded that morning by John M.
Stone, its senior colonel. Like the rest of Henry Heth's division, Stone's
men had been sadly smashed in Hancock's early morning attacks. Rallying, they played a peripheral role in Longstreet's stirring counterattack.

Somewhere in the course of the morning's action, Union attacks combined with the virtually impenetrable woods to sever the brigade. Its two non-Mississippi units wandered north of the Plank Road while the remaining four regiments found themselves south of the road. Sketchy evidence indicates that they attached themselves to the edge of the flanking force like some wayward appendage.[13]

Longstreet chose his chief of staff Lt. Col. G. Moxley Sorrel—"a particularly gallant officer," in Brig. Gen. E. Porter Alexander's judgment—to assemble the force. As Sorrel recalled, Longstreet beckoned to him and confided, "There is a fine chance of a great attack by our right. . . . Hit hard when you start, but don't start until you have everything ready. I shall . . . be on hand with fresh troops for further advance." Looking back in 1905, Sorrel aptly concluded that for "an aspiring young staff officer" it was a splendid moment of promise.[14]

Although the entire plan hinged on the secret movement and surprise assault of the flanking party, the attackers badly needed a cooperative eastward push from their comrades left behind on the Plank Road. While Sorrel maneuvered the flanking party, Longstreet would press eastward with everyone else. A simultaneous attack from two directions, abetted by the dense growth indigenous to the Wilderness, could bring panic to Hancock's men. Perhaps the Federals might even be dislodged from the Brock Road intersection.

The question of which officer actually commanded the attack has been controversial since 1864 and remains only unsatisfactorily resolved. William Mahone was the senior general in the group. If the various officers involved actually had time to ponder military protocol, Mahone clearly would have emerged as the leader of the attack. Shortly after the battle he identified himself as having been "charged with the immediate direction" of the attack by Longstreet. While that may have been technically true, there is scant evidence that Mahone played any part in the maneuver of the force. He seems instead to have spent the entire morning amidst his own brigade, exerting no control over the bigger picture. In direct contrast to the Virginian, Moxley Sorrel operated everywhere. Men from both Mahone's and Wofford's brigades saw the excited staffer astride a horse in front of the line.[15]

General Longstreet further confused the issue by crediting several people for virtually the same things in different terms. He identified Mahone as most senior in the attack, and to him "was entrusted its immediate direction." Longstreet's official report did not mention Mahone's elevation, instead noting that "special directions were given to

*Lt. Col. Gilbert Moxley Sorrel
(shown later as a brigadier general).
Gilbert Moxley Sorrel,* Recollections
of a Confederate Staff Officer
*(Wilmington, N.C.: Broadfoot, 1987),
plate 1 following p. 34*

Lieutenant-Colonel Sorrel to conduct" the attack. "Much of the success of the movement," he continued, "is due to the very skillful manner in which the move was conducted by Lieutenant-Colonel Sorrel." A different Longstreet letter (to Robert E. Lee) recommended Sorrel's promotion to brigadier general on May 19, 1864. It credited the staff officer again, remarking that he "was assigned to represent me in this flank movement, with instructions as to the execution of it." The same letter later made reference to "the attack made under the supervision of Lieut Col Sorrel." Still another war-date Longstreet letter praised William T. Wofford in familiar language. "Much of the success attending the movement is due to General Wofford," he wrote. Longstreet obviously felt Wofford's role substantial, as he recommended the Georgian for promotion to major general based specifically on his May 6 performance.[16]

Fighting sputtered along the Plank Road while Sorrel struggled to shift his four brigades into position along the unfinished railroad. He found it "difficult to assemble them in that horrid Wilderness." Meanwhile Robert E. Lee impatiently strained to hear the first sounds of the important movement. Somewhere to the west of the Tapp field, Third Corps staff officer William W. Chamberlaine found Lee uneasily awaiting news from the flank attack. Musket balls landing around the general prompted Lee to mutter to himself, "Those balls keep coming this way." Only later did the nonplussed Chamberlaine discern that Lee knew the westward-flying lead would only stop once the flank attack commenced.[17]

Having moved south from the Plank Road, Sorrel's men struck the unfinished railroad and turned east "for some distance." General Wofford had requested the easternmost position for his brigade knowing that it would be farthest behind the Federal flank, but G. T. Anderson's brigade arrived there first. To conserve time Wofford conceded the honor and formed on Anderson's left in the railroad cut. Mahone's Virginians occupied a spot in the woods angling obliquely northwest away from the railroad. The four fragmented Mississippi regiments of Davis's brigade probably hovered on Mahone's left flank closer to the Plank Road.[18]

With everything in order the infantry left the shelter of the railroad bed and moved into the confusing Wilderness "with a step that meant to conquer." Lt. Col. E. M. Feild had scattered the 170 men of his newly formed sharpshooter battalion as a screen in front of Mahone's brigade. One of Wofford's soldiers in the 3rd Georgia Battalion recalled that the members of his unit deployed with eight to ten feet between each man. The other regiments involved must have been less widely spaced.[19]

The Union flank rested without support halfway between the unfinished railroad and the Plank Road. Col. Robert McAllister, a testy brigade commander from Gershom Mott's division, had the nine regiments of his brigade posted in the woods facing west. Somewhere nearby lay the remnants of a New York brigade commanded by Col. Paul Frank— "a whiskey-pickled, lately-arrived, blusterous German," in the eyes of one Federal staff officer. Mott's other brigade and most of David B. Birney's division rounded out the Union presence south of the Plank Road. All were oriented west with their attention fixed on Kershaw's division, which continued to demonstrate.[20]

After crossing a network of small streams and tributaries, the Confederate line enjoyed its first view of the Union flank, still in woods. Mahone's men had performed a delicate wheel into line and now faced due north. Wofford's brigade to the east caught sight of the foe at about the same time. Sorrel's strike force had miraculously mastered the obstructing thickets and stood ready to hit the Union flank with nearly parade-ground precision. One final bog separated Mahone's brigade from its target. The 12th Virginia's color-bearer, Ben May, his progress "somewhat embarrassed by the bushes" and swampy terrain, struggled to carry his flag across the stream. From horseback Lt. Col. Sorrel offered to assist the process; May, "knee deep in mud," sternly refused to relinquish the colors but shouted, "We will follow you." Dozens of soldiers saw this episode and cherished its memory many years afterward.[21]

By the time of the Sorrel–May encounter, secrecy no longer mattered.

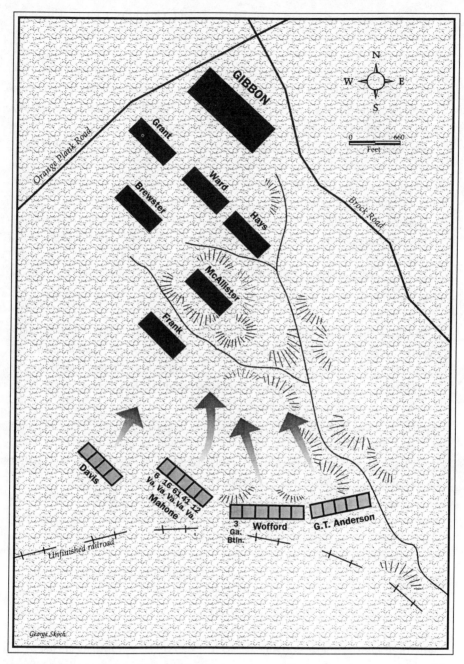

Sorrel's late morning attack, May 6, 1864.

The Union line lay in sight just ahead, and Confederates to the east already were charging loudly toward Hancock's exposed flank and rear. When their attack orders came, Wofford's men (in the quaint Georgia language of a participant) "raised the old rebel yell and went on them like a duck on a June bug." The landscape at the point where Mahone's men struck consisted of "scrubby" oak trees on ground that gently ascended to a slight hillock where the Union flank rested.[22]

McAllister maintained after the battle that he had divined the Confederate intentions but had not been able to counteract them. When the attack hit, McAllister wrestled his brigade through a maneuver that changed its front almost ninety degrees to face the onslaught. That merely exposed both his flanks to overlapping southerners and barely dented the momentum of the attack. Panic spread through Mott's entire force with increasing urgency. A sprinting soldier in the 3rd Maine found that the notorious undergrowth of the Wilderness so impeded everyone's progress that they had to keep their eyes shut "or we would have had our eyes put out."[23]

Most of the Confederates enjoyed the "highly exciting" chase, dashing forward with "overwhelming impetuosity." James A. Reynolds of the 16th Georgia wrote with relish that his regiment "drove them like a storm." Another man in the same brigade recalled that "some few of them [Yankees] fired, and a good many of them ran, throwing down their guns as they went; some lay flat on the ground." From horseback Moxley Sorrel supervised the rout and continued to cheer forward his line; men of the 12th Virginia saw him in front of their regiment wildly waving his hat and crying out, "Follow me, Virginians! Let me lead you."[24]

Union soldiers stationed along the Orange Plank Road soon felt the influence of the wild events occurring in the woods to their south. Like most flank attacks, the ramifications of this one spread over a far greater area than the small number of Confederates would suggest. The collapse of Hancock's southern flank telescoped units there into troops farther north, increasing the chaos exponentially. An astonished officer in Ward's brigade thought that he "might as well have tried to stop the flight of a cannon ball by interposing the lid of a cracker box." The fleeing crowd overwhelmed his regiment and shattered it. The "terrific tempest of disaster" roared onward, "tearing to pieces regiment after regiment." On other parts of the Plank Road the blossoming disaster seemed less intense. Well-behaved fugitives emerged from the woods almost quietly, "without any apparent cause," like men "returning dissatisfied from a muster."[25]

A few Federal officers began to understand their danger. Those near the Plank Road with the most initiative wheeled their men south to face the increasing noise. By late morning the collection of units patched together around the road even included men from Ambrose Burnside's Ninth Corps mixed among tired soldiers from the Second, Fifth, and Sixth Corps. Some of those fresh Ninth Corps units established themselves in the ditch paralleling the southern edge of the Plank Road and peered anxiously into woods "thick and heavy with sulphurous smoke." The crush of fleeing men from Mott's division constricted the view and for a time prevented any shooting toward the approaching threat.[26]

While Sorrel's men continued to roll up Hancock's flank "in the usual manner," Longstreet offered crucial assistance by aggressively probing eastward along either side of the road. What few bluecoats remained in the woods south of the road soon crumbled before the converging Confederates. To the north Charles W. Field ably led his Confederate brigades against Wadsworth's division, engaging in short-range duels over ground that already had changed hands numerous times in the past day. Perhaps Wadsworth did not fully comprehend the serious danger his division faced. His solution to the deteriorating situation was to attack west along the Plank Road, which only further exposed his men and hastened the collapse of his command. Confederates answered the new thrust with violent musketry that injured many officers. The noise reached new levels, reminding one soldier of "the boiling cauldron of hell, as it is represented to us by our good Chaplains." Mississippian W. M. Abernathy viewed it as "pandemonium worse confounded. . . . The Yankees were driven back and shriveled up."[27]

General Wadsworth fell with a fatal head wound in the course of his ill-fated attack. His nearly lifeless body lay on the edge of the Plank Road for the rest of the morning. Virtually everyone who passed remembered seeing the Yankee general indecorously propped against a tree beside the road. Several soldiers claimed souvenirs from among Wadsworth's personal effects.[28]

The mortal wounding of Wadsworth corresponded with the final collapse of Hancock's front. A Ninth Corps officer standing in the line along the Plank Road looked beyond his right flank to the west; to his horror, he could see Confederates crossing the road, "at first two or three and then whole squads, pushing for the shelter of the bushes on the north side." Sorrel's men had reached the Plank Road.[29]

No better illustration of the power of a flank attack can be found in Virginia during the Civil War. Once the Confederate line struck, Union defenses toppled in sequence. Those that changed their front to face the new threat merely opened themselves to envelopment and fresh trouble. Only four Confederate brigades had participated in the actual flanking maneuver. The role of Davis's Mississippians is uncertain, although it must have been small, nor did George T. Anderson's Georgia regiments carry much weight during the attack. As a contemporary newspaper correspondent described it, "Anderson's brigade was so far to the right and rear of the enemy that it met with little or no opposition."[30]

Wofford's and Mahone's eleven regiments, at their much reduced 1864 strength, had driven in the equivalent of at least one Federal corps. Certainly the Confederates pressed home their attack with vigor and skill, but some of the credit for their astounding success must be attributed to the character of the battlefield. Almost unbroken woods added to the Federal disorder by mixing up units and simultaneously concealing Confederate strength. Even had the ground been more open, the generally flat terrain offered few natural points on which to rally.

It was close to noon when the main body of the Confederate force approached the road. Moxley Sorrel immediately dashed west "with great speed" in search of his chief to report the complete success of the attack and to seek further instructions. In the excitement of the moment, Wofford's brigade continued to slice north all the way across the Orange Plank Road and into the midst of Wadsworth's retreating masses. Mahone lagged slightly behind, having met the most resistance along his route.[31]

For the second time that morning the Army of Northern Virginia's soldiers enjoyed a thrilling surge of adrenaline. They had won a clear-cut tactical victory, swinging the balance of the battle in their favor. Confidence abounded among officers and men alike. A First Corps staffer noticed that "almost every face wore a smile, and . . . each officer and man felt disposed to congratulate every one he met on our success." General Longstreet found Charles Field along the road and "seizing my hands," Field recalled, "congratulated me in warm terms on the fighting of my troops." An ebullient Moxley Sorrel encountered Longstreet shortly afterward, hastening to the front with reinforcements, "happy at the success" and ready to "finish it" with fresh infantry. Brig. Gen. Micah Jenkins rode nearby at the head of his South Carolina brigade, flashing his "charming smile." He appeared that morning to an admiring friend as "my ideal as a soldier." Always considered a Longstreet man in the cliquish First Corps, Jenkins rather transparently prodded his brigade into delivering cheers in honor of Longstreet's success. The Plank Road corridor echoed with the noise of yelling Carolinians.[32]

Brig. Gen. Micah Jenkins.
Robert Underwood Johnson and
Clarence Clough Buel, eds., Battles
and Leaders of the Civil War, *4 vols.*
(New York: Century, 1887–88), 4:125

Despite the confusion of the last hour's events, Longstreet clearly understood that the victory was not yet entire. The intersection of the Brock and Plank roads offered an easy point of reorganization for Hancock. As long as Grant's army retained that crossroads, the Confederate success would be incomplete. Longstreet gathered his top subordinates to plot another phase to the flank attack that would drive the Union army away from the southern boundaries of the Wilderness. Martin L. Smith reappeared to report on a second reconnaissance he had performed toward the new Union left flank. He had discovered that it, too, dangled invitingly. Longstreet gave Smith command of another flanking force, again spearheaded by the industrious Wofford. While Smith descended on Hancock's left, Longstreet would bring Kershaw's division and all remaining fresh troops into the fray with a headlong attack. If executed quickly and simultaneously, the operation had prospects of catching Hancock regrouping. Daylight did not offer any obstacle; for once in the army's history, a full half-day remained in which to pursue great things.[33]

In this mixed atmosphere of giddiness and grim determination, Longstreet collected a considerable entourage. As key figures in the forthcoming second attack, Generals Wofford, Jenkins, and Kershaw rode with the First Corps commander along the Plank Road. Chief of Staff Sorrel stayed

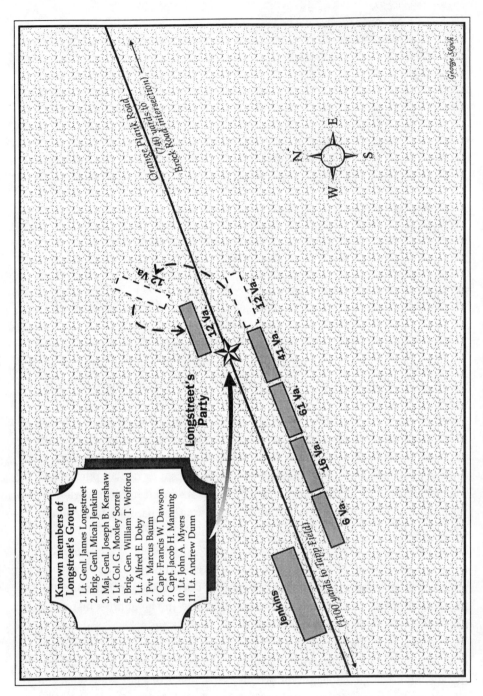

Known members of
Longstreet's Group
1. Lt. Genl. James Longstreet
2. Brig. Genl. Micah Jenkins
3. Maj. Genl. Joseph B. Kershaw
4. Lt. Col. G. Moxley Sorrel
5. Brig. Gen. William T. Wofford
6. Lt. Alfred E. Doby
7. Pvt. Marcus Baum
8. Capt. Francis W. Dawson
9. Capt. Jacob H. Manning
10. Lt. John A. Myers
11. Lt. Andrew Dunn

Longstreet's
Party

Orange Plank Road

Brock Road intersection)

(740 yards to

12 Va.

12 Va.

12 Va.

41 Va.

61 Va.

19 Va.

6 Va.

Jenkins

(1100 yards to Tapp Field)

N
W   E
S

George Skoch

Confederate deployment along the Plank Road at the time of Longstreet's wounding, May 6, 1864.

by Longstreet's side, bantering over his shoulder with Micah Jenkins. Two members of General Kershaw's staff rode with their patron, while at least three others of Longstreet's personal staff accompanied him.[34]

Full of zeal to implement the next attack, Longstreet rode with his cavalcade into dangerous territory. Some slow-footed Union soldiers still lurked in the woods, maintaining a halfhearted duel with advancing southerners. The command party traveled amidst fresh casualties on all sides, passing the body of General Wadsworth still lying against the base of a roadside tree. Andrew Dunn of Longstreet's staff imprudently reminded his general that they were in a volatile situation, to which Longstreet gruffly replied, "That is our business."[35]

In fact the woods of the Wilderness proved to be Longstreet's direst foe. Their choking density limited everyone's view to only a few yards. Once away from the Plank Road, soldiers quickly became disoriented, and units lost cohesion. Mahone's men encountered still another obstacle. Burning powder from the morning's incessant musketry had ignited scattered fires. In its position on the right end of Mahone's line, the 12th Virginia Infantry found its path to the Plank Road blocked by a burning patch of woods. They detoured to the east around the hot spot, striking the road well away from the other regiments of the brigade.[36]

After harassing fleeing remnants of Wadsworth's division, officers in the 12th realized that their regiment alone had crossed the road. They turned everyone around 180 degrees and soon had the line moving south toward the Plank Road. The other four regiments of Mahone's brigade were "lying down or kneeling" between thirty-five and seventy-five yards south of the road and facing north. A Union officer recently driven from that section of the field considered the woods there "so dense that one could distinguish nothing" from the road. While the two separate parts of the brigade faced each other obliquely across the narrow woods byway, Longstreet's cluster of horsemen unwittingly rode between them. Coincidence and ill luck had united to deliver another ugly blow to the Army of Northern Virginia.[37]

The command party reached the point between Mahone's wings very shortly after noon. A "shot or two" rattled from the woods to the north, "then more, and finally a strong fusillade" from Mahone's regiments to the south of the road. The friendly fire killed Micah Jenkins, one staff officer, and a courier. James Longstreet sagged in his saddle, badly wounded.[38]

After the war two distinct versions of the event emerged. Men from Micah Jenkins's brigade—who were horrified eyewitnesses to the death of their general—reported that some unnamed officer in the Longstreet group had stopped to pick up an abandoned Union flag. They believed that the sight of an enemy banner bobbing through the woods and heading toward the Brock Road led Mahone's men into a natural misidentification and prompted the fatal volley.[39]

The other explanation came from General Mahone's Virginians, who reminisced extensively about the unhappy episode. They candidly admitted having fired the shots and indicted themselves for the confusion. Most of their accounts blame the mistake on the re-arrival of the 12th Virginia at the northern edge of the Plank Road. Seeing shadowy figures coming from the direction of Wadsworth's division, Mahone's men fired at their comrades in the 12th, accidentally shooting down part of Longstreet's group, of which they previously had been unaware.[40]

George S. Bernard of the 12th Virginia recalled that when the volley erupted from the southern side of the road, he had a fearful thought: "*The enemy are in our rear, and we are in a bad box.*" Ben May of the 12th, who minutes earlier had refused Moxley Sorrel's request to carry the regiment's flag, hastily jumped out into the Plank Road and waved the colors with "a smile upon his face." Regimental adjutant Hugh R. Smith tried to avert further disaster by leaping into the road near May and brandishing a handkerchief on the point of his sword.[41]

Lt. Col. E. M. Feild of the brigade sharpshooters was south of the road when the firing started. He heard someone yell, "Look out boys, they are coming back!" General Mahone agreed, cautioning his men to be steady and "get in your places!" Although Mahone clearly thought his regiments confronted Federals across the Plank Road, there is no evidence he ever gave the order to fire the deadly shots; indeed, the volley seemed to spring to life on its own, file by file from the right of the brigade. In the sudden silence afterward, Mahone asked a bystander where the firing had started. Told that it had commenced on the right of his line, Mahone hastened in that direction "in a very agitated state."[42]

When the first shots began to crackle from the woods, the party of officers reacted in various ways. Jenkins rose in his stirrups and yelled out, "Steady men! For God's sake, steady!" He almost immediately fell senseless to the Plank Road, shot through the head. His lifelong friend Col. Asbury Coward of the 5th South Carolina arrived moments later and tried to speak with Jenkins, but convulsions wracked the general. He never regained consciousness.[43]

Moxley Sorrel was looking at Longstreet when the volley hit. He saw a heavy bullet strike Longstreet with such momentum that the burly general "was actually lifted straight up and came down hard" in his saddle.

The wounding of General Longstreet at the Wilderness, May 6, 1864. This postwar engraving depicts the forest at a more mature stage than would have been the case in 1864.
James Longstreet, From Manassas to Appomattox: Memoirs of the Civil War in America *(Philadelphia: Lippincott, 1896), plate 10 following p. 502*

Longstreet rode on for another moment, waving his uninjured left arm at Mahone's men. Shortly the heavy flow of blood caused him to reel in the saddle and convinced him that "my work for the day was done."⁴⁴

Staff officers made up the majority of Longstreet's group. Lt. Alfred English Doby of Kershaw's staff had been aide-de-camp to his general through nearly all the army's battles, only to fall in Mahone's volley. His death at friendly hands, after surviving "storms upon storms" of Yankee bullets, seemed to his friends to be an especially hard fate. A bullet also instantly killed Pvt. Marcus Baum of the 2nd South Carolina Infantry, who had been serving as one of Kershaw's couriers. The thirty-one-year-old Prussian Jew was "a handsome fellow" who rode a white horse that day. His blood-stained mount wandered into the hospital at Parker's Store later that afternoon, but Baum's body was never recovered.⁴⁵

Members of the group not injured by the volley responded with predictable alarm. Capt. Francis W. Dawson thought the enemy had surrounded them, deciding somewhat dramatically that "nothing remained but to sell our lives dearly." General Kershaw obeyed "my first impulse," which was to spur his horse into the roadside bushes. Peering out from his tangled haven, a sense of responsibility overtook Kershaw when he saw Jenkins's brigade in the Plank Road readying itself for a retaliatory volley. Drawing his sword, Kershaw returned to the road and began yelling, "F-r-i-e-n-d-s!" Capt. Jacob Hite Manning of Longstreet's staff "deliberately, calmly" rode toward the Virginians with extended palms, while Capt. Robert Moorman Sims of Jenkins's staff raced to the 5th South Carolina and warned them not to fire.[46]

From his position some thirty yards farther west on the road, Charles W. Field heard the shots. Looking ahead, he "saw General Longstreet's party in great confusion." Men swarmed from all directions to stare at the scene. Some of Mahone's infantry entered the road from the southern side and immediately began to apologize to the 12th Virginia, exclaiming, "Boys, we are *so sorry*! We are *so sorry*!!" Distraught South Carolinians gathered to look down at Micah Jenkins, unconscious on the ground with matter oozing from the wound in his forehead.[47]

Nearly everyone clustered around Longstreet, who seemed on death's edge. Three staff members struggled to remove the ponderous general from his horse, finally propping him against the roots of a large roadside tree in similar fashion to General Wadsworth just down the road. As Longstreet blew gory foam from his lips, he managed to give General Field instructions on how to continue the pending attack. The corps medical director, Dr. John Syng Dorsey Cullen, arrived quickly and assumed command of the patient. Much as it had after the fatal wounding of Stonewall Jackson the year before at Chancellorsville, Union artillery suddenly found the range and began dropping inconvenient shells along the Plank Road. General Kershaw spurred about urging haste and managed to see Longstreet into a nearby vehicle.[48]

The ambulance made for the complex of Confederate hospitals at Parker's Store. An inquisitive artillerist rode along for a spell and looked in once to observe Longstreet. He found the general awake, but the loss of blood had "paled out his face and its somewhat gross aspect was gone. I noticed how white and dome-like his great forehead looked." Various staff officers surrounded the ambulance, "literally bowed down with grief." The forlorn little cluster encountered General Lee on the rearward ride, "sadness in his face" prompted by his subordinate's injury. Sometime that same day Lee received word that Longstreet's wound was "not necessarily fatal."[49]

The question of which regiment wounded Longstreet and killed Jenkins has always been unanswerable. Nearly every regiment in the vicinity had accusers. The acrimonious debates started at once and were played out in various newspapers. A telegram published in the Richmond *Dispatch* of May 9 accused the 6th Virginia Infantry. George Bernard wrote in his diary for May 7 that the deadly fire came from the 41st Virginia, "and I hear also a part of the 61st regiment." Col. David A. Weisiger of the 12th Virginia informed his wife on May 7 that the 41st "mistook us for the enemy" and fired the fatal shots.[50]

Despite a considerable body of evidence to the contrary, some of Mahone's brigade initially denied any role in the affair. Responding to the standard newspaper reports, Mahone's adjutant general Robertson Taylor (brother to the army's chief of staff Walter H. Taylor) protested the accusation. Writing to the Richmond *Enquirer* in late May, Taylor made reference to a letter from Longstreet "in which he exonerates the brigade from the charge." The Richmond *Sentinel* confirmed the story, noting that Longstreet's letter "is a great relief to the brigade." Nonetheless, Longstreet correctly identified Mahone's men as the culprits in his memoirs.[51]

The loss of Longstreet disarranged Confederate plans for the next few hours. Lee soon arrived to assess the situation and "was most minute in his inquiries." The new attack planned before Longstreet's fall never occurred. The awkward configuration of his force bothered Lee, who preferred a more symmetrical arrangement that would allow for the best exploitation in the event of success. Charles W. Field, for one, thought it the proper decision. His division lay perpendicular to the Plank Road, while the remnants of Sorrel's flanking force mostly lay parallel. "The two were somewhat mixed up," admitted Field, upon whom rested tactical responsibility for much of the attack.[52]

After delaying until nearly 4:00 P.M., Lee assaulted the new Federal line along the Brock Road. The advantages won in Sorrel's flank attack of that morning no longer applied completely, though Hancock admitted as late as 3:00 P.M. that his force was still in "partially disorganized condition." Artillerist E. Porter Alexander considered the Confederate effort "more like an apology" for the original attack. "This attack ought *never*, *never* to have been made," he complained. "It was discouraging pluck & spirit by setting it an impossible task." Despite those feelings, the Confederate attack actually enjoyed brief success. At least two brigades fractured the new Union lines, only to be evicted by timely Federal reinforcements.[53]

Most Confederate participants and many subsequent historians have maintained that the untimely fall of General Longstreet deprived the army of a sweeping victory. Fred W. Cross, an early historian of the Wilderness, called Longstreet's flank attack "perhaps the most brilliant action of the day," only robbed of "complete success" by the injury to Longstreet. William Mahone wrote after the war that the accidental wounding of Longstreet "frustrated what I thought was an opportunity for a large success." Walter H. Taylor of Lee's staff concurred, writing that "I have always thought that had General Longstreet not been wounded he would have rolled back that wing of General Grant's army in such a manner as to have forced the Federals to recross the Rapidan." Even the judicious Alexander felt that his commander had briefly glimpsed a rare opportunity of following up the flank attack with another blow that would "have resulted in Grant's being forced to retreat back across the Rapidan."[54]

What would it have taken to drive Grant back across the Rapidan? Many Confederates rightly felt cheated by the bad fortune that had sabotaged their plans. Perhaps frustration obscured a few salient points that should have loomed large in their analysis. Only overwhelming defeat could have stalled Grant's campaign, and that degree of failure seems unlikely. Even had Longstreet been present to deliver his second flank attack in a timely fashion, the best result the Confederates could have hoped for would have been the collapse of Grant's southern flank. The Wilderness that ensnared the Army of the Potomac would have been its ally in time of need. The vast body of woods had somewhat equalized the disproportionate strengths of the two armies and rendered most of Grant's powerful artillery useless. Those same thickets, bisected only by a few country roads, also would have prevented Lee's winning a monumental victory over an army nearly twice the size of his own.

It is easy to draw interesting comparisons with Chancellorsville (fought on the fringe of the Wilderness), but ultimately the similarities break down. On the decisive day of the 1864 battle the Army of Northern Virginia lay stretched over a five-mile front, its two wings tenuously connected between the Orange Turnpike and the Orange Plank Road. Under those circumstances decisive victory seems unrealistic. The difference in Union leadership is of equal importance. In 1863 tactical defeat equaled strategic failure for Joe Hooker. Although Grant suffered numerous tactical setbacks in 1864 (and left himself open for many unrequited others), daily operations did not dictate his strategic view. It seems sound to conclude that nothing short of the wholesale destruction of the southern half of Grant's army would have prompted a withdrawal north of the Rapidan River. Longstreet's second flank attack could not have achieved that.

Moxley Sorrel's attack on the morning of May 6 typified the incredible havoc engendered by Civil War flanking maneuvers. Soldiers of all eras, in all wars, have an aversion to being flanked that often is out of proportion to the actual danger. A makeshift Confederate force numbering no more than 4,000 men inflicted thirty minutes of terror on at least five times their number that morning. In the process, Sorrel's men restored Confederate spirits to a new high and set the scene for yet another plummet. Few days in the army's history were so uneven. The exciting arrival of the First Corps had provided a memorable moment that caused many to forget the near-obliteration of A. P. Hill's corps. The Lee-to-the-Rear episode and an indecisive morning had sobered many until the flank attack suddenly brought everyone to joyous new heights.[55]

The death of Micah Jenkins and the wounding of James Longstreet finally brought the day to a "melancholy termination." Few failed to notice the coincidence: friendly fire along the Orange Plank Road had knocked out essential leaders in the euphoric aftermath of a successful flank attack. Stonewall Jackson had fallen under nearly identical circumstances not three miles distant just one year and four days earlier. Dispirited southerners pondered their ill fortune. Col. William F. Perry decided that some "evil genius of the South" hovered over the Wilderness. The midday events of May 6 must have prompted many men to agree with his sad observation: "We almost seem to be struggling against destiny itself."[56]

NOTES

The author would like to acknowledge particularly Keith S. Bohannon of Smyrna, Georgia, for his usual superb help with sources on Georgia troops. John R. Bass and Wilderness historian Gordon Rhea also generously helped the author hunt down elusive items.

1. Leigh Robinson, *The South Before and at the Battle of the Wilderness* (Richmond, Va.: James E. Goode, 1878), 80.

2. Charles H. Banes, *History of the Philadelphia Brigade* (Philadelphia: Lippincott, 1876), 230. Considerable controversy exists regarding the mild mid-morning attacks south of the Plank Road. Hancock complained that he had ordered all of Barlow's division into the assault but that only Frank's New York brigade had moved. See U.S. War Department, *The War of the Rebellion: A Compilation of the Official Records of the Union and Confederate Armies*, 127 vols., index, and atlas (Washington: GPO, 1880–1901), ser. 1, 36(1):321 (hereafter cited as *OR*).

3. *OR* 36(1):321–23, (2):442. Heavy skirmishing between cavalry detachments created the perplexing noise on Hancock's flank. Pickett's missing division actually was below Richmond countering the fresh expedition launched by Benjamin F. Butler. While May 6 proved to be one of the best days in the history of Longstreet's corps, it also ranks as one of the most useful in Pickett's otherwise uninspired career.

4. *OR* 36(2):952; James Longstreet, *From Manassas to Appomattox: Memoirs of the Civil War in America* (Philadelphia: Lippincott, 1896), 561–63; Jedediah Hotchkiss to his wife, April 21, 1864, Hotchkiss Papers, reel 4, Library of Con-

gress, Washington, D.C. It is unclear from the surviving evidence whether it was Lee or Longstreet who sent Smith to the far south flank on his reconnaissance.

5. *OR* 36(1):1055; Edward Porter Alexander, *Fighting for the Confederacy: The Personal Recollections of General Edward Porter Alexander*, ed. Gary W. Gallagher (Chapel Hill: University of North Carolina Press, 1989), 359. Alexander remarked that Moxley Sorrel of Longstreet's staff accompanied Smith; but Sorrel's own writings made no mention of personal participation, and Alexander might have been confused.

6. The railroad finally was finished as far as Orange in 1877 and operated at various times as the Potomac, Fredericksburg & Piedmont Company and the Virginia Central Railway. Locals termed it the "Poor Folk and Preachers" railroad. It ceased operation in January 1938 (*Orange County Historical Society Newsletter* 20 [October 1989]). One of the engineers involved in preparing the route for the railroad in 1853 was Carter Moore Braxton, who commanded a battalion of Second Corps artillery during the 1864 battle (Robert A. Hodge, *Fredericksburg to Orange by Rail* [Fredericksburg, Va.: Privately published, 1966], 3). For a good history of the railway, see John J. Hilton, "The Virginia Central Railway," in *The Headway Recorder* (National Capitol Historical Museum of Transportation, Bethesda, Md.) 29, no. 1, December 1969. Its use in the Civil War is documented in the unfinished railroad entry of Noel G. Harrison's manuscript "Gazetteer of Historic Sites Related to the Fredericksburg and Spotsylvania National Military Park," a copy of which is in the Fredericksburg and Spotsylvania National Military Park Library, Fredericksburg, Va. (repository hereafter cited as FSNMP).

7. Nelson M. Blake, *William Mahone of Virginia: Soldier and Political Insurgent* (Richmond, Va.: Garrett & Massie, 1935), 22–23; William Mahone to Francis H. Smith, February 1, 1853, William Mahone Papers, Virginia Military Institute, Lexington; "A Map of a Survey for the Rappahannock and Blue Ridge Rail-Road Made Under the Direction of Charles B. Shaw, Pr. Engr. of Va. by S. Eastman U.S.A. and D. B. Gretter, Asst. Engrs., 1836," Board of Public Works Records, entry 518, no. 2, Virginia State Archives, Richmond. These sources offer concrete circumstantial evidence that Mahone was very familiar with both the unfinished railroad and the Orange Plank Road in the Wilderness.

8. *OR* 36(1):697, 699.

9. James Longstreet to Robert E. Lee, May 19, 1864, in the Compiled Service Record (hereafter cited as CSR) of G. Moxley Sorrel, M331, roll 233, National Archives, Washington, D.C. (repository hereafter cited as NA).

10. "Wofford's Georgia Brigade: Its Conduct in the Recent Engagements," Atlanta *Southern Confederacy*, June 15, 1864; James A. Reynolds diary, May 6, 1864, copy at Richmond National Battlefield Park, Richmond, Va.; *OR* 36(1):1061–62; James Longstreet to Samuel Cooper, July 14, 1864, CSR of William T. Wofford, M331, roll 272, NA; James M[adison] Folsom, *Heroes and Martyrs of Georgia* (Macon, Ga.: Burke, Boykin, 1864), 19–20; James M. Goggin to James Longstreet, August 10, 1887, James Longstreet Papers, Southern Historical Collection, Wilson Library, University of North Carolina, Chapel Hill (repository hereafter cited as SHC).

11. John A. Everett to "Ma," May 5, 1864, Everett Papers, Emory University, Atlanta, Ga. For two other early May examples from this brigade, see John G. Webb to his father, May 7, 1864, Lewis Leigh Collection, U.S. Army Military History Institute, Carlisle, Pa., and May 15, 1864, letter of Lewis H. Andrews printed in Macon *Daily Telegraph*, May 26, 1864.

12. William F. Perry, "Campaign of 1864 in Virginia," in *Southern Historical Society Papers*, ed. J. William Jones and others, 52 vols. (Richmond, Va.: Southern Historical Society, 1876–1959), 7:59 (hereafter cited as *SHSP*); Richard H. Anderson to Edward B. Robins, May 14, 1879, Massachusetts Military History Society Papers, Boston University, Boston, Mass. (hereafter cited as BU); Charles E. Denoon, *Charlie's Letters: The Civil War Correspondence of Charles E. Denoon*, ed. Richard T. Couture (Collingswood, N.J.: Civil War Historicals, 1989), 96.

13. "Mississippians at the Wilderness," *Confederate Veteran* 9 (April 1901): 165. Most Confederate accounts of the flank attack ignore Davis's brigade. Longstreet (*OR* 36[1]:1055) mentioned it in his report using language that shows he was unaware of its presence at the time. See also P[eter] W[ellington] A[lexander], "From General Lee's Army," Columbia *Daily South Carolinian*, May 28, 1864, for another contemporary reference. One rumor in the army after the battle identified Davis's brigade as the culprit in the wounding of Longstreet (James F. Barron to "My own dearest Annie," May 9, 1864, typescript in the author's collection). The best evidence—albeit somewhat oblique—comes from a soldier of the 55th North Carolina of Davis's brigade, who wrote that his brigade "got cut in too" and that he joined one of the Mississippi regiments and participated in a big successful movement, presumably the flank attack (G. W. Pearsall to "My Dear Wife," May 11, 1864, Pearsall Letters, North Carolina Department of Archives and History, Raleigh). Traditional orders of battle for this brigade are incorrect. On May 6 it consisted of the 55th North Carolina, 1st Confederate Battalion, and four Mississippi regiments—the 2nd, 11th, 26th, and 42nd.

14. Gen. Edward P. Alexander, "Grant's Conduct of the Wilderness Campaign," *Annual Report of the American Historical Association for the Year 1908*, 2 vols. (Washington: GPO, 1909), 1:226; G. Moxley Sorrel, *Recollections of a Confederate Staff Officer* (New York: Neale, 1905), 231–32.

15. *OR* 36(1):1090; "Wofford's Georgia Brigade," Atlanta *Southern Confederacy*, June 15, 1864. Writing in 1879 Mahone reiterated that the brigades were "all under my immediate command" (William Mahone to Edward B. Robins, May 9, 1879, BU). Even if Mahone's claims are legitimate, their point of origin must be questioned. In 1880 Mahone reminisced further that he usually commanded at least two brigades in battles, "and was always . . . given the immediate command of the field. . . . Neither Gen. Lee nor Gen. Hill ever put me under command of other officers" (William Mahone in Richmond *Whig* supplement, August 23, 1880). This shocking remark prompted one of Mahone's many postwar enemies to observe, "Why, with this opinion of him, Gen. Lee did not abdicate the command of the army in Gen. Mahone's favor I cannot see" (William L. Royall to Editor, Richmond *State*, September 22, 1880).

16. James Longstreet to Samuel Cooper, July 14, 1864, CSR of William Mahone,

M331, roll 162, NA; *OR* 36(1):1055; James Longstreet to R. E. Lee, May 19, 1864, CSR of G. Moxley Sorrel, M331, roll 233, NA; James Longstreet to Samuel Cooper, July 14, 1864, CSR of William T. Wofford, M331, roll 272, NA.

17. Sorrel, *Recollections*, 232; William W. Chamberlaine, *Memoirs of the Civil War* (Washington, D.C.: Byron S. Adams, 1912), 95.

18. A. J. McWhirter, "General Wofford's Brigade in the Wilderness, May 6th," Atlanta *Journal*, September 21, 1901. All previous maps and explanations of this affair have placed Mahone between the two Georgia brigades. That interpretation seems to have been based entirely on Longstreet's official report, which doubtless suffers from his personal absence on that part of the line. Numerous accounts, both contemporary and postwar, make it clear that Wofford was in the middle, with Mahone's brigade on his left angling away northwestward. This stretch of railroad in 1995 is mostly deep cut (rather than graded earth), and it must have looked similar in 1864. For clues on alignment, see "Wofford's Georgia Brigade," Atlanta *Southern Confederacy*, June 15, 1864, and George S. Bernard, *War Talks of Confederate Veterans* (1892; reprint, Dayton, Ohio: Morningside, 1981), 87–106, 311–12.

19. *OR* 36(1):1090–91; statement of Col. Feild in Bernard, *War Talks*, 98. The Wilderness contents of Bernard's important book also appeared separately in two other places: John R. Turner, *The Battle of the Wilderness!: The Part Taken by Mahone's Brigade. An Address Delivered by . . .* (Petersburg, Va.: Fenn & Owen, [1892]), and *SHSP*, 20:68–95. A letter documenting the formation of Mahone's sharpshooter battalion appeared in the Richmond *Sentinel*, April 23, 1864. It is not clear whether the other brigades employed organized skirmish battalions. For distance between men, see McWhirter, "General Wofford's Brigade."

20. *OR* 36(1):323, 488–89; Morris Schaff, *The Battle of the Wilderness* (Boston: Houghton Mifflin, 1910), 260.

21. Bernard, *War Talks*, 88, 90, 95; Leroy Edwards to George S. Bernard, March 1, 1891, original in possession of Robert K. Krick, Fredericksburg, Va. This apparently is the original letter from which Bernard made slightly altered extracts in *War Talks*, 93–94. For an indirect reference to catching the Yankees squarely on the flank, see William R. Montgomery diary, May 6, 1864, typescript at Kennesaw Mountain National Battlefield, Kennesaw, Ga.

22. McWhirter, "General Wofford's Brigade"; Bernard, *War Talks*, 91.

23. *OR* 36(1):488–89; Samuel B. Wing, *The Soldier's Story: A Personal Narrative* (Phillips, Maine: Phonographic Steam Book and Job Print, 1898), 65. It is unclear just what position Frank's brigade occupied relative to McAllister's. Several sources confirm that Frank was hard hit by the flankers, among them Francis A. Walker, *History of the Second Army Corps* (New York: Scribner's, 1887), 427, and Banes, *Philadelphia Brigade*, 232.

24. Reynolds diary, May 6, 1864; "Wofford's Georgia Brigade," Atlanta *Southern Confederacy*, June 15, 1864; Bernard, *War Talks*, 92, 95–96.

25. Charles H. Weygant, *History of the One Hundred and Twenty-fourth Regiment N.Y.S.V.* (Newburgh, N.Y.: Journal Printing House, 1877), 293–94; Banes, *Philadelphia Brigade*, 231.

26. Z. Boylston Adams, "In the Wilderness," in [Massachusetts Commandery, MOLLUS], *Civil War Papers Read Before the Commandery of the State of Mas-*

sachusetts, M.O.L.L.U.S. (1900; reprint in 3 vols., Wilmington, N.C.: Broadfoot, 1994), 2:378; Charles W. Cowtan, *Services of the Tenth New York Volunteers* (New York: Charles H. Ludwig, 1882), 252. Some Confederate sources suggest that the Plank Road's defenders may even have erected hasty fortifications. See "Wofford's Georgia Brigade," Atlanta *Southern Confederacy*, June 15, 1864, and Bernard, *War Talks*, 94.

27. Charles S. Venable, "The Campaign from the Wilderness to Petersburg," *SHSP*, 14:526; Edward Steere, *The Wilderness Campaign* (1960; reprint, Mechanicsburg, Pa.: Stackpole, 1994), 399; D. G. Crotty, *Four Years Campaigning in the Army of the Potomac* (Grand Rapids, Mich.: Dygert, 1874), 128; W. M. Abernathy, "Our Mess: Southern Army Gallantry and Privations, 1861–1865," Abernathy Collection, Mississippi Department of Archives and History, Jackson, Miss. (repository hereafter cited as MDAH).

28. Wadsworth's field glasses were on public display in Richmond later that month (Richmond *Examiner*, May 27, 1864). Other interesting eyewitness accounts to Wadsworth's condition include Sorrel, *Recollections*, 232–33; Chamberlaine, *Memoirs*, 96; and "Rogers' Bloody 6th Regiment," Norfolk (Va.) *Ledger-Dispatch*, April 16, 1935.

29. Adams, "In the Wilderness," 379. These troops may have been Mahone's left-flank regiments or perhaps even parts of Davis's Mississippians. Maj. Richard W. Jones of the 12th Virginia wrote after the war, "I did not see the plank road until we were within a few feet of it" (Bernard, *War Talks*, 312).

30. "Wofford's Georgia Brigade," Atlanta *Southern Confederacy*, June 15, 1864.

31. Bernard, *War Talks*, 88; Sorrel, *Recollections*, 233. Kershaw's report states that Wofford came within "a few hundred yards of the Germanna Road," which seems improbable (*OR* 36[1]:1062). "Wofford's Georgia Brigade," Atlanta *Southern Confederacy*, June 15, 1864, states that the Georgians pursued "a half a mile beyond" the Orange Plank Road.

32. Unidentified 1867 newspaper clipping (possibly by James M. Goggin of Kershaw's staff) in the Edward Porter Alexander Papers, SHC; Charles W. Field, "Campaign of 1864 and 1865," in *SHSP*, 14:545; Sorrel, *Recollections*, 233; John C. Haskell, *The Haskell Memoirs*, ed. Gilbert E. Govan and James W. Livingood (New York: Putnam's, 1960), 65; Asbury Coward, *The South Carolinians*, ed. Natalie J. Bond and Osmun L. Coward (New York: Vantage Press, 1968), 134; "ideal soldier" from Col. J. R. Hagood quoted in John P. Thomas, *Career and Character of General Micah Jenkins* (Columbia, S.C.: State Co., 1903), 7; Edward Porter Alexander, *Fighting for the Confederacy*, 359; James B. Rawls, "Veteran's Sketch of Life from Battle of Chickamauga to Arrival at Home," *United Daughters of the Confederacy Magazine* 52 (June 1989): 17. Although nearly everyone agrees that Jenkins seemed unusually happy that morning, it is known that back ailments had confined him to an ambulance during the march, and "he was evidently in pain" (letter of unidentified surgeon in Yorkville [S.C.] *Enquirer*, June 29, 1864). Two separate sources also suggest that Jenkins felt uneasy about his fate in the spring campaign (obituary in Yorkville [S.C.] *Enquirer*, May 25, 1864, and John M. Jenkins, cited in Coward, *South Carolinans*, 139).

33. J. M., "Battle of the Wilderness"; *OR* 36(1):1055; Longstreet, *From Manas-*

sas to Appomattox, 562–63. M. L. Smith's performance in early May 1864 apparently impressed Lee, as Smith wrote home on May 29, "I seem to have acquired the confidence of Genl Lee to the extent of his being willing to place his troops on the lines of my selection" (M. L. Smith to "My Dear Sarah," May 29, 1864, James S. Schoff Collection, William L. Clements Library, University of Michigan, Ann Arbor).

34. Sorrel, *Recollections*, 233; Lancaster (S.C.) *Ledger*, May 24, 1864; Longstreet, *From Manassas to Appomattox*, 563. Capt. Francis W. Dawson wrote home that Captain Dwight of Kershaw's staff was part of the group, which certainly is possible; however, Dawson damaged his credibility as a witness by recording that Dwight was killed, which is incorrect (Francis W. Dawson, *Reminiscences of Confederate Service*, ed. Bell I. Wiley, [1882; reprint, Baton Rouge: Louisiana State University Press, 1985], 115, 196).

35. Andrew Dunn in Bernard, *War Talks*, 106.

36. Ibid., 94.

37. Adams, "In the Wilderness," 378; Bernard, *War Talks*, 92, 104; Coward, *South Carolinians*, 134; P[eter] W[ellington] A[lexander], "From General Lee's Army"; *OR* 36(1):1055.

38. Sorrel, *Recollections*, 234. Most sources place this episode at around noon or just later.

39. For sources on the flag, see Frank M. Mixson, *Reminiscences of A Private* (Columbia, S.C.: State Co., 1910), 70–71; Col. J. R. Hagood quoted in Thomas, *Career and Character of General Micah Jenkins*, 7. Coward, *South Carolinians*, 134–35, identifies the flag as belonging to the 2nd South Carolina Rifles rather than to some Yankee unit. General Mahone himself wrote after the war that Longstreet's group "were mistaken for a body of Federal Horse" (William Mahone to Edward B. Robins, May 9, 1879, BU). One account blames the accident on the uniforms of Jenkins's men, which were of a new, dark-blue cloth (Haskell, *Memoirs*, 65).

40. Bernard, *War Talks*, 88–106. This version is the more plausible of the two, especially because the soldiers involved voluntarily admitted to having done the deed.

41. Ibid., 92, 94–95, 105. At least two sources remark that Longstreet's group detoured around a thicket into a roadside turnout just prior to the fatal volley (John D. McConnell, "Recollections of the Civil War," 1918 typescript at Winthrop College, Rock Hill, S.C., and testimony of Col. E. M. Feild in Bernard, *War Talks*, 100).

42. Bernard, *War Talks*, 100; Dawson, *Reminiscences*, 115; Coward, *South Carolinians*, 135.

43. Dawson, *Reminiscences*, 115; Coward, *South Carolinians*, 135; William McWillie notebook and diary, May 6, 1864, McWillie Family Papers, MDAH; Rev. James McDowell in Thomas, *Career and Character of General Micah Jenkins*, 20. Jenkins died before sunset on May 6. Friends shrouded his corpse in a battle flag while the 6th South Carolina band played a funeral dirge.

44. Sorrel, *Recollections*, 233; Haskell, *Memoirs*, 65; Dawson, *Reminiscences*, 115; Longstreet, *From Manassas to Appomattox*, 564.

45. D. Augustus Dickert, *History of Kershaw's Brigade* (1899; reprint, Dayton, Ohio: Morningside, 1973), 349; Mac Wyckoff, *A History of the 2nd South Carolina Infantry: 1861–65* (Fredericksburg, Va.: Sgt. Kirkland's Museum, 1994), 158, 177; Dr. Simon Baruch, "The Heroic Death of Marcus Baum," *Confederate Veteran* 22 (April 1914): 170. Typescripts of eight letters written in January 1863 by Captain Doby are at the Museum of the Confederacy in Richmond, Va.

46. Dawson, *Reminiscences*, 115; Kershaw quoted in Thomas, *Career and Character of General Micah Jenkins*, 11; Longstreet, *From Manassas to Appomattox*, 564; Sorrel, *Recollections*, 234; McConnell, "Recollections of the Civil War," 8.

47. In his account of the episode, Field implied that R. E. Lee was within sight of Longstreet's group at the time of the volley (Field, "Campaign of 1864 and 1865," 14:545); Bernard, *War Talks*, 92; Chaplain James McDowell in Thomas, *Career and Character of General Micah Jenkins*, 9.

48. Dawson, *Reminiscences*, 197; John W. Fairfax quoted in Longstreet, *From Manassas to Appomattox*, 567; Sorrel, *Recollections*, 233; Coward, *South Carolinians*, 135. A 1906 obituary for Thomas R. Edwards of the 1st Texas Infantry (*Confederate Veteran* 14 [June 1906]: 277) reported that he "assisted in carrying him [Longstreet] from the field."

49. Robert Stiles, *Four Years under Marse Robert* (New York: Neale, 1910), 247; *OR* 36(2):893.

50. Richmond *Dispatch*, May 9, 1864; Bernard, *War Talks*, 93; David A. Weisiger to "My darling little Wife," May 7, 1864, Weisiger Papers, Virginia Historical Society, Richmond, Va.

51. Richmond *Enquirer*, May 24, 1864; Richmond *Sentinel*, May 25, 1864. The abundant correspondence addressing this matter in Bernard, *War Talks*, makes it clear that the fatal shots originated with either the 12th or the 41st Virginia. Most of the veterans accused the 41st, although two companies of the 12th had stayed attached to the right flank of the 41st and probably were closest to Longstreet's party. Further evidence (admittedly circumstantial) comes from the nature of Longstreet's wound. The bullet pierced both his throat and right shoulder (Longstreet, *Manassas to Appomattox*, 564). Although the chronological order of those wounds is uncertain, it seems most likely that the bullet went through his right shoulder and into his throat, unless he somehow was twisted around in the saddle when the projectile hit. Assuming the shoulder-to-throat chronology is correct, it can be tentatively deduced that the shot came from south of the road and thus likely from the 41st Virginia.

52. Field, "Campaign of 1864 and 1865," 14:545; Sorrel, *Recollections*, 234–35. For an excellent discussion of this issue, see Steere, *Wilderness Campaign*, 406–9.

53. *OR* 36(2):445; Edward Porter Alexander, *Fighting for the Confederacy*, 362–63; Coward, *South Carolinians*, 135–37; "Wofford's Georgia Brigade," Atlanta *Southern Confederacy*, June 15, 1864.

54. Untitled Fred W. Cross memoir of 1922 visit to the Wilderness, copy in bound vol. 223, FSNMP; William Mahone to Edward B. Robins, May 9, 1879, BU; Walter H. Taylor, *General Lee: His Campaigns in Virginia, 1861–1865* (Norfolk: Nusbaum, 1906), 236; Edward Porter Alexander, *Fighting for the Confederacy*, 360.

55. Confederate casualties in the flank attack were modest. Mahone's five regiments lost 20 killed and 126 wounded (*OR* 36[1]:1091). The only other unit from which casualty figures survive is the 18th Georgia, which lost 7 killed and 37 wounded. Extrapolating that sum to include the other regiments and battalions in Wofford's brigade brings that unit's total to 32 killed and 166 wounded (Folsom, *Heroes and Martyrs*, 20).

56. Edward Porter Alexander, *Fighting for the Confederacy*, 360; Perry, "Campaign of 1864 in Virginia," 7:59.

The notes for the essays provide a good guide to much of the literature pertaining to the Wilderness. Few of the titles stress the broader political and social context within which Grant and Lee commenced their operations in May 1864. The field of Civil War history remains sadly divided between historians interested in martial affairs and those drawn to nonmilitary aspects of the war.

The best source for printed primary materials on the Overland campaign is U.S. War Department, *The War of the Rebellion: A Compilation of the Official Records of the Union and Confederate Armies*, 127 vols., index, and atlas (Washington: GPO, 1880–1901), ser. 1, vol. 36, pts. 1–3. Unfortunately the vast majority of the reports, correspondence, and other documents in these three thick volumes relate to the Federals—roughly 2,750 pages compared with about 270 pages on the Confederates. *Supplement to the Official Records of the Union and Confederate Armies*, ed. Janet B. Hewett and others, 22 of a projected 100 vols. published to date (Wilmington, N.C.: Broadfoot, 1994–), will contain additional material about both armies, but the volumes covering the Wilderness have yet to appear.

Abundant postwar testimony about the Confederate side of the campaign is in the *Southern Historical Society Papers*, 52 vols., ed. J. William Jones and others (1876–1959; reprint, with 3-vol. index, Wilmington, N.C.: Broadfoot, 1990–92); *Confederate Veteran*, 40 vols. (1893–1932; reprint, with 3-vol. index, Wilmington, N.C.: Broadfoot, 1984–86); and *Histories of the Several Regiments and Battalions from North Carolina in the Great War, 1861–'65*, 5 vols., comp. Walter Clark (Raleigh: E. M. Uzzell, 1901). For the Union side readers should consult the *Papers* of the Military Order of the Loyal Legion of the United States, 66 vols. and 3-vol. index (Wilmington, N.C.: Broadfoot, 1991–96). Read before the state commanderies of the MOLLUS, many of these papers shed light on the Wilderness. Excellent material contributed by former Federals and Confederates is in vol. 4 of *Papers of the Military Historical Society of Massachusetts*, 14 vols. (1895–1918; reprinted in 15 vols. with a general index, Wilmington, N.C.: Broadfoot, 1989–90), and vol. 4 of *Battles and Leaders of the Civil War*, ed. Robert Underwood Johnson and Clarence Clough Buel (New York: Century, 1887–88).

Several monographs treat the tactical details of the battle. By far the best is Gordon C. Rhea's deeply researched and crisply written *The Battle of the Wilderness: May 5–6, 1864* (Baton Rouge: Louisiana State University Press, 1994). Edward Steere's *The Wilderness Campaign* (Harrisburg, Pa.: Stackpole, 1960) relies almost exclusively on printed sources and lacks Rhea's stylistic vigor but offers sound analysis buttressed by more than two dozen detailed maps. Clifford Dowdey's *Lee's Last Campaign: The Story of Lee and His Men against Grant, 1864* (Boston: Little, Brown, 1960) benefits from the author's compelling writing style but reflects his usual bias against James Longstreet; Noah Andre Trudeau's *Bloody Roads South: The Wilderness to Cold Harbor, May–June 1864* (Boston: Little, Brown, 1989), although unannotated, draws on manuscripts as well as published sources for its skillful narrative. Grady McWhiney's *Battle in the Wilderness: Grant Meets Lee* (Fort Worth, Tex.: Ryan Place, 1995) provides a spirited overview of the campaign, while Dayton Kelley's *General Lee and Hood's Texas Brigade at the Battle of the Wilderness* (Hillsboro, Tex.: Hill Junior College Press, 1969), focuses on accounts of the most famous incident of the battle.

A pair of older titles by Union officers merits the attention of modern students. Morris Schaff served during the battle as a junior officer on Gouverneur K. Warren's staff. His *The Battle of the Wilderness* (Boston: Houghton Mifflin, 1910) boasts a well-informed analytical narrative strengthened by numerous personal observations. Andrew A. Humphreys's more scholarly *The Virginia Campaign of '64 and '65: The Army of the Potomac and the Army of the James* (New York: Scribner's, 1883) suggests some of the qualities that made Humphreys an excellent chief of staff. Knowledgeable, restrained, and careful about details, Humphreys used records from the War Department, corresponded with officers from both sides who had been at the Wilderness, and produced a book that ranks among the best written by any Civil War general officer.

For the Union high command, vol. 10 of *The Papers of Ulysses S. Grant*, ed. John Y. Simon (Carbondale, Ill.: Southern Illinois University Press, 1982), includes letters and telegrams from January 1 to May 31, 1864. Grant's *Personal Memoirs of U. S. Grant*, 2 vols. (New York: Charles L. Webster, 1885) include the Federal commander's entertaining but scarcely evenhanded postwar interpretations. George Gordon Meade Jr.'s *The Life and Letters of George Gordon Meade*, 2 vols. (New York: Scribner's, 1913), traces through Meade's letters the difficult transition in command occasioned by Grant's joining the Army of the Potomac. John Sedgwick's *Correspondence of John Sedgwick, Major General*, 2 vols. ([New York: De Vinne Press], 1902–3), reveals much about the conservative chief of the Union Sixth Corps; Philip H. Sheridan's *Personal Memoirs of P. H. Sheridan*, 2 vols. (New York: Charles L. Webster, 1888), blends in about equal measure self-serving and dissembling passages with solid narrative flecked with useful insights.

R. E. Lee left a much smaller published literary legacy than Grant. For letters and other documents regarding the background and progress of the Wilderness campaign, see Robert E. Lee, *The Wartime Papers of R. E. Lee*, ed. Clifford Dowdey and Louis H. Manarin (Boston: Little, Brown, 1961). Also useful for events at Confederate headquarters is Walter H. Taylor's *Lee's Adjutant: The Wartime Letters of Colonel Walter Herron Taylor, 1862–1865*, ed. R. Lockwood Tower (Columbia: University of South Carolina Press, 1995). Although deeply flawed by its author's willingness to stretch the truth while answering postwar critics, James Longstreet's *From Manassas to Appomattox: Memoirs of the Civil War in America* (Philadelphia: Lippincott, 1896) remains essential on the Confederate high command.

A few highlights from the massive biographical literature deserve mention. Bruce Catton's *Grant Takes Command* (Boston: Little, Brown, 1969) is easily the best treatment of Grant in the spring and early summer of 1864. Although very admiring of its subject, Douglas Southall Freeman's *R. E. Lee: A Biography*, 4 vols. (New York: Scribner's, 1934–35), remains by far the most detailed analysis of the Confederate chieftain during the Wilderness campaign. Freeman Cleaves's *Meade of Gettysburg* (Norman: University of Oklahoma Press, 1960), is the standard life of a figure badly in need of a full, manuscript-based treatment.

Other worthwhile biographies include David M. Jordan's *Winfield Scott Hancock: A Soldier's Life* (Bloomington: Indiana University Press, 1988), Jeffry D. Wert's openly favorable *General James Longstreet, the Confederacy's Most Controversial Soldier: A Biography* (New York: Simon and Schuster, 1993), and James I. Robertson Jr.'s perceptive *General A. P. Hill: The Story of a Confederate Warrior* (New York: Random House, 1987).

A rich store of reminiscences, sets of letters, and diaries sheds light on various facets of operations in the Wilderness. Unrivaled for their perceptive and blunt analysis are Edward Porter Alexander's *Military Memoirs of a Confederate: A Critical Narrative* (New York: Scribner's, 1907) and *Fighting for the Confederacy: The Personal Recollections of General Edward Porter Alexander*, ed. Gary W. Gallagher (Chapel Hill: University of North Carolina Press, 1989). Gilbert Moxley Sorrel of James Longstreet's staff, who played a key role at the Wilderness, sketched many memorable scenes in *Recollections of a Confederate Staff Officer* (New York: Neale, 1905). Few printed primary sources from either army are as useful as Federal artillerist Charles S. Wainwright's *A Diary of Battle: The Personal Journals of Colonel Charles S. Wainwright, 1861-1865*, ed. Allan Nevins (New York: Harcourt, Brace & World, 1962), and Daniel M. Holt's *A Surgeon's Civil War: The Letters and Diary of Daniel M. Holt, M.D.*, ed. James M. Greiner, Janet L. Coryell, and James R. Smither (Kent, Ohio: Kent State University Press, 1994). For a common soldier's point of view about the campaign, Wilbur Fisk's *Hard Marching Every Day: The Civil War Letters of Private Wilbur Fisk, 1861-1865*, ed. Emil and Ruth Rosenblatt (Lawrence: University Press of Kansas, 1992) (originally published privately as *Anti-Rebel: The Civil War Letters of Wilbur Fisk*), is exceptional.

Finally, a quartet of general works stands out. Herman Hattaway and Archer Jones's *How the North Won: A Military History of the Civil War* (Urbana: University of Illinois Press, 1983) firmly locates the campaign within the larger strategic picture. Volume 3 of Douglas Southall Freeman's *Lee's Lieutenants: A Study in Command*, 3 vols. (New York: Scribner's, 1942-44), assesses Confederate leadership in memorable prose, and Bruce Catton's *A Stillness at Appomattox* (Garden City, N.Y.: Doubleday, 1953) tells the Army of the Potomac's part of the story in a stunningly effective narrative. Also powerfully written is Shelby Foote's *The Civil War: A Narrative*, 3 vols. (New York: Random House, 1958-74), vol. 3 of which includes a long section on the Wilderness.

Contributors

Peter S. Carmichael earned his doctoral degree in history at Pennsylvania State University. The author of *Lee's Young Artillerist: William R. J. Pegram*, as well as several essays and articles in popular and scholarly journals, he is completing a study of the sons of Virginia slaveholders and the formation of southern identity in the late antebellum years.

Gary W. Gallagher is a member of the Department of History at Pennsylvania State University and editor of the Civil War America series at the University of North Carolina Press. He has edited *The Third Day at Gettysburg and Beyond*; *The Fredericksburg Campaign: Decision on the Rappahannock*; and *Chancellorsville: The Battle and Its Aftermath*, three previous titles in the Military Campaigns of the Civil War series.

John J. Hennessy, a graduate of the State University of New York at Albany, has written widely on the Civil War, including *The First Battle of Manassas: An End to Innocence, July 18-21, 1861*; *Second Manassas Battlefield Map Study*; and *Return to Bull Run: The Campaign and Battle of Second Manassas*.

Robert E. L. Krick, a Richmond-based historian, was reared on the Chancellorsville battlefield. The author of *The Fortieth Virginia Infantry* and a number of essays and articles, he is completing a biographical register of the staff officers of the Army of Northern Virginia.

Robert K. Krick grew up in California but has lived and worked on the Virginia battlefields for more than twenty years. He has written dozens of articles and ten books, the most recent being *Stonewall Jackson at Cedar Mountain* and *Conquering the Valley: Stonewall Jackson at Port Republic*.

Carol Reardon is the military historian at Pennsylvania State University and author of *Soldiers and Scholars: The U.S. Army and the Uses of Military History, 1865-1920*. A former holder of the Harold Keith Johnson Visiting Professorship in Military History at the U.S. Army Military History Institute and U.S. Army War College, she recently completed a book on the image of Pickett's Charge in American history.

Gordon C. Rhea resides in St. Croix, U.S. Virgin Islands, and Mt. Pleasant, South Carolina. He is the author of *The Battle of the Wilderness: May 5-6, 1864* and *The Battles for Spotsylvania Court House and the Road to Yellow Tavern: May 7-12, 1864*.

Brooks D. Simpson is a member of the Department of History at Arizona State University. His books in the field of Civil War history include *Let Us Have*

Peace: Ulysses S. Grant and the Politics of Reconstruction, 1861–1868 and *America's Civil War.* He also has completed an edition of William Tecumseh Sherman's Civil War letters.

the Potomac); Third Corps Corps (Army of the Potomac); Twelfth Corps (Army of the Potomac); individual army, corps, division, and brigade commanders

Army of the Tennessee, 1, 5, 6
Associated Press, 18
Atlanta, Ga., 6, 37
Atlanta campaign, 31
Atlanta *Southern Confederacy*, 40, 41
Austerlitz, battle of, 5

Banes, Charles H., 237
Banks, Nathaniel P., 37
Banks Ford, 203
Barclay, Ted, 47, 56
Barnard, Vt., 203
Barney, Elisha R., 203, 228, 230
Barrow, H. W., 41
Bates, Edward, 18
Battle's Alabama brigade, routed near Saunders's field, 148
Baum, Marcus, 253
Belle Plain, Va., 21
Benedict, George G., 217
Bennett, James Gordon, 10
Berkeley, Henry Robinson, 52
Bernard, George, on Longstreet's flank attack, 252, 254–55
Birney, David Bell, 81, 214
Birney's division (Army of the Potomac), 220, 221, 244
Bixby, Orville, 223
Blackford, Charles Minor, 52
Blair, Frank, 7
Blake, Henry, critical of William H. French, 83–84
Blessing, Sam, 182
"Bloody Angle," 24, 186
Boswell's Tavern, Va., 164
Bragg, Braxton, 57, 58
Brandy Station, Va., 70, 72, 75, 80, 107, 109, 205; battle of, 106
Brinton, William P., 122, 126
Bristoe Station, battle of, 88, 90, 143

Brock Road, 119–29 passim, 149, 151, 206, 207, 216, 223, 225, 237, 240, 242, 249, 252, 255
Brooks, Noah, 8, 23–24, 29
Brooks, William T. H., 79, 91
Brown, G. Campbell: on Lee's contradictory orders, 147–48; criticizes Lee for vague orders, 154
Brown, Joseph E., 38, 44, 46, 48
Brown, Lizinka Campbell, controls Ewell, 142
Brush, Henry B., 212, 229
Bryan, Goode, 168
Bryan, Timothy H., 108
Bryan's Georgia brigade, 113, 118, 119, 121–22
Buford, John, 106
Bureau of War (Confederate), 54
Burnside, Ambrose E., 11, 51, 67, 68, 72, 79, 83
Butler, Benjamin F., 7, 19, 23, 27
Butterfield, Daniel, 72
Butterfield, Joseph E., 229

Cadwallader, Sylvanus, 17
Caldwell, Susan Emeline Jeffords, 40
Carpenter, Frank, 15
Carroll's brigade (Army of the Potomac), 215
Carter, Albert, 216, 227
Carter, Edward, 229
Carter, Robert G., 78
Cary, William B., 118
Catharine Furnace, 126, 129
Catharpin Road, 115–25 passim
Chamberlaine, William W., 243
Champlain Valley, 202
Chancellorsville, Va., 113, 115, 126, 239; battle of, xiv, 8, 19, 27, 67, 70, 88, 145, 203, 236, 256
Chapman, George H., 108, 109, 113
Chapman's brigade (Army of the Potomac), 113, 119–20, 122, 126
Charleston *Daily Courier*, 39, 40
Chase, Peter, 202, 211–12, 215–16, 219, 227–28, 229

136, 140; role in Gordon's flank attack, 136–37, 140; criticized by Lee, 138, 153–55, compared to Jackson, 141; eccentric behavior, 141–42; marriage to Lizinka Brown, 142; actions on May 5, 146–48; praised by E. P. Alexander, 148; pressured by Early, 154; and vague orders from Lee, 154; actions defended, 155–56. *See also* Second Corps (Army of Northern Virginia)

Faulkner house, 121
Favill, Josiah, 70, 86, 87, 94
Feild, Everard M., 244, 252
Field, Charles W., 166; at the Tapp field, 177; during Longstreet's flank attack, 247, 248, 254, 255
Field's division (Army of Northern Virginia), 165, 237, 240
Fifth Corps (Army of the Potomac), 11, 26, 67, 71, 81, 85, 88–89, 94, 113, 115, 118, 205, 207, 220, 222, 237, 247; Sykes replaced as commander of, 84; attacks Ewell, 148. *See also* Warren, Gouverneur K.
Finegan, Joseph, 37
First Corps (Army of Northern Virginia), 57, 79, 81–83, 138, 145, 220, 222, 237, 257; reunites with Lee's army, 50–51; at Mechanicsville, 145; approaches Wilderness battlefield, 162–69. *See also* Longstreet, James
First Corps (Army of the Potomac), protests reorganization, 85–86
Fish, Fred, 215
Fisher, Abial, 216
Fisk, Wilbur, 204, 206–7, 211, 212, 214, 216, 220, 221, 223, 224; on the Christian Commission, 75–77
Fitzgerald, Ben, 183
Fitzhugh, Charles L., 121
Fitzpatrick, J. C., 17
Flagg, George, 202, 214

Florida, 41, 42
Florida troops: 5th Infantry, 56
Forrest, Nathan Bedford, 37
Forsyth, James W., 108, 109
Fort Pillow, battle of, 37
Foster, George P., 203
Frank, Paul, 244
Frankenstein, George Leo, 170
Frank Leslie's Illustrated Newspaper, 21, 24
Franklin, William B., 79, 91
Fredericksburg, Va., xi, 18, 113, 116, 122, 170; battle of, xii, 19, 67, 77, 85, 88, 113; compared to Mine Run, 70; Confederate Cemetery at, 188; medical facilities at, 226–27
Fredericksburg and Gordonsville Railroad, 238
Freeman, Douglas Southall, accepts Gordon's and Heth's memoirs, 138–39
French, Horace, 216
French, William H., 82, 86, 102 (n. 39); relieved by Meade, 83–84

Gaillard, Franklin, 51
Gaines's Mill, battle of, 85, 88, 189, 236
Gallagher, Gary W., critical of Ewell, 139–40, assesses Hill, 142–43
Garrett, Jesse M., 47
Gee, Leonard Groce, 182, 183
Georgia, 46, 50
Georgia *Messenger & Journal*, 41
Georgia troops: Cobb's Legion, 51; 3rd battalion, 244; 7th Infantry, 240; 8th Infantry, 240; 9th Infantry, 240; 11th Infantry, 240; 14th Infantry, 48; 15th Infantry, 186; 16th Infantry, 246; 22nd Infantry, 44; 31st Infantry, 47; 35th Infantry, 47; 45th Infantry, 45, 47, 54; 51st Infantry, 42, 48; 60th Infantry, 54
Germanna Ford, 11, 113, 115, 143, 145, 154, 205
Germanna Plank Road, 205

Getty, George W., 119, 201; at the Wilderness, 205–7, 214–17

Gettysburg campaign, x, xi, xii, xiv, 2, 36, 43, 66, 67, 83, 88, 90, 106, 130, 143, 153, 203, 229, 230; shapes Ewell's reputation, xiii, 136, 140; increases confidence of Army of the Potomac, 78; Lee questions Hill's abilities in, 142–43; Hill and Ewell serve as scapegoats for, 155–56

Getty's division (Army of the Potomac), 205, 206, 209, 220, 224, 225

Gibbon's division (Army of the Potomac), 215

Gordon, James B., 125

Gordon, John B., 186; influence of memoirs, 137, 140–41, 155; plans flanking maneuver, 137, 154–55

Gordon's Georgia brigade, 54

Gordonsville, Va., 145, 164

Goree, Thomas J., 43, 51

Gorgas, Josiah, 46

Graham, James A., 45, 46, 211

Grant, Lewis A., xiv, 201, 203, 231; attacks Heth's division, 207–17, actions on May 6, 219–26; reflects on battle, 226. *See also* Vermont Brigade

Grant, Ulysses S., ix, x, xi, 1, 18, 19, 21, 24, 26, 29, 81, 90, 109, 125, 143, 146, 201, 204, 213; accepts overall command of Union armies, 2; strategic designs, 4–7, 30; assessed by northern press, 8–11; sensitive to public opinion, 10–11, 22, 30–31; composure in battle, 11–13; judged by Army of the Potomac, 12, 93–94; evaluates the battle of the Wilderness, 14, 19, 22; Lincoln's confidence in, 19; influences northern reaction to the Wilderness, 23; relations with Meade, 30, 94–95, 130; southern reaction to, 40–41, 51–52; supports Sheridan, 85, 107, 130. *See also* Army of the Potomac

Greeley, Horace, 10, 20

Gregg, David McMurtrie, 106, 109, 113–15, 117, 122–24, 126–27, 129

Gregg, John, 167; at the Tapp field, 178–81, 186

Gregg, Maxcy, 168

Gregg's division (Army of the Potomac), 111, 115

Haley, John, 84, 85

Halleck, Henry W., 6, 11, 16, 19, 21, 22, 26

Hamilton, Eugene, 215

Hamilton's Crossing, 117, 122, 126

Hammond, John, 116–19, 126, 130

Hampton, Wade, 52

Hancock, Winfield Scott, 79, 126–29, 161, 163, 164, 167, 217, 220–21, 224, 237, 246, 255; separates political and military matters, 80; respected as a corps commander, 86–88; slights the Sixth Corps, 225; fails to use unfinished railroad, 240. *See also* Second Corps (Army of the Potomac)

Hannibal, 236

Hanover Junction, Va., 164

Harper's Weekly, 9

Harris, Luther B., 204, 205, 207, 209, 211, 213, 217, 220, 224–25

Harris's Mississippi brigade, 186, 184

Hart, James H., 123

Hartshorn, Ephraim, 229

Haskell, Alexander Cheves, 58

Haskell, Frank, 70

Hassler, William Woods, 139

Hatcher, J. J., 184

Hattaway, Herman, 142

Heaton, Edward, 126

Heaton's Battery (Army of the Potomac), 127

Henagan, John W., 169

Heth, Henry, 178, 206, 213, 217; reliability of memoirs, 137, 152, 155; criticizes Hill, 137–38, 152, 162; during the morning of May 6,

Lee, Fitzhugh, 117, 122, 124, 126, 129
Lee, George Washington Custis, 166
Lee, Robert E., ix, 4, 5, 6–8, 11, 13, 19–22, 24, 26, 29, 45, 48, 67, 111, 117, 125, 130, 160, 166, 201, 213, 236–38, 243, 254, 255; opinion of Grant, xi; considers Ewell and Hill unreliable, xiii, 137, 138, 142–43, 153; leading the Texans, xiii–xiv, 176–90; soldiers' trust in, 2–3, 41–42, 49–52; laments lack of supplies, 42–43; compared to George Washington, 49–50; affection for Longstreet, 50–51; religious convictions, 56–57; requests reinforcements, 57–58; offensive designs, 58; criticizes Hill and Ewell at the Wilderness, 138–39; opinion of Gordon's flank attack, 140, 154; accountable for subordinates' mistakes, 140, 155–56; slow to concentrate army, 143–46, 155–56; desires a reconnaissance in force, 145–47; instructions to Hill, 147, 149; sends Ewell contradictory orders, 147–48; responsible for Third Corps collapse, 152–53; instructions to Ewell, 154; style of generalship, 154; defines subordinates' actions, 155; headquarters, 162–63; tries to rally Hill's men, 176; welcomes Longstreet, 176; demeanor in battle, 176–77; approves Longstreet's flank attack, 240, 241
Lee's Mill, Vt., 202–3
Lewis, Jackson, 171
Lewis, John R., 203, 214, 227, 230–31
Lillie, Daniel, 203, 223, 228
Lincoln, Abraham, xii, 1, 2, 7, 21–22, 55, 79; frustrated by public's expectations, 4, 30; considers Lee's army the primary objective, 6; faces mounting political pressures, 8; stays out of Grant's plans, 10; anxious about the Wilderness,

14–16; reaction to the Wilderness, 18–19; confidence in Grant, 19; challenges northern press, 28–29; meets with Sheridan, 107, 130
Little Round Top, 88, 189
Lockhart, William G., 180, 183
Lomax, Lunsford L., 124, 125
Lone Star Preacher, 189
Long, Alexander, 53
Longstreet, James, 57, 126–28, 140, 142–43, 146, 147, 151, 153, 184; role in flank attack, xiv, 240–57 passim; soldiers admire, 50–51; march to the Wilderness, 162–69; compared to Jackson, 164; criticized by contemporaries, 166–67; welcomed by Lee, 176; evaluates battle, 222–23; impact of flank attack, 223, 247–48, 255–57; wounding of, 251–55, 257, 263 (n. 51). *See also* First Corps (Army of Northern Virginia)
Louisiana, 6, 41, 53
Louisiana troops: 14th Infantry, 53
Lyman, Theodore: assesses Meade, 67; rates Butterfield, 73; on William H. French, 84; describes Hancock, 86–87
Lynchburg, Va., 6, 26

McAllister, Robert, 66, 77, 244
McArdle, Harry Arthur, 183, 187
McClellan, George B., 10, 30, 31, 51, 67, 68, 79, 80, 83, 84, 88, 93, 95; legacy in Army of the Potomac, 5; supported by Sedgwick, 91
McClellan, Henry B., 166
McDowell, Irvin, 81
McGowan, Samuel, confronted by Lee, 168
McGowan's South Carolina brigade, 168
McGuire, Judith W., 41
McIntosh, John B., 118
McLaws's division (Army of Northern Virginia), 55
McPherson, James B., 5

11th Infantry, 43; 18th Infantry, 168; 21st Infantry, 41; 27th Infantry, 45; 37th Infantry, 153; 44th Infantry, 43

Northern press: shapes public reaction to the Wilderness, 4–5, 16–3; evaluates Grant, 8–11

Northern public: desires a decisive victory, 9–10; unrealistic expectations of Union generals, 30–31

Ohio troops: 6th Cavalry, 123

Okolona, battle of, 37

Old Wilderness Tavern, 205

Olustee, battle of, xii, 37

Orange Court House, Va., 113, 125, 146, 205, 206, 238

Orange Plank Road, xiii, 115, 116, 117, 118, 119, 121, 125, 128, 149, 160, 164–76 passim, 183, 187, 189, 209, 217, 219–20, 221, 225, 237–57 passim

Orange Turnpike, 11, 115, 116, 118, 160, 205, 207, 256

Ormsbee, C. J., 207, 209, 214

Overland campaign, 70, 71, 88, 94, 143

Owen's brigade (Army of the Potomac), 215

Page, Charles A., 9, 12

Palmer, William H., 169; defends A. P. Hill, 152–53

Palmetto Sharpshooters, 165

Parker, Tully Francis, 53

Parker's Store, 115, 116, 117, 119, 125, 163, 165, 172, 205, 253, 254

Parker's Store Road, 118

Patrick, Marsena, 67, 73, 91, 93

Patterson, Josiah Blair, 48

Pemberton, John, 42, 52

Pendleton, Alexander "Sandie," 142, 147

Pendleton, William N.: nearly captured, 161; at the Tapp field, 172–73, 177, 179–80, 182

Peninsula campaign, 6, 31, 88

Pennington, Alexander C. M., Jr., 121

Pennsylvania, 36, 54

Pennsylvania troops: 1st Cavalry, 124, 129; 2nd Cavalry, 129; 4th Cavalry, 129; 8th Cavalry, 129; 16th Cavalry, 115; 18th Cavalry, 122, 124; 141st Infantry, 214–15, 217

Perry, William F., 257

Petersburg, Va., 7

Petersburg campaign, 143

Philadelphia Inquirer, 17

Pickett's Charge, 230

Pickett's division (Army of Northern Virginia), 58, 237,

Piney Branch Church, 129

Pingree, Stephen M., 209, 230

Pleasant Hill, battle of, 37

Pleasonton, Alfred, xiii, 106–7; removed by Meade, 84–85, 102 (n. 43)

Plymouth, battle of, xii, 37, 41

Poague, William T., at the Tapp field, 153, 162, 163, 172–73, 177

Poague's battalion, 175–76, 177, 179, 195 (n. 40); repulses Hancock's attack, 172–73

Pollard, Edward A., 37

Polley, Joseph B., 178, 183

Pope, Daniel, 47

Pope, John, 68, 107, 236

Po River, 124, 125

Porter, Fitz John, 79, 80; rejects emancipation, 71

Port Royal, Va., xi

Potomac River, x, 54

Prior, E. W., 219

Pulliam house, 172

Ramseur, Stephen Dodson, 47; confident of Confederate success, 42; desires a northern raid, 54–55

Rapidan River, ix, x , xiv, 4, 11, 15, 19, 20, 42, 52, 53, 58, 95, 106, 113, 115, 117, 137, 143, 145, 201, 205, 256

Wilcox, Cadmus, 170, 213; believes
Confederates unprepared on May
6, 152, 161–63, 166; division col-
lapses, 152–53, 167–68
Wilcox's division (Army of Northern
Virginia), 140; routed on May 5,
151, 161–62
Wilderness, battle of: Lee-to-the-
rear, xiii–xiv, 176–90; Grant's
strategic designs, 4–7, 30; Grant
assesses battle, 14; casualties, 19;
Lee's plan for, 58; Union cavalry
operations in, 106–30; terrain of,
113, 169; Gordon plans flanking
maneuver, 137, 154–55; Lee slow
to concentrate army, 143–46, 155–
56; fighting at Saunders's field,
147–48; Hill unprepared on May 6,
152, 161–63; collapse of Third
Corps, 153, 161–62, 167–69; First
Corps marches to, 162–69; impact
of Longstreet's flank attack, 223,
247–48, 255–57; wounding of
Longstreet, 251–55, 257, 263
(n. 51)
Wilderness Church, 117
Wilderness Run, 115

Wilderness Tavern, 11, 113, 115, 116
Wiley, Bell I., gauges Confederate
morale, 36–37
Wilkerson, Frank, 95
Willard's Hotel (Washington, D.C.), 2
Williams, Seth, 73
Williamsburg, battle of, 88
Wilson, James H., xiii, 106, 111; sup-
ported by Grant and Sheridan,
108–9; at the Wilderness, 113–17,
118–26, 130; fails Grant, 117
Wilson, William L., 56
Wing, Henry, 15
Wofford, William T., role in Long-
street's flank attack, 240, 243, 244,
249
Wofford's Georgia brigade, 240, 246,
248
Wood, Fernando, 54
Woodward, A. T., 226
Wooster, Winfield Scott, 216
Wyatt, James W., 172

Yellow Tavern, battle of, 130
York River, xi
Yorktown, siege of, 88
Young, Abram Hayne, 46